Surveys of Australian Economics

Volume II

Surveys of Australian Economics

edited by

F.H. GRUEN

for the
Academy of the Social Sciences in Australia

Volume II

Income Distribution and Poverty
Urban Economics
Economics of Education
Radical Economics
Australian Economics 1968–78

Sydney
George Allen & Unwin
London · Boston

First published in 1979 by
George Allen & Unwin Australia Pty Ltd
8 Napier Street
North Sydney
NSW 2060

National Library of Australia
Cataloguing-in-Publication data:

Surveys of Australian economics. Volume 2.

Bibliography
ISBN 0 86861 137 9
ISBN 0 86861 129 8 Paperback

1. Australia—Economic conditions. I. Gruen, Fred Henry George, 1921–, ed. II. Academy of the Social Sciences in Australia.

330.9′94

Library of Congress Catalog Card Number: 78-55055

Set in 10 on 11½ point Plantin by Filmset, Hong Kong
Printed in Australia by Watson Ferguson, Brisbane

Contents

Preface

This is a companion volume to the Survey of Australian Economics published in 1978 at the Seventh Conference of Economists at Macquarie University. Decisions about the placing of the surveys in the different volumes was partly a question of their time of completion. However, in addition, an attempt was made to put the more technical macro- and micro-economic surveys in the first volume and to include in this volume surveys which would be of greater interest to other social scientists. A good deal of the literature surveyed here is widely dispersed and has appeared in non-economic journals.

The instructions to authors, the procedures for their selection and the refereeing process was outlined in the Preface to the first volume. Identical procedures were followed in the case of the surveys assembled here. I would like to thank the anonymous referees who helped us; and to thank again Heinz Arndt, Alan Boxer, Max Corden and Max Neutze, who served conscientiously as members of the Project Committee which planned and carried through the project and Charles Rowley who acted as Executive Officer to the Committee (and to the Academy) during the project.

Finally I would like to express our thanks to those who supported us financially: CSR Ltd, Esso Australia, General Motors-Holden, Trustees of S.B. Myer, the Reserve Bank of Australia (Economic and Financial Research Fund), the Shell Company of Australia, the State Savings Bank of Victoria and the Utah Foundation. Without their help, it is doubtful whether the project would have been possible.

F.H. Gruen
October 1978

Chapter 1

Income Distribution, Poverty and Redistributive Policies

S. RICHARDSON

University of Adelaide

Contents *Page*

A first draft of this paper has benefited greatly from the thoughtful comments of a number of people. For this I am grateful to Heinz Arndt, Geoff Brennan, Keith Hancock, Geoff Harcourt, Nanek Kakwani, Henry Phelps Brown, Peter Saunders, Fred Gruen and an anonymous referee. They should not, however, be held responsible for the remaining inadequacies.

Section 1 Introduction

Every economic change involves some impact on the distribution of income and most probably also on the degree of inequality. In this sense the entire Australian economic discussion over the last decade could be the subject of this survey. Since such an approach is plainly impractical, the topic will be interpreted more narrowly to comprise only discussion which is directly concerned with questions of distribution, poverty and redistribution. It should be remembered that this restriction is necessarily somewhat arbitrary.

Even thus confined the literature to be reviewed is diverse and on the whole fragmented.[1] If a common theme can be found it is perhaps the attempt to piece together the empirical jigsaw depicting who gets what in the Australian economy.

It may appear that analysis of the distribution of income will be intimately connected with policies to redistribute income and to reduce poverty. By and large this is not so. Discussion of the observed distribution of income has mostly concentrated on full-time adult male earnings. Policies to redistribute income, on the other hand, are concerned primarily with family incomes and especially with the relation between family income and need. Even a perfect understanding of the dispersion of adult male full-time earnings would only partly illuminate the distribution of family incomes because it would fail to encompass the issues of labour force participation, female earnings, household composition and non-labour income. It is even less suited to explaining poverty since it appears that in Australia most of the poor are not in the workforce at all.

This survey seeks to describe the major points developed in the Australian literature over the preceding decade, with some comment and suggestion for further work. The way in which the material is presented thus reflects the nature of the literature, including the relation between the topics mentioned above. The international debate is referred to only where it throws light on issues in the Australian literature, or on its relative strengths and weaknesses. Since the local discussion does not encompass the full range of topics being considered elsewhere, this survey should not be seen as attempting a comprehensive review of the field.

Generalisations across a heterogeneous literature are hazardous, but several such observations can be made without too much injustice being done.

All three topics covered in this survey have experienced a burst of activity during the last decade, and especially the last five years. Prior to 1968 research had been severely hampered by lack of data. Since then there have been major efforts to provide new information on income and expenditure at the individual and family level. Both the Australian Bureau of Statistics and academic researchers have been involved, providing in all six new sets of survey data.[2] The research which has been done in recent years has in large part been based on this newly available information: overall it has advanced on a very uneven front.

An unusual feature of the debate on poverty and redistributive policies is the dominant part played by the reports of government appointed commissions of enquiry. Of the four reports most relevant to this survey,[3] two were headed by academic economists (K. Hancock and R. Henderson).

The substance of the paper begins in Section 2 with the issue of income distribution. This has several dimensions, though only that of the size distribution of family income is related to the subsequent topics of poverty and redistributive policies. Other aspects concern the determination of relative wages, the size distribution of pre- and post-tax individual income from all sources, and the division of income between the factors of production. Although they do not contribute to a common theme, these latter topics have an interest in their own right and have attracted considerable attention (relatively) among Australian economists. They will therefore be discussed, briefly, in this survey before we proceed to the more cohesive welfare-related questions. The welfare topic starts with the distribution of income among households and leads into Section 3, the investigation of poverty. Finally in Section 4 we look at possibilities for redistributing income, where the prime interest has been the derivation of policies for the reduction of poverty.

Section 2 Income Distribution

2.1 Distribution of Earnings

Aggregate income comprises income from several different sources. These may be classified as income from employment (wages and salaries), income from property and income from government social welfare payments. Earnings are quantitatively by far the most important. Labour economists have investigated several characteristics of the structure of earnings, some of which are pertinent to the issues of income distribution. Generally earnings are taken to mean rates paid to adult males in full-time employment. They may be classified according to the types of jobs for which a given wage is paid or according to the numbers of individuals who receive a given wage. While it is the latter classification which is particularly relevant for the overall distribution of income, the former has been of most concern to labour economists.[4] Bearing this in mind we may see how the structure of earnings has varied over time, how it compares with Britain and America and how it may influenced by factors such as the Arbitration Commission and earnings drift.

A careful examination of some Australian data suggests that the dispersion of award rates shows no apparent trend over time.[5] This conclusion contrasts with earlier views, firmly held both in Australia and in comparable overseas countries, that there was a long-run trend for the distribution of earnings to become more equal.[6] The Australian evidence from the 1950s onward in fact suggests a reverse trend. The lesson from this, Hancock and Moore (1974, p.108) suggest, 'is *not* that assertions about secular stability should be substituted for earlier claims about secular compression' but rather that one should simply 'seek explanations for the observed fluctuations in wage relativities' without adopting a prior view about secular trends. The behaviour of the Australian evidence certainly lends support to this view. The period from 1914 to 1920 showed a reduction in the dispersion of award wages, then relative stability in the twenties followed by a dramatic rise in inequality in 1931, a gradual decrease in inequality until 1948–9 when the dispersion suddenly was subject to a strong compression until 1952. From 1953 on dispersion has tended to increase once more, though the dispersion of earnings, as distinct from award wages, decreases again quite sharply in 1975 (Hancock and Moore 1974; Lydall 1968, pp.190–193; Norris 1977).

To understand the dispersion of earnings it is helpful to consider separately the influence of earnings drift and of the award structure. The evidence suggests a positive correlation between the rate of earnings drift and changes in the employers' capacity to pay (this latter measured via the proxies of change in value added or change in gross profits per worker (Hancock 1966, pp.173–75; Dufty 1971, p.186).) The wages in industries which are becoming increasingly profitable and have relatively high excess demand for labour can be expected to exhibit above average earnings drift. The impact of this on dispersion depends on whether such industries initially had levels of wages above or below average. This relation has not been investigated. Norris (1977) tests explicitly the hypothesis that dispersion is positively related to the proportion of earnings accounted for by the two components of over-award pay, namely overtime and over-award payments. He finds that both, but expecially overtime, are significant in explaining the dispersion of earnings which are below the median, but not those above the median.

The extent to which the Arbitration Commission can influence the structure of earnings through its determination of award rates of pay has yet to be fully resolved. One test is to see whether the structure of earnings in Australia differs from that overseas, and in particular whether less powerful groups of workers are relatively better off under the Australian system of compulsory arbitration. The conclusions must as yet be tentative, in part because of the variability over time in the Australian dispersion of earnings. They suggest that the Australian wage structure is remarkably similar to the British, but rather more compressed than that in the United States. Differences show up most clearly for the highest and lowest paid workers.

(Brown 1978; Hughes 1973; Lydall 1968; Norris 1977). Hughes (1973, p.20) concludes that 'the Australian arbitration framework did not at that time exert much of an equalizing effect on the industrial wage structure'. This is contrary to the evidence on the impact of arbitrated decisions on earnings inequalities produced by Hancock and Moore (1974). They show that, prior to 1967, the decision of the Commission on whether to use margins or the basic wage as the vehicle for a wage increase had a considerable impact on the degree of earnings dispersion: increases via the basic wage decreased inequalities while increases in margins had the reverse effect.

Hancock and Moore (1974, pp.118–19) argue that the 'alternate stretching and compression of the wage structure has not generally been due to the explicit pursuit of such results' by the Commission. If these effects on relativities are the unintentional by-products of judgements based on other criteria then there is no reason to suppose any particular net impact on dispersion over time. Norris concurs in this view of the impact of the Commission, arguing that it causes considerable short-run fluctuations in the inter-industry dispersion of earnings, but little net change over the longer period.

If one accepts this perception of the Commission's impact on the earnings structure then it is to be expected that the conclusions from international comparisons will depend importantly on the years chosen for the comparison; that is, whether it is a period of 'stretching' or of 'compression' of the wage structure. Reinforcing this is the fact that, as Hughes notes, the ability of the Arbitration Commission to influence relative wages is likely to be minimised in periods of high levels of employment, when employers are competing for labour. High demand for labour characterised the period considered by Hughes, and in fact most of Australia's post-war experience.[7] When one considers also the strong tendency to allow margins for skill 'to bear the brunt of economic adjustments' (Hancock and Moore 1974, p.122), it appears the macro-economic forces of inflation and unemployment modify both the nature of decisions made by the Arbitration Commission and the actual effects of these decisions.

We may conclude that if, as seems likely, the Arbitration Commission has not sought systematically to alter the dispersion of earnings, then its power to do so in the longer run remains untested. If the opposite view is held of the Commission's policy then the evidence suggests that the Commission's short-term impact on dispersion does not endure.[8]

Few labour economists have faced the issue of the relation between market forces and institutional factors in wage determination. Should the Commission adopt some explicit notion of equity such as comparative wage justice, it is not clear whether pursuit of this goal would coincide or conflict with market forces of supply and demand. In the event of a conflict it is not known which set of influences would prevail. It has been argued outside Australia that the virtue of adopting maintenance of customary differentials as the equity goal of institutions is reinforced by the fact that this is consistent with market forces (Turner and Jackson 1969). At a theoretical level this conclusion has been shown to be premature (Manning, Richardson and Webb 1972). The consistency or conflict between these two sets of forces depends on empirical factors such as the price elasticity of demand for products and the elasticity of supply of labour.

The use of a simplified formal model of economic behaviour as in Manning, Richardson and Webb is notable for its rarity in the Australian literature on the determination of earnings. It may be that the labour market is peculiarly unsusceptible to formal theorising which has its roots in competitive theory. Nonetheless there do seem to be regularities in aspects of the earnings profile, between countries and over time, which suggest the need to look for forces which are reasonably enduring and which may possibly be identified with the aid of theoretical speculation.

In contrast with the overseas literature, there has been little analysis of why individuals, as distinct from occupations, receive the incomes they do. There are many aspects being discussed elsewhere even in the field of income from employment which have yet to appear in the Australian literature. In Britain, for example, it has been observed that the distribution of earnings for full-time male manual workers has remained almost stable for the hundred or so years for which data have been collected (Lydall 1976). The shape of the earnings distribution is also found to be similar in comparable countries. Perhaps provoked by observation of these regularities, but at any rate seeking to explain them, a number of theories of the size distribution of earnings between individuals has emerged. Excellent summaries can be found in Lydall (1975 and 1976) and Tinbergen (1975).

2.2 *The Functional Distribution of Income*

A second dimension of the distribution of income concerns the division of the national product between the factors of production. Ideally this would describe and explain the relative rewards of all the factors of production—land, capital, entrepreneurship and labour. In practice, the factors have been summarised as labour and non-labour and in Australia the contemporary focus has been on description rather than explanation of relative factor shares. In particular there has been considerable interest in the proposition that the ratio of labour to non-labour shares has been extremely stable for the whole of the twentieth century and perhaps even before that. How best to measure this ratio is controversial and it is this empirical problem which has been the centre of recent Australian debate. Little has been added to the still inadequate explanation of factor shares. We here exclude the Cambridge capital controversy, though this complex debate has had one or two lively Australian participants.[9] Fortunately it has already been summarised and assessed by Harcourt (1976).

Careful definition of the items being compared is critical both to the values of the measures of factor shares which result, and to the interpretation to be placed upon them. There is general agreement that a suitable measure of labour income is that used in the national accounts, namely the total of wages, salaries and supplements paid by employers. Slightly more controversial is whether gross domestic product should be measured at market prices or at factor cost, or alternatively whether domestic factor incomes[10] should be used as the denominator. A major study by the Department of Labour calculates the labour share using as a base both gross domestic product (which avoids the problem of depreciation) and domestic factor incomes. Their figures show that, taking series which differ only in the base used, the change in labour share from 1948–49 to 1970–71, varied by as much as six percentage points (Department of Labour 1974, pp.27–8).

Other difficult questions arise in selecting the portion of the economy to be considered and the extent to which adjustments should be made for changes in the proportion of wage and salary earners in the labour force.[11] This latter question arises from uncertainty about how to determine the proportion of the income of the self-employed to allocate as labour income. The theoretical difficulties are aggravated by the extraordinary variety of such enterprises.

It is possible to generate at least 32 plausible measures of labour's share, matched by an almost equal variety of conclusions on the direction and extent of changes in labour's share (Department of Labour 1974, pp.27–28). The alternatives are the product of combining the plausible approaches to industry coverage with constant or current industry weights and alternative techniques for the allocation of unincorporated income. Ingenious minds could no doubt extend the list of 32 plausible measures of labour's share. But 32 are enough to demonstrate that the conclusion about what has happened to labour's share of output in Australia in the post-war period depends greatly on how this is measured. The range of values contained within this group of 32 possibilities extends from a decline in labour's share of 6.4 percentage points to a rise of 10.2 percentage points.

Interest in these calculations is not confined to academic economists. They are seen also to have ideological and welfare implications, some of which have been espoused by unions and Australian political parties and argued before the Arbitration Commission (James 1974, p.1). Given an imputed ideological content of a kind to stir the blood and a smorgasboard of statistics large enough to cater for the most varied tastes, one expects dispassionate reason to play a minimal role in the debate.[12]

Much of the dispute over the facts of the matter could be resolved if the question the data are to illuminate was first clearly and precisely articulated. If one simply wants to know what portion of total income is received in the form of wages and salaries then all sectors should be included, except perhaps those where the factor shares are determined by arbitrary convention. Then no attempt should be made to remove changes in the relative size or factor ratios of industries. If the interest is in how the private market sector operates to determine factor shares then plainly it is inappropriate to include sectors which function outside the market or have politically determined prices. Examples could be multiplied but the point is obvious: which measure is the proper one depends on the question being asked. The only curious thing is that this approach has played almost no part in the dispute over what is the appropriate measure of labour's share, and how this share has changed over time.

If the purpose is to assess changes in the relative material well-being of employees, none of the measures is sufficient. They say nothing about the distribution of income between workers, or the distribution of the income share which accrues to non-labour factors. It may be that equity in the profitable big corporations is owned by society's widows and orphans, and the income of unincorporated enterprises which is attributed to non-labour factors is received predominantly by small scale dairy farmers, fishermen and bottle-os. We know little about these matters, but perhaps the most effective way to promote an equitable distribution of total income is to have more equal ownership of non-labour factors of production, rather than to attempt, or rely upon, changes in factor shares (Stretton 1976).

Examination of the 'most preferred' measure chosen by the Department of Labour reveals two interesting facts. First, the fall in labour's share (from 80.6 per cent to 76.6 per cent) which appears over the period 1948–49 to 1970–71 was concentrated almost entirely in the early 1950s. (The exact years depend on which measures are used.) Second, there are cyclical fluctuations in labour's share associated with the level of economic activity. Specifically, labour's share shows a marked tendency to rise during periods of recession. The converse movement during the recovery period is not so pronounced but appears to be spread over a number of years (Department of Labour 1974, chap. 3; Clark 1970, pp.59–60). The explanation seems to be related to short run changes in labour productivity. During a recession, the reduction in output (or in its rate of growth) is greater than the reduction of labour employed.

The remarkable variety of conclusions which may be supported by plausible measures of labour's share suggests there is an interesting project to be done on identifying the causes of these divergent outcomes.

The sharp changes in both factor shares and the dispersion of incomes which were observed in the early 1950s, and will probably show up in data for the early 1970s, raise the issue of whether such events are temporary aberrations or the crucible in which longer term shifts in relativities are formed. Phelps Brown has argued for the latter interpretation (1957, pp.49–65) but the issue has yet to attract the attention of Australian economists.[13]

Curiously there has been no attempt to compare labour's share with that observed in other countries. It may be that the variety of possible measures make commensurability difficult, but that comparison would be interesting if it could be made.

Kakwani (forthcoming) uses data from the Macquarie/Queensland survey to link the functional distribution of income with the distribution between households. Specificially he identifies the contribution that each of seven sources of income (excluding social welfare benefits) makes to total income and to total inequality. Since earnings comprise about 88 per cent of mean income their distribution necessarily dominates the overall distribution. Income from property, unincorporated enterprises and capital gains contribute more to total inequality than they do to total income. Serious doubts about the reliability of the data (discussed below on pp.21–23) mean little confidence can be placed in the calculation of precise percentage contributions of each income source to total inequality.

The early 1960s saw a vigorous exchange on the possibilities of a wages policy which restricted increases in award wages to the average rate of productivity growth. The chief virtue of such a policy was claimed to be a costless reduction in the rate of inflation. That it would be costless (in the sense of causing no real changes) was argued on two grounds. First, it was held that the share of labour in total income could be observed to be stable in the long period and by implication could be relied upon to remain stable in the future regardless of the behaviour of money wages.[14] Second, and more modestly, it was argued that the rate of growth of money wages does not affect the rate of growth of real wages, but only the rate of growth of prices.

Confidence in the existence of powerful macro-economic forces which ensure stability of labour's share over long periods must be hard to sustain in the face of some persuasive arguments presented by Solow (1958). Seeking to establish some standard by which constancy may be assessed (in the absence of *a priori* expectations), Solow examines whether the aggregate share has fluctuated less than the weighted fluctuations in sector shares would suggest. He concludes that for the United States between 1929 and 1954 'the aggregate share varied just about as much as it would vary if the individual sector shares fluctuated independently' (1958, p.624). A selected group of manufacturing industries showed the share of wages of production workers in manufacturing value-added fluctuated much *more* in aggregate than it would have, had the individual sector shares fluctuated independently (1958, p.624), though the extent of this is somewhat reduced in the longer run. A similar test has been applied to a group of Australian manufacturing industries from 1948–49 to 1967–68 and similar conclusions emerge (Hancock 1971, p.24).

The extent to which changes in money wages cause corresponding movements in real wages remains unclear. One view is that the available evidence—which in fact is rather slender—'*points to the conclusion that the relative shares of profits and wages are not influenced by the rate of growth of money wages*' (Whitehead 1973, p.49, italics in original). In partial support of this an examination of the relation between costs of inputs (including capital), productivity and prices of outputs in Australian manufacturing (Hancock 1971, 1976) finds no evidence that changes in money wage rates on their own alter the equilibrium ratio of wages to prices. However, recognition that wages and price adjustments are not made instantaneously makes it clear that real wages can be increased for periods by high rates of money wage increase, and decreased by low rates of money wage increase. 'It is the short-term adjustment mechanism which, apparently, provides the main scope (other than 'squeezing' the export sector) for manipulating the level of real wages' through varying money wages (Hancock 1971, p.38).

2.3 The Size Distribution of Income and Wealth

Definitions

The distribution of income is not an unambiguous concept. Both the income unit and income itself may be variously defined. Since the welfare implications of the distribution of income derive from the relation between income received and the people to be supported by that income, the family is usually adopted as the relevant income unit. However, the concept of family is itself ambiguous. One definition of family uses kinship relations, another uses actual living arrangements (e.g. the sharing of common cooking facilities.)[15] Neither is entirely satisfactory, and the results from the application of each are not strictly comparable.

Income is normally defined as cash receipts from all sources. A major problem arises from a failure to impute a rental value to owner-occupied houses. The economic welfare of two comparable families receiving the same income may be very different if one owns and the other is renting accommodation. Similar difficulties apply to the value to a family of a housewife's unpaid services. A choice must also be made whether to use income before or after income taxes (or all taxes) have been paid, and whether to include cash social services benefits. A value is rarely imputed for benefits in kind.

Data

Empirical, rather than theoretical, investigations dominate the Australian literature on the size distribution of income. Until recently the inadequacy of the available data has meant that the limits on the depth and coverage of attempts to describe the facts of Australia's income distribution were quickly reached.

The main sources of information on the distribution of income are income tax statistics and surveys. Neither is likely to be fully accurate, though for different reasons. With tax data inaccuracy arises from the incentive deliberately to misrepresent income. This is aggravated by arrangements to receive income in non-taxable forms, such as capital gains, and by devices, such as discretionary trusts, for dividing large incomes between multiple recipients for tax purposes. Survey data suffer from sampling error, genuine mistakes and lack of full co-operation from respondents.

Taxation data have several additional limitations when used to describe the distribution of income. First, not all incomes received are covered, since those whose incomes are below the minimum level which attracts tax need not submit a return. Furthermore, the exemption level is changed from time to time, which reduces the comparability of data derived from different years. More importantly, there is a whole variety of reasons why people have different income levels in a given period, and it is not possible to discriminate between these using income tax figures. Thus income from property is not distinguished from income from personal exertion and it is not possible to distinguish full-time from part-time earnings or temporary from permanent employment (Hancock 1970, p.20).

The Australian tax data describe the distribution of income between individuals. Since generally people live in groups this distribution is not very interesting from a welfare viewpoint. Instead one needs information on family incomes, preferably related to both the size and composition of the family (the latter on the premise that the expenditure needs of children are less than those of adults). As Hancock (1970, p.20) remarks 'our use of statistics derived from the Reports of the Commissioner of Taxation to measure changes in distribution is due entirely to the lack of any alternative.' 1966 saw the first (apart from a pilot study in the mid-1950s (Harcourt and Ironmonger 1956)) of a number of surveys which, *inter alia*, provide a definition of a household and use this to seek information on the total income of the household and the numbers of people supported by that income.

The 1966 survey was the joint project of Macquarie and Queensland Universities. It was a pioneering effort and for many years it had no rival as a source of information on household and individual income, expenditure and wealth. It has now been superseded by the four surveys undertaken by the Australian Bureau of Statistics. Two of these, the 1968–69 and 1973–74 surveys of income distribution, are part of what was intended to be an ongoing series conducted at five-yearly intervals.[16] In each, one half per cent of the total population over 15 years of age (excluding those normally not counted in ABS surveys) were asked questions about their incomes for the preceding financial year.[17] Income is classified by source and age, marital status, education and labour force experience. Similar information is also presented using households rather than individuals as the income unit. It is the household information which is particularly helpful for those interested in the welfare implications of the distribution of income, though it is regrettable that the ABS has chosen to exclude one-person households when presenting these data.

The third ABS survey of income distribution was conducted in 1973 on behalf of the Commission of Inquiry into Poverty for use in the *First Main Report* (Henderson Report). It sought more detailed information, including questions on expenditure, than the 1968–69 and 1973–74 surveys, but did not ask these questions of high income earners. It is thus not comparable with the other two.

The final set of relevant data come from the Household Expenditure Survey. This is in two parts, with capital cities being surveyed in 1974–75 and non-metropolitan areas in the following year. The chief purpose of the exercise was to provide information on expenditure patterns, but households were also asked to give details of their income. The definitions used differ from those in the income surveys, again making the results difficult to compare with the two major income surveys.

There is plainly a rich pool of information awaiting analysis here. The data on families include information on the number of income earners, the contribution of government social service benefits to family income, the position of families with female heads, the relation between income and family size, and the impact on family income of a second adult wage.

Many important questions can be illuminated by examination of these data. The information on second earnings allows some assessment of the impact on family income of the dramatic rise in the labour force participation rate of married women, and the implications for income differences compared with families where only one spouse earns an income. Such a change in work-force behaviour may generate a whole new aspect of income inequality dividing one-income from two-income households.[18] The implications of having no household member currently employed can be examined using information provided on sources of income and relating unearned income to family size. Mean and median incomes are classified according to the list of 69 occupations used for the 1966 population census and by years and type of education. Plainly there is scope here for both the human capital theorists and those concerned with the occupational dispersion of earnings. Something may also be learned from the separate calculation of male and female incomes in many occupations.

A major interest in assessing inequality lies in comparison both between countries and over time. The Australian Bureau of Statistics has itself calculated the Gini coefficients, Lorenz curves, and deciles for family income and individual male and female incomes.[19] Comparison of these measures for the two sets of income data indicates how inequality has behaved in the five years since 1968–69. The measures for family income indicate some reduction in inequality. The Gini coefficient has fallen from 0.33 to 0.31.[20] At the same time the deciles suggest that the groups in the bottom half of the income distribution have maintained their share of income but that the sixth, seventh, eighth and ninth deciles have increased their share, largely at the expense of the tenth decile.

Undoubtedly imaginative researchers could think of many other fruitful uses to which these important new data sources can be put. Although this unique mine of data is only just now being exploited, we can look forward to much new work in this area in the next few years.

Since the ABS survey data first became available only in 1973, most of the currently available work on the distribution of income among families uses the Macquarie/Queensland data. Thus, while we can here avoid a detailed discussion of the procedures used in the latter survey (spelled out in Edwards, Gates and Layton 1966), some discussion of the quality of the data is warranted. The sample comprised about 5500 families and was confined to urban areas. The extent of non-response is not stated for the first stage, which sought information on gross family income, the number of people in the household and expenditure on specified groups of commodities. Two pieces of evidence cast doubt on the reliability of this first stage. One-person households comprise only nine per cent of the total surveyed whereas in the larger and more comprehensive ABS household expenditure survey of 1974–75 they comprised about twice that percentage. In addition, data from the 1968–69 ABS income survey (conducted no more than three years after the Macquarie/Queensland survey) produce a Gini coefficient and deciles for household income which are remarkably similar to those derived from the Macquarie/Queensland data. Podder (1972, p.188) calculates the latter Gini coefficient of before-tax family income to be 0.335, while the comparable figure for the ABS survey is 0.33 (p.8). For any one decile, the maximum difference between the two sets is one per cent of income.

The puzzling aspect of this close coincidence is that the definition of 'family' used in the two surveys is not the same. The most important difference is that the Macquarie/Queensland definition includes single person households, while these are excluded by the ABS. This is especially significant because the distribution of income among the approximately one million single people (predominantly juveniles and the aged) differs substantially from that of families of two or more people. First, the distribution of income *within* the group is more unequal for single people. In 1973–74 the Gini coefficient for non-family individuals was 0.44 whereas for families it was 0.31. Second, the average income of non-family individuals was only 40 per cent of that of families. For 1973–74 inclusion of non-family individuals increases the Gini coefficient from 0.31 to 0.36.[21]

The other main difference in definition of family is that the ABS includes only those having a relationship to each other by blood, marriage or adoption (referred to as 'families'), whereas the Macquarie/Queensland definition includes all those, other than boarders, living in the same dwelling and relying upon common cooking facilities (referred to as 'households').

This distinction is not trivial. Households include many individuals who would not constitute part of a family, such as young people sharing a flat or elderly brothers and sisters living together. The incomes of members of such households are aggregated for the purpose of identifying household income. The more inclusive is the notion of income unit used, the lower we would expect inequality between income units to be. Therefore, *a priori* we expect inequality among families to be less than inequality among households and this in turn to be less than inequality among families plus non-family individuals. Statistics from the 1973–74 income survey and the 1974–75 Household Expenditure Survey support this expectation. The respective Gini coefficients are 0.31, 0.33 and 0.36 (though note that the 1974–75 Household Expenditure Survey covered capital cities only, where the distribution is more equal than for the population as a whole).

Using the information now available we can infer an approximate expected value of the Gini coefficient for households in the mid-1960s (i.e. when the Macquarie/Queensland survey was taken). We would expect it to be greater than the 0.33 actually found for several reasons. First, it should be higher than the coefficient for families at the same time (approximately 0.33). Second, it should be higher than the coefficient for households in 1974–75, since inequality among families has declined over the period and we would expect this decline to affect households similarly. Third, it should be higher than the coefficient for capital city households only (0.33). The author's best guess is about 0.36.

The second stage of the Macquarie/Queensland survey involved a return visit to the 5,500 households first interviewed to seek more detailed information on income and expenditure and some information on wealth. The non-response rate at this stage was almost 50 per cent. The low response rate compounds the problems arising from the apparent unrepresentativeness of the first stage, though it is alleviated somewhat by a comparison of demographic data between the second and the first stages. This shows that the representation of each age group of the family head was fairly similar in the the two samples, with the exception of household heads under 30 years of age. These were significantly under-represented in the second survey (Kakwani and Podder 1975, pp.76–78).

Individual Incomes

Inferences about the distribution of income prior to 1968 rely mainly on income tax data. These enable, of course, analysis only of individual incomes.

Using these data it can be seen that the distribution of individual income became more equal in Australia during the 17 years from 1950, but that most of the reduction in inequality occurred in the early years and is partly illusory. The starting year of 1950–51 was a period of exceptionally severe inequality, owing to high primary producer incomes (Hancock 1970). It appears that the absence of any clear trend in degree of inequality of the taxable incomes of males between 1952 and 1967 is the result of two offsetting changes. The ratio of the incomes of the highest quartile of taxpayers to those of the lower quartile declined while the ratio of the second to the third quartiles, if anything, increased. Remarking on the latter change, Hancock lays stress on the policy reversals of the Arbitration tribunals. In the early 1950s, the tribunals granted wage increases largely in the form of increases in the basic wage. This had the effect of compressing wage relativities. On three subsequent occasions wage increases were given in the form of substantial rises in margins. Each occasion is accompanied by a noticeable rise, of two to three per cent, in the percentage value of second to third quartile incomes.

There are several questions yet to be answered which are amenable to the use of tax data. These include the relative positions of the highest incomes, say the top five or one per cent; the extent to which the incomes generated in each state have similar degrees of inequality; and the influence, if any, of short-run fluctuations in the level of economic activity on the inequality measures. Related to this last point, it would be of considerable interest to know whether changes in the ratio of profits to wages were associated with noticeable changes in the distribution of income.

The ABS survey data of 1968–69 have been used to examine the change in the degree of income inequality which has occurred in Australia in the period from 1915. In 1915 the Commonwealth Government undertook a population census which sought to identify *inter alia* the wealth which could be called upon to finance the war effort. Information on income was sought, in addition to that on wealth (Lancaster-Jones 1975, p.22). Lancaster-Jones has used the 1915 and 1969 figures to calculate a number of inequality measures which indicate the direction and extent of change in that 54 year period. He concludes (p.32) that

> it would require a mind peculiarly resistant to evidence to deny that over the last half century there has been a significant reduction in inequality of income distribution among men.

Both skill and imagination are required to make the figures from the two sources comparable. Adjustments were made to allow for differences in the data base, including the definition of income; changes in the structure of the population; and changes in the number of income categories. After these adjustments are made the Gini coefficient falls from 0.42 in 1915 to 0.338 in 1968/69. Supplementary evidence suggests that much of the reduction in inequality has resulted from a decline in the relative position of the highest income earners. In 1915 the top one per cent of male income earners received 14.6 per cent of *net* income, whereas in the later year this group received 7.9 per cent of *gross* income (Lancaster-Jones 1975, p.30).

The normative and policy implications of any observed degree of inequality depend a great deal on the reasons why incomes are not equal. Annual incomes, for example, may vary even though lifetime incomes are identical. Differences in hours worked, the propensity to save and the costly acquisition of skills are examples of sources of income difference which may be acceptable even to an egalitarian spirit. Thus great caution is required in drawing normative inferences from movements in (or the absolute level of) aggregate inequality measures. (Rivlin 1975; Paglin 1975; Murray forthcoming; Murray 1978). Recent theoretical developments coupled with the detail available from the ABS income surveys enable some systematic examination of the characteristics correlated with income inequality in Australia. It is possible to avoid the controversial issue of which sources and amounts of inequality are acceptable and which are not if attention is confined to identifying the sources of income differences.

The population may be classified into mutually exclusive groups based on some characteristics believed to be associated with income differences, such as age, sex, hours worked and education. Differences of mean income between the groups thus classified will indicate the contribution of the relevant characteristic to total inequality. There will still remain income differences within the groups, which are not explained by the chosen characteristic. The details of the results vary with the technique of decomposition used, though Murray obtains consistent rankings of characteristics in order of importance. The 1968–69 ABS data for individuals indicate that differences in income by sex and then age (in that order of importance) account for a substantial amount of total inequality—about 65 per cent according to one measure. Classification of the income of the group comprising fully employed workers by age, education and sex suggests that together these characteristics account for a large proportion of total inequality, with education and then age being the most important factors (Murray forthcoming).

Work done overseas makes clear that it cannot be inferred from the observed correlation between income and education that differences in income are *caused by* differences in education. Attempts to find an independent role for education, having standardised for IQ, family background and age, for example, have produced very modest results (Rivlin 1975; Lydall 1976b; Phelps Brown 1977).

Decomposition of the aggregate inequality measures also enables *changes* in total inequality to be examined. In Australia this has been made possible by the existence of the two comparable ABS income surveys conducted five years apart. Over the five year period to 1973–74 the aggregate Gini coefficient for individuals fell from 0.33 to 0.31. Classification of the population into income—related sub-groups enables the source of this decrease in the aggregate Gini coefficient to be decomposed into changes in the relative mean incomes of different groups and changes in the degree of inequality within groups.

Application of this approach suggests that the decline in aggregate inequality was the result of a fall in the dispersion of the mean incomes of different groups rather than a fall in the dispersion within groups. The male/female, education and age related differentials have all diminished (Murray 1978). The improvement in the relative position of women is probably explained by both the move to equal pay and the substantial increase in the relative mean incomes of those principally dependent on government social services benefits. The sources of the other changes are not so obvious.

Disaggregation of the sort undertaken by Murray greatly enhances our understanding of changes in the distribution of income. It is clear that aggregate results, as is so often the case, can conceal a great variety of movement in the components of the aggregate. Both understanding *per se* and the development of effective policies are aided by decomposition when the aggregate experience is not typical of that of each of the constituent parts.

Family incomes

The only work which has been done on inequality in family, rather than individual, incomes relies on data from the Macquarie/Queensland survey (Kakwani 1976; Podder and Kakwani 1975; Podder 1972). These data suggest that family incomes are more equally distributed than individual male incomes,[22] and that the degree of inequality in the distribution of pre-tax family incomes is reduced further (the Gini coefficient falls from 0.33 to 0.29) if families are converted to an equivalent scale to allow for differences in size and composition (Kakwani 1976, p.18).

Podder (1972) seeks to identify the impact on income inequality of several socio-demographic factors; specifically age, family size, occupation, and education. Classification of the total sample according to these characteristics means that the actual numbers in some categories are quite small and must raise the possibility of significant sampling error. With this reservation, we can note that age of the family head emerges as one of the most important influences on the difference in income between families. On average, income rises with age until the family head reaches age 45–49, and then declines. It would be interesting to test for the impact of the other characteristics while standardising for age. Attempts to do this using the Macquarie/Queensland data will encounter the problem of small absolute numbers. However, the data from the 1968–69 and 1973–74 ABS surveys include these socio-demographic characteristics and would be satisfactory for this purpose.

The Macquarie/Queensland data are sufficiently detailed to allow for distribution of family expenditure to be calculated.[23] There are several reasons why this may have a separate interest. First, expenditure may for some purposes be considered a better indicator of economic welfare than income. It also appears to be more equally distributed than income (Podder 1972, p.185).[24] Finally, an expenditure which exceeds one's income suggests an ability either to borrow or to use previously acquired assets. Both, but especially the latter, lend some weight to the idea that one's position in the income hierarchy varies during the life cycle, and to the idea that some people's income varies more from year to year than their expenditure.

International Comparisons

The hazards of international comparisons of income distribution are severe. Briefly these hinge on the non-comparability of definitions of family and income; the possibility of substantial sampling error; and the inability of any existing measure of private income to reflect the value of government-provided goods and services. It is plain that even the most careful analysis should be taken as suggestive rather than conclusive. Despite the difficulties and the very tentative nature of the conclusions, a number of studies attempt this comparison of family incomes.

Several inequality measures have been used. Although the Gini index of family incomes calculated for other developed countries varies between studies, the index for Australia consistently has a value amongst the lowest. (Kakwani forthcoming; Podder 1972, p.199; OECD 1976; Roberti 1978).

This indicator is supported by several percentile measures. A study involving 56 countries calculated the proportion of total pre-tax income received by the top five per cent of households. Australia, along with the United States and the Scandinavian countries, was placed among the group for which this top five per cent received the smallest share, i.e. about 15 per cent (Paukert 1973). In a sample of 17 developed countries, only in Hungary is the income share of the top 20 per cent less than in Australia. Similarly the income share of the bottom 40 per cent in Australia is exceeded only in Hungary (Kakwani, forthcoming). Lydall (1968) uses Australian taxation data of 1959–60 to estimate the incomes of non-farm, full-period workers receiving predominantly non-property income. In comparison with 25 other countries Lydall's inequality measures consistently put Australia, along with New Zealand, Czechoslovakia and Hungary, in the group with the lowest degree of inequality.

Despite the overwhelming consistency of the evidence suggesting Australia has a relatively very equal distribution of income, reservations remain. All the studies, except those of Lydall and Roberti, rely on the Macquarie/Queensland data base. We have noted earlier some reasons for doubting its reliability. Particularly pertinent here is its apparent under-representation of single-member households, for they are a group which has been identified as having a relatively high risk of poverty. The OECD study chooses the Macquarie/Queensland data in preference to the 1968–69 ABS survey results precisely because the latter's definition of a household excludes single people. Paradoxically, it makes no difference which one is used, since the inequality measures for the two are virtually identical.

Distribution of Wealth

There is some tentative evidence to reinforce the commonsense expectation that wealth and asset ownership is distributed among households less equally than income.[25] Kakwani and Podder (1976) calculate the shares of households in disposable income, assets and net worth. They also show shares in assets and net worth when families are ranked by disposable income.

The inequality in the distribution of net worth as compared with income is striking whether one compares Gini indices, the share of the top 5 or 20 per cent, or the share of the bottom quintile. The correlation between family rankings according to income and rankings according to wealth is not exact. As a consequence 'the distribution of wealth between *income* groups is somewhat more equal than the distribution of wealth between *wealth* holders.' (Kakwani and Podder 1976, p.85, emphasis added.)

The impact of the sex, age and occupation of the family head on the inequality of wealth distribution has been assessed in the same paper. However, this disaggregation of the sample produces quite small numbers in some categories. The addition of the problem of small numbers to the other doubts about the reliability of the data on wealth so reduces confidence in the results that they will not be reported here.

Section 3 Poverty

Poverty is one aspect of the distribution of income which—after a long drought—has seen some concentrated research in recent years.[26]

Until the publication in 1967 of the results of a survey of poverty in Melbourne, there had been no systematic attempt to identify the extent, location and characteristics of poverty in Australia.[27] Since then there has been a major investment in improving understanding of Australian poverty, including some analytical work. The empirical information has largely been generated under the auspices of the Commission of Inquiry into Poverty and forms the basis of its *First Main Report* (referred to hereafter as the Henderson Report 1975).

The Commission organised three main sources of information about the extent and nature of poverty in Australia. First, as noted earlier, in 1973 the Australian Bureau of Statistics undertook a survey of lower incomes for 1972–73, assessed on both an individual and a family basis. Second, 34 studies of specific aspects of poverty were commissioned. Of these, 19 have been published as separate reports. Third, written and verbal submissions were made to the Inquiry by a diverse range of individuals and organisations. By and large the impressive collection of information about poverty thus generated has confirmed and extended the findings of the Melbourne Survey.

Several conceptual puzzles need to be resolved before even the most comprehensive data can be organised to provide an indication of the extent of poverty.

3.1 Measurement of Poverty

How should poverty and changes in poverty be measured? There is no simple answer to this question, though the homogeneous approach in most of the Australian literature would imply otherwise.

In its simplest sense poverty implies material deprivation. Deprivation may be absolute—i.e. inadequate means to sustain health—or it may be relative. This distinction may also be characterised as objective/subjective. The requirements for health can be established through assessment of minimum quantities of food, housing, clothing and access to medical care. The cost of providing these minima identify an objectively determined income requirement below which people are in absolute need. In principle such a minimum income requirement is determined independently of the material conditions of the community as a whole.

On the relative/subjective view deprivation occurs because some people have incomes which impose a standard of living much below that of the community norm. The identification of such relative poverty need make no reference to minimum physical requirements. It may be measured, for example, by the proportion of the population with incomes below some nominated percentage of an indicator of average income such as average weekly earnings.

The above are caricatures of the two competing notions of poverty or deprivation. Actual poverty measures usually combine elements of both. In particular the absolute approach cannot be pursued in its pure form for there is no unambiguous measure of minima, especially for housing, clothing, and medical requirements.[28] Such measures will inevitably be influenced by the general standards of the relevant community. The purely relative notion of poverty is at odds with its commonsense meaning and is thus likely to cause ambiguity in interpretation. Further, there are no clear criteria for identifying a relative poverty line.

Thus, a strong case can be made for the most appropriate concept of poverty being one which incorporates both relative and absolute dimensions. A sense of deprivation does have both physical and social roots and to focus on one to the exclusion of the other is to deny the complexity of the problem.[29] Any definition of poverty must thus in part be arbitrary and hence disputable. Even the proper mix between the absolute and relative components is controversial. The part played by the personal views and judgements of the researcher in defining poverty needs emphasis because the definition chosen will have an important impact on the extent of measured poverty and the perceived characteristics of the poor. This is precisely the information which usually is being sought in such investigations.

This raises the issue of the appropriateness of a single index by which absolute levels of poverty, changes in those levels and the characteristics of the poor could be measured. While such an index is extremely convenient, its use involves a number of hazards, of the sort inevitable in any attempt to express a complex human situation in terms of a single number.

Unless the poverty line is set at a fairly high level there will be some people whose incomes exceed the poverty line but who nonetheless are in need. Perhaps they are committed to especially high housing costs, or have accumulated debt or simply do not spend their income 'in ways which would be regarded as appropriate by scientific investigators' (Wilson 1974, p.7).[30] Conversely there will be some with incomes below the poverty line whom closer investigation reveals are not in need. A person may, for example, have considerable wealth, or be one of the 28.6 per cent of unmarried women who in 1976 kept house, as an occupation, without pay (Social Indicators 1976, p.43). Low income was found to be a particularly inadequate indicator of need among the aged. The Melbourne survey found that on the basis of income alone 15 per cent of the aged were below their poverty line. However only 2.3 per cent were identified as being in need, once allowance had been made for the cheapness of accommodation, the value of assets owned and private assistance from family and others (Henderson, Harcourt and Harper 1970, p.63). Further, people's needs for income are not uniform. It is difficult to be precise but one could expect wide agreement on the proposition that the needs of a person with other disabilities, such as a physical handicap or old age, exceed those of a fit young adult. This dimension of hardship is obscured by a single-minded concentration on income as the index of poverty or deprivation.[31]

Both the Melbourne survey and the Henderson Report have chosen to express the extent of poverty in terms of a single 'poverty line', expressed as a weekly income such that a person receiving less than this amount per week is classified as living in poverty. On a number of occasions percentages have also been given of those receiving incomes up to 20 per cent above the poverty line. The issues considered above suggest great care and some discussion should attach to the choice of any measure of poverty. The discussion of the poverty line, if not the care taken in its selection, is inadequate in the report of the Melbourne survey. The discussion begins with the observation that the choice 'depends on an assessment of what seems appropriate in a particular situation, taking account of community attitudes, economic conditions, customs and tradition' (Henderson, Harcourt and Harper 1970, p.29). The reader is then offered scarcely more than a page (pp.1 and 29), in all in explanation of the figure chosen and almost no discussion of the limitations of the single index approach.

The poverty line is set to equal the basic wage (which still existed in 1966, when a poverty line was first determined) plus child endowment payments, for a family comprising a married couple plus two dependent children. The basic wage is deemed appropriate because it is the minimum which meets, in the words of Mr. Justice Higgins, 'the normal needs of an average employee regarded as a human being living in a civilised community' (quoted by Henderson, Harcourt and Harper 1970, p.1). Even if one accepts that the basic wage of Higgins' day (1907) was a suitable measure of minimum standards it does not follow, as Henderson, Harcourt and Harper imply, that the basic wage of 1966 had the same implication. For many years prior to 1966 the Arbitration Commission had abandoned 'minimum needs' as the sole criterion for determining the basic wage, and had referred in particular to capacity to pay.

A second problem arises with the need to update the poverty line to allow for growth and inflation. The chosen updating procedure is to adjust for both price and productivity changes by linking the poverty line to movements in pre-tax average weekly earnings per employed male unit (Henderson, Harcourt and Harper 1970, p.30). As the Priorities Review Staff (1975) point out, this implies a secular increase in the poverty line as a proportion of some measure of average disposable income such as median post-tax income. It is also hard to reconcile this updating procedure with the choice of the basic wage for the initial poverty line. The combination implies that until 1966 movements in the basic wage reflected changes in minimum acceptable standards of living, but after that date such changes become embodied in changes in pre-tax average earnings.

If the poverty line had been derived from a study of the costs of providing for specified minimum needs then the appropriate updating procedure would be to reassess the relevant costs. A related procedure would be to retain the poverty line at the same real value. It may be preferred that the poverty line retain a constant relative, rather than absolute, value. The choice between the two embodies different perspectives on the nature of poverty and perhaps also on the community's obligations to the poor: it needs careful consideration and explicit justification. Where it is held that the appropriate poverty line is a relative one it remains necessary to decide whether or not its relative position (e.g. to median/average disposable income) should improve over time. With virtually no defense of their choice, the Henderson Report opts for a rising relative poverty line. This should be borne clearly in mind when comparing percentages of the population below the poverty line in different years.[32]

Given the subjective nature of the poverty line it would have been a most valuable exercise to establish and report the extent to which the percentages in poverty and the socio-economic characteristics of the poor were sensitive to changes in the poverty line chosen. Cox (1976), using the data from the 1973 ABS income survey, finds that the composition of the group with an income between 100 and 140 per cent of the Henderson poverty line is rather different from that with an income below the poverty line. Specifically the former group has a substantially smaller proportion of family heads who are single or under 20 years of age, and a substantially higher proportion of heads who are over 60 years of age, and of married couples, than does the group below the poverty line. (Cox, 1976, pp.436–37).

3.2 Household Equivalence Scales

People live in households which vary in both size and composition. These differences result in different income needs. Since poverty is viewed as an income insufficient to meet minimum needs, an income which is just adequate for some households will place others in poverty and still others in relative comfort. Thus measures which enable heterogeneous households to be expressed as multiples of some chosen standard household are required. Differences in needs between adults and children of different ages, between males and females, between those in the workforce and those not, have both a physiological base and a social base. To identify these with any confidence requires detailed information on either the requirements for physical and psychological health, or the actual expenditure patterns of households in the relevant income range.[33] Such information was not available for Australia when the results of the Melbourne survey were being assessed. The Henderson Report (p.13) implies that the data from the Australian Bureau of Statistics expenditure survey of 1974–5 will be usable for this purpose. Both the Melbourne survey and the Henderson Report resort to a scale prepared in 1954 by the Budget Standard Service of New York.

This scale (information for which excluded home owners) sought to identify minimum cost relativities for low income families rather than actual expenditure relativities. As the Melbourne survey points out (p.27), the use of this scale 'assumes that the relationship between the costs of living of, say, a pre-school child and a working adult male is similar in New York in 1954 and in Melbourne in 1966' and, we might add, for Australia as a whole in 1973. This is a very strong assumption and again some discussion of the sensitivity of results to the scale chosen would have been most welcome. Adjustment for family composition that considers only the number (and not work status as in the New York scale) of adults and children gives rather different conclusions about who is poor. In particular the simplified approach substantially increases the proportion of poor households which are headed by a person over the age of 60 (Cox 1977, pp.436–37).

At the time the Henderson Report was written there was some information available on Australian household expenditure patterns, derived from the Macquarie/Queensland survey. The data can be used to identify expenditure by household composition and income level. A cross-section study has been used to derive a scale which 'converts the income of a non-standard household into the income of a standard household while the household remains at the same level of utility' (Kakwani 1976, p.6). Kakwani's rather tersely presented technique is the most sophisticated available, though the reliability of the scale it produces is diminished by doubts about the data. He also assumes an identical utility function for all households. The technique takes advantage of the classification of families by both composition and level of income and is a variant of the 'observed behaviour' approach. Kakwani finds considerable economies of scale in household size, which are not apparent in the New York scale.

The Kakwani and New York scales diverge markedly for households with more than three children, the divergence increasing with household size (Kakwani 1976, p.16; Henderson Report 1975, p.14). This produces important differences in the composition of families below the poverty line. Specifically, the Kakwani ratio produces a substantially higher proportion of small families among the poor.

Using the same data as Kakwani, Podder (1971) produces an equivalence scale which differs from both the Henderson scale and the Kakwani scale. He defines families of different composition to have the same level of welfare if they spend the same proportion of their income on food. The ratio which converts the expenditure needs of a child to an adult equivalent is constant for families of different size (in contrast with Kakwani's more plausible economies of scale). In this the Podder scale is quite similar to that of Henderson but it is markedly different in its treatment of an additional adult. Podder claims that the costs of a single adult are half that of a married couple. Henderson's figures put a single adult's costs as at least 70 per cent of those of a married couple.

It is apparent that equivalence scales can differ substantially even when constructed from the same data set. It is important, therefore, to establish the sensitivity of results to the measure used. The Australian studies suggest the different scales cause important differences in the measurement of poverty and the identification of groups most in need.

Differences in need can also occur when there are large variations in housing costs borne by different households. Poverty estimates thus are made separately for income before and after housing costs have been considered. The technique for adjusting for housing costs is virtually the same in both the Melbourne survey and the Henderson Report. Basically because 'it is a fairly common assumption that housing costs for low income families should represent not more than 20 per cent of income' (p.30) the Melbourne survey defined the poverty line after housing costs had been met to be 18 per cent below its standard poverty line. It noted, however, that the survey data show a great deal of variation in the relation of housing costs to total costs.

3.3 Empirical Findings

Not surprisingly, the Melbourne survey and the Henderson Report can be seen as complementary. The Melbourne survey did the pioneering work of providing figures about poverty where there were none before and attempting answers to the issues discussed above. Since then a considerable literature has developed overseas on these questions. Despite this development, the methods and concepts of the Melbourne survey have been adopted virtually without change by the Henderson Report. Equipped with a ready-made framework the Henderson Report concentrated on generating information about poverty which had a broader and perhaps more reliable base than that already available.

This article cannot do justice to the volume of information now available about poverty and the poor. Convenient summaries of their findings are provided by both the Melbourne survey and the Henderson Report, to which the interested reader is referred. We can, however, note some of the main patterns to emerge.

The Henderson Report (p.15) found that after housing costs had been considered 6.7 per cent of households had incomes below the poverty line used in that Report (10.2 per cent before housing costs). This figure is similar to the percentage identified as being in poverty by the Melbourne survey, though the Henderson poverty line implies a higher absolute and relative standard of living.

The Melbourne survey sought to identify the socio-economic and demographic characteristics of those receiving the lowest incomes. Its purpose was to locate those features which make an individual or household most at risk of being poor. The characteristics considered are family composition plus the following 'disabilities'—old age, female head without dependent children, fatherless family, large family (four or more dependent children), recent migration, low skill, sickness or accident, and unemployment (pp.38–

39). This same approach has been used in the Henderson Report, though with a slightly more disaggregated set of disabilities (p.17). Kakwani (1976) follows this procedure also, though with some different categories.

Perhaps the dominant finding is that poverty is overwhelmingly concentrated among households which do not have an adult, especially a male, earning an income. The exceptions are those with large numbers of children and those who are recent migrants.[34] The Melbourne survey and the Henderson Report both attribute an important role to Australia's high level of employment, until 1974, in helping to keep families from poverty.

The insecure financial position of women also comes through strongly. The group with the highest incidence of poverty, both before and after allowing for housing costs, is fatherless families (Henderson Report 1975, p.19; Henderson, Harcourt and Harper 1970, p.39; Kakwani 1976, p.27). About one third of these families were found to have incomes below the poverty line, with a substantial number not much above this level. In addition, the Henderson Report found that by far the largest group having incomes of less than 40 per cent of the poverty line were non-aged single women with no dependents. In fact being a single female is classified as a disability. Why these women should be so poor is not entirely clear. About 7000 of them were in religious orders, hence low income was not an indication of need. Of the remainder, it seems that a large proportion were entitled to some pension or benefit, such as the widow's pension, but were not receiving one, through ignorance or pride (Henderson Report 1975, p.22). The other group with a very high incidence of poverty (before adjustment for housing costs) is the aged. As noted earlier, however, the position of the aged is influenced by a number of factors other than simply recorded income.

The other disability characteristics most likely to be associated with low incomes were sickness and invalidity, unemployment and the presence of more than one disability, such as being a recent migrant with a large family (Henderson Report 1975, p.18). Probably associated with the high incidence of poverty among families with female heads is the high incidence also found where the household head is widowed, divorced or separated (Kakwani 1976, p.27). There may also be a relation between the risk of poverty and the level of education attained by the household head. Those with education below complete secondary schooling, and especially those with no secondary education, appear to have a much higher incidence of poverty than the more educated. The relation breaks down for higher levels of education (Kakwani 1976, p.29).

This identification of the characteristics which are strongly correlated with poverty is plainly most valuable, especially for policy purposes. However, two caveats are required. First, as discussed earlier, the above conclusions are probably sensitive to both the definition of the poverty line and to the household equivalence scale used. Second, almost a quarter of the poor had none of the 'disabilities' as listed in the Henderson Report.

3.4 Poverty Gap

Poverty can be more or less severe, and one measure of its severity is the 'poverty gap'. This records the difference between the relevant poverty line and the actual income received. It is useful for assessing where the most severe poverty is located, and for estimating the minimum transfer of funds necessary to raise the income of a particular group at least to the poverty line. If we apply this not to income actually received but to social service entitlements of pensioner income units with different family compositions, it emerges that in 1973 single pensioners and fatherless families with two or more children were the worst off, with a poverty gap of about 20 per cent. A similar exercise applied to families receiving the minimum wage shows a poverty gap which becomes severe as the number of children rises to four or more (Henderson Report 1975, pp.23–24). Kakwani (1976, pp.27–33) calculates poverty gaps, based on recorded incomes, for families classified in a variety of ways, e.g. by education, occupation, age and country of origin. The size of the poverty gap typically varies substantially within a particular classification and it is not always clear what interpretation should be placed on this. When poor families are grouped according to the educational level of the head, for example, the greatest poverty gap occurs for those who have completed a general tertiary course, while the second lowest gap is for those with no secondary education. To improve our understanding of the nature and causes of poverty, such data require a closer inspection than they have been given.

The poverty gap can be used to calculate the minimum amount of redistribution necessary to ensure that everyone receives an income at least equal to the poverty line (Kakwani 1976). Of course the poverty line which is chosen will have a critical effect on the size of the poverty index, while the social welfare system has yet to be devised which would ensure that this minimum transfer occurred continuously and with a neutral impact on the incentive to qualify for assistance. In a more extensive discussion of the poverty index, Kakwani (forthcoming) notes that the index for the whole population may be expressed as a weighted average of the indexes for mutually exclusive sub-sets of the population. The disaggregation may be based on pertinent socio-economic characteristics of households, to see where poverty is most strongly concentrated.[35]

3.5 Changes Over Time

We have as yet little information on changes over time in the effectiveness of efforts to reduce poverty and otherwise to redistribute income. The only study done of this (Hancock 1970) uses tax and social welfare data to pick up some of the shifts in income distribution before 1967. We expect many changes to have occurred since then.

The events of the mid-1970s require a whole new analysis of movements in real social welfare benefits, the effects of inflation, and the role of high employment in minimising poverty. At the time of writing these events were too recent to have been the subject of serious empirical analysis.[36] The available survey data only just encompass the period 1973–74, when the real break in the previously established patterns occurred. The net effect on poverty of these changes is therefore as yet unknown.

However, some assessment of the distributional impact of recent fiscal changes is possible. The Federal budgets from 1974–75 to 1977–78 introduced important amendments to the structure of personal income tax, associated concessional deductions, health benefit levies and levels of welfare payments.[37] These changes are quantitatively large and must nave had a substantial effect on the distribution of household disposable income.

The major redistributive change in the 1974–75 budget was an increase in the real value of the age, widow's and supporting mother's pensions. Unemployment and sickness benefits were also raised substantially following earlier large increases. The changes from June 1972 to June 1975, expressed as a percentage of average weekly earnings, are shown in Table 1.

TABLE 1
*Weekly Benefit Rate as a percentage of Average Weekly Earnings**

	Age & Invalid		Widows' Pension		Unemployment & Sickness		
	Standard	Married	Class A	Class B	Married	Single Adult	Single 18–20 years
June 1972	19.1	33.5	28.0	16.7	26.2	17.8	11.5
June 1974	20.5	35.8	27.5	20.5	35.8	20.5	20.5
June 1975	23.3	38.8	30.4	23.3	38.8	23.3	23.3

*During June 1974–June 1975 the real value of average weekly earnings rose by six per cent.
Source : Social Indicators 1976, pp.66, 68, 71.

The substantial rise in the real value of social services benefits evident in the table occurred during a period of rapid inflation. This rise, which by and large has been sustained, must have an important effect on reducing poverty. The data on poverty all suggest that those dependent on government social service benefits are among the most needy: perhaps inevitably so given that at the time of the surveys the poverty lines were chosen to exceed the level of pension benefits. In addition to the rise in the value of pensions the eligibility conditions for the age pension have also been relaxed. The means test has been replaced by a more liberal income test and removed entirely for all those of age 70 years or more.

The real income changes experienced by the aged during the 1970s varies, depending on their initial primary source of income. The poorest among the aged, those dependent on the age pension, have experienced a rise in their real incomes, at a rate similar to that for the population as a whole. In addition, liberalisations of the tests for obtaining a pension have partially protected those who initially relied on income from past savings. Retired people who continue to rely on interest, dividends and rent are undoubtedly worse off (Murray 1977). It appears that the distribution of income among the aged has become more equal, while the impact of this on the aggregate distribution remains unclear.

There are three aspects to the changes in the structure of personal income tax which occurred over the years 1975–76 to 1977–78. First, the tax structure has been very much simplified (and average rates reduced), with only three different marginal rates to apply from February 1978. In addition an automatic minimum rebate, sufficient to encompass the claims of most taxpayers, has replaced the previous concessional deductions from taxable income. There has also been a substantial rise in the level of real income at which tax first becomes payable. Second, the whole income tax structure, except the ceiling above which rebates are allowed for concessional expenditure, has been indexed annually to changes in the consumer price index, excluding the effects of indirect taxes. Third, tax rebates for dependent children have been replaced by much increased child endowment payments (now referred to as family allowances).

The net effect of the changes in the 1975 and 1976 tax rates, the treatment of dependent children and the health insurance levy is complex because the final impact on the individual taxpayer depends critically on the amount of concessional expenditure normally incurred. While acknowledging this, Scotton and Sheehan (1976, p.20) conclude that

> the big gainers are taxpayers with dependents, especially those at the lowest end of the income scale. The income effect is U-shaped: the greatest benefits flow to those at both ends of the income scale. The greatest losers are taxpayers without dependents and with income around the average.

The figures supplied by the Australian Treasury suggest that, while the 1977–78 budget changes reduce income tax for all taxpayers, the distribution of the gains has the same U-shape as identified for the earlier measures (Budget Speech 1977–78, Statement Number 4, p.125). In all it seems very likely that the federal tax and benefit changes have reduced the extent of poverty, especially among large families and those wholly dependent on social welfare payments. We cannot, however, predict the net impact on inequality measures such as the Gini coefficient. The progressive simplification of the income tax structure has increased the share of disposable income going to the high income groups, especially at the expense of middle income earners. We must await further survey data to learn how the shares of different income groups in household disposable income have been altered. Even then it will be difficult to separate the effects of the budgetary from the non-budgetary changes which occurred during the same period. The most important of the latter were unemployment and high rates of inflation, though non-trivial effects can also be expected from the increasing participation of women in the workforce and the compression of relative wages.

We know as yet very little about the distributional impact of these events, but it is clear that the effect of high rates of inflation can be separated into the implications for incomes and the implications for wealth. Information is sparse in both areas, but we can be confident that wage earners still in employment have not yet suffered from an overall reduction in real wages as a result of the post-1973 inflationary burst. This is not to say that efforts to reduce inflation will not have this effect sometime in the future. Income from property ownership has not fared so well. This is partly because of the taxation of profits on the basis of historical cost accounting, which was modified in the 1977–78 budget, and partly because of the prevalence of negative real rates of interest not fully offset by capital gains. If only the wealthy received property income this would have little import for a study of poverty. But it is unlikely that this is so. The aged are one obvious group where relatively large asset holdings (owned directly or in the form of superannuation and life assurance entitlements) need not be correlated with relatively high incomes. Those dependent on interest, dividends and superannuation benefits (i.e. non-wage, non-pension incomes) have seen the real value of their incomes substantially eroded by the high rates of inflation.

Inflation may also affect the distribution of income and the extent of poverty through its implications for unemployment. There is dispute over the extent to which high rates of inflation *per se* cause unemployment. But there is no doubt about the effect on unemployment of cures for inflation based on deflationary measures. In this context it is interesting to recall the important role attributed to low levels of unemployment in enabling households with adult members of working age to stay out to poverty. Of course whether or not an increase in unemployment increases the percentage of the population who are defined as poor depends on the relation between the poverty line and the level of unemployment benefits.

3.6 Life Cycle Poverty

An important but virtually unexplored aspect of poverty in Australia is the extent to which it is a temporary or permanent state for those involved. Poverty experienced for a short period—especially if expected to be temporary—is likely to be much less demoralising than more enduring poverty. It can also be eased by dissaving. On the other hand, it has been argued that it is the experience of a *decrease* in living standards that is especially painful, so that a given low income (above some subsistence level) will cause more hardship for a family accustomed to a significantly higher income than for a family for whom that income is the norm. If much poverty is associated with particular stages in life, and is temporary, then this may have implications for the planning of measures to prevent people becoming poor (rather than subsidise them after their income has fallen). For example, assistance may be given to encourage the distribution of lifetime income according to the needs of particular stages of life. Superannuation is an obvious illustration of this sort of policy.

On the basis of long and detailed observation of poverty in Australia, Professor Henderson describes the life-cycle income experience of many as 'snakes and ladders'. There is

> a slip down the snake, so to speak, if you become unemployed or sick or lose your husband by death or desertion when you have young dependent children, then you go up again when that situation is past, and perhaps down again when you retire. (Henderson 1978, p.35).

The ideal data for a more formal exploration of lifetime patterns of income and need are derived from longitudinal studies, where the fortunes of selected families are followed over a period of years. No such studies of any size have been undertaken in Australia. However a six-year study in the United States found a considerable movement of individuals in and out of the poorest group during the period. Only about one quarter of those classified as poor in any one year were poor in all six years (*Five Thousand American Families—Patterns of Economic Progress*, quoted in Cox 1977, p.423). The other important finding noted by Cox is that changes in family composition and in the labour force participation of family members occurred frequently and were the most important influences on changes in their economic well-being.

If the propensity to be poor is related to stages of the life cycle then this may emerge from an examination of cross-section data, provided the relevant socio-economic characteristics are included in the data. The contention that 'rather than being a lifetime phenomenon much poverty is temporary and is associated with the life cycle of family income' (Cox 1976, p.423) has been tested so far as is possible by the use of cross-section data from the 1973 Australian Bureau of Statistics Income survey. Cox tested the following three propositions: that poverty is related to age (the old and the young being over-represented among the poor), family composition (especially where the family is headed by a single adult), and number of adults in the family. Further, it was expected that the composition of the poor will depend on where the poverty line is set; that the incomes of many tenants of subsidised public housing will no longer meet the means test (given that existing tenants are not obliged to shift when their income rises) and that expenditure will be distributed more evenly than income. To varying degrees the evidence is consistent with each of these. The last point is supported also by data from the Macquarie/Queensland survey which show that the Gini coefficient for household expenditure was 0.281, whereas for income after tax it was 0.317 (Podder 1972, p.198). At the same time it should be noted that those most vulnerable to poverty caused by changes in their circumstances are those who have the lowest lifetime incomes.

Section 4 Redistributive Policies

Policies to redistribute income may operate through two main vehicles. One is the structure of pre-tax earnings, the other is the taxation and government expenditure system. They cannot be perfect substitutes, of course, since the former affects only those receiving a taxable income. One may argue that the preferred arrangement is to have the payments to factors of production distributed in an equitable manner in the first place, so that coercive government action is minimised. But successful intervention in the structure of private sector factor payments is difficult and likely to have unintended consequences. This problem applies in part also to tax policy, where the ambiguity of incidence and possibilities for avoidance mean the intended redistributive effects are unlikely to be realised fully. Transfer payments and, to a lesser extent, provision of benefits in kind appear to offer the most reliable opportunities for redistribution.

The government's role in altering the market-determined distribution of income has been subject to vigorous scrutiny during the first half of the 1970s. This has come mainly from committees of enquiry appointed to report on and make recommendations for particular areas of government activity, specifically taxation (Asprey 1975, Mathews 1975), compensation and rehabilitation (Woodhouse 1974), superannuation (Hancock 1976) and the general alleviation of poverty (Henderson 1975). It is not possible in this survey to examine the findings and recommendations of each of these committees. Thus brief reference only will be made to all but the Henderson Report. This latter is centrally concerned with efforts to redistribute income, in a way which the others are not.

4.1 Negative Tax Schemes

A question of particular interest in Australia, as overseas, is the role which a negative tax scheme has to play in the alleviation of poverty. Both the Henderson Report and the Priorities Review Staff (1975) support the introduction of a guaranteed minimum income (a form of negative tax), while the Hancock Report opposes the idea in so far as it involves the removal of specific benefits. The two supporters of the idea propose very similar schemes.[38]

The many specific negative tax schemes take the form of either a negative income tax or a social dividend (or guaranteed minimum income). The negative income tax schemes identify some level of income (which varies with family composition) below which households receive cash subsidies and pay no income tax. The subsidy increases as the amount of other household income falls. Social dividend schemes make an automatic payment to all households and levy a positive tax on all other income. The main difference between the two is that with a social dividend approach every income unit in the community receives a regular payment, whether or not it is in need. In all other respects the two approaches can be made to produce schemes which are identical. Any negative tax scheme can be decomposed into three components—the level of the guaranteed minimum income; the level of the marginal tax/retention rate; and the breakeven level of income, at which there is no net income tax paid or subsidy received. Possible variations abound, but the common elements include a floor level of income below which no family should fall; determination of entitlement to benefit based only on current income; the payment of benefits in cash rather than in kind; and the substitution of this cash subsidy for most existing social welfare benefits, such as age and widow's pensions, unemployment and sickness benefits and student living allowances. It is usual also to specify a constant retention rate of private income, from the first dollar earned up to some high level at which a surtax may be imposed.

Many virtues are claimed for such a scheme. In the simplest versions all tests other than that on income are removed, so potential beneficiaries need not subject themselves to detailed personal enquiry; the guarantee of an income to all and its integration within the tax system reduce the affront to pride involved in 'being on welfare'; and the single benefit rationalises the many separate forms of assistance available for specific categories. In doing so it simplifies administration, makes it easier for an individual to ascertain his or her eligibility for benefit and ensures a complete coverage of all in need. The fact that benefits are received in cash provides maximum freedom of choice for beneficiaries. As the Priorities Review Staff (1975, p.19) note the evidence that much poverty is temporary suggests that 'policy should be flexible, aware that family circumstances will change and quick to respond to such changes'. They claim that a guaranteed minimum income will have these attributes. It concentrates assistance on those with the lowest incomes, while ensuring that all those in need are covered. Finally, it avoids the 'poverty trap', where at low levels of income the effective marginal tax rate can be even more than 100 per cent as a rise in private income simultaneously removes eligibility for a range of benefits.

With such a splendid list of desirable characteristics it is little wonder that the idea has evoked much interest among academics and policy makers alike. Both the United Kingdom and the United States have seriously considered variations of the negative tax approach. Both schemes were abandoned before being introduced, so that currently such a scheme is yet to be implemented.

The Hancock Report argues strongly that the administrative difficulties of tax credits (a form of negative income tax) are severe and 'it is at that level that minimum income schemes, if regarded as substitutes for social welfare payments, are defective' (1976, p.18). The administrative difficulties hinge on the need to cope with the heterogeneous circumstances of families, which may change rapidly. The proposals put forward in the Henderson Report and basically endorsed by the Priorities Review Staff handle this need by specifying a social dividend scheme. The minimum income guaranteed to each family would actually be paid at regular intervals, by cheque, to *all* families regardless of their current income (family here includes single people). The size of the payment would vary with the composition of the family, in line with the relative poverty lines used in the Henderson Report. The recommended marginal tax rates on non-grant income are 35 and 40 per cent, depending on the generosity of benefits preferred (43 per cent in the Priorities Review Staff scheme). The level of the minimum guarantee would be more generous for defined categories of families—namely those now entitled to pensions of various sorts owing to a 'permanent disability hindering their earning of a private income by working' (Henderson 1975, p.73). For these groups the guaranteed income should be set at slightly above Henderson's poverty line. The guarantee for all other families would be half this amount (55 per cent in the Priorities Review Staff scheme).[39]

One consequence of this two-tier system is that the guaranteed minimum for those meeting the categorical test can be made reasonably adequate (the Henderson Report recommends 106 per cent of its poverty line, though note that the poverty line was chosen to be 'austere') without the need to make marginal or average tax rates excessive. On the other hand, the use of different benefit categories reduces the supposed advantages of ensuring an adequate income to all, of removing the stigma of being classified as in need, and of doing away with the administrative procedures necessary to make such classifications.

The provision of a regular (say fortnightly) non-taxable automatic payment to all families overcomes the objection that such schemes cannot meet rapidly changing circumstances and respond quickly to a newly developed need. It will, however, involve substantial administrative costs. The Henderson Report believes 'the increased payment load should not be impossible' (p.74) and this may be right, though we are given no evidence of this in the Report.[40]

One substantial difficulty which may emerge from an integrated tax/welfare structure with a constant marginal retention rate of private income is its inflexibility. For instance, the degree of progression of the tax system can only be altered by changing the level of the grant or tax credit, i.e. the guaranteed minimum, or the marginal tax rate. This would require lower marginal income retention rates if the change is not to increase the net costs of the scheme (Saunders 1976, Pritchard and Saunders forthcoming). The alternative is to forgo the advantages of a constant retention rate and introduce further surtaxes. A second problem arises from marrying two systems which have rather different functions. The tax system is concerned, at least in part, to identify capacity to pay, whereas the welfare system is concerned to identify need. The appropriate definition of family unit and income (e.g. should imputed rent, capital gains, private transfers be included?) and the treatment of wealth may not be the same in each case (Treasury 1974).

One of the claimed advantages of a negative tax scheme is that the size of any grant paid is determined solely on the basis of a family's income. Yet this is not of indisputable benefit. It may be held that low incomes impose greater hardship on some groups than on others, for example widows as compared with students, or that some groups—e.g. the handicapped—have a special claim to be relieved of the worst hardships of poverty. The Hancock Report for one is of the opinion that

> the aged have a claim to economic assistance which does not inhere equally in many other sections of the community (though it may inhere in *some* others, such as invalids and widows) (1976, p.15).

The Henderson Report concurs in part for it argues that priority should be given to those who are hindered in earning an income (1975, p.74). This view would support the payment of higher benefits to some groups using criteria other than simply the level of family income.

A second concern is that reliance on a simple income test may reduce work incentives. There is very little empirical evidence on this question. A much quoted American experiment, which provided income guarantees to a group of families in New Jersey, concluded that there was no significant decline in earnings as a result of the assistance guaranteed (*New Jersey Experiment* quoted in Treasury 1974, p.16). The results refer to an eighteen month period only and the total sample of families was not very large. It derives its importance in part from the fact that there is very little other evidence available. The disincentive effect can be expected to vary, in particular with age. Where an adult responsible for a family may not be much affected, others, for example young people who place a high priority on leisure and who have yet to acquire financial commitments, may respond quite differently. The concern expressed in Australia with the efficacy of the work test in ensuring that unemployment benefits are paid only to those genuinely in the workforce suggests that a simple income test may not be welcomed by everyone. An unequivocal view on this matter comes from the Asprey Committee, which remarks that 'such schemes are likely to have consequences for incentives to work and save which make it impossible to consider them seriously' (p.180).

The Henderson Report largely ignores the above disincentives. Instead it emphasises the positive work incentive effects that a guaranteed minimum income may have for low income groups now subject to very high effective marginal tax rates. But, as Pritchard and Saunders (forthcoming) emphasize, there will necessarily also be changes in the average and marginal tax rates facing most other income groups. It is therefore not sufficient to look only at the incentive effects on the poor. They note, for example, that the marginal tax rate for the large lower middle income group would rise substantially.

The Henderson and Priorities Review Staff schemes avoid a number of serious difficulties confronting versions of negative tax schemes developed elsewhere—in particular the difficulties of accommodating rapidly changing circumstances while retaining acceptable marginal and average rates of tax. Yet the modifications which allow this make it necessary to ask whether the attributes of the proposed scheme could not be as, or more, effectively attained by modification of existing welfare provisions.

An argument given prominence in the support of a negative tax scheme in other countries is that this is the one acceptable way of introducing a means test on benefits. It appears that means tests have objectionable connotations of poor laws and intrusive investigation of private circumstances which lead them to be resented by those who are subject to them. Australia has been described as 'the only advanced country to retain a means test as a central feature of most of its cash social service benefits' (Henderson, Harcourt and Harper 1970, p.10). Several commentators have observed that the particular history and manner of administration of the means test in Australia has enabled it to remain largely free of the strong negative connotations observed elsewhere. The main objection to the means test in Australia seems instead to come from those who are excluded by its provisions from receiving benefits (Henderson, Harcourt and Harper 1970, p.10; Horne 1970, p.118). Further, in most cases the means test is tapered so that there is not a 100 per cent effective marginal tax rate on the private income of beneficiaries, as occurs in some other countries. The political acceptability of the means test has enabled social welfare benefits to be concentrated more effectively on those in need 'with very few extraneous flows of funds' (Henderson 1975, p.67).[41] The argument that a guaranteed minimum income would enable a socially acceptable test on means which is otherwise unobtainable thus does not carry great weight in the Australian context. In fact one consequence of the two schemes proposed for Australia would be the introduction of substantial 'extraneous flows' to all those families now able to support themselves adequately.

In assessing the need for such a comprehensive change, an important question is who will benefit who cannot now, without too much difficulty, be brought under the income security umbrella. One substantial group may be the 60,000 income units with no disability which entitled them to assistance who were found to be below Henderson's poverty line in the ABS 1973 survey of income distribution. Not all this group would benefit since they would be entitled only to the lower guaranteed income. This is recommended to be 62 per cent of the poverty line. Who were these people? Unfortunately, we are given little information about the composition of the group. It contains a relatively high proportion of non-aged single adult males and a significant number of couples with three children (Henderson Report p.21). Without knowing why this group is poor it is not possible to judge the extent to which they need assistance or the ease with which they could be incorporated into the existing welfare system. Another group to be benefitted, though not appearing among current statistics as low income receipients, may be those who choose to avail themselves of the guaranteed income to supplement their savings while having an unpaid holiday.

The other major group which appeared to be at risk of poverty when the income survey was taken in 1973 was families with four or more children. The Henderson Report itself proposed a solution to this which has since been implemented, namely that a greatly increased level of child endowment payment replace the then existing tax deductions for children.[42]

Categories of need would be retained and to qualify for the higher minimum, potential beneficiaries would presumably have to apply. Thus the problem of take-up would remain, though modified by the fact that those who failed to apply would still receive the lower minimum rather than nothing as at present.[43] When acknowledging that poor people dependent on the lower minimum may be left below the poverty line, the Henderson Report (p.82) remarks that 'the categories are defined so generously that no person in need is likely to be left out'. Why then is the payment of a lower guaranteed minimum to millions of families which are not in need really necessary?

One possible answer to this question concerns the role the universal social dividend could play in enabling the combination of a progressive total tax system and constant marginal retention rates of income. If the personal income tax continues as a major revenue source then this combination can be achieved, as at present, by nominating a tax free level of private income. However, the Asprey Committee has recommended the substitution of a broad based tax on consumption for a substantial part of the income tax, and this appears to have some political support. If the incidence of a consumption tax does in fact fall on the consumer, such a move would generally be regressive on the lowest incomes (given that the rate of tax was uniform across commodities). Social welfare recipients could be compensated by raising the level of benefits. Such an avenue is not readily available for those supporting themselves and some form of government grant does seem to be worth exploring as a means of making the consumption tax progressive (Manning and Saunders 1978).

The absence of the need for any separate mechanism for enquiring into a person's means remains an advantage of the proposed income guarantee. Even the more enthusiastic supporters of the means test see it as a method of concentrating benefits where they are most needed rather than as desirable in itself. A broadly similar alternative within the existing tax and welfare system would be to pay benefits to all who qualify for the nominated categories, irrespective of personal income and wealth, and then to tax the benefits. This is the proposal of the Hancock Report, which advocates the payment of fully taxable national superannuation benefits to all persons over the age of 65, irrespective of private means. The Asprey Committee also remarks favourably on such a possibility, which would ideally cover most benefits and substitute for most means tests (1978, p.130). Subjecting a benefit to tax does not, of course, fully offset the payment to people who are not in need.[44]

Although the two guaranteed minimum income schemes developed for

Australia are very similar, the overseas literature is rich with variations. A technique for comparing the effectiveness of alternative plans in redistributing income has been devised by Kakwani (1977b). It also permits an assessment of the sensitivity of the redistributional impact to parameters such as the marginal tax rate, the breakeven level of private income, the procedure adopted to allow for differences in family composition, and the basic tax credit received by all families. Illustration of the technique is so far confined to U.S. data, and does not cover the Australian schemes.

4.2 Should Benefits be Earnings Related?

Conflicting views on an important principle of social welfare have emerged in the reports of the Asprey, Hancock, Henderson and Woodhouse Committees. The issue is whether any benefits ought to be earnings-related, so that recipients who had relatively high incomes prior to becoming eligible for benefit receive more than those with a relatively low earnings history. This is vigorously opposed by the Henderson Report as it seems a perverse way of redistributing income. But earnings-related schemes may have some appeal even to the most egalitarian. It is argued that citizens will be more ready to make payments (even compulsory payments) for some area of government expenditure if the size of the benefit they will receive subsequently is related to the size of their prior contribution. Then, *ceteris paribus*, a government can raise more revenue for that expenditure area using earmarked contributions than it could by simply raising taxes of the conventional sort. For this mechanism to work it is necessary for expected benefits to vary demonstrably with contributions (Asprey 1975, p.181; Hancock 1976, pp.13–14, 22–25) and it can be expected to be stronger the more certain is the individual of ultimately receiving the benefit. Clearly this approach cannot be used for all forms of government expenditure; it is appropriate only where identifiable benefits accrue to specific individuals. The Hancock Report is based on the presumption that funds to provide universally adequate retirement benefits for the aged will not be forthcoming from conventional tax sources (pp.22–25). The extra revenue to meet the substantial increase in the level of the minimum pension recommended by the Report is to come from the levying of contributions. Some of this extra revenue can then be redistributed to those with small earnings histories, while paying additional earnings-related benefits which it is hoped are sufficient to induce the higher contributors to accept the level of contribution required of them.

A second argument supports earnings-related benefits as intrinsically desirable. Adherence to the view that 'the disruption of customary patterns of life can be a serious hardship. (p.25), enables the Hancock Committee to welcome the modest element of income maintenance which is embodied in their financing arrangements for a national superannuation scheme. The strongest support for the principle of income maintenance in social security is expressed by the Woodhouse Committee on compensation and rehabilitation. In their view a large part of the hardship imposed by a fall in income arises from the *difference* between the new low level of income and that which was expected and on which present commitments were based. They further regard it as equitable that in times of adversity people should receive a level of support which is related to the 'important contributions they had made earlier to the economy in general and the social welfare fund in particular' (Woodhouse 1974, p.100). There seems to be embodied in this latter view the belief that income inequalities reflect differences in the individual's contribution to total output, and that such differences reflect on the effort made by the individual rather than on inherited ability, luck or favoured childhood. This does not accord with the judgements of any of the major theories of the determinants of income distribution, with the possible exception of human capital theory.

The strongest objection to the income maintenance principle comes from those who believe that funds for social welfare are strictly limited and independent of the manner in which they are raised. Any arrangement which makes payments to the relatively well off (even if their incomes have fallen substantially) then implies fewer funds for the poorest members of the community. The Henderson Report for one appears to make this judgement and holds that this is an unacceptable diversion of funds while real hardship caused by lack of income continues to exist. This paramount concern for those with the lowest income also justifies the use of the means test even for benefits paid only to those who meet some test of disability. It does seem naive to respond to this concern by asserting that

> An annual domestic product that is accelerating past $48,000 million per annum is the answer to any economic argument that there should be exclusions of those in higher income brackets from a comprehensive scheme of social welfare. (Woodhouse 1974, p.101).

The Henderson Report is implacably opposed to any use of earnings-related benefits (which it describes as 'Government efforts to maintain the rich in their accustomed luxury while leaving the poor in penury' (p.35)), or the insurance principle in the social welfare field.

The differing views of the Woodhouse, Hancock and Henderson Committees no doubt partly reflect differences in values. But their disagreements are likely to arise also from the nature of the problem considered by each Committee and their judgements of fact. Governments do many things other than redistribute income. One of these may be to substitute an orderly and economical compensation system for the present inefficient and expensive private system. Further, the empirical issue of whether or not earnings-related benefits enable more revenue to be raised appears to be an important part of the conflict between the Hancock and Henderson Committees. Also in dispute is the importance attached by the Hancock Committee to goals other than the reduction of poverty, such as income maintenance, protection against contingencies and the reduction of inequality.

The issue of the appropriate role of the insurance principle in social welfare underlies much of the above disagreement. The insurance approach views social welfare as providing support in the event of specified contingencies, such as old age and unemployment. Schemes are financed through contributions, often compulsory, paid prior to the contingency arising. The levels of contributions (and benefits) frequently vary with income. This insurance analogy plays an important part in the social welfare systems of most of the developed Western world. It has yet to do so in Australia. Here the basis has been to provide government funds to people who would otherwise be very poor. Thus minimum benefits are paid subject to a means test to categories of people most prone to poverty (such as single mothers and invalids).[45] [46] Kaim-Caudle (1973, p.34) identifies three bases for income redistribution: to those experiencing certain contingencies such as widowhood and unemployment; redistribution over the life-cycle; and redistribution from high to low income groups. The Australian system has concentrated on the last of these, while requiring low income to be linked with specified contingencies. The insurance approach reflects more a combination of the first two types of redistribution. In these terms the Henderson Report can be seen as advocating an extension and improvement of the unusual Australian approach whereas the Hancock Report argues for some shift of emphasis to the first two forms of income redistribution.

4.3 Redistribution Through the Tax System

A comprehensive discussion of the taxation system will not be attempted; however it is relevant to report here some findings on the redistributive impact of the taxation system and compare it with that of social welfare payments. Work based on the Macquarie/Queensland survey data (Bentley, Collins and Drane 1974; Bentley, Collins and Rutledge 1975) concludes that the aggregate burden of local, state and federal taxes is regressive on the lowest incomes, proportional on the bulk of incomes in the middle ranges and progressive on the highest incomes (above $13,000 in December 1973)—at least as reported. These broad features are very pronounced and are likely to survive variations in assumptions about incidence. When the impact of cash social welfare benefits, including child endowment, is included with taxes the overall impact becomes significantly progressive at low incomes before becoming proportional and then progressive as before (Asprey 1975, p.26). Personal income tax is the dominant source of the taxation system's reduction in income inequality. The most regressive taxes are indirect taxes followed by local government taxes. Overall, the tax system reduced inequality by 5.5 per cent in the year the survey data were collected (Kakwani 1977, p.76). The income tax scale, at the time the Macquarie/Queensland data were collected, appeared to be strongly progressive. Yet this 'is not reflected in the actual income taxes paid by families' (Kakwani and Podder 1975, p.117). Perhaps the system of concessional deductions from taxable income, the existence of several income earners in a household, and exploitation of tax avoidance possibilities help to explain this. It certainly appears that the progressive income tax structure does not have a large impact on the distribution of household income. It is far less important in this regard than the system of social welfare benefits. Table 2, again based on Macquarie/Queensland data, illustrates these points.

TABLE 2
The Effect of Redistributive Policies—1966

	Original Income %	Original Income plus Social Welfare Benefits %	Disposable Income %
Share of			
bottom 20%	2.9	6.4	7.0
top 20%	41.0	39.0	37.3
Concentration ratio*	0.368	0.318	0.296

*The concentration ratio, which differs slightly from a Gini coefficient, is 'calculated by using the cumulative proportion of families in terms of original income and the corresponding cumulative proportions of income defined in different ways.' (Kakwani and Podder 1975, p.119).
Source: Kakwani and Podder 1975, p.118.

4.4 *Housing*

Some of the government's impact on the distribution of real income occurs through the direct provision of goods and services. The redistributive impact of such expenditure is virtually unknown, except in the broadest terms. This is partly because of the difficulty of allocating units of expenditure per family and partly because there are few statistics relating receipt of these benefits to levels of family income. One expenditure area of particular distributional significance is housing. The poverty studies show that housing costs can be a major factor in determining whether or not a family on a given income is in need. This applies particularly, though not exclusively, to the aged.

There is reason to believe that existing housing policies are not effective in minimising the burden of high housing costs for the poor. First, waiting lists for those eligible for public housing are long, maybe several years. Second, many families with quite adequate incomes remain in subsidised public housing, while others in much greater need are excluded. Some evidence of this is provided by the *Survey of Income* (ABS 1973) undertaken for the Poverty Inquiry. It was found that although the number of renters who had incomes below the Henderson poverty line was significantly less than the number of housing authority rental units, rather less than half these households were housing authority tenants. Seventy-two per cent of the public tenants had incomes exceeding 120 per cent of the poverty line (Burbidge 1975; Henderson 1978, p.35).

The existing policy of public housing authorities is to subsidise the purchase or rent of housing which they own. To benefit from the subsidy it is necessary to live in housing authority dwellings.

Disadvantages arise because subsidies attach to dwellings rather than households. First, inequity exists between those who obtain such accommodation and those who remain on waiting lists with no subsidy. Second, a shift in locality may be necessary to take up the offer of a particular dwelling. This causes disruption of schooling, jobs and social contacts. Third, stigma attaches to welfare housing estates. Finally, those who are subsidised are allowed little choice in the form of their housing and no choice in the priority they place on housing as against other needs. The provision of a rent subsidy would avoid these problems. This could take the form either of higher cash pensions (Burbidge 1975) or rent vouchers (Paterson 1975).

Compared with a cash payment the voucher approach has the disadvantage for the recipient of reducing choice. It may, however, have a revenue-raising advantage. A recent development in theoretical welfare economics argues that donors gain some utility from giving and thus Pareto-optimal redistributions of income are possible. Without making claims about Pareto-optimality, the relevant point is that people may give more willingly if the funds are to be used for specific expenditures of which they approve. Taxpayers may thus be prepared to support subsidised housing for the poor where they would not support cash grants of an equal amount.

Arguments against subsidising the tenant rather than providing public authority dwellings focus on the fear that landlords rather than tenants will be the ones to gain, and the belief that housing authorities gain scale economies not available in the private building sector. Burbidge has examined some evidence on both points. He finds several private builders with costs equivalent to those of the Housing Commissions. He concludes also that rents currently received by landlords provide a return on capital which is quite low. Further, the conditions for rental exploitation, such as a shortage of of dwellings and difficulties in increasing supply, do not characterise the Australian housing market of the 1970's.

Vouchers assist only those who are renting. There are arguments also for assisting low income families who own or would like to purchase their own homes. The financial cost of maintenance may be lower for owner-occupiers, in part because they have an incentive to avoid behaviour which accelerates depreciation. In addition Henderson points out (1978, p.36) that large landlords such as a housing commission must pay full commercial rates for many maintenance jobs an owner-occupier would do for himself. The pattern of home ownership also has a profound influence on the distribution of wealth. If low income families can be helped to buy their own houses this may not only make wealth more evenly distributed, but also assist such families to have reasonable standards of living in the future, and especially in old age. One proposal is to offer a means-tested subsidy which tapers off if income rises and is subject to a ceiling on the maximum value of the dwelling (Henderson 1978, p.36).

The Victorian Housing Commission is pursuing a related idea directed specifically towards the aged. Where maintenance costs become a serious burden for a home owner, the Commission will offer to buy the house, take responsibility for the maintenance and offer the owner a choice of either life tenancy in the house or alternative Commission accommodation (Henderson 1978, p.38).

The principle of using cash grants for explicit redistribution to the poor is not confined to housing. It is embodied also in many of the specific recommendations of the Henderson Report. The Report acknowledges that a guaranteed minimum income, even were it to be accepted, would not replace the existing social welfare system for a number of years. It therefore makes many proposals for improving the current social welfare system. These are presented in detail in the discussion of each of the major disabilities identified as being associated with poverty. They reflect the basic views underlying the Report—that no one should be forced to endure a material standard of living which is well below that of the community average; that ideally people should start with an equal opportunity in life; and that social welfare payments should be determined by the test of financial need (Henderson Report 1975, p.2).[47]

In their actual implication, welfare policies appear to face political constraints which are not fully recognized by economists. The experience of the Whitlam Government suggests that to concentrate redistributive benefits solely on the poor, which is the central principle of the Henderson Report recommendations, has limited political appeal. Certainly that Government directed considerable funds to some of the poorest groups in the community, such as Aborigines, single mothers and those on the old age pension. Yet even though they claimed a dominant concern for the most disadvantaged they also introduced a number of important policies whose impact was regressive. The major examples are the abolition of tertiary education fees and the provision of grants (rather than loans) for tertiary students; the allowance of mortgage payments as tax deductable for incomes below a specified (quite high) level; and the removal of the means test on old age pensions for those aged 70 years or more.

Section 5 Conclusion

We are now in a position to make some sense of Rivlin's paradox (1975, p.8) that what economists think of as 'income distribution theory' relates to the distribution of earnings of fully employed males, while what they think of as 'income distribution policy' means almost everything else.

Income distribution policy has been largely associated with the alleviation of poverty. In Australia most of the poorest members of the community have been found to be not in receipt of full-time earnings. Thus the structure of earnings is not immediately relevant to the income position of the very poor. It remains indirectly relevant if there is substance in the life cycle poverty hypothesis: then the level of earnings received when employed will affect the ability and need to supplement current income during periods when income is very low.

The information on income distribution and poverty which has become available in the last ten years provides the basis for a great deal of further research on both the existing state of distribution and on redistributive policies. Already our knowledge of the characteristics associated with poverty and the overall degree of inequality of income in Australia has markedly increased. The stage is set for an informed and thoughtful debate on the specifics of welfare policy, including schemes such as medibank, national superannuation and national compensation. There is now a base enabling future comparison of inequality and poverty. Changes over time are of particular interest to researchers and policy-makers alike. Awareness of any trends which exist, or of the absence of a trend, enables policies to be formed with more understanding of the future circumstances they are designed to alter. In addition, comparison over time, especially if the time intervals are not too long, may make it possible to identify whether major welfare policy changes have any distributional effects, and if so whether they are the intended effects.

We have learnt also that there now appear to be no clear secular trends in the post-war period in either the dispersion of earnings or the functional distribution of income. Yet the belief that stability is imposed by powerful macro-economic forces must be viewed with some scepticism.

A point which has emerged in several different contexts is the important role played by the full employment experienced during most of the post-war years. It is claimed to affect significantly the dispersion of earnings, the impact of the Arbitration Commission and the nature of poverty. This takes on a new significance at a time when unemployment is very high by recent standards.

Much remains to be done. Our new knowledge is almost overshadowed by our remaining ignorance. We still do not know with any certainty the relation between institutions and market forces in the determination of pay, nor how far the earnings structure may be compressed and with what consequences. Almost no work has been done on household labour supply patterns though this has become a pertinent issue with the increasing involvement of married women in the labour force. The failure to understand what causes the earnings of a job or an individual to be what they are means that policy proposals to alter these earnings cannot be offered with any confidence.

It is fortunate that Australian policy discussion can poach insights from the considerable work being undertaken overseas on the determinants of earnings. This work includes both theoretical and empirical assessment of the roles of education, intelligence, genetic inheritance, early family environment and luck.

Although the work of Henderson and others has vastly expanded our knowledge of poverty there remain several issues which require more attention. These include the extent to which poverty is a permanent or temporary state for the individuals concerned; the relation between income and need—or more broadly, the most appropriate practical indicator of need; the virtually untouched question of the intra-family distribution of income; and the application of a more soundly based poverty line and family equivalence scale.

The impressive efforts of recent years to devise redistributive policies have identified some basic unresolved issues in social welfare policy. These hinge on the extent to which benefits ought to be related to previous earnings; the relevance of the insurance principle; and the role of the means test. Economists, of course, cannot settle these 'ought' questions. They can, however, seek to ensure that whichever approach is adopted is pursued efficiently, and they can spell out the values implied in alternative schemes. They have an important role also in settling the issues of fact on which much controversy is based. Important examples are the relation between methods of revenue raising and taxpayer's willingness to pay and the incentive effects of specific social welfare provisions. Two further aspects of redistribution which have yet to be subject to any systematic research are redistribution across the entire income range and redistribution through government provision of goods and services and regulation of private economic activity.

Finally, the fundamental question arises why a society such as Australia's generates poverty at all. Must there always be a sizeable group at risk of poverty, to be rescued only by the generosity of an effective welfare system? Or is it possible that the social and economic system may be modified in such a way that people are assured an opportunity to provide adequately for themselves in all circumstances? This question is intrinsically very difficult and perhaps ultimately unaswerable. It is also, however, important and intriguing.

Notes

[1] The most integrated work is to be found among the writings of the labour economists and those concerned with policies for reducing poverty.

[2] These are the Macquarie/Queensland survey of household income and expenditure (1966); the Melbourne Poverty survey (1966); two surveys of individual and household incomes undertaken by the Australian Bureau of Statistics (ABS) for 1968–69 and 1973–74; a detailed survey of low income households undertaken by the ABS on behalf of the Commission of Enquiry into Poverty, in 1973; and an ABS survey of household expenditure taken in 1975 and 1976.

[3] The Asprey Report (1975), the Hancock Report (1976), the Henderson Report (1975) and the Woodhouse Report (1974).

[4] The distribution of income—even the individual labour income of adult males—may vary while the structure of rates paid for particular jobs remains constant because the proportion of the workforce in each occupation changes.

[5] This may differ from the dispersion of earnings when there is earnings drift (i.e. a change in the amount by which the rate actually paid for a standard week exceeds the award rate) and when there are changes in overtime.

[6] See, for example, Reynolds and Taft 1956; Turner 1957; Reder 1962; Leiserson 1966. These references are cited in Hancock and Moore (1974, pp.107–08).

[7] The Commission's influence may also be greater in the tertiary sector, which was not included in the comparison.

[8] In the 1970's major changes have occurred in the wages area which post-date the preceding discussion. The years 1972 to 1975 saw a sharp increase in the move to equal pay for women (universally required by 1976); the virtual elimination of lower rates of pay for juveniles; and an historically unprecedented shift in the distribution of income from profits to wages. The profit/wage shift had been partially reversed by 1978 but the change in relative award wages for women and juveniles has a legal status which is not readily eroded. The overall structure of award rates has also been compressed as a consequence of Arbitration Commission decisions to give tapered wage increases in some national wage cases. The impact of these events on earnings and the distribution of income has yet to be assessed.

[9] The Australian author to contribute most significantly to the debate is G.C. Harcourt. His many writings include 1972, 1975, 1976.

[10] Domestic Factor Incomes replaces the previously used concept of Net National Product.

[11] It can be argued, for example, that those parts of the economy where a variation in labour's share is not possible should be excluded. Predominantly these are the public service (where the value of production is defined to equal wages and salaries paid) and the housing sector (where the imputed value and rents are attributed entirely to housing capital). Two elements support the exclusion of the primary sector (in Australia). Changes in total income and the share of labour are dominated by external events where both prices and quantities sold need bear little relation to trends in the domestic economy. Further, sharp fluctuations in the value of output occur in this sector, which are reflected in a comparable variability in labour's share.

Thus inclusion of the primary sector may confuse the identification of trends in the rest of the economy.

Exclusion of sectors dominated by public enterprises, such as electricity, gas and water supply, and transport and communications is argued for on related grounds. That is, the relative shares in these industries do not reflect some notion of the 'normal outcome of the domestic market economy', since their prices are often set by reference to political or administrative criteria. Coincidentally, these industries experienced sharp changes in technology resulting in more capital—intensive forms of production. This is reflected in corresponding decreases in labour's share and it has been argued that the industries should be excluded for this reason also (Isaac 1967, pp.67–69).

[12] This expectation is contradicted in the case of the thorough and conscientious study by the Department of Labour.

[13] The exception is the Department of Labour Report which gives a brief discussion of the matter on p.45.

[14] Exactly what constitutes stability has not been established satisfactorily.

[15] Even this is not straightforward since a decision must be made about whether, where appropriate, to include relatives outside the nuclear family; whether to include adult student children and so on.

[16] The future of this series is in doubt following cutbacks in the activities of the ABS.

[17] Details of the surveys can be found in *Income Distribution 1968–69* (ABS 1975).

[18] A quick look at the numbers from the two ABS income surveys supports this expectation. Between 1968–69 and 1973–74 the ratio of one- to two-income families fell from 1.03 to 0.87. The ratio of mean incomes of these two groups also fell, from 0.72 to 0.70. In 1973–74 14.6 per cent of one-earner families had incomes of $4000 or less and 47.9 per cent had incomes of $6500 or less. The corresponding figures for two-earner families are 8.5 per cent and 18.2 per cent.

[19] These are measures of inequality. The Gini coefficient is derived from the Lorenz curve, which relates the cumulative proportion of income recipients to the cumulative proportion of income received. The Gini coefficient summarises the Lorenz curve as a single ratio. It may take on values between zero and one with zero indicating perfect equality. The Gini coefficient is calculated as

$$G = \sum_{i=1}^{N} X_i Y_{i+1} - \sum_{i=1}^{N} X_{i+1} Y_i$$

where the data have been grouped into income classes i, X is the distribution of the cumulative proportion of income earners in each income class and Y is the distribution of the cumulative proportion of income in each income class. The deciles are calculated by ranking individuals in ascending order of taxable income. The bottom decile contains the ten per cent of people with the lowest incomes and so on. This is an example of the more general percentile approach to measuring inequality.

[20] 'Family' is defined to consist of two or more people.

[21] Perhaps the similarity of inequality measures derived from the two sets of data can be explained by the underepresentation of single households in the Macquarie/Queensland survey. This would have the effect of making their sample more like the population surveyed by the ABS—i.e., families excluding single-person households. Data for non-family individuals are not available for the 1968–69 ABS income survey.

[22] This observation is supported by the Gini coefficients calculated by the ABS from its two income distribution surveys.

[23] At the date of writing (August 1978) no analysis of the ABS Household Expenditure Survey was available.

[24] If, as is commonly supposed, the average propensity to save rises with income then it necessarily follows that the inequality of expenditure will be less than that of income (Kakwani 1977b). Note also that British evidence suggests expenditure is less likely to be under-reported in surveys than is income.

[25] The data came from the second stage of the Macquarie/Queensland survey.

[26] Credit for much of this work is due to the initiative and stimulus provided by Professor Ronald Henderson. His pioneering work with the Melbourne Poverty survey was followed by appointment to head a commission to investigate poverty on behalf of the Federal Government.

[27] This survey was undertaken in 1966 by the Institute of Applied Economic and Social Research, University of Melbourne. A full discussion of the findings of this survey is to be found in Henderson, Harcourt and Harper 1970, while the central results are available in Harper 1967.

[28] See, for example, Townsend 1970.

[29] In saying this it should be acknowledged that for *some* questions, such as a study of inequality, it will be sensible to concentrate on only one aspect.

[30] This last problem is referred to as secondary poverty. In a survey of 220 large families in inner Sydney, Halliday (1972, pp.454–5) found that an adequate income was by no means perfectly correlated with adequate housing, food, clothing, dental care, or the absence of a sense of deprivation.

[31] This issue is raised again in the discussion of a guaranteed minimum income (p.40).

[32] For some further discussion of the problems of the Henderson poverty line see Priorities Review Staff 1975, pp.13–16 and Social Welfare Commission 1974, pp.1–2 and appendix 1. It should be noted that in the period between the Melbourne survey and the Henderson Report a considerable overseas literature has developed on the measurement of poverty and the related issue of family equivalence scales.

[33] One way to establish a household equivalence scale is to observe how differently composed families actually behave. Alternatively, as with an absolute poverty line, one can calculate the expenditures required to allow differently composed families to achieve a common consumption level. Regrettably, the relative merits of these alternatives have not been considered in the Australian literature.

[34] The generalisations which follow exclude Aborigines and juveniles. The characteristics of these two groups are rather different from the remainder.

Note also that the position of large families depends in an important way on the family equivalence scale used and the extent to which it allows for economies of scale.

[35] The attempt to apply this, however, produces a statistic which must be interpreted with caution. The problem arises from the way the index is calculated. It shows the proportion of income received by those of the relevant group above the poverty line which needs to be transferred to those below it to bring all the latter to an income just equal to the poverty line. When this is applied to sub-sets of the population, such as males and females, it measures the amount of transfer of income which is

needed *within* each sub-set: e.g. from non-poor females to poor females and from non-poor males to poor males. The value of the index will depend in part on the average income of those members of the group above the poverty line (possibly reflecting the influence of a small number of very high incomes).

An alternative may be to calculate the poverty index for each group as the proportion of income received by the whole of the population above the poverty line which must be transferred to the members of the group below it in order just to lift them to the poverty line.

[36] The effects of inflation on the distribution of income in Australia are to be discussed in a forthcoming book by D.H. Whitehead.

[37] The 1977–78 budget was the most recent at the time of writing.

[38] Note that these are rather like that advocated by Brown and Dawson (1969).

[39] A discussion of this scheme is included in a review of the Henderson Report by Pritchard and Saunders (1978).

[40] Rough calculations based on the number of single income earners and non-pensioner couples without children, who would be receiving a payment for the first time, and the number of families with children who would be receiving payments fortnightly rather than monthly as at present with family allowances, suggest that the volume of payments would approximately double under the Henderson Report scheme.

The ABS survey of *Income Distribution*, 1973–74, Parts I and II provides the basis for these calculations.

[41] Debate on these issues over the last decade owes a considerable debt to the pioneering efforts of the late Professor R.I. Downing. He did much of the original work on tax reform, the virtues of the means test, and possibilities for national superannuation. See, for example, Downing 1974, a, b, c, Downing, Boxer and Arndt 1964.

[42] The Social Welfare Commission (1974) is critical of this remedy for the poverty of large, low-wage families, and offers an alternative scheme of means tested family supplements. Its prime objection to the Henderson proposal is that funds are not concentrated on those most in need. In support of this it notes that the greatest single cost of the proposal will be payments for the first child in a family, which does indeed seem not to provide special assistance for large families. However an adjustment of rates paid for the first as compared with subsequent children should overcome this objection. In addition the Social Welfare Commission means-tested family supplements could be introduced as a scheme *complementary* to the existing universal allowances.

[43] This assumes that the government will be able to identify and keep track of every family unit. We are not told how this is to be done.

[44] In response to this the Asprey Committee has suggested that a separate rate of tax may be made applicable to welfare benefits, superimposed on the standard tax scale at some nominated level of income (p.178).

[45] My thanks to an anonymous referee for emphasising this distinction.

[46] For a history of the Australian social security system see Kewley, 1973. Kaim-Caudle 1973, in a ten country study, and the OECD 1974, compare the Australian social security system with that of other developed Western Countries.

[47] The recommendations include 1) an increase in all pensions and benefits to the level of the Report's poverty line, this line to be adjusted for changes in average weekly

earnings or gross domestic product per head; 2) a discretion be given to the Department of Social Security to make emergency grants and capital grants to cover the debts of new pensioners; 3) a large increase in child endowment, to be converted to a tax credit to replace existing tax deductions for children (this was implemented in the 1976–77 Budget); 4) an acceptance by the Australian Government that wage differentials should be reduced and part-time work should be made more readily available; 5) abolition of the seven day waiting period for unemployment benefits and the undertaking of active job creation programmes, aimed at those least able to obtain private employment; 6) the introduction of a tax credit scheme for low income renters; 7) the provision of benefits equivalent to the widow's pension to lone fathers; 8) the removal of the age pension for women aged 60 to 65 and its replacement by a pension available to breadwinners aged 50 to 65 'if for any reason they are finding difficulty in working for an adequate private income' (p.238); 9) entitlement to benefits be made available to all migrants who intend to remain permanently in Australia; 10) greater involvement of aborigines in the formulation and implementation of welfare policies for their assistance.

Bibliography

Australian Council of Social Service (1975), *Guaranteed Minimum Income: Towards the Development of a Policy* (ACOSS).

—— (1975), *Seminar on Guaranteed Minimum Income* (ACOSS).

Asprey (1975), *Taxation Review Committee Full Report* (AGPS, Canberra).

Australian Bureau of Statistics (1975), *Income Distribution, 1968–69 Consolidated and Revised Edition* (ABS, Canberra).

—— (1976, 1977 and 1978), *Income Distribution, 1973–74, Part I, Part II and Part III* (ABS, Canberra).

—— (1978), *Household Expenditure Survey 1974–75* (Bulletin 7 (Income Distribution), ABS, Canberra).

Bentley, P., D.J. Collins and N.T. Drane (1974), 'The Incidence of Australian Taxation' (*Economic Record*, 50, pp.489–510).

—— and D.J.S. Rutledge (1975), 'Incidence of Australian Taxation: Some Further Results', published in *Taxation Review Committee: Commissioned Studies* (AGPS, Canberra).

Brennan, G. (1973a), 'Pareto Desirable Redistribution: The Case of Malice and Envy', *Journal of Public Economics*, 2, pp.173–183.

—— (1973b), 'Pareto Desirable Redistribution: The Non-Altruistic Dimension', *Public Choice*, 14, pp.43–67.

—— and C. Walsh (1973), 'Pareto-Optimal Redistribution Reconsidered', *Public Finance Quarterly*, 1, pp.147–168.

Brown, C.V. and D.A. Dawson (1969), *Personal Taxation Incentives and Tax Reform* (P.E.D. Broadsheet No. 506, London, 1969).

Budget Speech, 1977–78 and Statements, 1977, AGPS, Canberra.

Burbidge, A. (1975), 'Improving Low Income Housing', *Shelter*, 19, Special Edition, 1975.

Broom L. and F. Lancaster-Jones (1969), 'Father-to-Son Mobility: Australia in Comparative Perspective', *American Journal of Sociology*, 74, pp.333–342.

Brown, W. (1978), 'Does Arbitration Deny Australia an Effective Labour Market?', mimeo.

Clark, C. (1970), 'Net Capital Stock', *Economic Record*, 46, pp.449–466.

Creighton, L. and S. Geis (1976), 'Income Maintenance and Then What?', *Social Policy*, 6, pp.47–52.

Cox, J.P. (1977), 'The National Survey of Income, Income Distribution and Temporary Poverty', *Economic Record*, 52, pp.423–442.

—— (1976), Conference paper of the same title.

Department of Labour (1974), *Labour's Share of the National Product*, a discussion paper published by the Department of Labour.

Downing, R.I. (1974a), 'Inflation: Incomes, Prices and Social Welfare', *Australian Quarterly*, 56, pp.9–19.

—— (1974b), 'National Superannuation', *Australian Economic Review*, 27, pp.53–58.

—— (1974c), *Social Reconstruction, Social Welfare and Self-reliance* (George Judah Cohen Memorial Lecture, University of Sydney, 1974).

Downing, R.I., A. Boxer and H. Arndt (1964), *Taxation in Australia: Agenda for Reform* (Melbourne University Press, Melbourne, 1964).

Dufty, N.F. (1971), 'Earnings Drift in Australian Secondary Industry', *Economic Record*, 47, pp.410–417, reprinted in J.R. Niland and J.E. Isaac (eds.) *Australian Labour Economics Readings* (new edition, Sun Books, Melbourne, 1975).

Edwards, H.R., R.C. Gates and R.A. Layton (1966), *Survey of Consumer Finances* (University of Sydney and University of New South Wales, Sydney, 1966).

Encel, S. (1970), *Equality and Authority* (Cheshire, Melbourne, 1970).

Halliday, A. (1972), 'The Extent of Poverty Among Large Families in the Heart of Sydney', *Economic Record*, 48, pp.483–499.

Hancock, K.J. (1966), 'Earnings Drift in Australia', *Journal of Industrial Relations*, 8, pp.128–157 reprinted in J.R. Niland and J.E. Isaac (eds.) *Australian Labour Economics Readings* (new edition, Sun Books, Melbourne, 1975).

—— (1970a), 'The Economics of Social Welfare in the 1970's,' in H. Weir, (ed.) *Social Welfare in the 1970's* (ACOSS, 1970).

—— (1970b), Review of *The Structure of Earnings* by H. Lydall, *Economic Record*, 46, pp.276–279.

—— (1971), 'The Real Wage Cost of Wage Restraint', mineo. paper given at seminars at the ANU, La Trobe and Monash Universities.

—— (1976), 'The Relation Between Changes in Costs and Changes in Product Prices in Australian Manufacturing Industries 1949–50 to 1967–68', *Economic Record*, 52, pp.53–65.

Hancock Report (1976), *A National Superannuation Scheme for Australia* (National Superannuation Committee of Enquiry, Part One of Final Report, AGPS, Canberra, 1976).

Hancock, K.J. and K. Moore (1972), 'The Occupational Wage Structure in Australia Since 1914', *British Journal of Industrial Relations*, 10, pp.107–122.

Harcourt, G.C. (1972), *Some Cambridge Controversies in the Theory of Capital* (Cambridge University Press, London, 1972).

—— (1975), 'Theoretical Controversy and Social Significance: An Evaluation of the Cambridge Controversies' (Edward Shann Memorial Lecture).

—— (1976), 'The Cambridge Controversies: Old Ways and New Horizons—Or Dead End?', *Oxford Economic Papers*, 28, pp.25–65.

—— and D. Ironmonger (1956), 'A Pilot Survey of Personal Savings', *Economic Record*, 32, pp.106–118.

Harper, J.A. (1967), 'Survey of Living Conditions in Melbourne—1966', *Economic Record*, 43, pp.362–388.

Henderson, R.F. (1977), 'Why Have a Guaranteed Minimum Income Scheme?', in *Poverty in Australia* (papers given at a conference organized by Workers' Educational Association of NSW, 1976, WEA of NSW, Sydney, 1977).

—— (1978), 'Housing Policy and the Poor', *Australian Economic Review*, 41, First Quarter, pp.34–39.

Henderson, R.F., A. Harcourt and R.J.A. Harper (1970), *People in Poverty: A Melbourne Survey* (University of Melbourne, Melbourne, 1970).

Henderson Report (1975), *Poverty in Australia*, Vol. I (Commission of Inquiry into Poverty, AGPS, Canberra, 1975).

Horne, S. (1970), 'A Comparative Annual Income', *Australian Journal of Social Issues*, 5, pp.117–119.

Hughes, B. (1973), 'The Wages of the Weak and the Strong', *Journal of Industrial Relations*, 15, pp.1–24.

Isaac, J.E. (1967), *Wages and Productivity* (Cheshire, Melbourne, 1967).

James, D.W. (1974), *What is the Share of Wages in the National Product?* (Australian Industries Development Association, Canberra, 1974).

Jones, M.A. (1972), *Housing and Poverty in Australia* (Melbourne University Press, Melbourne, 1972).

Kaim-Caudle, P.R. (1976) 'Poverty in Australia, review article', *Journal of Social Policy*, 5, pp.401–406.

Kakwani, N.C. (1976), 'Household Composition and Measurement of Income Inequality and Poverty with Application to Australian Data', *Discussion Paper No. 19* (School of Economics, University of New South Wales, Sydney, 1976).

—— (1977a), 'Measurement of Tax Progressivity: An International Comparison', *Economic Journal*, 87, pp.71–80.

—— (1977b), 'Redistributive Effects of Alternative Negative Income Tax Plans', *Public Finance*, 32, pp.77–91.

—— (1977c), 'Measurement of Poverty and Negative Income Tax', *Australian Economic Papers*, 16, pp.237–248.

—— (forthcoming), *Income Distribution: Methods of Analysis and Applications* (to be published by Oxford University Press for the World Bank).

Keating, M.S. and O.F. Gascoine (1970), 'Average Earnings Per Employee and Product Per Worker in Australia, 1959–60 to 1965–66', *Economic Record*, 46, pp.250–253.
Kewley, H.T. (1973), *Social Security in Australia 1900–1972* (Second Edition, Sydney University Press, Sydney, 1973).
Kravis, I.B. (1962), *The Structure of Income* (University of Pennsylvania Press, Pennsylvania, 1962).
Lancaster-Jones, F. (1975), 'The Changing Shape of the Australian Income Distribution, 1914–15 and 1968–9', *Australian Economic History Review*, 15, pp.21–43.
Leiserson, M.W. (1966), 'Wage Decisions and Wage Structures in the United States', in E.M. Hugh-Jones (ed.) *Wage Structure in Theory and Practice* (North Holland, Amsterdam, 1966).
Lydall, H. (1968), *The Structure of Earnings* (Oxford University Press, London, 1968).
—— (1976a), 'The Economics of Inequality', *Australian Bulletin of Labour*, 2, pp.29–52, reprinted from *Lloyds Bank Review*, 117, 1975.
—— (1976b), 'Theories of the Distribution of Earnings', in A.B. Atkinson (ed.), *The Personal Distribution of Incomes* (Allen and Unwin, London, 1976).
Mackrell, N.C., J. Frisch and P. Roope (1971), 'Equations for Business Fixed Investment', in W.E. Norton (ed.), *Three Studies of Private Fixed Investment* (Occasional Paper No. 3E, Reserve Bank of Australia, Sydney, 1971).
Manning, R., S. Richardson and R. Webb (1972), 'Market Forces and the Principle of Comparative Wage Justice: Discord or Harmony?', *Australian Economic Papers*, 11, pp.131–44, reprinted in J.R. Niland and J.E. Isaac (eds.), *Australian Labour Economics Readings* (New edition, Sun Books, Melbourne, 1972).
Manning, I. and P. Saunders (1978), 'On the Reform of Taxation and Social Security in Australia', *Australian Economic Review*, 41, First Quarter, pp.51–57.
Mathews Report (1975), *Report of the Committee of Enquiry into Inflation and Taxation* (AGPS, Canberra, 1975).
Mincer, J. (1974), *School, Experience and Earnings* (National Bureau of Economic Research, New York, 1974).
Murray, D. (1977), 'The Changing Incomes of the Aged in Australia', (mimeo).
—— (1978), 'Changes in Income Inequality: Australia 1968–69 to 1973–74', (mimeo).
—— (forthcoming), 'Sources of Income Inequality in Australia, 1968–69', *Economic Record*.
Nevile, J. (1969), *The Share of Wages in Income in Australia*, Economic Monograph, 286, (Economic Society of Australia and New Zealand, New South Wales Branch, 1969).
Norris, K. (1977), 'The Dispersion of Earnings in Australia', *Economic Record*, 53, pp.475–489.
OECD (1976), *Public Expenditure on Income Maintenance Programmes* (OECD Studies in Resource Allocation, No. 3, Paris, 1976).
—— (1976), *Occasional Studies*, 'Income Distribution,' by Malcom Sawyer.
Paglin, M. (1975), 'The Measurement and Trend of Inequality: A Basic Revision', *American Economic Review*, 65, pp.598–609.
Paterson, J. (1975), 'Home Owning, Home Renting and Income Redistribution', *Australian Quarterly*, 47, pp.28–31.
Paukert, F. (1973), 'Income Distribution at Different Levels of Development: A Survey of Evidence', *International Labour Review*, 108, pp.97–125.
Phelps Brown, E.H. (1957), 'The Long-Term Movement of Real Wages', in J.T. Dunlop (ed.), *The Theory of Wage Determination* (Macmillan, London, 1957).
—— (1977), *The Inequality of Pay* (Oxford University Press, Oxford, 1977).
Pitchford, J. (1967), 'Wage Policy and Distribution Theory', *Economica*, 34, pp.167–180.
Podder, N. (1971), 'The Estimation of an Equivalent Income Scale', *Australian Economic Papers*, 10, pp.175–187.
—— (1972), 'Distribution of Household Income in Australia', *Economic Record*, 48, pp.181–200.
Podder, N. and N.C. Kakwani (1975), 'Distribution and Redistribution of Household

Income in Australia', *Taxation Review Committee* (Commissioned Studies, AGPS, Canberra, 1975).
Podder, N. and N.C. Kakwani (1976), 'Distribution of Wealth in Australia', *Review of Incomes and Wealth*, pp.75–92.
Priorities Review Staff (1975), *Possibilities for Social Welfare in Australia* (Parliamentary Paper No. 163, Canberra, 1975).
Pritchard, H. and P. Saunders (1978), 'Poverty and Income Maintenance Policy in Australia—A Review Article', *Economic Record*, 54, pp.17–31.
Reder, M.W. (1962), 'Wage Differentials: Theory and Measurement', in NBER, *Aspects of Labour Economics* (Princeton University Press, Princeton, 1962).
Reynolds, L.G. and C. Taft (1956), *The Evolution of Wage Structure* (Yale University Press, New Haven, 1956).
Rivlin, A.M. (1975), 'Income Distribution—Can Economists Help?', *American Economic Review*, 65, Papers and Proceedings, pp.1–15.
Roberti, P. (1978), 'Income Inequality in Some Western Countries: Patterns and Trends', *International Journal of Social Economics*, 5, pp.22–41.
Samuelson, P., K. Hancock and R. Wallace (1975), *Economics* (Second Australian Edition, McGraw-Hill, Sydney, 1975).
Saunders, P. (1976), 'A Guaranteed Minimum Income Scheme for Australia? Some Problems', *Australian Journal of Social Issues*, 11, pp.174–186.
Scotton, R.B. and P.J. Sheehan (1976), 'The New Personal Income Tax', *Australian Economic Review*, 34, pp.13–24.
Social Indicator (1976), *Social Indicators, 1976* (ABS, Canberra, 1976).
Social Welfare Commission (1974), *Review of the Interim Report of the Commission of Inquiry into Poverty* (Discussion Paper, 1974).
Solow, R. (1958), 'A Skeptical Note on the Constancy of Relative Shares', *American Economic Review*, 48, pp.618–631.
Stretton, H. (1976), 'The Road Ahead—Australia's Options', in T. van Dugteren (ed.), *Who Gets What?* (Hodder and Stoughton, Sydney, 1976).
Tinbergen, J. (1975), *Income Differences: Recent Research* (Professor Dr. F. De Vries Lecture, North Holland, Amsterdam, 1975).
Townsend, P., ed. (1970), *The Concept of Poverty* (Heinemann Educational Books, London, 1970).
US Department of Health, Education and Welfare (1974), *The Changing Economic Status of 5000 American Families—Highlights from the Panel Study of Income Dynamics* (Washington, 1974).
US Department of Health, Education and Welfare (1973), *Summary Report: New Jersey Graduated Work Incentives Experiment* (Washington, 1973).
Wallace, R.H. (1975), 'Taxation Reform: But What is the Agenda? (Review Article)', *Economic Record*, 51, pp.564–575.
Whitehead, D.H. (1973), *Stagflation and Wages Policy in Australia* (Longman, Melbourne, 1973).
Wilson, T., ed. (1974), *Pensions, Inflation and Growth* (Heinemann Education Books, London, 1974).
Woodhouse Report (1974), *Compensation and Rehabitation in Australia* (Report of the National Committee of Inquiry, AGPS, Canberra, 1974).

Chapter 2

Urban Economics

MAX NEUTZE

Australian National University

GRAEME BETHUNE

Department of Housing & Urban Affairs, Adelaide

Contents

The authors wish to acknowledge the very helpful comments of the editor and two referees on an earlier draft.

Section 1 Introduction

As an area of study urban economics is not much more than a decade old either in Australia or elsewhere. Wilbur Thompson's *A Preface to Urban Economics* was published in 1965, and all the other commonly used texts and books of readings are more recent. Some parts, such as the economics of housing, go back much further, but it was only in the 1960s that economists became interested in urban transport. Although courses are taught at many tertiary institutions there is no Australian journal. The Australian urban economics literature is found partly in economics periodicals but also in geography, planning, transport and sociology journals and often in overseas publications. Economic geographers and other non-economists have contributed much to our knowledge of the economy of Australia cities. If this survey were to confine itself to the writings of economists alone it would be unduly narrow.

Two books that served to awaken interest in urban questions among Australian economists were Butlin's (1964) account of Australian economic development which emphasised the importance of urban development and Mathews' (1967) estimates of the volume of public investment in urban development and criticism of the lack of planning.

In most countries the development of urban economics has been closely related to policy issues. Books of readings such as Gordon (1971) and Edel and Rothenberg (1972) demonstrate the importance of race, poverty, and public finance as issues in US cities. Australian economists have been more concerned with the problems of urban growth, leading to research on the process of urban development, decentralisation and urban land markets, with almost no contributions to the development of theoretical models of cities. Both the strengths and weaknesses of the work in this area are reflected in a book of readings published in 1976 (McMaster and Webb).

Although this survey is divided into a number of sections some of the divisions are difficult to maintain because different sections deal with closely related issues. Each topic area is discussed in two or more sections dealing first with analysis and then with policy. For example the section on the supply and demand for housing is followed by a section on housing policy. The second and third sections of the survey deal with the distribution of activities and population between cities. All the other sections deal mainly with the use of resources and the distribution of welfare within cities.

The predominant change that has occurred within urban areas in recent decades is the suburbanisation of living and working places. Its causes and consequences are discussed in sections on residential density, causes of, and policies towards, suburbanisation. The next section outlines the general role of government in urban development. It is followed by sections dealing with specific functions of local government, public utilities and land use controls. The discussion of urban land economics deals mainly with the causes of land price inflation and policy measures to dampen it. The two sections on housing economics come next and are followed by the last major topic, urban transport economics. It includes sections on the demand for transport, transport planning, pricing and policy.

Section 2 The Growth and Size of Cities

Most of the economic studies of urban growth in Australia have been concerned with whether the existing distribution of population between cities is likely to be optimal, or whether a policy of diverting some growth from the largest cities to smaller centres should be undertaken. Unfortunately, these studies have not always been based on a good understanding of the reasons for the present distribution. Commentators differ on the effects that changes in the distribution would have on national welfare. This is partly because the size and location of cities influence welfare both directly through the environment and life style opportunities they offer and indirectly through the efficiency of production.

Two main approaches have been taken to explain geographic distribution. The first emphasises the effect of natural resources. Towns and cities process the output of farms and mines and provide services for them and their workers. This approach was developed into a formal structure by Losch (1954) and has been used frequently in Australia (Butlin 1964; Linge 1963). It lends itself to an historical explanation of the development of a hierarchy of towns as an agricultural economy changes into an industrial and service economy. It also helps to explain the concentration of metal processing industries in the major urban areas of New South Wales, and can incorporate the effects of government policy (Linge and Rimmer 1971).

Economic development in Australia proceeded from urban settlements outward rather than by commercialisation of self-sufficient agriculture (Butlin 1964). Consequently the size and location of cities is to a considerable extent independent of the output of resource-based industries in their hinterlands. This is becoming increasingly true as farming and mining become less important as users of labour. The second approach has therefore put its main emphasis on the cities themselves as generators of employment. This approach was first spelling out fully by Evans (1972), who developed a model in which the efficiency of production depends only on the size of a city and, as a consequence, wages vary with city size. It has also been used by Tisdell (1975).

Colin Clark (1964) emphasised the very long periods that are involved in changes in the geographic distribution of economic activities. Equilibrium models like Tisdell's are of value mainly in helping to explain the direction of marginal changes. Like firms, cities experience economies of scale and diminishing returns. Economies of scale and specialisation with city growth occur in many local personal and business services—education, recreation, entertainment, inter-city transport, water supply, sewage treatment, legal, accounting and financial services. Together with economies of agglomeration they largely explain the growth of cities. In larger cities there may be diseconomies of scale, resulting mainly from increasing costs of communication and transport (Neutze 1965).

Diminishing returns to city growth result from the limited area of land (natural resources) that can be used for building sites, transport routes, recreation space, water supply and waste disposal, requiring people, water and wastes to be transported over increasing distances. The growing use of its limited land resources is also reflected in traffic congestion, air, water and land pollution and crowding of recreation areas. As a result of the scarcity of accessible land people have to live at higher densities if they want to avoid spending long periods travelling. Many would agree with Tisdell's assumption, that there are increasing returns with growth of most cities up to some stage and decreasing returns thereafter. However because of theoretical and practical difficulties it is unlikely that these relationships can be measured. Nor is it clear that any Australian cities are 'too large' in this sense (Alonso 1974).

Unlike firms, cities are not decision-making units and cannot readily control their own growth. Some of Tisdell's models, using quite plausible assumptions, result in the whole population living in one city, demonstrating the limits of an explanatory model which ignores historical and resource influences. Decisions about location involve a long-term commitment of capital. The minimum risk location for many firms and families is the large city with its large pool of labour, wide range of jobs and services and large and varied market (Webber 1972).

One approach to analysing urban or regional growth is to break it into its component parts. Shift-and-share analysis allocates growth in employment into (1) the part which is simply the city's share of national growth, (2) the part which is due to the city's having more than its share of fast or slowly growing industries, and (3) the part due to particular industries in the city growing faster or more slowly than the national average for that industry. Kerr (1970) and Stilwell (1974) show that the more rapid growth of the state capitals between 1954 and 1966 was primarily due to their concentration on fast-growing industries.

Growth of population can be divided into the parts due to natural increase, overseas migration and internal migration (National Population Inquiry 1975). During most of the post-war period growth in the state capitals has resulted primarily from overseas migration and natural increase, and only to a minor extent from internal migration. It does not necessarily follow that a lower rate of overseas migration would have led to a much more dispersed population: there may then have been more internal migration to the state capitals. However the decline in overseas migration since 1971 has been accompanied by a dramatic fall in the proportion of national population growth occurring in the state capitals.

The 1971 Census results provided the first detailed statistics on internal migration. An economic study for the Cities Commission (1975) found that a region's out-migration is roughly proportional to its population but that the number of in-migrants attracted to the capital cities rises less than proportionately with their population. In-migration is much more sensitive to labour market conditions.

Section 3 *City Size Policies*

Using some quite simple models Tisdell (1975) shows that only in a few special circumstances will the market produce a distribution of population between cities that maximises welfare. If a city's growth depends on its average income, but the average income varies with its population, the social returns from growth (marginal addition to city income) differ from the private returns (average income). In small centres growth produces net external economies whereas in large centres it may produce net external diseconomies. External diseconomies result mainly from physical interaction and, because large numbers normally preclude negotiation, their effects can only be offset by either controls or continuing taxes or subsidies. Most of the advantages from city growth result from economies of scale and specialisation in local service industries and are therefore reflected in lower prices and wider availability of goods and services in larger cities. In order to realise these advantages it may be necessary to plan and coordinate city development for much the same reasons as are often given for planning the development of under developed countries: what Tisdell calls myopia and Paterson (1973) describes as 'gaps in the market for cities of various types which make some feasible forms of urban living unattainable to private decision makers'.

Stilwell (1974) argues that producers have more control over location than consumers, but gives only very general reasons. One possible reason is that wage rates vary little between different cities and towns. In other countries one of the main incentives for manufacturing and some services to locate outside large cities has been to find cheaper labour. Australia does not have such pools of relatively cheap labour because it has no large pool of rural underemployed. But the uniformity of wages, resulting from the strength of the national and state-wide wage-fixing system, may also discourage decentralisation. A study by the Department of Labour and National Service for the Committee of Commonwealth/State officials on Decentralisation (*Studies on Decentralisation*, 1975) found that wages were only 0.6 per cent lower in country centres.

The Committee of Commonwealth/State Officials carried out the most exhaustive empirical investigation of the case for and against a policy of decentralisation (*Report of the Committee*, 1972, and *Studies on Decentralisation*, 1975). Comparisons between the costs of production for manufacturing firms operating in both metropolitan and non-metropolitan locations showed very small differences. Comparisons between the costs of providing public services in cities of varying size were not very conclusive because of the small numbers of large centres. However the services required to cater for expansion of Sydney cost significantly more than if the same growth was distributed among a number of smaller centres. The Committee's conclusion was that, from the point of view of economic efficiency, there is no very strong case either for or against decentralisation.

The Committee admitted that it paid little attention to social, defence and aesthetic issues. It interpreted economic issues as solely concerned with efficiency whereas some of the strongest criticism of the existing concentration of population is based on equity grounds (Stretton 1975). People in rural areas and country towns have poor access to many services. In large cities competition for space forces poorer people to live either in poor quality inner city areas, close to jobs and services, or in better but less accessible housing on the suburban fringes. Equality of access to jobs and services would be maximised by a relatively even distribution of medium-sized cities.

There are at least two kinds of policy which may be both feasible and desirable. The first is diversion of some metropolitan growth to a limited number of regional centres, variously called selective decentralisation and growth centres policy (Neutze 1974a). Attempts to boost the growth of all country centres have not succeeded and seem unlikely to succeed because the available incentives will be spread too thinly to allow any to reap the economies of scale available in medium-sized centres. The second is diversion of growth to satellite centres near the existing metropolitan areas, such as Newcastle, Wollongong, Gosford-Wyong and Geelong. This amounts to a redirection of metropolitan growth within the broad metropolitan regions. Joy (1968) and Braby (1973) argue that many of the advantages claimed for decentralisation could be achieved by dispersing jobs and services to suburban centres. The National Population Inquiry (1975) pointed out that serious problems of over-concentration are mainly confined to Sydney and Melbourne and argued that decentralisation to the smaller states could be more easily achieved and bring more benefits than establishing growth centres in south-east Australia.

The concentration of jobs in a few cities facilitates transfers of workers and is probably one reason that unemployment in Australia has generally been relatively low. It eases the transfer from one job to another. On the other hand Stilwell (1974) claimed, and some of the *Studies on Decentralisa-*

tion (1975) support his claim, that there is a good deal of unused labour available in non-metropolitan centres because of the lack of job opportunities, especially for women. If more expansion occurred outside the main centres it would generate fewer inflationary pressures.

The slow-down in population growth since 1971 has reduced the growth pressures in the large cities, and has led to falling populations in most of the inner and middle suburbs. Since much of the slow-down has resulted from a decline in the birthrate, the number entering the work-force and household formation are still likely to be nearly as large between 1975 and 1990 as between 1960 and 1975. The slow-down in metropolitan growth has generated pressures for it to be stimulated on the somewhat questionable grounds 'that economic development . . . takes place, at least initially, within our larger centres and then increases directly with the size of the city' (Little 1977).

The main reason for the agnostic views of the Committee of Commonwealth/State Officials is that the evidence about the magnitude of the costs and benefits of decentralisation is very slim. Since special factors affect costs and living conditions in individual cities a large number of cities of varying size is required before there can be any confidence in the shape of the relationships. In addition many of the costs and benefits are very difficult to measure—pollution, traffic congestion, access to jobs and services, quality and costs of services, economies of agglomeration.

Decentralisation, especially to 'new cities', usually involves heavy investment in infrastructure in advance of growth. These costs may be no higher in a new city that grows rapidly, but the need to invest in advance without an assurance that growth will occur makes them a risky venture. Paterson (1973) therefore argues that the limited resources available for influencing the location of employment would be better used where there is already a backlog of demand for services and where the return is more certain. The past record of the effectiveness of decentralisation policies, apart from the special case of Canberra, is scarcely reassuring but this may be because the policy efforts were so dispersed (Development Corporation of NSW 1969). Another alternative would be to concentrate on providing more work in established centres where there are few jobs for women, such as Wollongong, or where structural unemployment is becoming significant, such as Whyalla and Newcastle (Hunter Regional Planning Committee 1977).

The policy instruments available for influencing the location of employment—provision of infrastructure, location of government agencies, subsidies—are not very powerful (Linge 1976). As Rhodes and Kan (1972) point out, Australia has relied entirely on a system of 'carrots' whereas other countries have also used various 'sticks' to control expansion of employment in congested metropolitan areas. The case for decentralisation continues to rely heavily on qualitative judgements. The feasibility of establishing new regional centres has not yet been adequately tested.

Section 4 Residential Density

Economists have contributed little to understanding of the pattern of land use within Australian cities or how it has changed over time. One reason is that there is little data about the variation in income, residential density, house and land prices between parts of cities. Another is that economic theories to explain urban structure have provided only limited insights. In order to be manageable they concentrate on a single spatial variable, distance from the city centre, and ignore other aspects of location.

These urban models first developed by Wingo (1961), Alonso (1964) and Muth (1969), assume that the city centre contains all its jobs and services and predict the declining population density with distance from the city centre observed by Clark (1951). The density gradient has also become less steep as a result of falling transport costs, as the theory would predict. Clark later showed that sub-areas of individual cities were tending towards a common (he called it a pivotal) density of about 3,000 persons per square kilometre in Brisbane and nearly 4,000 in Sydney and Melbourne (Clark 1970). The models' predictions relate to the density of population per unit of *residential land* but frequently the only data available for testing it are population per unit of *all land*. Neutze (1977a, Ch.3) has shown that, beyond quite a short distance, residential densities in Australian cities vary little with distance from the centre, and suggests that historical factors have had a greater influence on residential density (Harrison and Kain 1974). Daly (1967a) has also shown that distance from the city centre explained relatively little of the variation in density in Newcastle.

The largest concentrations of jobs and some specialised services are still found in the city centres. Geographical and sociological examinations of residential structure by Johnston (1971), Timms (1971) and Jones (1969) all show that, as the theory would predict, families with young children who have a high demand for space, but commonly only one member in the workforce, are most likely to live in the outer suburbs. Parts of cities differ markedly in terms of income, age and ethnic composition. The causes of segregation, including the role of the property market, require much more research.

Section 5 The Causes of Suburbanisation

Most of the growth of Australian cities since the second world war has been accommodated by extension of suburbs rather than by increased density. The reasons for this have been subject to very little economic analysis.

Increased car ownership has both facilitated urban spread, and been forced on people living in outer suburbs because of poor public transport. Survey results suggested that closeness to the city centre is not a very important determinant of choice of housing, especially as the centre contains a declining proportion of jobs, shops and other services. Price and congenial neighbours are more important (Daly 1968; Urban Research Unit 1973). Another contributing factor has been the greater willingness of institutions to lend for new houses (Hill 1959, p.141). Increasing incomes have also resulted in a growing demand for larger houses with more outdoor space. As the post-war housing shortage eased, the population in the inner suburbs actually fell in spite of an increased rate of flat building in the 1960s.

The movement of jobs to the suburbs lagged behind their residential development and occurred mainly in retailing, manufacturing and wholesaling (Neutze 1977a, chap.4). The main reasons why manufacturers have moved from inner city to suburban locations are described by Logan (1966). Availability of cheap land has become increasingly important to manufacturers needing larger sites for horizontal movement of goods during processing, storage at ground level and on-site parking. Motor trucks have freed most kinds of manufacturing from the need to be close to city transport terminals. With the growth of residential suburbs it has also become easier to recruit workers in suburban industrial areas (Logan 1964). Rimmer (1969) described a process of diffusion as Melbourne manufacturing spread from the inner suburbs, but noted that most moves were short or within the same sector of the city because firms try to keep their workers and their customers. Availability of a suitable site or rental factory is a major determinant of location; operating costs for most firms do not vary greatly between parts of a city (Vandermark 1970; Neilson 1972).

Wholesaling has tended to follow manufacturing, and retailing and other services have followed their markets, often into large, land-intensive, suburban shopping centres. Most of them have been located away from established suburban centres (Johnston and Rimmer 1969). A high proportion of office jobs, however, has remained in the city centre. None of the suburban centres provides more than a small fraction of the number or range of shops and services found in the city centre, and none of the suburban industrial areas rivals the inner suburban industrial zone (Harrison 1977). Suburban concentrations remain relatively small because they have relatively poor public transport and, if they grow too large, suffer from severe congestion and parking problems.

Suburbanisation is only partly a result of market forces. Investment and pricing policies of government authorities that provide roads, public transport, water, electricity, telephones and sewerage often encourage suburban development. In addition, planning authorities, through control over land use, can influence the direction and shape of development (Archer 1976a). But service authorities appear to respond to demand rather than either anticipating or seeking to influence it (Urban Research Unit 1973).

Logan (1966) argues that residential zoning prevented expansion of inner city factories after the war. However, the surrounding housing was too expensive for single-storey factories and for parking. The main effect of land use controls has been to separate industrial and residential development, to consolidate both, and to preserve areas of open space for recreation and other public purposes (Harrison 1978).

There has been a significant amount of development in the established urban areas, much, but not all of it, replacing existing houses, factories, shops or office buildings. One reason for the extent of office construction has been their value as a hedge against inflation. The oversupply which emerged in the mid-1970s, partly as a result of the long gestation period, has made office buildings a much less attractive investment.

Flats, mostly privately built, have been the other major form of redevelopment. Most have been built at only modest density. Rising interest rates with inflation in the 1970s, and increased opposition from local residents who fear external diseconomies, have resulted in fewer flats being built during the 1970s.

Section 6 Policies towards Suburbanisation

Urban structure has been a matter for active policy debate. The extent of low-density suburban spread has been criticised and more high-density housing redevelopment advocated. Some have applauded the decentralisation of jobs from the city centre and others have deplored it. Some have argued that suburban employment should be more concentrated in and around a few suburban centres. There have been no careful comparisons of costs and benefits and it is possible only to review the arguments on each side briefly.

The main argument in favour of encouraging decentralisation of jobs and services from the central area is that it shortens the journey to work and increases the accessibility of people living in the suburbs to jobs and services (Joy 1968; Braby 1973). The argument concerns both efficiency and equity. Public transport and, it can be argued, roads serving the central area are heavily subsidised mainly in order to cater for peak demands for the journey to work. As a result employment is excessively concentrated. If jobs were more dispersed such subsidies would be lower.

Measures of accessibility to jobs and services (e.g. Black 1977) show that people living in outer suburbs are relatively disadvantaged, and that the difference between inner and outer suburbs is greater than the difference between income groups. On the other hand people travelling to suburban work places are much more likely to drive (Lanigan 1976) and thereby add to congestion and air pollution. Public transport cannot efficiently cater for dispersed trips between suburban residences and suburban jobs.

Local councils frequently use the 'plot ratio' (ratio of floor area to site area) as a way of determining development rights and limiting the density of development in central business districts. However, a fixed plot ratio high enough to encourage redevelopment is not an efficient means of avoiding the problems of excessive density—traffic and pedestrian congestion and daylight in buildings (Paterson 1972). It can be argued that unrealistic expectations of capital gains have resulted in too many resources being used to increase the volume of office space during the 1960s and 1970s for only a small increase in the office workforce. Partly because of long cycles in development, much of the building has been speculative and by January 1976, when there was already much vacant office space, twenty-five buildings with an average of 25 storeys each were still under construction in the Sydney Central Business District.

The more specialised services can only be attracted to large suburban centres. Parramatta, the largest suburban centre in Australia, has less than five per cent of the number of jobs in the Sydney Central Business District. Offices, that house many of the city's clerical, professional and administrative workers, seem reluctant to move from the centre (Alexander 1976). Some government services, such as public hospitals, are also highly concentrated even though their clients are quite widely dispersed. Since the main attraction of a suburban location is its freedom from congestion and ease of parking it seems unlikely that suburban centres will grow large enough to attract much office development or to become the focus of a network of public transport services. A disadvantage of continuous outward spread of cities is the lack of differentiation, and the diffusion of demand for transport. If expansion could be focussed into a limited number of corridors or separate satellite towns there would be more chance of providing a wider range of jobs and services outside the central areas. Furthermore, corridor development can be more efficiently served by public transport. Green wedges between the corridors can be used for open space and institutions (Stretton 1975). The plans for most Australian cities provide for growth corridors. There has been some success especially, as in Sydney, where corridors follow established transport routes.

The compactness and continuity of urban expansion also influence its cost. It is expensive to provide urban services—water, sewer, roads, telephone lines—past vacant land to service houses some distance from the urban fringe. A study of Sydney showed the very considerable savings from filling in the established area, compared with continuing scattered development (Cumberland Country Council 1958).

There are also strong arguments for maintaining a large number of jobs in the central area. There is already a large amount of capital invested in the public transport system, buildings, streets, parklands and other services in the central areas. It would be inefficient to duplicate many of these facilities elsewhere. Furthermore, a declining number of manufacturing and wholesaling jobs in the inner areas might lead to increased unemployment among the predominantly blue-collar workers who live in the inner suburbs (Melbourne and Metropolitan Board of Works 1977). There is, though, still a large excess of jobs compared with resident workers in the inner areas and, so far, the latter are declining faster than the former.

Maintaining a high level of employment in the central area is made easier in one respect if more people live in the inner suburbs. They can work locally and demand local services. Non-residential activities also compete for space with housing and one of the direct reasons for loss of population in inner areas is that houses have been converted for use as, or demolished to provide sites for, offices, factories, warehouses, hospitals and universities. The fact that there has been little increase in the workforce employed in these areas reflects partly the fall in labour used per unit of output in all industries and also the increasing space used for each worker.

Section 7 The Role of Government in Urban Development

The government and private sectors of a mixed economy are particularly closely related in urban development and the operation of cities. Consequently market failures, which may require government involvement in and regulation of private activities, are particularly important. However government actions often fail to correct or compensate for market failures and sometimes create further inefficiencies.

One kind of market failure that has received little attention in Australia, results from 'natural monopolies'. In public utilities (electricity, gas, telephones, water, sewerage and public transport) economies of scale in the links in the distribution network are so great that competition between private suppliers would be very inefficient. As a result they are either provided by government authorities or their production and pricing are regulated by governments. Governments also became heavily involved in urban development in the course of providing education, health, transport and other services.

A second kind of market failure results mainly from interdependence between activities that occur close to one another. (Paterson 1973; Urban Research Unit 1973). Physical externalities can cause the socially optimal location to be different from the private optimum. Those activities that produce only externalities that cannot be appropriated (public goods) are normally performed by governments. There is also an argument for improved information about likely future developments, and even for coordination of related developments that occur at different times.

The two major functions of governments that derive from analysis of market failures, provision of services and planning and regulating development, should be performed by governments representing people living in the affected areas. Such 'optimal jurisdictions' range from small localities through regions to the whole nation in the case of national settlement policy. However, interdependencies are especially great between parts of an urban area.

Section 8 Local Government

Australian local governments have fewer functions than comparable governments in other western countries. In addition the fragmentation of the country into some 900 local government areas means that some have very few resources. Many of the equity problems which result from variations in resources available to different councils could be solved by amalgamation of councils covering large sections or the whole of metropolitan areas. Nevertheless attempts to amalgamate local councils have borne relatively little fruit in Australia. There have been moves for metropolitan government since early in the century. The only notable success occurred in Brisbane in 1925. There were also less significant amalgamations later in Newcastle and Wollongong. Instead, services such as water, sewerage, electricity, major roads and public transport are provided by metropolitan semi-government or state authorities. (Neutze 1974c). Because they provide relatively few of the labour-intensive personal services such as education, health, police, welfare, Australian local governments have suffered less than the states from increasing labour costs, and the consequent 'urban crisis' (Baumol 1967).

Local governments and special purpose authorities are, primarily, concerned with the allocative functions of government. However their pricing and investment decisions, the taxes they levy and their land use control decisions inevitably influence the distribution of welfare, so that the distributive effects of their policies constrain their activities (Bentley 1973; Voumard 1972). Indeed, as Henderson and Lewis (1974) argued, local councils have advantages in providing some health and welfare services that redistribute in kind rather than in cash. Stilwell (1974) also argues the importance of distributive objectives in urban policy.

Some of the services provided by governments in cities are financed either by charges or special taxes, but others, especially the general functions of local governments, including local roads, bridges and drains, libraries, recreation facilities and regulatory functions are financed from general revenue. The main source of that revenue for local councils is the property tax (rate). Local governments in Australia are chronically short of funds and all states have instituted inquiries to examine the adequacy of rates as a source of revenue and to look for alternative or additional sources of revenue.[1]

All the inquiries recommended that rates should remain the major source of revenue, and some also pointed out that rate revenue has not risen as rapidly as revenue from other taxes or the property tax base. This suggests that, despite the complaints of councillors that they 'cannot' raise more revenue from rates, they could do so simply by maintaining the rate in the dollar. The Voumard Report suggested that it may not be possible to raise more revenue because of the regressivity of property rates. It quotes a submission by the Local Government Engineers Association of Victoria:

> It is a political fact of municipal life that the rate of municipal taxation tends to be fixed on the ability to pay of those on the lower incomes.

Bentley (1973) also argues that rates are very regressive, using incidence data from the Macquarie University Survey of Consumer Finances. To make matters worse, he argues, the expenditures of Australian local governments probably also have a regressive effect on the distribution of welfare. None of the reports considers the possibility that the property tax is capitalised into the value of the property (Neutze 1977b). Bentley argues that capitalisation does not occur, and even if it did, some aspects of regressivity would remain. It is not clear whether the progressivity of a tax which results in a once-over reduction in capital values should be assessed by comparison with income or wealth levels.

Several of the reports recommended additional sources of tax revenue for local government. One of the few to be implemented was the recommendation by the Else-Mitchell (1967) Inquiry that a betterment tax be collected in New South Wales. The results are described in the section on land policy.

Tiebout (1956) argued that resources could be allocated quite efficiently by local councils since residents could choose to live in the municipality that provides the combination of services and local tax rates that best suits them. This neglects the fact that low-income families can only afford to live where housing is cheap. For this and other reasons rich and poor families frequently live in different municipalities. Local rates, as a source of revenue, are often criticised because residents in poor, or rapidly growing, municipalities often have to pay higher rates in the dollar to provide any given level of services (Manning 1973).

This distributive problem arises with any local tax and led the Voumard Report (1972) to accept the recommendation of Henderson and Lewis for more state government funds for local governments, especially for health

[1] The most useful are Voumard (1972) and Else-Mitchell (1967). In addition a *Joint Study into Local Government Finances, Australia and New Zealand* (1976) has considered the same questions.

and welfare services. Most of the inquiries recommended the distribution of state funds to needy local authorities and some states now do so. This was taken further under the Whitlam Government when the Grants Commission recommended grants from the Commonwealth to individual local governments using criteria similar to those used in making grants to claimant states (Mathews 1974). Groenewegen (1976) has compared the ability of local councils in New South Wales to raise revenue. Like most other Australian analysts he neglects the possibility of capitalisation of property taxes. American studies suggest that, as a result of capitalisation, housing is cheaper in municipalities where rates are high relative to services received. If this occurs it almost precludes horizontal inequity (Hamilton 1976).

Section 9 Public Utilities

Water, sewerage and drainage services are the only utility-type services that raise most of their revenue from taxation, again property taxes. The main argument of the Sydney and Hunter Water Boards for retaining this method of financing is that a high proportion of the costs of water and sewerage services are independent of the volume of water used in any one year (Else-Mitchell 1967). In addition, installing and reading meters at all properties would be expensive. As the Else-Mitchell Report pointed out, if volume charges discourage use of water there would be less need for capacity for storage and transmission. The Boards argued, however, that demand is price inelastic. In the absence of usable Australian data Gallagher and Robinson (1977) examine the overseas evidence on demand elasticity and argue the case for metering and the use of prices to ration consumption (see also Binnie 1977). They recognise that some of the costs, especially the cost of providing water to each property at a pressure and volume sufficient for fire fighting, are indeed independent of the volume used. For this reason they recommend a combination of volume charges and property rates. For most of the other utility services production costs are higher relative to distribution costs. Both electricity and telephones use a fixed charge to cover the cost of connection.

Discussions of electricity pricing (e.g. McColl 1976) focus on the implications of temporal variation in demand for pricing and investment but ignore the implications of its spatial distribution. For the authorities involved in providing these services, the location of the growth in demand is very important. Mushkin (1972) has shown that growth in demand within the geographic area already served by a utility can often be met at decreasing average cost whereas extending the service area is likely to result in increasing average costs. As long as the costs of extending the network are spread over all users, there will be no disincentive to developments in scattered locations and at low densities that require high cost extensions of mains by the utility authorities.

It was partly to discourage excessively scattered development, but mainly to get more revenue, that from the mid-1950s part of the cost of installing services has been shifted to developers. Pollock and Neutze (1976) argue that such 'requirements' form part of an optimal charging system for water and sewerage.

Section 10 *Land Use Controls*

Scattered and excessively low density development, or development in areas that are very expensive to service, can be prevented by land use controls. While service costs are a legitimate criterion for land use planning they cannot be over-riding (Paterson 1968). Furthermore, the cost and efficiency of servicing may be affected more by the ability of the service authority to predict when and where development occurs, than by its particular location. This is particularly important for telephone services (Reubenicht 1968).

It is difficult to forecast the location of urban development. Even with developers responsible for service reticulation and an optimal set of service prices there is a case for land use controls as a means of improving predictability in order to improve the dynamic efficiency of resource allocation, especially since public authorities are responsible for nearly half the investment in urban development. Most decisions about location commit resources to one place for a considerable time. Many of those decisions, taken at different times, are inter-dependent and therefore not readily coordinated by the private market.

Urban planning attempts to coordinate public and private development decisions. Even coordination of the various public authorities is difficult to achieve, given the number of authorities and different levels of government involved (Neutze 1972b). At the state level alone, even when the interests of two authorities coincide, coordination can be difficult. An example involving the planning and the water and sewerage authorities in Sydney occurred when planning controls were used to force developers to pay for servicing land released from the green belt (Gibbons 1976).

The main means by which private location decisions can be influenced are controls over the use of land. They confer benefits on some land owners but reduce the value of land whose development is restricted. If all owners injuriously affected by those controls were compensated land use planning would be so costly as to be impossible (Davidson 1955). In addition, compensation would be almost impossible to assess. Rather, all property rights are limited by land use controls. The effects of such controls on property values sometimes seem like a lottery and set up formidable market pressures against planning measures. Given these problems it is not surprising that the achievements of urban planning in Australia have been modest (Harrison 1978).

Land use planning and land use controls bring their own inefficiencies. It is argued that local councils use their powers to control the standard of development in order to upgrade the local environment and thereby exclude those who cannot afford the higher standards (Paterson 1975a; Paterson **et al** 1976). Paterson can be accused of over-stating his case when, ignoring the segregative effects of an unconstrained property market, he argues that this is the main reason for residential segregation. Nor does he recognise that land use controls are simply the tools used by local community groups to protect the local environment. If these particular tools were not available others would probably be devised. Furthermore, as recent American studies have shown (Hamilton 1976), controls over land use can be part of an efficient system of local government in metropolitan areas. Such a system would need to have many jurisdictions to give people a wide choice. It can become inefficient if all municipalities with room to grow attempt to exclude the poor. Avoidance of this problem may require controls from some higher level of government.

Section 11 Urban Land Price Inflation

As a result of rapid increases in land prices between the mid-1960s and 1974 there has been a good deal of interest in the urban land market (Department of Urban and Regional Development 1974a). Much of the writing was concerned with policy measures to contain the rate of inflation, and with analysis of the effects of proposed measures.

Land price inflation became a major issue in Perth in the mid-1960s and resulted in the Premier appointing the McCarrey Committee. Its Report (*Land Taxation and Land Prices in Western Australia* 1968) attributed such inflation to increased demand resulting from metropolitan growth, restriction of supply as a result of speculative holding of vacant land, land use controls, the time required to get development permission, and the financial inability of public authorities to keep up with the demand for their services (especially sewerage). In addition it noted that the costs of subdivision had increased as developers were required to install some services within their subdivisions, and assumed that such costs would be passed on to the final buyers of developed land.

Much of the traditional analysis of urban land markets has assumed a completely inelastic supply of urban land, even though land can be converted from rural to urban use. The production of urban sites from rural land can be analysed like other production processes and factors likely to affect the supply of, and demand for land for urban development explored (Neutze 1970). In particular, the effect on prices of the requirements that developers provide or pay for some services can be analysed as if they were taxes on conversion of land to urban use. What proportions of such charges fall on the price of raw land and developed sites depends on the relative elasticity of supply and demand.

If location could be ignored the supply of raw land would be almost infinitely elastic at its value for non-urban use. However, only land near the city can be used for urban purposes. Access to the city's jobs and services falls off quite rapidly with distance from the built-up area. Land near a growing city can be expected to appreciate because of the increase in demand for a scarce resource. The owner can either develop it for urban uses or hold it for capital gains. The supply of land for urban development can be analysed by studying what determines when the owner will decide to develop (Bentick and Fischer 1975). The analytical problem is similar to deciding when to cut maturing trees for timber or to sell (or drink) maturing wine. The greater the rate of expected appreciation the greater the incentive to hold the land vacant and take the capital gains. The supply of developed land is highest when the price is high but not expected to rise. These influences are reflected in the instability that has been observed in the supply and price of allotments (*Report of the Working Party on the Stabilisation of Land Prices* 1973). Since there is a relatively long delay between the decision to create allotments and their availability for use, and there is no ready substitute for land near the city, it is not surprising that the market is characterised by quite large fluctuations.

The opportunity cost of land for urban use is its value for non-urban use near the city plus the costs of development. Observed prices are generally much higher than this, and indeed raw land for urban use usually sells for much more than its rural value. The reason is that supply is restricted and demand, at least over a range of prices, is relatively inelastic. Although there have been allegations that monopoly land owners restrict supply there is no evidence of concentrated ownership of development land near the larger cities. Reasons for supply restriction must be sought elsewhere.

Land owners who expect future appreciation will withhold land from development. Such speculative holding is the mechanism by which the market, responding to a limited stock of developable land, reduces the rate of development of that stock. Speculative holding of selected sites to provide for later, higher-density, development improves resource allocation (Bentick 1972). However, such selective withholding can occur at any general rate of development.

While there are natural limits to the land with access to the city the stock of land available for development is further restricted by actions of public authorities in zoning of land near the city for rural use or for open space. Even those areas that are planned for eventual development are usually released progressively to avoid urban sprawl and so avoid the need for costly and inefficient extensions of services to areas that are only partly developed. Land-use controls are used for this purpose partly because most government services are either provided at uniform prices or financed by special taxes which do not vary with the costs of the services.

Increased concern about the environment has led to demands that unsewered areas and all new developments be sewered, and that levels of treatment be improved. The loan funds of sewerage authorities have been limited by the Loan Council and by their unwillingness to raise taxes or charges to cover interest costs on larger borrowings. Requiring developers to pay for reticulation and connection to existing mains both discourages scattered development and reduces the investment funds needed by the service authorities.

The efficiency gains from requiring developers to pay more of the costs of servicing may have been partly offset by efficiency losses when service authorities demand higher standards than buyers would otherwise want to pay for, or planning authorities require higher standards of subdivision (Paterson *et al* 1976). In some cases of course these standards are designed to protect the welfare of non-residents. Another unfortunate consequence is that public authorities now take longer to consider development applications to ensure that all their requirements are met (Bromilow and Meaton 1974).

The equity effects of developer requirements depend on their incidence. There is a widespread belief that they are passed on as higher allotment prices (Bromilow 1975; *Land Taxation and Land Prices in WA* 1968), partly because a serviced lot is worth more than an unserviced lot. However, there is some evidence that at high prices demand for lots may become quite elastic and at least part of the cost is passed back as lower raw land prices. When costs are passed on they cause house prices to rise so that more of the cost of servicing is paid by first-time home buyers at a time when their resources are heavily strained. The wealth of established home owners increases but their housing costs are unaffected. It seems particularly inequitable that the owners of homes for which developers paid to reticulate services should have to pay the same rates as those whose homes were serviced by the authorities. Despite their equity disadvantages during the long transitional period while they are being introduced, because of their efficiency and financing advantages, developer requirements are part of an optimal pricing system.

Most of the enquiries and reports recognise developer requirements and land use controls as the main contributors to the high price of building sites (e.g. Department of Urban and Regional Development 1974a). The Hayes Report (1975) emphasised their effects in creating what turned out to be a short-term shortage of building sites.

Section 12 Urban Land Policy

In a period of shortage of developed lots and rapid price increases, the South Australian Working Party recommended temporary price control and a government land commission to develop land in competition with private developers (Bentick 1974). It also suggested that developers should have access to lower-interest finance, though Bentick and Fischer (1975) recognised that this could encourage speculative holding of vacant land. The later report by the Department of Urban and Regional Development (1974b) analysed the cause of land price inflation in some detail and, among the policy options proposed, placed most of its emphasis on land commissions.

Equity has been the main objective of Australian urban land policy. Efficiency considerations would also suggest that the price of land for housing should not exceed its opportunity cost. It is commonly recognised that increases in the value of land resulting from urban development are 'unearned' and could be taxed away without any effect on resource allocation (Taxation Review Committee 1975, pp.432–3; Commission of Inquiry into Land Tenures 1973, pp.15–17), though the same arguments apply to all other kinds of pure economic rent (Parish 1977). There have been many attempts in Britain to capture this so-called 'unearned increment' in land value. In Australia developer requirements have sometimes been justified as being such a tax. A more specific attempt to tax betterment was made in Sydney between 1969 and 1973 with the introduction of a levy on the difference between the base-date rural land value and its value after rezoning for development (Pullen 1971). Although the levy was widely criticised because, in the buoyant market conditions of the period, it was thought to be being passed on, Archer (1976b) defended it as a useful source of finance for services, which was only beginning to yield substantial revenue when it was abolished.

There has been some theoretical analysis of the effect of a betterment tax on the time of development and therefore supply and price. Bentick and Fischer (1975) argue that it will have no effect if the non-urban value is correctly defined. However, they also note that if land owners expect the tax to be passed on, and act accordingly, their belief is likely to be justified by their actions. An exchange in *Urban Studies* (Rose 1973; 1976; Neutze 1974b; Foster and Glaister 1975) demonstrated that the effects of such a tax depend on how the base is defined, and on when the tax is payable. One conclusion is clear. If owners expect the tax to be removed in the near future they will delay development, which will result in higher prices. The relevant taxes in both Britain and Australia have all been short-lived, and owners might well expect future similar taxes to suffer the same fate. The *Preliminary Report* of the Taxation Review Committee (1974) recommended a development gains tax but the *Full Report* (1975) withdraw that recommendation, mainly because of difficulties in administration.

Land Commissions or similar bodies competing with private developers have been established in four Australian States more or less in line with the blueprint set out by the *Report of the* [South Australian] *Working Party . . .* (1973) and the Department of Urban and Regional Development (1974b). More radical policies have been advocated by the Australian Institute of Urban Studies (1972), that all non-urban land for development should pass through public ownership, and by the Commission of Inquiry into Land Tenures (1973) that the development rights of all land be 'reserved' (pass into public ownership)—a proposal which was criticised as both impractical and inefficient by Parish (1977). Neither has been implemented.

Speculative land holding is a result of a decision about the form in which wealth is held. Bentick (1972) suggested the creation of a paper asset indexed to the price of land as a means of reducing the demand for land as an appreciating asset. The consequent fall in the price of both real and paper land would result in more land being developed and less being held vacant. This approach accepts the limits to the stock of land that can be developed and attempts to ameliorate its effects.

Australia is well known among analysts of property taxes as one of the few countries where Henry George's tax on unimproved value is used quite widely. Yet analysis of the effects of local rates and land taxes as policy measures is almost non-existent. If a tax on unimproved value is capitalised, it encourages development only if its introduction allows the abolition of a tax on rental or improved value that discourages development.

The usual objective of taxes on land for development is to capture part of its increase in value that results from permission to develop. Bentick and Fischer (1975) suggest a specifically designed tax to encourage development, but they have doubts about it. In order to give an incentive for development the Western Australian Report (*Land Taxation* . . . 1968) recommended a surcharge on land tax on undeveloped land zoned for urban use. The surcharge was in force until 1976. Like the basic land tax the surcharge was progressive and, as well as the speculator, penalised the large scale developer who needed to develop a large area slowly.

A more radical way to capture increases in the economic rent of land and to control land use is to give the state greater rights in some or all land through a change in tenure. One possibility is the reservation of development rights (Commission of Inquiry into Land Tenures 1973). Another is that development land that is purchased by a government authority should be leased rather than sold. This has been the practice in Canberra and, through lease conditions, allows the government to exercise control over land use (Archer 1974). As land rents are adjusted part or all of the increase in value accrues to the lessor. (They have not been collected at all in Canberra since 1971.) The Commission rejected leasehold for residential land for two reasons. First, a home owner with a leased site cannot hedge against price inflation. Second, residential leases from an elected government are politically vulnerable. However, it recommended leasehold tenure for non-residential land.

Urban land markets are poorly understood and the consequences of urban land policy are often unexpected. Few countries satisfactorily reconcile the interests of private land owners and the local community. This is an area in which economists have made relatively little contribution because externalities and inter-dependencies abound. However urban economists and lawyers are beginning to learn by comparing the different experience of a number of countries in land policy (Neutze 1973; Roberts 1977).

Section 13 Housing Demand and Supply

One of the most important determinants of housing preferences is stage in the family life cycle—the age and marital status of adults and the age of any children. Families, for example, are more likely to want to buy and to live in a house than young, single householders who often prefer rented flats (Gibbings 1973, Urban Research Unit 1973).

Income and savings also exert a powerful influence on housing tenure and expenditure. Once savings (reflecting income over a number of years) exceed a certain minimum (the buying threshhold) there is a high probability that most households will buy. Few studies have been able to explore the relationship between net worth and ownership. Struyk (1976) made a detailed study of the relationship between ownership and permanent income among a large sample of US households. The marginal influence of income was found to be lower at higher levels of household income and to vary widely between different types of households, being greatest among young husband-wife families.

The estimation of demand elasticities has received a great deal of attention in the United States. De Leeuw (1971) surveys a large number of cross-sectional studies of income elasticity and suggests that the elasticity of demand with respect to permanent income lies in the range 0.8–1.0 for tenants and 1.1–1.5 for home-owners. However, more recent studies surveyed by Polinsky (1977) imply true income elasticities closer to 0.75. The only published cross-sectional estimate of income elasticity based on Australian data is by Podder (1971). He estimated elasticities with respect to permanent income of 0.5 to 1.2 for the six capital cities, based on individual data collected in 1966–67. This estimate relates to expenditure on house maintenance and overhead, furnishing and rent. It omits the imputed rent of home-owners—a large part of the value of housing services. A further difficulty with most cross-sectional studies is that they ignore variations in house prices with accessibility within metropolitan areas, variations which the theory of residential location suggests are likely to be related to income. As Polinsky argues, this leads to a downward bias in estimates of the income elasticity of expenditure based on comparisons within a metropolitan area.

Income and price elasticities have also been estimated using time series data. However the published Australian estimates all have limited value for housing analysis, perhaps because they have been calculated as parts of wider consumption studies. Powell (1966) and Hoa (1968) derived estimates of 1.167 and 2.385 for the income elasticity and −0.543 and −0.976 for the price elasticity of demand respectively. However, both studies use a house price index which excludes land and interest costs and applies to capital cities only (Neutze 1972a). Since land prices and interest costs have increased at quite different rates from construction costs this is likely to affect estimates of the elasticities.

Tucker and Woodhead (1975) conclude that home-ownership is likely to be cheaper than renting for a household planning to live in a dwelling for more than five years. The main cost savings are in the costs of management, maintenance and mortgage interest rates. Some first-time home buyers qualify for a Home Savings Grant. Home-owners also receive taxation concessions from the tax rebate on rates, limited interest deductibility and exclusion of imputed rents and capital gains from the income tax base (Apps 1973). Given this price differential we would expect most households who can afford it to buy. However in times of inflation the difference in costs may be reduced somewhat through an implicit tax concession to landlords: although they pay tax on their rental incomes, all interest expenses are deductible (including that part of the interest rate which compensates the lender for inflation) whilst capital gains are usually tax-free.

Variations in the price of housing also affect where people decide to live. Within an urban area, other things being equal, the price of housing and land is likely to be higher in locations that are more accessible to employment, retailing and entertainment facilities (Evans 1973), reflecting travel costs in both time and money. A number of attempts has been made to relate observed variations in house and land values to differences in accessibility, type of dwelling and environment (Ball 1973; Clark 1970). Daly (1967b) shows that, at least in one urban area, Newcastle, distance from the centre is a major determinant of residential land value only within the inner suburbs. Elsewhere, closeness to sub-centres and to the cost and elevation are more important. In a more recent study Abelson (1977) has compared the relative importance of differences in dwelling structure and environment (particularly exposure to airport noise) in determining house prices in two Sydney suburbs. Generally, structural variables were found to be more significant than environmental ones.

Most of the building in the post-war period has been for owner occupation and, during the 1950s, large numbers of rented dwellings were sold to owner-occupiers. Accordingly the rate of home-ownership increased dramatically between the 1947 and 1961 censuses. The increase was partly a result of rent control (Johnson 1974), and a decline in house prices relative to incomes in most cities (except Sydney) and relative to rents during the 1960s (Neutze 1977a).

During the second half of the 1960s interest rates began to increase, reflecting both a rise in the rate of inflation and changes in the structure of housing finance. During the 1950s the most important lenders for housing were the savings banks and life offices (both directly and through terminating building societies), trading banks and the Defence Service Homes Scheme. After the 1950s the importance of life offices, terminating societies and Defence Service Homes declined while that of two more expensive lenders, finance companies and permanent building societies, increased (Hill 1974).

Increases in interest charges were accompanied by rising land prices. From the late 1960s rising interest charges and land prices caused the cost of purchasing a home to increase more quickly than the costs of renting. Landlords are also affected by rising land costs and interest rates but expectations of capital gains have probably helped to moderate rent increases. There may also have been lags in adjusting rents (Neutze 1977a). Part of the fall in the aggregate home-ownership rate since the 1966 Census is also due to the increasing propensity of young people to leave home and establish separate households, often in 'groups' renting houses or flats (Gordon, 1977).

This appears to be one of the reasons for the rapidly growing importance of flat building from the late 1950s. In the years 1954–59 flats comprised only 4 per cent of all dwellings completed, rising to 30 per cent in 1966–71 and declining somewhat in the 1970s. Other causes of the increase have been the relaxation of rent control, the increasing inaccessibility of the urban fringe where new houses are built (Cardew 1970) and the increase in the cost of buying the traditional detached house.

At any time the available supply of housing depends on the level of vacancies in the existing stock and the rate of new construction. Even when the market is tight there will be some vacancies because of the time and costs involved in acquiring information about such heterogeneous capital goods. If an occupant moves to a new house his previous dwelling becomes vacant and a chain of moves through the housing stock follows, truncated either by new household formation, immigration or demolition.

Chains of moves may be associated with filtering, in which the relative market value of a dwelling gradually falls with age, bringing it within reach of households with lower incomes (Smith 1964). Alternatively, if average incomes rise over time, existing houses are likely to be occupied successively by households lower in the income distribution. In this way the housing needs of low income households may be met, even if they are unable to afford new homes. Theories of filtering ignore spatial considerations. Although houses depreciate with age, improvements in their relative accessibility may impede filtering. Furthermore, in a growing city there may be a number of housing sub-markets with few links between them. Most of the published research on filtering relates to the United States.

Recent Australian work by Maher (1976) suggests that vacancies created by new construction may be filled by households at different life-cycle stages rather than by those on different income levels. Working-class families in

Australian cities generally have had the choice of a small, old house in an inner suburb or a larger, new house on the less accessible fringe. Maher's findings receive some indirect support from Malinauskas' (1977) study of vacancy chains started by construction of public housing in Adelaide. It was found that dwellings constructed specifically for low income tenants, such as the aged, brought about more moves by low income earners within the existing stock than did construction of housing for better-off owner-occupiers. This suggests that housing sub-markets are heavily stratified by income.

In many cities flat development is closely controlled to limit the external diseconomies which can arise if flats are built in an area of single family houses. The controls may have become too stringent, increasing the rents paid by tenants (Paterson 1975a). The economic effects of flat control, though, are by no means clear. Information about investment in rental housing is also scanty. Most investment appears to be on a small scale and many investors have close connections with the building and real estate industries. Many properties, particularly houses, are let for *ad hoc* reasons. Such housing investments probably dominate the portfolis of most landlords.

Section 14 Housing Policy

During the 1970s there has been a re-awakening of interest in housing policy in Australia. In 1971 at least, there was no absolute housing shortage (King 1973). However, the rapid rise in interest rates and land prices since the late 1960s has reduced the proportion of people able to afford to buy a home (Bromilow 1975). Increases in interest rates, due to a rise in the rate of inflation, increase loan repayments as a proportion of incomes in the early years of a loan and reduce it in later years (Priorities Review Staff 1975). This is because interest rates reflect inflation anticipated over the whole term of the loan whilst incomes only increase gradually during the term. Indexation of the loan principal or of repayments has been suggested to overcome this mismatch (Priorities Review Staff 1975). Some slow-start mortgages are available which partially index repayments. However, many borrowers will not readily accept the possibility that their debt may increase whilst lenders have been wary of schemes which reduce their cash flow.

It has long been the policy of savings banks to maintain low interest rates for depositors and housing loans. Consequently the total funds available for lending have been limited and loans for housing have had to be rationed by size of loan and by restricting loans to established customers. Although the aims of this policy have been egalitarian, it has been an inefficient way of achieving equity objectives (Hill 1974). While there is little evidence that savings bank borrowers have lower incomes than those borrowing elsewhere the less financially sophisticated are most likely to keep their savings in savings banks and thus subsidise borrowers. Under the influence of inflation and competition from building societies the banks have been forced to take a more competitive approach to housing finance.

Prior to the 1970s banking policy also tried to encourage new construction by offering lower rates on loans for new rather than for established houses, and restricting loans for alterations and additions. This may have restricted alterations, and depressed the relative prices of existing houses, resulting in losses for some owners but little change in housing behaviour.

The Priorities Review Staff (1975) has estimated that exclusion of imputed rent reduced tax revenue by $500 million 1974–75. Deductibility of interest and rates each cost a further $120 million in that year, but have since been restricted. These estimates are only rough orders of magnitude as introduction of a tax on imputed rents would bring about changes in the housing consumption and financing of household expenditure.

The benefit to households may be less than the cost of the subsidies because interference with consumer preferences creates a dead weight loss. Reece (1975) estimates the dead weight loss resulting from the tax treatment of imputed rent as only $7 per dwelling per annum in Sydney in 1966–67, an amount which could easily be offset by the external advantages of the supposed higher standards of maintenance of home owners. Taxation of imputed rent would increase horizontal equity between tenants and owners but reduce the vertical progressivity of the tax system because many aged households who own their homes outright have very low incomes. The Home Savings Grant is again becoming an important subsidy to home purchasers (expected cost in 1977–78 is $20.8 m).

The Taxation Review Committee (1975) did not recommend taxing imputed rents but did suggest that comparable subsidies to renters might be usefully investigated. None of this discussion has considered the possible benefits accruing to tenants under inflation. If capital values increase with inflation and landlords can afford to wait to realise these gains, they may be willing to accept a lower current return from their tenants. The dimensions of this effect are not clear but it could offset much of the taxation bias in favour of home-owners when there is rapid inflation (Kiefer 1976).

There has been wide-spread criticism of public housing policy as a means of income redistribution. Although assistance is subject to means test, the test is applied only at the time of application. At the same time many authorities base their rents on historic costs. Accordingly, given the limited stock of public housing, many on low incomes are excluded whilst long-time tenants may have higher incomes but pay lower rents than those housed more recently. Some housing authorities have also been criticised for the social environments provided in large-scale outer-suburban estates and in high-rise inner city development. (Commission of Inquiry into Poverty 1975).

Since 1956 a minimum of 30 per cent of funds advanced under the housing agreements has been lent to low-income purchasers through terminating building societies. This scheme has also been inefficient in reaching those with the greatest need since the deposit needed is too great for many low income earners (Jones 1972).

Suggestions for reforming public housing fall into two groups. First, are those aimed at ensuring that the maximum benefits go to those with the greatest need by setting rents and sale prices at market levels with rebates for those on low incomes. A second group go further and suggest that, as a means of improving consumer choice, housing assistance should be separated from dwelling provision. In economic terms the aim is to remove the welfare losses which occur when consumers have limited choices among types and locations of public housing. The Poverty Inquiry and the Priorities Review Staff (1975) both suggested rent supplements for low-income families in private as well as public housing. The Housing Allowance Voucher Experiment, plans for which were dropped in 1978, would have provided rent supplements. The main economic argument against provision of assistance in cash is that supply may be price inelastic (Australian Institute of Urban Studies 1975). This is less likely to be a problem as long as governments still construct housing for rent and sale (Stretton 1974).

Some housing authorities also enforce minimum housing standards. Maintenance orders can be placed on dwellings in a poor state of repair. As Kiefer (1977) shows this could lead to earlier demolition if the owner is thereby forced to make losses.

Public housing authorities are also concerned with urban redevelopment. Some cost-benefit analyses have been carried out to decide whether redevelopment or rehabilitation is the better way to provide accommodation in the inner city (Stretton 1975). Pugh (1976b), Pak-Poy (1973) and Beattie (1973) each compared the costs and benefits of redevelopment or renovation in an inner suburb with outer suburban development. The Housing Commission of New South Wales (1976) compared the costs of alternative means of providing housing on its site at Waterloo. The studies not only considered different alternatives but varied in the range of costs and benefits they considered. Beattie and Pak-Poy estimate variations in consumer benefits between locations from differences in travel costs whilst Pugh uses differences in market rents. Finally Pak-Poy also takes account of differences in infrastructure costs between established and developing areas. These are usually difficult to measure and the results tend to be very area-specific.

The inner city has traditionally been an area of low cost rental housing. However in recent years it has become increasingly attractive to young middle-class households because of changes in housing tastes, the growing number of white-collar jobs in the city centre, the increasing cost of new housing, the remoteness of fringe areas and the increasing propensity of groups of young people to form separate households. At the same time some of the existing inner city housing has been destroyed by road building (itself a result of urban growth), slum clearance and the encroachment of non-residential uses. This process has been documented in Sydney by Kendig (1977) and Melbourne by Madden (1977).

In an economic sense, the process of gentrification represents an efficient response to changing patterns of accessibility: people with a high marginal valuation of travel time will want to live close to the city centre. However, the costs of adjustment are borne by the existing rather than the new residents, particularly private tenants whose dwellings may be sold. Such pressures have generated a great deal of land-use conflict in inner areas in recent years. Ensuring that the urban housing stock is used efficiently without making many low-income households worse off is likely to remain one of the most important issues in urban housing in the future.

Section 15 Urban Transport Demand

Transport has probably received more attention from economists than any other aspect of urban development. Almost all the work in this area has a strong policy orientation. Much of the research has been concerned with incorporating explicit economic criteria into decisions about transport investment.

The urban transport task can be conveniently divided into the movement of goods and people. Thirty per cent of the distance travelled by motor vehicles in Sydney in 1971 was by commercial vehicles (Commonwealth Bureau of Roads 1975). Movement of freight is thus an important and neglected issue in road planning.

The individual demand for travel is related to the choice of a place to live. Households trade-off variations in house prices against accessibility. Those who locate at greater distances from employment and shopping centres will have a greater demand for travel. Similarly, the cheaper transport is, the more decentralised the city and the greater the volume of travel.

The longest trips and those that make the greatest demands on the transport system, are journeys to work, partly because they are highly peaked. Some two-thirds of work trips are taken by car, mostly as the driver, and the fraction is increasing (Neutze 1977a). Travel to the central business districts (CBDs) of the large cities, however, is mostly by public transport. Road congestion and parking costs make cars less attractive for these trips, whilst public transport is efficient at carrying large numbers of people to concentrated destinations (Bureau of Transport Economics 1976).

Since the Second World War car-ownership has increased dramatically whilst use of public transport has declined. The increase in car-ownership has resulted more from rising per capita incomes than from the fall in the relative price of motoring (Talbot and Filmer 1973). The income elasticity of per capita car ownership is falling over time, suggesting that the market is approaching saturation (Bureau of Transport Economics 1977). However, some 20 per cent of dwellings were still without cars in 1971. The growth in car-ownership has directly reduced the use of public transport. It has also meant that cities have become more decentralised. The lower densities are more difficult to service with public transport—one of the reasons for its decline. The fact that fares have increased relative to other prices has also made public transport less attractive. (Bureau of Transport Economics 1976). Poorer public transport services have reduced the overall accessibility of those who do not have access to a car, including many housewives, those who are too young or too old to drive, the handicapped and those who cannot afford a car. For most other people accessibility has been increased.

Demand projections play a critical part in determining optimal transport investment. The usual approach has been to collect information on trips made by people living in each zone in a city. The observed trips are then modelled in four stages: trip generation (in each origin zone), distribution (to destination zones), modal split and route assignment. This is what Hensher (1977) in a comprehensive review of demand studies calls the aggregate sequential model. Given population and land-use forecasts these sub-models are then used to forecast travel demand.

Economists have made a number of criticisms of this approach. Although breaking up the travel decision into four stages is a useful simplification, it ignores feedback effects such as those between modal choice and the decision whether or not to travel (Blackshaw 1974). Trip generation sub-models usually relate the number of trips originating in a zone to land use and the social status of the population in that zone rather than to its location (Paterson 1970). In addition, the supply of transport services is generally ignored, implying that travel demand is completely insensitive to the adequacy of capacity. However, construction of new facilities may lead to increases in demand, in the short run by reducing congestion costs, and in the long run through its influence on land use. Transport studies usually make insufficient allowance for interactions between transport and land use (Paterson 1977). Finally, the practice of basing time series forecasts of demand on cross-sectional relationship can also be criticised.

Obviously not all these criticisms apply to all demand studies. Furthermore most of the criticisms are *a priori* rather than being based on an *ex post* evaluation of past demand forecasts. However, there seems to be wide agreement that the models would be more soundly based if they reflected hypotheses about actual human behaviour and much of the recent research has been directed towards establishing this kind of base.

Shepherd (1973), for example, has estimated a simultaneous demand model for Perth based on zonal data in which demand for inter-zonal travel by each mode is a function of income and the cost of travel, in both money and time. A number of attempts has also been made to estimate models based on individual rather than zonal data as a way of avoiding the problems of intra-zonal heterogeneity. Most of these have been concerned with explaining the probability of using public transport. Smith (1976) applied such a model to Sydney CBD work trips and Hensher (1973) shows how such a model can be derived from utility theory.

One of the interesting issues is how sensitive public transport use is to variations in fares compared to other factors such as comfort and waiting times. Most studies have found that the demand for public transport is very price inelastic: fare elasticities for work trips by public transport appear to be in the region of −0.3 (Smith undated). Time series estimates usually show that the use of public transport is more sensitive to level of service than to fares. The Bureau of Transport Economics (1977) obtained an elasticity of 0.63 for bus and 1.10 for rail patronage. Shepherd (1973) and Smith (1976) estimated elasticities of public transport choice with respect to in-vehicle time of −0.3 and −0.22 in cross-section studies (with even lower estimates for access and waiting time). In a detailed study that confirmed the significant effect of comfort and convenience factors on public transport use Hensher and McLeod (1977) included exposure to weather, level of crowding and number and duration of stops.

Section 16 *Transport Planning*

Demand studies play an important part in the formulation of transport investment proposals. In the traditional study facilities are designed to meet the end-state demand forecast and the alternative is selected which minimises the flow/capacity ratio, subject to a budget constraint. Studies of this kind have been carried out for all of the larger Australian cities. The most recent was in Sydney, the results of which were released in 1974 (Black 1974).

As well as criticising their demand analysis, economists have also made wider criticisms of traditional transport studies (Blackshaw 1974; Duhs and Beggs 1977). The orientation of the plans towards a distinct planning year ignores questions of phasing and biases the recommendations towards investment strategies. The complexity of the planning process also restricts the number of transport and land-use alternatives which can be tested. For this reason Blackshaw (1974) argues that the planning procedures should be simplified, perhaps by splitting metropolitan areas into relatively self-contained planning regions. Finally the traditional studies have also been criticised for their failure to incorporate economic evaluation criteria. Unlike cost-benefit analysis there is usually no estimate of the rates of return on the recommended investment.

Cost-benefit analysis has been used in evaluating urban transport investment since the late 1960s. In fact the Commonwealth Bureau of Roads, established in 1964, has based its advice to government mainly on the results of CBA. The benefits of transport investment include lower journey time and running costs, better service quality and fewer accidents. The most important costs are usually the initial capital costs. Kolsen and Forsyth (1968) applied CBA to the Sydney eastern suburbs railway, the Bureau of Transport Economics (1972) to public transport and the Bureau of Roads (Thompson, Delaney and Lees 1970) to urban road improvements.

One difficulty in using CBA is in quantifying the costs and benefits, particularly of accidents involving injury or loss of life (Troy and Butlin 1971) and of savings in travel time. One common way of valuing time savings has been to observe travellers making a choice between a slow, inexpensive and a faster, more expensive mode or route. The values of travel time saved imputed from this trade-off have usually been between 30 and 50 per cent of the average hours wage rate, although time spent walking or waiting is usually valued more highly than in-vehicle time (Hogg 1970). Few studies allow for variations between individuals.

Hensher (1976) has developed an alternative way of valuing time savings by asking what increase in money cost would induce a traveller to change mode. The total cost difference at the point of indifference is then related to the difference in travel time. On average the results are not very different from those estimated using traditional models. However he found that values increase with the amount of time saved and with the proportion of the total trip time saved, but not with the level of income.

Urban road projects frequently require the acquisition and demolition of occupied housing. Compensation to owner-occupiers has generally been limited to the market value of their homes. Stanley *et al* (1973) have argued that this is inadequate, the proper measure being that sum which would leave the householder as well off as before: the loss of consumer surplus. It should include moving costs, search costs and any loss of satisfaction caused by a forced move. In principle all calculations of benefits and costs in CBA should be based on variations in consumer surplus (Blackshaw 1975).

CBA of transport proposals can incorporate equity considerations. Most analyses identify possible improvements and evaluate their social costs and benefits. An alternative approach adopted by the Commonwealth Bureau of Roads (1976) begins by identifying transport-and-location-disadvantaged groups and then goes on to evaluate alternative facilities designed to meet their needs.

Section 17 Transport Pricing

Investment criteria are inextricably linked with pricing policy. If user charges are lower than short-run marginal social costs, demand will be too high and estimates of benefits will also be too high. In equilibrium prices should be equal to both short and long run marginal social costs. If short run marginal cost exceeds long run marginal cost and capacity can be expanded by marginal units, it should be increased. However, in many kinds of transport investment there are economies of scale in construction which make it inefficient to expand capacity marginally, and make it necessary to use CBA (Neutze 1966).

Most of the discussion of transport pricing has related to roads. Three major kinds of costs are incurred in the operation of roads: capital, maintenance and user costs. While capital costs—mainly interest—do not vary with use in the short run, user costs—time and operating costs—and maintenance costs increase with the volume of traffic on any road. Since each additional vehicle on a congested road slows down the others the social marginal cost of a trip exceeds its private marginal cost by the extent of the externality. Road users should cover short-run marginal social cost, including road maintenance, their own costs and the external congestion cost of a trip. They should also cover long run marginal costs such as capital costs, though preferably in a way which does not restrict use of uncongested roads. Kolsen, Ferguson and Docwra (1975) suggest some appropriate pricing methods. By comparison, present charges are too high on uncongested roads and too low on those which are most congested.

Jacobi (1973) raises some of the problems associated with road pricing. He argues that the externalities of road congestion are reciprocal and there can only be a net gain if the receipts from road pricing are used to subsidise those tolled off the road. Otherwise, those still using the road are left paying more than before and any road is less intensively used, giving the impression that no one has gained. However, this is erroneous. Although those still using a road may have higher out-of-pocket costs, Neutze (1964) demonstrates that the savings in operating costs and journey times on those trips still made on a road will exceed the welfare loss resulting from those not made.

A second problem is how to estimate the demand curve to show that there is a welfare gain, and to set prices. However, Hicks (1973) shows that even charges substantially below optimum levels could produce significant benefits. The more price elastic the demand for road use the larger these benefits are likely to be. Finally, on equity grounds, congestion probably favours relatively low-income drivers whilst congestion pricing would favour those on higher incomes (Commonwealth Bureau of Roads 1975, p.130).

The cost to a car-owner of making a particular journey by car is his short run marginal cost. Without subsidies someone using public transport, on the other hand, would have to pay fares based on longrun average cost. Even if the marginal cost of a trip by public transport was lower it could still be cheaper for someone who has a car available to drive, unless roads are very congested or there are heavy parking charges. This has led to suggestions that public transport pricing be based on a two-part tariff (Webb 1972b). Potential passengers would pay a fixed annual fee to belong to a public transport club and fares would reflect short-run marginal costs. Accordingly, while fares might be quite high during peak period, travel at other times would probably be free.

If it is not possible to use a two-part tariff, but the transport authority is still constrained to cover long-run costs, the setting of an optimal set of prices becomes extremely complex. One way of approaching the problem is to ask how users of public transport could be taxed to raise a given amount of revenue whilst at the same time minimising distortions in resource allocation (Forsyth 1977). Distributional constraints could also be analysed within the same framework. Another complication is that much transport is an intermediate rather than a final good and heavy taxation may distort production decisions.

Section 18 Urban Transport Policy

Relatively little consideration has been given to the appropriate goals for transport policy. Low-level objectives, like reducing congestion or increasing traffic speed, are too narrow to be applied to the entire transport system. It could be argued that there should not be any transport oriented goals at all, only goals of accessibility for which transport and land-use planning are the major instruments. Land-use planning attempts to reduce the need for movement whilst transport policy aims to reduce its costs in both time and money.

While some people believe that mobility should be enhanced others believe that such a policy is likely to impose serious social costs, such as those accompanying urban freeway construction, in return for diffuse and nebulous benefits. This line of thought suggests that transport policy not aim to promote mobility in general but rather concentrate on assisting the transport disadvantaged, such as those who do not own cars.

This debate tends to revolve around the question of how far transport policy should aim to encourage public transport at the expense of the private car. Cars create more pollution and cause more accidents, and road building in urban areas imposes social costs on the households that have to be relocated. Furthermore, public transport is a decreasing cost industry whilst private urban road transport experiences increasing costs. If prices cover opportunity costs too few resources will be devoted to the former and too many to the latter.

Another argument used against investment in facilities for the car is that the increasing cost of petrol will make them uneconomic. However, although rising fuel costs may lead to some fall in rates of car ownership, it is expected to have more influence on the type of car used, encouraging people to buy smaller and more efficient models (Commonwealth Bureau of Roads 1975). In 1974–75 fuel costs were only 3 per cent of total household expenditure and less than a fifth of total transport expenditure (ABS 1977).

What are some of the alternatives to increased investment in road facilities? One is investment in public transport facilities such as new rail tracks, busways and new rolling stock for all modes. This is the current trend in Australian cities. Since 1972–73 real capital expenditure on roads has fallen whilst expenditure on urban public transport doubled over the period 1970–71 to 1974–75 (Bureau of Transport Economics 1977). Rail accounts for the greater share of capital expenditure on urban public transport. The Commonwealth Government has provided specific purpose grants for roads since 1923 but grants for urban public transport only commenced in 1974–75.

Another alternative is to make more efficient use of existing resources. Many of these options have been discussed by the Commonwealth Bureau of Roads (1975) and the Bureau of Transport Economics (1977). Most are aimed at reducing peak hour congestion. For example, traffic management techniques can be used to give priority to high-occupancy vehicles through use of transit lanes. Such a lane has successfully operated in Sydney since 1974.

Sometimes road pricing is suggested as a way of reducing congestion. Given the high level of car ownership in Australia road pricing seems unlikely. Singapore is the only country in which a limited system of pricing has been introduced. Costs of collection are likely to be high. Road use in congested areas is being restricted simply by limits to capacity. Capacity is no longer being expanded in such areas, and parking is being restricted and made more costly. Charging for a previously-free facility of such importance is not likely to be readily accepted. Other means of reducing car use need to be sought.

An alternative to road pricing is to reduce fares on public transport. The New South Wales Government recently reduced public transport fares by 20 per cent. With a price elasticity of about -0.3 we would expect this to lead to an increase in patronage of 6 per cent. To date there has only been a very small increase in patronage in Sydney although it may take some time for people to adjust to new fare levels. However this does suggest that across-the-board fare cuts are not likely to be as efficient as those applied to sub-markets with a more elastic demand.

One clear result of the fare reduction has been to further increase the public transport deficit. Deficits have been growing rapidly in recent years. The loss on urban public bus and tram services in Australia increased by 179 per cent between 1972–73 and 1974–75 and the loss on urban rail services in New South Wales increased by 80 per cent between 1972–73 and 1973–74 (Bureau of Transport Economics 1977).

Almost any pricing policy which reduces the peakedness of demand would reduce the losses made by public transport. For example, peaked demand means that buses and trains are idle for much of the day, labour is underutilised and high wages must be paid for split shifts (Webb 1972a). Government bus services generally make losses, partly because of the fact that they often have to provide a minimum level of service, even when it is not profitable to do so. Some private bus services are subsidised but their relative profitability reflects the narrower range of services they provide. They may also benefit from their smaller scale and lower labour costs. Although private services in many cities have been taken over by government authorities, Gilmour (1973) argues that, because of their lower costs, private services should be encouraged at the expense of public.

It is more difficult to assess the financial position of urban railway services because of the difficulties of separating the costs of suburban services. Clark (1975) estimated that revenue covered only about 40 per cent of the 1970–71 cost of operating urban railway services. This loss appears to be substantially greater than that incurred on government buses. Accounting losses suffered by the railways have been understated because of inadequate depreciation allowances (Webb 1973), a policy which has made it difficult to replace obsolete equipment. Webb (1972b) argues that the railways should be allowed to operate as business enterprises, with any services provided for social reasons being explicitly subsidised. Alternatively, it could be argued that public transport, at least at off-peak times, should be provided free as a social service, especially if the cost of collecting fares is high relative to the revenue collected.

Most public transport, then, makes substantial losses which have to be financed by the general community. Do the taxes and fees which road users pay cover the operating costs of roads?[1] The Commonwealth Bureau of Roads calculates that revenue and costs roughly balance out. However, their estimates ignore land rent.

Altogether the subsidies to urban transport appear to be extremely large but there has been relatively little work done to estimate their incidence. Bentley, Collins and Rutledge (1977) have calculated that the net benefits of road programs are distributed progressively, favouring those on higher incomes. As for public transport, a high proportion of the benefits of investment flow to peak-hour CBD travellers who tend to have higher than average incomes whilst off-peak users tend to come from households with below average incomes and low levels of car ownership. The Bureau of Transport Economics (1977) uses this as an additional reason for increasing fares for peak-hour travel to and from the CBD which would reduce deficits and increase the resources available to support off-peak travel.

Whilst the benefits of transport programs appear to favour those on higher incomes, there are many for whom the time and money costs of mobility

[1] It can be argued of course that road users should not cover all road costs as some of the benefits also accrue to property owners.

are very high. Studies by the Commonwealth Bureau of Roads (1975, p.106) show that households in some of the outer western suburbs of Sydney allocate twice the average proportion of their time and income to the journey to work. A small difference in income can lead to a very large difference in transport costs, depending on whether a family can afford a car (Paterson 1974). Manning (1977) has estimated that in Sydney in 1971 18 per cent of all households could not afford a car and had none whilst 12 per cent had a car even though it absorbed a very high proportion of their low incomes. Those who cannot drive—the young, the old and the invalid—are also disadvantaged in cities built around the car (Black 1977). The problems which these people face—problems which are neglected in the traditional transport study—are rapidly becoming major issues in transport policy.

Section 19 Concluding Comment

The significance of urban economics derives from the fact that it deals with an important dimension of the economy—the spatial relationship between activities. One approach has been to transfer 'how much' decisions to 'where' decisions within the traditional micro-economic framework. For example, in residential location theory the traditional price-quantity diagram of price theory becomes a price-distance diagram. However, urban economics is more than this. The relative location of activities within cities affects not only travel and transport cost between them but also the amount of smoke, dirt, noise and traffic in nearby residential areas. Urban economics thus has to allow for the complications of externalities and for activities with both public and private good dimensions.

Governments play a large role in urban development both as providers of services and as planners and controllers. Too frequently the contributions of economists to the analysis of urban policies have been limited to pointing out the cost of any interference with the market without asking why the controls were adopted and looking for better ways of achieving their objectives, or recognising the extent to which property and other prices are influenced by widely accepted functions of government. Urban economists have to recognise that different parts of the urban economy interact not only through the market but also through the physical environment. Where people live in cities directly affects their welfare. Urban investments and policy measures affects the distribution of welfare by changing the environment, accessibility and the value of property, as well as by changing money incomes. The economist who wants to understand cities and to provide useful policy advice to governments on urban issues, needs to encompass this wide range of relationships.

He must also communicate with those working in other disciplines such as sociology and geography. In urban studies the disciplines overlap a great deal, as the literature covered in this survey shows. While urban economics can take a great deal from longer-established areas of economics, it also benefits from contacts with other disciplines, many of which have a much longer tradition of research in urban issues.

Bibliography

Abelson, P. (1977), *The Impact of Environmental Factors on Relative House Prices* (Bureau of Transport Economics, Occasional Paper No. 7, 1977).

Alexander, Ian (1976), 'The suburbanization of private sector office employment: fact or fiction?', in G.J.R. Linge (ed.), *Restructuring Employment Opportunities in Australia* (Department of Human Geography, Publication HG/11, Australian National University, Canberra, 1976).

Alonso, W. (1964), *Location and Land Use: Toward a General Theory of Land Rent* (Harvard University Press, Cambridge, Mass., 1964).

—— (1974), 'A report on Australian urban development issues', *Overseas Experts' Reports* (Cities Commission, Occasional Paper No. 1, 1974).

Apps, P.F. (1973), *Tenure, Real Housing Costs and House Price Inflation* (Department of Architecture, University of Sydney, Sydney, 1973).

Archer, R.W. (1974), 'The leasehold system of urban development: land tenure, decision making and the land market in urban development and land use', *Regional Studies*, 8, pp.225–38.

—— (1976a), *Planning and Managing Metropolitan Development and Land Supply* (Committee for Economic Development of Australia, Melbourne, 1976).

—— (1976b), 'The Sydney Betterment Levy, 1969–1973: an experiment in functional funding of metropolitan development', *Urban Studies*, 13, pp.339–42.

Australian Bureau of Statistics (1977), *Household Expenditure Survey 1974–75* (Bulletin 4, Ref. No. 17.22, ABS, Canberra, 1977).

Australian Institute of Urban Studies (1972), *Second Report of the Task Force on The Price of Land* (Canberra, 1972).

—— (1975), *Housing for Australia: Philosophy and Policies* (Canberra, 1975).

Ball, M.J. (1973), 'Recent empirical work on the determinants of relative house prices', *Urban Studies*, 10, pp.213–33.

Baumol, W.J. (1967), 'Macroeconomics of unbalanced growth: the anatomy of the urban crisis', *American Economic Review*, 57, pp.415–26.

Beattie, D. (1973), 'Economic evaluation of the proposal to acquire residential property in Glebe', *Urban Economics Paper No. 1* (Department of Urban and Regional Development, Canberra, 1973).

Bentick, B.L. (1972), 'Improving the allocation of land between speculators and users: taxation and paper land', *Economic Record*, 48, pp.18–41.

—— (1974), 'Land market legislation in South Australia', *Australian Economic Review*, 1st Quarter, pp. 45–8.

—— and A.J. Fischer (1975), 'To have and to hold—some aspects of the economics of land subdivision', *Australian Economic Papers*, 14, pp.57–74.

Bentley, Philip (1973), 'The Australian local government tax base: revenue potential', *Australian Economic Papers*, 12, pp.21–35.

Bentley, P., D.J. Collins and D.J.S. Rutledge (1977), *The Distributional Impact of Road Expenditure and Finance in Australia* (Research Paper No. 140, School of Economic and Financial Studies, Macquarie University, Sydney, 1977).

Binnie International (1977), *Development Study* (Metropolitan Water Supply, Sewerage and Drainage Board, Perth, 1977).

Black, John A. (1974), 'Techniques of land use/transportation planning in Australian cities', *Transportation*, 3, pp.255–288 reprinted in G.R. Webb and J.C. McMaster (eds.) (1975), *Australian Transport Economics* (Australia and New Zealand Book Co., Sydney, 1975).

Black, John (1977), *Public Inconvenience* (Urban Research Unit, Australian National University, Canberra, 1977).

Blackshaw, P.W. (1974), 'The Sydney Area Transportation Study—an economic review', *Australian Quarterly*, 46, No. 4, pp.56–67, reprinted in G.R. Webb and J.C. McMaster (eds.) (1975), *Australian Transport Economics* (Australia and New Zealand Book Co., Sydney, 1975).

—— (1975), 'The treatment of cross-modal effects in transport evaluations', *Transport Economics and Operational Analysis*, 1, pp.34–44, reprinted in G.R. Webb and J.C. McMaster (eds) (1975), *Australian Transport Economics* (Australia and New Zealand Book Co., Sydney, 1975).

Braby, R.H. (1973), 'Urban growth and policy: a multi-nodal approach', *Economic Analysis and Policy*, 4, pp.43–58, reprinted in J.C. McMaster and G.R. Webb (eds.) (1976), *Australian Urban Economics, A Reader* (Australia and New Zealand Book Co., Sydney, 1976).

Bromilow, F.J. (1975), 'The supply of land for urban purposes', *The Developer*, 13, No. 2, pp.32–7.

—— and M.L. Meaton (1974), *The Land Conversion Process: A Case Study* (Australian Institute of Urban Studies, Canberra, 1974).

Bureau of Transport Economics (1972), *Economic Evaluation of Capital Investment in Urban Public Transport* (AGPS, Canberra, 1972).

—— (1976), *Transport Outlook Conference 1975* (AGPS, Canberra, 1976).

—— (1977), *Urban Transport: Capital Requirements 1977–78 to 1979–80* (AGPS, Canberra, 1977).

Butlin, N.G. (1974), *Investment in Australian Economic Development 1861–1900* (Cambridge University Press, Cambridge, 1974).

Cardew, R.V. (1970), *Flats: A Study of Occupants and Locations* (Faculty of Architecture, University of Sydney, Sydney, 1970).

Cities Commission (1975), *Studies in Australian Internal Migration 1966–1971*, Occasional Paper No. 2, Canberra.

Clark, Colin (1951), 'Urban population densities', *Journal of the Royal Statistical Society*, Series A, 114, pp.490–6.

—— (1964), 'The location of industries and population', *Town Planning Review*, 35, pp.195–218.

—— (1970), 'The economics of urban areas', in N. Clark (ed.), *Analysis of Urban Development* (Department of Civil Engineering, University of Melbourne, Melbourne, 1970).

Clark, N. (1975), 'The costs of operating urban public transport services in Australian cities 1970–71', in G.R. Webb and J.C. McMaster (eds.) (1975), *Australian Transport Economics* (Australia and New Zealand Book Co., Sydney, 1975).

Commission of Inquiry into Land Tenures (1973), *First Report* (AGPS, Canberra, 1973).

Commission of Inquiry into Poverty (1975), *Poverty in Australia* (AGPS, Canberra, 1975).

Commonwealth Bureau of Roads (1975), *Roads in Australia 1975*, 2 Volumes (Melbourne, 1975).

—— (1976), *An Approach to Developing Transport Improvement Proposals*, Occasional Paper No. 2 (Melbourne, 1976).

Cumberland Country Council (1958), *Economics of Urban Expansion* (Sydney, 1958).

Daly, M.T. (1967a), *Land Use of the Newcastle and Lake Macquarie Regions* (Hunter Valley Research Foundation, Monograph 28, Newcastle, 1967).

—— (1967b), 'Land Value Determinants: Newcastle, N.S.W.', *Australian Geographical Studies*, 5, pp.30–9.

—— (1968), 'Residential location decisions, Newcastle, N.S.W.', *Australia and New Zealand Journal of Sociology*, 4, pp.36–48.

Davidson, F.G. (1955), 'Planning and compensation in Victoria', *Economic Record*, 31, pp.40–9.

de Leeuw, F. (1971), 'The demand for housing: a review of cross-section evidence', *Review of Economics and Statistics*, 53, pp.1–10.

Department of Urban and Regional Development (1974a), *Urban Land Prices 1968–1974* (AGPS, Canberra, 1974).

Department of Urban and Regional Development (1974b), *Urban Land: Problems and Policies* (AGPS, Canberra, 1974).

Development Corporation of New South Wales (1969), *Report on Selective Decentralisation* (Sydney, 1969).

Duhs, L.A. and J.J. Beggs (1977), 'The urban transportation study', in D.A. Hensher (ed.), *Urban Transport Economics* (Cambridge University Press, Cambridge, 1977).

Edel, M. and J. Rothenberg (eds.) (1972), *Readings in Urban Economics* (Macmillan, New York, 1972).

Else-Mitchell, Mr Justice R. (Chairman) (1967), *Report of the Royal Commission of Inquiry into Rating, Valuation and Local Government Finance* (Government Printer, Sydney, 1967).

Evans, Alan W. (1972), 'The pure theory of city size in an industrial economy', *Urban Studies*, 9, pp.49–77.

—— (1973), *The Economics of Residential Location* (Macmillan, London, 1973).

Forsyth, P. (1977), 'The pricing of urban transport: some implications of recent theory', in D.A. Hensher (ed.), *Urban Transport Economics* (Cambridge University Press, Cambridge, 1977).

Foster, C.D. and S. Glaister (1975), 'The anatomy of the development value tax', *Urban Studies*, 12, pp.213–8.

Gallagher, D.R. and R.W. Robinson (1977), *Influence of Metering, Pricing Policies and Incentives on Water Use Efficiency* (Australian Water Resources Council, Technical Paper No. 19, AGPS, Canberra, 1977).

Gibbings, M.J. (1973), *Housing Preferences in the Brisbane Area* (Australian Institute of Urban Studies, Canberra, 1973).

Gibbons, Robert P. (1976), 'Finance and planning: The Sydney Water Board and the 1959 Green Belt Releases', *Australian Journal of Public Administration*, 35, pp.147–59.

Gilmour, P. (1973), 'The economic condition of Australian urban bus transportation', *Growth*, 26, pp.26–36.

Gordon, A.R. (1977), 'Home ownership in Australia: 1966, 1971 and beyond' (paper presented to Sixth Conference of Economists, Hobart, 1977).

Gordon, D.M. (ed.) (1971), *Problems in Political Economy: An Urban Perspective* (D.C. Heath, Lexington, Mass., 1971).

Groenewegen, P.D. (1976), *The Taxable Capacity of Local Government in N.S.W.* (Centre for Federal Financial Relations, Research Monograph No. 13, Australian National University, Canberra, 1976).

Hamilton, Bruce W. (1976), 'Capitalisation of intrajurisdictional differences in local tax prices', *American Economic Review*, 66, pp.743–53.

Harrison, David, Jr. and John F. Kain (1974), 'Cumulative urban growth and urban density functions', *Journal of Urban Economics*, 1, pp.61–98.

Harrison, Peter (1977), 'Major urban areas', *Atlas of Australian Resources* (Second Series) (Map Commentary, Department of National Resources, Canberra, 1977).

—— (1978), 'City planning', in Peter Scott (ed.), *Australian Cities and Public Policy* (Georgian House, Melbourne, 1978).

Hayes, G.P. (Chairman) (1975), *Residential Land Development* (Report of Committee of Inquiry, Government Printer, Melbourne, 1975).

Henderson, Ronald F. and R.B. Lewis (1974), 'Urban local government and personal welfare', in R.L. Mathews (ed.), *Intergovernmental Relations in Australia* (Angus and Robertson, Sydney, 1974)

Hensher, D.A. (1973), 'A probabilistic disaggregate model of binary mode choice', in D.A. Hensher (ed.), *Urban Travel Choice and Demand Modelling* (Special Report No. 12, Australian Road Research Board, 1973).

—— (1976), 'The value of commuter travel time savings', *Journal of Transport Economics and Policy*, 10, pp.167–76.

Hensher, David (1977), 'Demand for urban passenger transport', in David Hensher (ed.), *Urban Transport Economics* (Cambridge University Press, Cambridge, 1977).

Hensher, D.A. and P.B. McLeod (1977), 'Towards an integrated approach to the identification and evaluation of the transport determinants of travel choices', *Transportation Research*, 11, pp.77–93.

Hicks, S.K. (1973), 'Demand behaviour and the evaluation of road pricing proposals', in D.A. Hensher (ed.), *Urban Travel Choice and Demand Modelling* (Special Report No. 12, Australian Road Research Board, Melbourne, 1973).

Hill, M.R. (1959), *Housing Finance in Australia 1945–1956* (Melbourne University Press, Melbourne, 1959).
—— (1974), 'Housing finance institutions', in R.R. Hirst and R.H. Wallace (eds.), *The Australian Capital Market* (Cheshire, Melbourne, 1974).
Hoa, T.V. (1968), 'Interregional elasticities and aggregation bias: a study of consumer demand in Australia', *Australian Economic Papers*, 7, pp.206–26.
Hogg, T.M. (1970), 'The value of private travel time savings—a review of the theoretical and applied literature', *Proceedings, Fifth Australian Road Research Board Conference*, 5, pt. 2, pp.73–87.
Housing Commission of N.S.W. (1976), *Waterloo Development Proposals* (Sydney, 1976).
Hunter Regional Planning Committee (1977), *Hunter Region: Problems and Proposals* (Newcastle, 1977).
Jacobi, S.N. (1973), 'Alternatives for relieving urban traffic congestion' (Occasional Paper No. 2, Department of Economics, University of Newcastle), reprinted in G.R. Webb and J.C. McMaster (eds.) (1975), *Australian Transport Economics* (Australia and New Zealand Book Co., Sydney, 1975).
Johnson, K.M. (1974), *People and Property in North Melbourne* (Urban Research Unit, Australian National University, Canberra, 1974).
Johnston, R.J. (1971), *Urban Residential Patterns* (G. Bell & Sons, London, 1971).
Johnston, R.J. and P.J. Rimmer (1969), *Retailing in Melbourne* (Department of Human Geography, Publication HG/3, Australian National University, Canberra, 1969).
Joint Study into Local Government Finances: Australia and New Zealand (1976), (Report of the Joint Steering Committee appointed by the Local Government Ministers Conference, Canberra, 1976).
Jones, F.L. (1969), *Dimensions of Urban Social Structure* (Australian National University Press, Canberra, 1969).
Jones, M.A. (1972), *Housing and Poverty in Australia* (Melbourne University Press, Melbourne, 1972).
Joy, S.C. (1968), 'Urban form and passenger transport problems', in *The Economics of Roads and Road Transport* (Commonwealth Bureau of Roads, Occasional Paper No. 1, 1968).
Kendig, H. (1977), 'The changing role of the inner suburbs' (ANZAAS Congress, Melbourne, 1977).
Kerr, Alex (1970), 'Urban industrial change in Australia, 1954–1966', *Economic Record*, 46, pp.355–67.
Kiefer, D. (1976), 'The equity of alternative policies for the Australian homeowner' (Discussion Paper No. 12, Department of Economics, La Trobe University, Melbourne, 1976).
—— (1977), 'Housing deterioration, housing codes and rent control' (paper presented to Sixth Conference of Economists, Hobart, 1977).
King, R. (1973), *The Dimensions of Housing Need in Australia* (Faculty of Architecture, University of Sydney, 1973).
Kolsen, H.M. and P.J. Forsyth (1968), 'Public investment in transport', *Australian Planning Institute Journal*, 6, pp.124–32.
Kolsen, H.M., D.C. Ferguson and G.E. Docwra (1975), *Road User Charges: Theories and Possibilities* (Occasional Paper No. 3, Bureau of Transport Economics, Canberra, 1975).
Land Taxation and Land Prices in Western Australia (1968), (Report of the Committee appointed by the Premier, Perth, 1968).
Lanigan, P.J. (1976), 'The spatial reorganisation of a federal government department', in G.J.R. Linge (ed.), *Restructuring Employment Opportunities in Australia* (Department of Human Geography Publication HG/11, Australian National University, Canberra, 1976).
Linge, G.J.R. (1963), 'The location of manufacturing in Australia', in Alex Hunter (ed.), *The Economics of Australian Industry* (Melbourne University Press, Melbourne, 1963).
—— (ed.) (1976), *Restructuring Employment Opportunities in Australia* (Department

of Human Geography, Publication HG/11, Australian National University, Canberra, 1976).
—— and P.J. Rimmer (eds.) (1971), *Government Influence and the Location of Economic Activity* (Department of Human Geography, Publication HG/5, Australian National University, Canberra, 1971).
Little, F.M. (1977), 'Socio-economic implications of urban development' (research report submitted by Urban Economic Consultants Pty. Ltd. to the Melbourne and Metropolitan Board of Works, 1977)...
Logan, M.I. (1964), 'Manufacturing decentralisation in the Sydney metropolitan area', *Economic Geography*, 40, pp.151–62.
—— (1966), 'Locational behavior of manufacturing firms in urban areas', *Annals of the Association of American Geographers*, 56, pp.451–66.
Losch, A. (1954), *The Economics of Location* (Yale University Press, New Haven, 1954).
Madden, P. (1977), *The Displaced: A Study of Housing Conflict in Melbourne's Inner City* (Centre for Urban Research and Action, Melbourne, 1977).
Maher, C.A. (1976), 'New housing construction and the filtering effect: some implications for policy formulation' (unpublished, Department of Geography, Monash University, Melbourne, 1976).
Malinauskas, P.S. (1977) *Vacancy Chains and Public Housing* (Australian Housing Research Council, Melbourne, 1977).
Manning, Ian (1973), *Muncipal Finance and Income Distribution in Sydney* (Urban Research Unit, Australian National University, Canberra, 1973).
Manning, Ian (1977), 'Car ownership in Australian cities' (Urban Research Unit (ANU) seminar paper, August 1977).
Mathews, Russell (1967), *Public Investment in Australia* (Cheshire, Melbourne, 1967).
Mathews, R.L. (1974), 'Fiscal equalisation for local government', *Economic Record*, 50, pp.329–45.
McColl, G.D. (1976), *The Economics of Electricity Supply in Australia* (Melbourne University Press, Melbourne, 1976).
McMaster, J.C. and G.R. Webb (eds.) (1976), *Australian Urban Economics* (Australia and New Zealand Book Co., Sydney, 1976).
Melbourne and Metropolitan Board of Works (1977), *Melbourne's Inner Area—A Position Statement* (Melbourne, 1977).
Mushkin, Selma (1972), 'An agenda for research', in S. Mushkin (ed.), *Public Prices for Public Products* (The Urban Institute, Washington, D.C., 1972).
Muth, Richard F. (1969), *Cities and Housing* (University of Chicago Press, Chicago, 1969).
National Population Inquiry (1975), *Population in Australia: A Demographic Analysis and Projection* (First Report, AGPS, Canberra, 1975).
Neilson, L.R. (1972), *Business Activities in Three Melbourne Suburbs* (Urban Research Unit, Australian National University, Canberra, 1972).
Neutze, Max (1964), 'Pricing road use', *Economic Record*, 40, pp.175–86.
—— (1965), *Economic Policy and the Size of Cities* (Australian National University, Canberra, 1965).
—— (1966), 'Investment criteria and road pricing', *The Manchester School*, 34, pp.63–73.
—— (1970), 'The price of land for urban development', *Economic Record*, 46, pp.313–28.
—— (1972a), 'The cost of housing', *Economic Record*, 48, pp.357–73.
—— (1972b), 'The government and administration of metropolitan development', *Economic Papers*, 36, pp.38–49, reprinted in H.W. Arndt and A.H. Boxer (eds.) (1972), *The Australian Economy* (Cheshire, Melbourne, 1972).
—— (1973), 'The price of land and land use planning' (OECD, Paris, 1973, mimeo), portions are reprinted in J.C. McMaster and G.R. Webb (eds.) (1976), *Australian Urban Economics* (Australia and New Zealand Book Co., Sydney, 1976).
—— (1974a), 'The case for new cities in Australia', *Urban Studies*, 11, pp.259–75, reprinted in J.C. McMaster and G.R. Webb (eds.) (1976), *Australian Urban Economics* (Australia and New Zealand Book Co., Sydney, 1976).

—— (1974b), 'The development value tax: a comment', *Urban Studies*, 11, pp.91–2.
—— (1974c), 'Local, regional and metropolitan government', in R.L. Mathews (ed.), *Intergovernmental Relations in Australia* (Angus and Robertson, Sydney, 1974).
—— (1977a), *Urban Development in Australia* (Allen and Unwin, Sydney, 1977).
—— (1977b), 'State and local property taxes', in R.L. Mathews (ed.), *State and Local Taxation* (ANU Press, Canberra, 1977).
Pak-Poy, P.G. and Associates (1973), *Inner Suburban—Outer Suburban; A Comparison of Costs* (Australian Institute of Urban Studies, Canberra, 1973).
Parish, Ross (1977), 'The Commission of Inquiry into Land Tenures', *Australian Journal of Management*, 2, pp.35–52.
Paterson, John (1968), 'Metropolitan water supply, sewerage and drainage', *Australian Planning Institute Journal*, 6, pp.81–3.
—— (1970), 'Predictive errors arising from transportation study techniques with special reference to Melbourne', *Proceedings of the Fifth Australian Road Research Board Conference*, 5, pt. 2, pp.373–96.
Paterson, John, Urban Systems Pty. Ltd. (1972), *Melbourne's CBD in the 1960s* (Australian Institute of Urban Studies, Canberra, 1972).
Paterson, John (1973), 'Economics of urbanisation policy', *National Bank Monthly Summary*, July 1973, pp.5–9, reprinted in J.C. McMaster and G.R. Webb (eds.) (1976), *Australian Urban Economics* (Australia and New Zealand Book Co., Sydney, 1976).
Paterson, John, Urban Systems Pty. Ltd. (1974), *Transport Services Available to and Used by the Disadvantaged Sections of the Community* (Commonwealth Bureau of Roads, Melbourne, 1974).
Paterson, John, Urban Systems Pty. Ltd. (1975a), 'Social and economic implications of housing and planning standards', in Priorities Review Staff, *Report on Housing* (AGPS, Canberra, 1975).
Paterson, John (1977), 'Transport and land-use determinants of urban structure', in D.A. Hensher (ed.), *Urban Transport Economics* (Cambridge University Press, Cambridge, 1977).
Paterson, John, David Yencken and Graeme Gunn (1976), *A Mansion or No House* (Hawthorn Press, Melbourne, 1976).
Podder, N. (1971), 'Patterns of household consumption expenditures in Australia', *Economic Record*, 47, pp.379–98.
Polinsky, A.M. (1977), 'The demand for housing: a study in specification and grouping', *Econometrica*, 45, pp.447–61.
Pollock, Richard and Max Neutze (1976), 'Alternative methods of financing water supply and sewerage services', in Department of Environment, Housing and Community Development, *Pricing and Demand Management in the Provision of Water and Sewerage* (AGPS, Canberra, 1976).
Powell, A. (1966), 'A complete system of consumer demand equations for the Australian economy fitted by a model of additive preferences', *Econometrica*, 34, pp.661–75.
Priorities Review Staff (1975), *Report on Housing* (AGPS, Canberra, 1975).
Pugh, C. (1976a), *Intergovernmental Relations and the Development of Australian Housing Policies* (Centre for Research on Federal Financial Relations, Research Monograph No. 15, Australian National University, Canberra, 1976).
—— (1976b), 'Older urban residential areas and the development of economic analysis: a comparative study', in J.C. McMaster and G.R. Webb (eds.), *Australian Urban Economics* (Australia and New Zealand Book Co., Sydney, 1976).
Pullen, John (1971), 'The N.S.W. Land Development Contribution Act 1970', *Royal Australian Planning Institute Journal*, 9, pp.5–11.
Reece, B.F. (1975), 'The income tax incentive to owner-occupied housing in Australia', *Economic Record*, 51, pp.218–31.
Report of the Committee of Commonwealth/State Officials on Decentralisation (1972), (AGPS, Canberra, 1972).
Report of the Working Party on the Stabilization of Land Prices (1973), (South Australian Government, Adelaide, 1973).

Rhodes, J. and A. Kan (1972), 'British regional policy—some implications for Australia', *Australian Economic Papers*, 11, pp.163–79.

Rimmer, P.J. (1969), *Manufacturing in Melbourne* (Department of Human Geography, Publication HG/2, Australian National University, Canberra, 1969).

Roberts, Neal A. (1977), *The Government Land Developers* (D.C. Heath, Lexington, Mass., 1977).

Rose, L.A. (1973), 'The development value tax', *Urban Studies*, 10, pp.271–6.

—— (1976), 'The development value tax: a reply', *Urban Studies*, 13, pp.71–3.

Shepherd, L.E. (1973), 'A probabilistic aggregate travel demand model', in D. Hensher (ed.), *Urban Travel Choice and Demand Modelling* (Special Report No. 12, Australian Road Research Board), reprinted in G.R. Webb and J.C. McMaster (1975), *Australian Transport Economics* (Australia and New Zealand Book Co., Sydney, 1975).

Smith, A.B. (1976), 'An econometric model of the modal choice of Sydney work trips', in Bureau of Transport Economics, *Australian Transport Research Forum* (AGPS, Canberra, 1976).

—— (undated), 'Urban public transport demand elasticity: some Australian estimates', Bureau of Transport Economics (unpublished).

Smith, Wallace F. (1964), *Filtering and Neighbourhood Change* (Center for Real Estate and Urban Economics, University of California, Berkeley), reprinted in part in M. Edel and J. Rothenberg (eds.) (1972), *Readings in Urban Economics* (Macmillan, New York, 1972).

Stanley, J.K., T.M. Hogg and D.J. Delaney (1973), 'The theory of benefit and cost measurement with reference to residential disruption costs of urban road improvements', *Australian Road Research*, 5, No. 2, pp.23–35.

Stilwell, Frank J.B. (1974), *Australian Urban and Regional Development* (Australia and New Zealand Book Co., Sydney, 1974).

Stretton, Hugh (1974), *Housing and Government*, 1974 Boyer Lectures (Australian Broadcasting Commission, Sydney, 1974).

—— (1975), *Ideas for Australian Cities* (Georgian House, Melbourne, 1975).

Struyk, R.J. (1976), *Urban Homeownership* (D.C. Heath, Lexington, Mass., 1976).

Studies Commissioned by the Committee of Commonwealth/State Officials on Decentralisation (1975), (AGPS, Canberra, 1975).

Talbot, S. and R. Filmer (1973), 'Demand for passenger motor vehicles' (Industries Assistance Commission, Canberra, 1973).

Taxation Review Committee (1974), *Preliminary Report* (AGPS, Canberra, 1974).

—— (1975), *Full Report* (AGPS, Canberra, 1975).

Thompson, K.E., D.J. Delaney and P. Lees (1970), 'A model for the economic evaluation of urban road projects', *Proceedings of the Fifth Australian Road Research Board Conference*, 5, pt. 2, pp.323–37.

Thompson, Wilbur R. (1965), *A Preface to Urban Economics* (Johns Hopkins Press, Baltimore, 1965).

Tiebout, Charles M. (1956), 'A pure theory of local expenditures', *Journal of Political Economy*, 64, pp.416–24.

Timms, Duncan (1971), *The Urban Mosaic: Towards a Theory of Residential Differentiation* (Cambridge University Press, Cambridge, 1971).

Tisdell, C.A. (1975), 'The theory of optimal city-sizes: elementary speculations about analysis and policy', *Urban Studies*, 12, pp.61–70.

Troy, P.N. and N.G. Butlin (1971), *The Cost of Collisions* (Cheshire, Melbourne, 1971).

Tucker, S.N. and W.D. Woodhead (1975), 'Economic aspects in the choice of a home' (paper presented to the Fifth Australian Building Research Congress, Melbourne, 1975).

Urban Research Unit (1973), *Urban Development in Melbourne* (Australian Institute of Urban Studies, Canberra, 1973).

Vandermark, Elzo (1970), *Business Activities in Four Sydney Suburban Areas* (Urban Research Unit, Australian National University, Canberra, 1970).

Voumard, L. (Chairman) (1972), *Report of the Board of Inquiry into Local Government Finance in Victoria* (Government Printer, Melbourne, 1972).

Webb, G.R. (1972a), 'The economics of government bus services in Australia', *Traffic Quarterly*, 26, pp.117–32, reprinted in G.R. Webb and J.C. McMaster (eds.) (1975), *Australian Transport Economics* (Australia and New Zealand Book Co., Sydney, 1975).
—— (1972b), 'The rail passenger problem in Australia', *Australian Quarterly*, 44, No. 1, pp.4–11, reprinted in G.R. Webb and J.C. McMaster (eds.) (1975), *Australian Transport Economics* (Australia and New Zealand Book Co., Sydney, 1975).
—— (1973), 'Railway depreciation in Victoria: some financial, economic and operating considerations', *Growth*, 25, pp.1–6.
Webber, Michael, J. (1972), *Impact of Uncertainty on Location* (Australian National University Press, Canberra, 1972).
Wingo, Lowdon, Jr. (1961), *Transportation and Urban Land*, Resources for the Future (Washington, D.C., 1961).

Chapter 3

The Economics of Education in Australia 1962–1977

RICHARD BLANDY
JOHN HAYLES
ALAN WOODFIELD

Contents

We wish to express our thanks to two anonymous referees for criticism and suggestions on earlier drafts. More particularly we owe a very large debt to the editor, Professor Gruen, whose help and advice went far beyond what we had any right to expect and hope for. We absolve the referees and editors for any responsibility for the general thrust of the essay and for residual errors and omissions.

Section 1 Introduction

This survey of the economics of education in Australia is largely concerned with issues of educational policy for two reasons. First, the largest volume, and most influential, of the contributions to educational debate have been policy-directed. Second, the opportunity provided by a survey of this kind to evaluate critically educational policy is irresistible. Our concluding post-script does take a partisan position on some controversial issues. It is critical of much current Australian educational policy. To those who would have preferred something less crusading we extend our apologies for our lapse in taste.

The present time is fortuitous as a point at which to make a retrospective assessment of the economics of education in Australia. The dominating issues of the post-war era are changing in response to unexpected demographic and economic circumstances. The post-war policy preoccupation with expanding educational resources is giving way to a preoccupation with the *effectiveness* with which those resources are used. In retrospect at any rate, Australia's past response has been relatively straightforward—'more'. Future responses will be much more complex. We need more concern with efficiency, flexibility and the responsiveness of the resources used in the education system—thus laying much greater claim on the economist's tool-kit than in the past.

The increase in our educational effort over the past three decades has been very great, first in response to the tidal wave of demographic pressures following the post-war baby-boom, and second in response to the politically-articulate view of the Australian people that 'needs' in education were not being adequately met. This view originated influentially at a particular date. On the 18th May, 1962, Professor P.H. Karmel delivered the Buntine Oration on 'Some Economic Aspects of Education' to the Australian College of Education in Melbourne. He argued that Australia spent too little on education compared with other advanced countries, that Australia was a relatively lightly-taxed country and could afford increased educational expenditure financed from increased taxes and that the post-war increase in educational expenditure to that date had largely resulted from demographic factors with little quality improvement (Karmel 1964, pp.24–48).

Despite Karmel's qualification that there was no particular reason why a country should spend any particular proportion of its GNP on education, and his counsel against a too-rapid increase in educational output, the ideas became the foundation for the phenomenal educational developments over the next fifteen years. In contrast to the pre-Karmel period nearly all the increase in our educational effort over this period has come from increased resource inputs per child in the education system ('quality' improvements) rather than from demographic pressures.

In a very real sense, we have witnessed the flowering of 'Karmelism' in educational policy. Not only has Karmel been a prolific writer on educational policy (1962, 1964, 1966, 1971, 1972, 1973, 1975, 1976, 1977a, 1977b) but he has been in an unprecedented position to give effect to his ideas, *inter alia* as Chairman of the Committee of Enquiry into Education in South Australia, of the Interim Committee for the Australian Schools Commission, of the Australian Universities Commission and, very recently, of the Tertiary Education Commission.

Over the next decade our educational effort will ebb. The ratio of the school-age population to the working population will fall back to early post-war levels. Hence, we will be able to provide educational services at existing 'quality' levels (real resource inputs per child) with a smaller proportion of our national output than at present. If downtrends in fertility persist, the possible release of resources to non-education uses will be accentuated. In the mid 1980s, Australia will be devoting a minimum of one per cent less of Gross National Product to education than at present—inputs per child being maintained at current levels.

The existing Australian literature on economic issues in education is widely dispersed. Much of it is contained in monographs, official reports, edited collections of papers and readings, conference documents, works published by the Australian Council for Education Research and by the *Current Affairs Bulletin*, theses and some mimeographed research papers. This makes the literature a formidable task to grasp as a whole. In our survey we have attempted to gather together this disparate set of contributions as a starting point for future research workers. The survey is organised along 'natural' topic lines into which the literature falls but with the imposition of the usual major demarcations familiar to those who have penetrated this swampy terrain: 'social' demand or 'needs' approaches; the economics of education 'proper', including questions of markets, prices, costs, returns on investments, production functions and government intervention; and finally, manpower planning for education.

Some readers may find a curious imbalance about the sections—for example, the lengthy discussion of equality. This imbalance in fact flows mainly from the weight given particular issues in policy discussion. What has seemed to weigh most heavily has received most treatment. This gives a peculiarly-Australian bias to the survey. The issue of equality in educational provision (in a variety of senses) has provided such a dominating focus over recent years that to downplay such an issue as being, say, 'non-economic' would be like surveying the superstructure of the QEII while ignoring its engines. On the other hand, *purely* theoretical contributions by Australians to the economics of education have been ignored.

Because little of our surveyed literature has appeared in the leading Australian economics journals many economists may be unaware of a number of the contributions. We found the work to be of uneven quality, ranging from pedestrian descriptions to perceptive analyses of fundamental policy problems. There has been some competent applied research in the examination of costs, returns and financing schemes relating to education. The main research *lacunae* would appear to be in five areas: work on educational production functions, on the ways in which labour markets for credentialled workers operate, on 'new home economics' analyses of education (especially informal education), on 'the economics of politics' of education, and on the role of 'in-kind' redistributions in egalitarian policy. We found no Australian literature of note in the last three of these areas.

Of course, one reason for the smallness of volume and scope of considered academic research in Australia, compared with the extensive United States work, for example, is the less extensive data series on education, earnings and incomes cross-classified by socio-demographic characteristics. The situation has improved markedly over the past five years, but the absence of long and detailed time series data may explain part of the essentially derivative nature of much of the Australian research. We do not, however, see the problem of data inadequacy as fundamental.

Section 2 *Education Effort in Australia*

The past decade has witnessed an unprecedented growth in *per capita* educational expenditures. Public spending on education increased by about 150 per cent in real terms over the decade 1964/5–1974/5 (Tomlinson 1976). Much growth, however, was not in *per capita* terms, and primary, secondary, and tertiary enrolments grew by 11, 45, and 89 per cent, respectively. The period was also characterized by a growing share of relatively expensive forms of education (secondary & tertiary) while average attendance rates for noncompulsory education grew rapidly. The growth rate in recurrent educational expenditures was approximately twice that of GDP, and came mainly from public funding.

An 87 per cent increase in capital expenditure was observed over the decade. 1973 saw tertiary education finance transferred entirely to the Commonwealth, and 1974 saw fee abolition in tertiary institutions and technical colleges. Education expenditure as a proportion of GDP rose from 1.6 per cent in 1950/1 to 3.3. per cent in 1960/1, to 4.3 per cent in 1970/1 and in 1976/7 stood in excess of 6 per cent.

The origins of this enormous growth in educational expenditures can be traced to Karmel's Buntine Oration. Here, Karmel cited a table (from Svennilson, Edding and Elvin 1961) demonstrating that Australia's expenditure on education as a percentage of GNP was 11th in terms of total expenditure and 15th in terms of recurrent expenditure in a league table of largely OECD countries. Karmel argued 'may I now say that I believe that in Australia we can and should spend very much more on education than we are doing' (p.44).

The reasons given for this conclusion include the following: (i) education aids growth and hence pays for itself, (ii) benefits from education are generally underestimated, (iii) rights to education were not then being met, (iv) Australia was seen as a country with a high *per capita* income, but spending relatively little of it on education. Fielding possible criticism that Australia's high income was produced in spite of low past educational expenditures, Karmel asserted that education is necessary for skill development upon which basis future income growth would strongly depend. As a programme of action, Karmel suggested that 'teacher-pupil ratios need to be greatly improved. Children need to be encouraged (or compelled) to remain at school longer. A diversified range of tertiary institutions needs to be established, and the area of educational opportunity widened. To do these things, there must be a considerable increase over a number of years in the share of resources devoted to education' (1964, pp.47–48).

A connection between education and economic growth has been asserted by a number of followers (e.g. Cochrane 1968, p.142; Archbold 1971, pp.103 and 107).

There were always some Jeremiah's over the 'education-yields-growth' issue, however. Abramowitz' celebrated review (1962) of Denison's United States work (1962) congratulated Denison on his ingenuity but found no reason to believe numbers like 40 per cent of growth in output per man being attributable to education. Denison's subsequent work (1967) on growth in Europe attributed very much less of growth to education there. Harbison and Myers' correlations (1964) showed significant positive correlations between *enrolment ratios* and GNP per head, but *no* correlation between science-oriented enrolments and GNP per head and *no correlation between expenditure on education as a percentage of GNP and GNP per head.* Bieda's (1970) cross-country study does find some significant correlations between educational expenditure and economic growth, although the results are sensitive to the lags adopted, and there is also a disturbingly high correlation between growth rates and *subsequent* expenditures on education. Other disturbing results from Bieda's paper include an absence of correlation between science-oriented educational effort and subsequent growth rates.

The most basic objections to the 'league-table' approach are, first, that the alternatives are not specified. Do we *really* want a greater share of output originating from the education sector at the expense of, say health—and if not, which sectors are to have their shares reduced? The second objection is that a country which has managed to achieve a high per capita income with only a small expenditure on education might equally well be regarded as doing better—if education is *the* key to economic growth it must have used its educational resources to great effect. It may be others which are out of step—wastefully spending an unnecessarily large amount on education.

The model which was to prove most influential makes no presumptions about education's role as an economic agent. The Svennilson, *et al.* (1961)

model adapted by Karmel (1966) is a descriptive framework (or identity) in which changes in recurrent educational expenditure can be ascribed either to 'demographic' or to 'quality' changes. The model first describes recurrent educational expenditure (E) as the product of the school-age population (S), the average enrolment ratio of the school age population (e), the teacher/pupil ratio (r) the average earnings of teachers (w), and the ratio of average expenditure per teacher to teachers' average earnings (k) (reflecting a 'betterment factor' of ancilliary expenditures associated with teachers in the schooling process). Second, Gross Domestic Product is described as the product of the labour force (L) and the average output of the labour force. If average output bears a constant relation, α, to average earnings of the labour force (Y), then the proportion of GDP devoted to recurrent expenditure on education can be written as

$$\frac{\mathrm{E}}{\mathrm{GDP}} = \frac{\mathrm{S}}{\mathrm{L}} \times e \times r \times \frac{w}{\alpha \mathrm{Y}} \times k \qquad (1)$$

The first two terms of the right hand side of (1) represent 'demographic' or 'quantity' factors while the last three terms represent 'quality' or 'policy' factors, i.e. the teacher/pupil ratio, the 'quality' of teachers insofar as this is captured by the earnings of teachers relatively to the work force, and the size of the 'betterment factor'.

Using this model, Karmel (1966) demonstrated that the increase in educational expenditure in Australia had largely been the result of *demographic* changes. His basic calculations are reproduced in Table 1, extended to 1974/75, and forecasted to 1985/86.

Since 1965/66, 'demographic' factors have been insignificant in raising recurrent educational expenditure. Between 1965/6 and 1974/5 the latter increased by 59 per cent as a percentage of GDP, and would have increased by only 1 per cent from demographic factors alone. 'Quality' improvements raised the percentage by 57 per cent, virtually accounting for the entire growth in expenditure. This pattern is the reverse of that described by Karmel from 1948/49–1965/6; over the entire period 'quality' improvements now outweigh demographic changes as a source of growth in recurrent educational expenditures.

Educational capital expenditure has also risen greatly over the period—from 0.16 per cent of GNP in 1948/49, to 0.93 per cent in 1965/66 and to 1.3 per cent in 1974/75. With the reduction of demographic pressures since 1965/66, the increased capital expenditures must have been associated with a significant quality improvement in the capital stock used in education.

Using the Australian Bureau of Statistics' population projections (1976, Ref. No. 4.13), Karmel's weights, and various assumptions about enrolment ratios and quality changes, we can make some estimates about the likely trends in educational expenditures (see Table 1). Given the projected demographic developments, and assuming the 1974/75 propensity to enrol and that there is no decline in the 'quality' index for education, the index for recurrent educational expenditure as a percentage of GDP falls from 329 in 1974/75 to 277 in 1985/86, or from 4.9 per cent to 4.1 per cent. Since this pattern of development is likely to be associated with some reduction in pressure for capital expenditure in the schools (but still allowing for quality improvement), we might estimate capital expenditure as the same as in the mid 1960s, or 0.9 per cent, yielding a total expenditure on education as a percentage of GDP at 5.0 per cent. If anything this estimate is likely to prove too high, because our assumptions appear to us to be rather 'generous'. Hence, educational expenditure as a percentage of GDP should fall significantly over the medium term future without assuming any deterioration in the 'quality' index of educational provision.

In his 1966 paper, Karmel suggested that total educational expenditure might reach 4.4 per cent of GDP by 1970 (actual = 4.5 per cent!) and in *Education in South Australia* (1971), Karmel (and others) suggested that total expenditure on education would reach 6.7 per cent of GDP if the programme of his Committee of Enquiry into Education in South Australia were implemented across Australia (the 1974/5 figure was already 6.2 per cent). Since the thrust of Karmel's 1971 ideas were carried through into the

TABLE 1
Expenditures on Education and Various Indices Affecting such Expenditure, Australia, 1948/49, 1965/66, 1974/75 (and forecast 1985/86)

	1948/49	1965/66	1974/75	(1985/8
(1) Total Expenditure on Education (as % of GDP)	1.65%	4.0%	6.2%	(5.0%)
(2) Recurrent Expenditure on Education (as % of GDP)	1.49%	3.08%	4.9%	(4.1%)
(3) Index of (2) $\frac{E}{GDP}$	100	207	329	(277)
(4) Pool for enrolments index (S)	100	180	206	(206)
(5) Working population index (L)	100	132	161	(191)
(6) $\left(\frac{4}{5}\right)\left(\frac{S}{L}\right)$	100	137	128	(108)
(7) Propensity to enrol index (*e*)	100	128	138	(138)
(8) Demographic factor index (6) × (7) $\left(\frac{S}{L} \times e\right)$	100	175	177	(149)
(9) Quality Index $\left(\frac{3}{8}\right)\left(r \times \frac{w}{\alpha Y} \times k\right)$	100	118	186	(186)

Sources: P.H. Karmel, (1966)
Australian Bureau of Statistics, *Social Indicators No. 1*, 1976
ABS, *Demography*
ABS, *University Statistics*
ABS, *Expenditure on Education*

1973 Report of the Interim (Karmel) Committee for the Australian Schools Commission—the target of 6.7 per cent might well have been achieved but for the mid-1970's recession. It now seems probable that the mid-1970's levels of expenditure will prove to be high-tide marks for the percentage of GDP devoted to education.

Some impression of the gains in 'quality' since the mid 1960's can be obtained from the pupil/teacher ratios in Table 2. Targets proposed separately by Wood (1969, p.177) and Karmel (1969, p.535) were achieved for Government schools as a whole by 1976. However, they were not yet achieved for Catholic schools. Finally, the gap in pupil/teacher ratios between the Government sector and the non-Catholic private sector has narrowed or even been eliminated entirely by 1976. The extent to which reductions in the pupil/teacher ratio represent improvements in quality is, in fact, very moot: '. . . within the practicable operating ranges of class sizes, *there is no evidence to show that smaller classes generally facilitate learning*. This is not to deny that important benefits might well flow from small classes: for example, teachers' job satisfaction might increase, and the possibility of improved relationships among the class group might be enhanced' (our emphasis) (*Schools in Australia*; p.63).

TABLE 2
Pupil/Teacher Ratios, Australian Schools, 1952, 1962, 1966, 1972 and 1976.

	1952	*1962*	*1966*	*1972*	*1976*
Primary					
Government	32	30	28	26	22
Catholic	—	—	—	31	27
Other	—	—	—	17	18
Secondary					
Government	19	20	19	16	14
Catholic	—	—	—	22	19
Other	—	—	—	14	14

Sources: Karmel (1966, p.157)
ABS (1976, p.33)

By 1974, Australia was no longer a relatively lightly taxed country and Australia's educational 'effort' is not obviously now 'below average'. In our view, however, such league-table analysis does not help much because the opportunity costs of moving to different expenditure and taxation patterns are not spelled out.

Section 3 *Financing Education in Australia*

How has this massive growth in education spending been financed? There has been a dramatic increase in the participation of the Commonwealth government over the past decade. The Commonwealth government is now wholly responsible for the financing of tertiary education, provides substantial grants for technical and further education, and 'needs-based' specific purpose grants for pre-primary, primary and secondary schools. Specific purpose grants have largely replaced matching grants.

This has not coincided with the development of *specific* machinery to integrate educational planning at State or national level; neither has there emerged a set of procedures for the evaluation of competing uses for government finance (Tomlinson 1976). With specific-purpose grants, Federal policy necessarily becomes State policy, possibly distorting a State's priorities, a problem also involved in matching requirements. Matching requirements prevent States from substituting Commonwealth grants for their own voluntary expenditures, but they lead to distortions in allocations if matching differs between sectors. In practice, matching encouraged State spending away from the sub-tertiary sector. (Mathews 1968, 1972, Wade 1974). In addition, differential matching requirements between capital and recurrent costs could have encouraged over-capitalisation within the tertiary sector. The distribution of outlays actually shows relatively reduced capital expenditure which Tomlinson attributed mainly to salaries escalation (an 82 per cent increase in teachers' salaries over the period 1971–1974), and reduced outlays on sub-tertiary relative to tertiary education. Tomlinson argued that the matching requirements induced the States to increase their own allocations to tertiary institutions in order to maximise such grants.

Jay saw the 'matching' and 'specific purpose' devices as means by which the Commonwealth *could* induce the States to adhere to a *national* plan of educational expenditure; thus 'the Australian government has imposed upon the States a national plan for primary and secondary school education, at the price of finding additional funds and assuming political responsibility for the aggregate level of expenditure' (1975, p.48). Tomlinson argued that executive responsibility for tertiary education resides *directly* with the Commonwealth and for sub-tertiary 'is being assumed by the Commonwealth by virtue of its fiscal dominance' (p.57). He suggested that local education taxes would yield an escape from these characteristics while Mathews (1968) suggested that distortions in spending patterns could be avoided (at least within the education sector) by the use of capital, sales, or value-added taxes. Such measures would also be compatible with more decentralised administration of education.

Much of the increased government spending may be considered a response to, and adoption of, many of the proposals set forth in a series of official reports commissioned to investigate Australia's educational requirements.

These include, *inter alia*, Murray (1957), Martin (1964–65), Sweeney (1969), Wiltshire (1969), Karmel (1973), Cohen (1973), Kangan (1974) and Cochrane (1974).

3.1 Some Theoretical Considerations

Under a system of private education, parents/children would buy educational services in a manner similar to other services. Their private demands would be reflected in their willingness to pay. Freedom of choice among institutions would exist, and profit-maximising producers (including those producing teachers) would be encouraged to produce those outputs most highly valued, and through competition, to adopt cost-minimising technologies. If parents are judged to know best the interests of their children, and are perfectly informed on all long-run outcomes of the educational process, just what is it that has led to such obvious devastation of this Panglossian vision?

Some would argue that a competitive market will fail to produce optimal quantities of educational services since there will generally be observed a divergence between marginal social benefits and marginal social costs, the equality of which is a necessary condition for a Pareto-optimal allocation of resources.

As far as market failure is concerned, Blaug (1970) argued that the concept provides little basis for the degree of intervention *generally* observed in market economies. For instance, economies of scale in schooling are highly limited, while external economies prevail only in the production (as opposed to the diffusion) of knowledge. Blaug considered that educational benefits are essentially captured by those undergoing education either as investment and/or consumption (including aspects of expanded choice). Regarding consumer ignorance, Blaug noted that the classical economists thought that parental incompetence or unconcern may well be characteristics from which children could usefully be liberated, yet these economists still emphasized that state education could crush spontaneity and diversity. The state's role in correcting any information deficiencies would not imply state *production* and *finance* of education: neither does the desire of the state to act *in loco parentis* necessarily imply absence of private production of schooling services—parents could be supplied with education-specific state grants.

A second potentially strong ground for intervention lies in capital market imperfection (or outright failure). Human capital cannot be separated from its owner; in a nonslave society borrowers cannot assign rights over their human capital. Consequently, rates of interest on loans to finance individuals' education may be much higher than market rates generally, since borrowers cannot protect themselves from default, even through risk-pooling devices. Generally, the acquisition of human capital will be greater if society as a whole bears the risk of lending to students. This provides the basis for the establishment of a state educational opportunity bank, but does not necessarily justify government subsidies, nor the production of education by the state.

If extensive state intervention in the production of educational services has little substantive basis in conventional (Paretian) welfare economics, what other basis can be offered? Of major importance in the Australian literature is the desire to alter the distribution of incomes, power and opportunity in the society, by altering the human capital endowments of individual children or classes of children through state intervention.

It is true that some income redistribution may be required to satisfy the Paretian conditions, that is redistribution which would make donors and recipients no worse off (and which arises because of interdependent household utility functions). The Australian literature, however, appears to take the stance that redistribution is not only 'good' *per se*, but is to be accorded a status which can only be described as pre-eminent. The implicit welfare function cannot be Paretian, and since it is unclear what the welfare function is, and in particular what role economic efficiency plays in it, economic evaluation of this literature is no easy task.

Our Australian point of departure is the set of influential contributions by Karmel (loc.cit.) and Mathews (1968, 1973). Mathews (1973) introduced objectives other than economic efficiency, including growth, social harmony, equity in wealth and income distribution, and the development of individuals' potential. Mathews applauded the market mechanism for imposing discipline on expenditure decisions, for achieving efficiency in allocation, as well as satisfying diversity, decentralisation of decisions, opportunities for innovation and/or parental and community involvement. But, claimed Mathews, distributional equity and external benefits of education are ignored, while the implicit voluntary restriction of schooling to a small fraction of the work-force was seen as highly inimical to income growth. Mathews concluded that 'for all these reasons, the pure fee-paying case is unacceptable as a general method of financing education' (1973, p.149).

Karmel's 1962 Buntine Oration isolated the following reasons for government intervention: underestimation by individuals of the private benefits to education, misguided parental decisions, socially beneficial externalities, household income as an inappropriate constraint on educational spending, and the impact of socially-contrived wants for private goods (reinforced by the advertising expenditures of private firms). In addition, Karmel noted that since the supply of skills responds with a lag, a competitive market might prove to be dynamically unstable, requiring further intervention in the form of manpower forecasting. As a consequence of the *assumed* existence (and presumably, importance) of such phenomena, Karmel recommended an expanded educational effort that stressed that rights to education be limited only by individuals' capacities to benefit.

Mathews (1968) assumed an educational 'crisis' existed—which could only be overcome by government action raising educational expenditures. 'Excessive' educational thrift was explained by Mathews 'to be found in the balance of financial powers and responsibilities between Commonwealth and State governments' (1968, p.80).

A striking aspect of these views is the absence of empirical evidence to substantiate the existence and importance of the various avenues of market failure. Even if pernicious private sector advertising, benefit miscalculation, and externalities are sufficiently significant to require 'correction', do these phenomena really justify the very rapid growth in our education expenditures? If one accepts that income redistribution and expansion of opportunities for social mobility are legitimate governmental functions, economists would be interested in the *efficiency* of various mechanisms for achieving such aims.

Moreover, to explain Australia's apparently low ratio of educational expenditure to GDP in terms of the above arguments requires demonstration that the alleged distortions and degree of income inequality are *more significant* in Australia than in most other countries in the league. No demonstration of this is offered, but on the income distribution question, it is (now) well known that the distribution of household incomes in Australia before and after income tax is amongst the most egalitarian in the world (Paukert 1974, Jain 1975, Tinbergen 1976, the Gini index of concentration in 1973/4 for all families before tax being 0.31.

Also, to some economists, incantation of potential sources of market failure are insufficient; thus Blaug argued that 'the idea that the external or indirect benefits of education to society as a whole are enormous in magnitude and vastly exceed the direct personal benefits to the educatees is one of the myths of our time . . .' (1970, p.107). Maglen (1976) considerably elaborated on this, arguing that the 'real substance' of external benefits to higher education were embodied in income gains of persons other than those receiving higher education. He pointed to the need to value these benefits properly by separating the other influences on earnings differentials—including changes in relative supplies of persons with varying educational attainments, and productivity changes related to capital accumulation and technological progress.

Maglen took an agnostic view of the nebulous 'atmospheric' externalities (e.g. the fostering of political stability and social cohesion) and was sceptical of the empirical significance of other alleged sources of external benefits of higher education including reductions in lawlessness, the raising of incomes of subsequent generations and increasing labour market mobility with reduced costs of search by firms for workers. In many cases, Maglen argued, externalities would be 'internalised' as private benefits. Finally, Maglen emphasised that only *marginal* externalities require 'correction' by subsidies and taxes, and that external benefits are not generally uniformly distributed and/or uniformly valued across all members of society.

Maglen's evaluation of the externalities issues threw 'serious doubt . . . upon the appropriateness of the present level of subsidies, and hence the amounts of public resources currently being devoted to higher education in Australia' (p.40). However, there is little uniquely Australian about Maglen's contribution; he attempted only to set a framework by which empirical research could proceed, and did not specify methods by which external benefits of education could be valued. Without evidence on these matters, assertion is likely to continue to rule the day.

If the problem of underestimation of benefits is essentially one of *information*, it is not evident that massive state subsidisation of education is the most efficient remedy. A massive educational boost across the whole population might cure the information inadequacies once-and-for-all, after which the state could retire; it is wasteful continually to duplicate well known information. Nevertheless, it must be admitted that homogeneous state education assists in preventing parental 'backsliding' in indoctrination of societal values. '*Tant pis*' for parents and children who do not desire to be socialised in the approved manner.[1] Also, the assumption that parents are ill-informed on matters of education, as Parish noted, 'has not very favourable implications about the consequences of the past eighty years of state education', (1964, p.232). What *is* important, on the other hand, is whether some people, especially low-income families, are somehow conditioned into wrongly viewing educational benefits as inaccessible to them, or to their children. The critical questions are whether there is evidence that bureaucrats are better informed on the advantages of education to low-income families than those families are. Is education an efficient redistribution device? How can a movement towards equality be expected to occur, and does such a movement take place? What are the costs in terms of reductions in freedom? Many of these issues are simply by-passed in the Australian literature.

3.2 Equality as a Consideration

Possibly the most important recurring theme in the literature is that of *equality*; used in a wide variety of senses. A major justification for government production and distribution is a desire to support certain 'fundamental rights' of access to education. Archbold argued that because *most* households cannot afford to bear the full cost of their education (*sic*), 'it is inevitable that there should be a considerable volume of public investment in education', (1971, p.103). This is a curious argument. If there is capital market failure, there would be a basis for the government's developing and underwriting a loan scheme, or a system of education vouchers if capacity to pay for education was desired to be augmented. This does not imply public *production* of education. In what sense is education a very special commodity? There is no technically fixed 'survival' level of education, so why cannot most households afford modest educational expenses? Most households agree that they cannot afford a Mercedes Benz, but governments do not seem obliged to fill the breach in cases like this.

In his more recent contributions, Karmel (1972, 1975, 1976, 1977a, 1977b) has provided some valuable clarification—especially for educational expansion at the tertiary level, for which costs per student are highest and for which externalities are minimal. In 1975, Karmel argued that public educational policy has two basic motivations, namely, that a highly educated, trained workforce is needed to improve productivity, and 'a belief that education is an avenue for the promotion of equality', (1975, p.257). The first is regarded as an investment motive, and the second as a consumption motive. Karmel distinguished four concepts of equality in relation to educational expenditures.

The first refers to equal provision of education to students, independently of the institution they attend. The second is equality of opportunity, to be achieved by removing financial barriers which prevent students staying as long as they desire, and by compensating for socio-economic disadvantage. Third, we have equality of attainment. As Karmel noted, this does not mean equal levels of skills for all persons, but that the distribution of attainment be independent of the initial distribution of socio-economic status. Finally, there is equality of income distribution, towards which education can contribute through the equalisation of the distribution of human capital.

Karmel then reviewed the extent to which these criteria have been met by the Australian system. First, he argued that 'the one major advantage which can be claimed for centralised systems is that they tend to produce equality of provision', (1975, p.270). If education is a normal good, income inequality among households would imply an observed inequality in educational provision and outcomes. If people are poor partly because they lack human capital, their poverty also imposes a constraint on their (and their children's) accumulating human capital, thus creating a 'vicious circle' of poverty. Poorly educated people may also be relatively inefficient in transforming purchased goods into meaningful activities (Becker Goods), so they end up both with few market goods and also unproductive time on their hands. We would agree that a humane society should change the rules of a game that permit such a state of affairs to persist. But is publicly-provided, subsidised education an appropriate vehicle? And if it is, what freight-loading can it efficiently carry compared with other transportation media to the egalitarian land?

A number of economists have rebelled against this notion of equal provision. One could equalise resources per child by providing a child with a lifetime fund to finance education, which could not be augmented by parental contributions. This would permit children and parents to exert major influences on education. Burke (1973) argued that the education system should give each child an opportunity to develop whatever personal assets he possesses. This may require the provision of quite diverse environments. The typical Australian State system 'does little to promote equality of opportunity as briefly outlined for the 'person-centered' society' (Burke 1973, p.235). Burke noted that inequality of provision occurs in Victoria despite compulsory school attendance until age 15, finance and staffing administered by the Education Department rather than school authorities, zoning, centralised allocation of teachers, and substantial excess payments above taxation contributions to opt out of government schooling. Moreover,

Burke argued that removal of parental choice leads to a 'hidden curriculum', the indoctrination of a particular form of authority, a hierarchy based on certification, and an alienation of the lower classes in the most general sense.

Equality of provision, then, has its price. Burke argued that permitting freedom of choice as well as providing the type of education wanted, would promote efficiency of resource use. There is now little pressure on State systems or their teachers to satisfy consumers' individual wants. At present, institutions are not really accountable to users. Efficiency incentives would have some scope if school authorities had freedom to choose appropriate input mixes and output composition. But it is hard to justify (on grounds of efficiency) a tenured staffing system which makes ineffective teachers virtually fixed factors of production, where seniority dominates performance in determining rewards—which may also require quitting the classroom in favour of administration—and where salary differentials cannot be used to affect teachers' subject specialisation. Until the 1970s, effective teachers really had to love their work to remain. But when salaries were subsequently raised substantially, tenure served, at least partly, to raise economic rents earned in the teaching profession.

Parish noted that education could be subsidised and provided competitively by private firms. He argued that 'our existing policy is a remarkably ineffective way of encouraging voluntary private expenditures on education' (1964, p.230) and that variety, innovation, and parental interest in education is effectively discouraged. Many parents who do seek alternative education do so at considerable hardship. Also, Selby Smith claimed that 'to speak of rich schools rather than schools attended by children whose parents are wealthy is a fundamental error with far-reaching implications. In fact, government schools, Catholic schools and other independent schools do not generally cater exclusively for the rich or the poor, but for pupils whose parents vary widely in income, wealth and taste for education', (1975c, p.125).[2]

Existing incentives are in favour of an increasingly elitist enclave of exclusive private schooling, because, increasingly, only wealthy people can easily accommodate their tastes for different education. As Parish put it, 'existing arrangements put a price on quality improvements which is absurdly higher than their real cost', (1964, p.231).

Karmel expressed some disquiet regarding the implications of mass tertiary education. 'There are no grounds for believing that the trend towards mass tertiary education in Australia will do anything but continue strongly for some time to come' (1972, p.5). Nevertheless, Karmel noted some genuine problems associated with the proliferation of post-school institutions. A major problem concerns that of academic excellence: thus 'there is a basic paradox in the notion of elite education for a mass clientele' (p.15); 'if the universities' main commitment is to rational enquiry, the main commitment of other institutions may be to vocational training', (p.17). Recent proposals to close some CAE's and retrench some staff at universities have brought forward somewhat the time when the trend towards mass tertiary education will grow less strongly. Contributing factors would include errors in demographic forecasting, occupational downgrading of tertiary credentials, and the compression of wage differentials for skill.

Karmel noted that the trade off between excellence and mass education depends on prevailing attitudes towards equality. If one wishes to use tertiary education as a compensating device for social disadvantage, the commitment to academic excellence and meritocratic sorting of students would be under considerable strain. Whatever may be concluded from this line of reasoning, two points stand out; first, whether tertiary education should (or even can) act as a compensatory device, and second, whether it is more efficient to engage in compensatory educational spending at a much earlier stage of the learning cycle, including the pre-school stage. As Karmel pointed out, 'the critical financial barriers may not be at the threshold of entry to tertiary education but may exist much earlier in the school system' (1972, p.11). In particular, subsidisation of mass tertiary education may not only be expensive, but it may also have socially *unequalising* influences. On the one hand, it is only the disadvantaged student one wishes to subsidise, rather than those who are willing to pay a nonsubsidised price. On the other, those (disadvantaged) who do not take up the offer of an education at subsidised prices are doubly disadvantaged. Many may be unwilling to forego current earnings, and/or may sensibly question their capacity to make fruitful use of the services offered.

Some of these tensions might be resolved by the parallel development of universities and other tertiary institutions, the former being rather few in number, and awarding conventional degrees at high standards of excellence, while other institutions of advanced education might award diplomas at lower levels, and in additional subject areas. This appears to have been the Martin Committee's role for CAE's, as essentially vocationally-based institutions not competing for the same students as universities. The practice has departed from this form. CAE's have striven to emulate the pretensions of the Universities.

As Karmel pointed out, we certainly have not got equality of attainment. 'Whether equality of attainment in the statistical sense . . . is possible is itself arguable. Nor is it obviously desirable because the costs of attempting it might be very great and, if achieved, it might be at a relatively low level of attainment' (1975, p.271). Yet even if absolute equality of attainment is not feasible, presumably satisfying the equal opportunity objective would go some of the way towards meeting the equal attainment criterion, otherwise equality of opportunity would not appear to be a very interesting objective. This is the sense of the equal opportunity objective in *Schools in Australia* (1973, p.23).

Finally, we have equality of income distribution. To quote Karmel again: 'there are no obvious reasons why greater educational opportunities should necessarily produce a more equal distribution of income' (1975, p.271).

Individuals' different endowments of *physical* capital, and the effect of different genetic and environmental backgrounds on their *human* capital endowments, will produce income and earnings differentials that equal opportunity for educational investment will not remove. One would then agree with Karmel that 'there may be all kinds of deficiencies in educational policy, but to accuse it of failing because it has not produced an equal income distribution is absurd' (1975, p.272).

As Karmel pointed out above, the theoretical basis for equalising incomes through expanded access to education is not unambiguous. Expanded opportunities will alter the distribution of human capital. Suppose the earnings distribution is split into separate returns to 'raw' labour and human capital. As Hartman (1973) notes, earnings dispersion depends on the degree of equality of distribution of each component, of the dispersion of returns in each category, of the relative importance of each in determining earnings, and on interactions between education and ability. When educational opportunities become more evenly distributed, opposing forces come into play, and it is not possible on *a priori* grounds to judge whether earnings dispersion will be reduced.

Karmel, however, invokes two separate arguments for assuming a (limited) contribution of education to income redistribution. First, education is used as a screen, affecting job sorting but not the distribution of wage offers. Second, wages and salaries are unrelated to skills (or, rather, qualifications).[3] Both are, of course, *possible* explanations, but Karmel gives no indication of their empirical significance. Snooks (1977) finds that education is not a significant determinant of income for Australian artists, but this is a very special case. The wealth of American studies on determinants of individual earnings generally finds a significant role for years of completed schooling, yet also finds that education explains little of the variance in individual earnings.[4]

Section 4 The Schools Commission and Equality: The Guardians Cometh

These issues have also been discussed in *Schools in Australia* (1973), in a book edited by d'Cruz and Sheehan (1975) given over to its critical evaluation and in a recent report by two members of the Schools Commission, McKinnon and Hancock (1976). In *Schools in Australia*, the Interim Committee for the Australian Schools Commission under Karmel argued that the standard of schooling a child receives should be independent of its parents' income level, that schools should compensate 'for unequal out-of-school situations', that 'greater than average public spending on education for children handicapped in various ways is involved', and that 'some altering of the balance of expenditure in favour of earlier stages of education to consolidate a more equal basic achievement between children is desirable' (p.11). The Committee's programme systematically attempts to reduce the variance in per child *resource use* between schools throughout Australia and to *increase* the *fee* gap between government schools and private schools (by indexing fee effort roughly to incomes rather than prices). In addition to this basic 'resource use equalisation' thrust is a compensatory thrust to provide extra resources to disadvantaged schools—identified as schools with pupils drawn from neighbourhoods suffering 'socio-economic disadvantage' (p.97). This is a measure involving three principal components—essentially occupationality, Aboriginality and migrancy. Relatively small funds ($20 million) were allocated for these schools in programmes to be devised by the schools and the groups served by them. The Committee was aware that 'quantifiable cognitive gains from many compensatory programs in the past have been slight and even ephemeral' (p.94), but argued

'. . . An acceptance of the view that the influence of schooling is limited does not imply that efforts to make schools more effective are futile, for it could be argued that we have not yet tried hard enough to assist disadvantaged children in their learning . . . However, if the ten years or more of life that a person spends in school can be lived in pleasant surroundings, in a satisfying community, and in a program of activities which is meaningful to its participants besides being relevant preparation for a later interest in work and learning, then this must justify the expenditure of additional resources . . .' (p.94).

Recognising that Jencks (1972) and others have urged a more direct attack on poverty through income redistribution—instead of compensatory schooling programmes—the Committee feared that such action would not materialise in this generation and claimed that 'the school provides a practical point of attack on the cycle of poverty, for it is a social institution more amenable to change than is the family, and an institution where deliberate social intervention is acceptable' (p.94).

McKinnon and Hancock (1976) is in lineal descent from *Schools in Australia*. They explored in greater depth the problems of meeting objectives outlined in *Schools in Australia* including not only equality but extra support for special groups, decentralising the locus of control of schools to the individual school and promoting diversity of choice. Only once is quality of education mentioned, in a sideways glance to a 'small but vocal group within the community arguing that current concepts of equality of opportunity inevitably lead to a general decline in excellence and intellectual aspiration' (p.34).

One of the key passages in McKinnon and Hancock ascribed (by implication) to the Schools Commission a perspective which 'accepts that schools have limited impact on social mobility but nevertheless supports the view that current evidence about the effectiveness of schools only deals with what has been, not with what might be' (p.33). Locus of control and diversity of choice objectives were associated by McKinnon and Hancock with the financial mechanisms of grants to non-government schools, tax deductability of educational expenditures and disadvantaged schools grants. But they were clearly uneasy about an extended range of choice in schooling and about shifting the locus of control to parents—although not about shifting the locus of control from the States to the Federal level. Choice is plainly to be subservient to equality: '. . . any method of assistance to promote diversity of choice through public financial aid must take into account the level and type of service offered and the openness and access to that service in order to guard against unjust discrimination among children according to parental income and preference . . .' (p.42).

They cautiously endorse the 'Supported Schools' concept (especially for low-fee, low-resource private schools) as a basis for the financing of all schools 'providing there was an acceptable nationwide policy on the tolerable limits of choice and diversity' (p.72). They mention preventing intolerable diversity and the inconsistency between subsidising choice and maintaining equality of opportunity (defined as reducing disparities in per child resource levels among schools) in spite of private sector schools having *lower* resource inputs per child on *average* than government schools. However, the disadvantaged schools programme deliberately seeks a disparity of *inputs* inversely associated with socio-economic background in order to strive 'for greater equality of *outcomes* across groups' (p.47). These funds are given provided schools use participatory decision-making procedures 'insisted on by the Commonwealth' putting the States 'under pressure to operate in ways they might not have adopted if there had been no programme' (p.48). Federal programmes have deliberately favoured the 'lagging States' in education creating the difficulty that 'States which have had least concern for education have benefitted most'. But the alternative matching grant approach would widen the (between-State) gap in resources.

Further, it is argued that several Australian minority groups, notably Aboriginals, rural dwellers, and migrants have suffered particular disadvantage. Yet equalisation expenditures to prevent discrimination in labour markets must recognize 'above all, that Australia should view itself as a multi-cultural society, accepting the cultural consequences and benefits of its diverse population'. (p.33). In a more general sense, McKinnon and Hancock wrote 'it is generally accepted that some sort of educational planning is desirable because the characteristics of Australia's economic and political system prevent educational services from reaching maximum efficiency without some external interference' (p.40), a justification by way of definition.

Many of the arguments in *Schools in Australia* have been criticised by contributors to a review volume edited by d'Cruz and Sheehan (1975). Crittenden, for example, argued that it is difficult to give operational meaning to some of the objectives which may turn out to be mutually inconsistent. Thus, 'equal educational outcomes' were ill-defined in any specific sense, as were concepts such as 'full participation' and 'social and individual needs' to which the Report refers. Again 'basic achievements', 'common minimal standards' and 'capacities for independent thought' do not get clearly defined, and one is consequently left without specific criteria to evaluate performance.

Crittenden also noted that *Schools in Australia* called for a massive expansion of government activities in schools, yet supported decentralised administration, local initiative and decision-making, and close mutual involvement of each school with its immediate community. This was seen essentially as lip-service to the radical view of autonomy, since a substantial core curriculum is favoured, administration is still to be centralised, while services such as continuing teacher education are seen as requiring central organisation. Again the concept of diversity gets strong approval and strong qualifications. Essentially, acceptance of common outcomes places strong constraints on admissible diversity. Although private schools are encouraged to co-exist, equality gets precedence over diversity in dealing with 'high-standard' private schools.

Regarding the conflict between equal opportunities and equal outcomes, Crittenden argued that the Committee was only giving effect to minimum acceptable educational standards. He questioned the efficiency of compensating for educationally hostile influences in home environments. Many writers have argued that *by itself*, education is a blunt instrument for social and economic reforms, and *Schools in Australia* acknowledges this. The Committee then appears to support a policy admitted to be of very limited effect. Crittenden concluded that 'if the main objective is to remedy poverty rather than the deficiencies of our education, the weight of evidence tends to show that the school is not a very effective instrument. Perhaps the Report should have examined the evidence for the view that simple income transfers are more effective in alleviating poverty than additional expenditure on education' (p.14). Interestingly, by 1975 Karmel did not accept that education had a major role in redistribution policy. Rather, 'wage fixing methods and tax policy are much more effective weapons' (1975, p.272).

Schools in Australia does attempt to measure educational need, by reference to average *per capita* resource costs in government schools. This standard, however, does not refer to minimum educational achievements, nor to the resource level required to attain equal outcomes, or even the objectives supposed to be served by the school.

These issues arise again in the Committee's attitude towards parental freedom of choice. Its Report 'values the right of parents to educate their children outside government schools' (p.12). But it then claims that if parents choose a school well above the desirable minimum, they should not be provided with government assistance to do so. The reason for this is that the upgrading of government schools is seen as an earlier priority. Crittenden argued that there was an inconsistency here: thus 'one cannot consistently grant that all parents have a right of choice . . . yet deny that they are entitled to expect that a fair estimate of the cost of educating a child in the government system should be applied to the education of their own children if they choose an alternative to that system' (p.17). In fact there may be no inconsistency; instead, the Committee may not be prepared to give parental choice a high weight in its objective function.

In a summary statement on *Schools in Australia*, Sheehan praised it for 'the humanity of its discussion of both educational ideals and deficiencies and for the freshness of its approach' (1975, p.163) but still regarded it as 'seriously flawed'. Sheehan's main worry was that the Report called for a massive increase in resources which only *might* have some desirable effect and some of which may be complementary to high-quality higher-motivated teachers, but are not necessarily substitutes for them. Thus, Sheehan would prefer a shift in emphasis away from the volume of generalised resource inputs, in favour of emphasis on the quality of educational *processes*.

Sheehan also noted a divergence in the short-run and long-run attitude towards private schools with high levels of assistance in the long term being frustrated by 'priorities' in the short term. Sheehan did not see this to be a very useful approach. To begin with, some *government* schools exceed the Commission's target standard. As Sheehan noted, 'it does seem highly anomalous that there can be wealthy parents who happily send their children to a high quality government school at public expense while parents on average incomes who choose an independent school of comparable quality have no right to public assistance' (p.171). Secondly, families choosing high-quality independent schooling are penalised *independently* of their wealth, clearly reducing the incentive to assign private funds for schooling and leading to the possible demise of high-fee schools. *Schools in Australia* suggested that parental contributions might be expected to cover a fair share of costs of operating non-government schools with perhaps some matching of fees to grants. Sheehan argued that this seems to acknowledge the inadequacy of the proposal itself! He saw these problems arising because the Report dealt with *schools* rather than *parents*, and points out that it is *children* who get educated, and *parents* who bear the major burden of financing. Consequently, Sheehan envisaged equitable funding mechanisms based on the varying circumstances of *parents*, rather than the varying circumstances of *schools*, but he did not explore the practical possibilities of this approach in any detail.

Even with the marked growth in educational expenditures over the decade, the Schools Commission would not accept current levels as optimal. It was argued in 1973 that primary and secondary recurrent expenditures per pupil would have to be raised by 40 per cent and 35 per cent, respectively, to meet perceived educational needs. In addition, Australian pre-school (November, 1973) and TAFE (April, 1974) committees recommended large-scale capital and recurrent grants to increase facilities at these levels. Tomlinson (1976), however, questioned whether these trends could continue, arguing that it is 'simplistic' to regard education of such importance that it should grow even at the expense of competing social services. Without market principles to obtain an assessment of public support for educational expenditures, the distant removal of educational finance from taxpayers, according to Tomlinson, would reduce the likelihood of opposition to additional public spending on education. Nonetheless, the tension between alleged demonstrated 'needs' and the clearly evident government budget constraint, led Tomlinson to recommend a measure of financial accountability which 'relates also to the broad concepts of establishing educational goals, of assessing educational outcomes, and of evaluating the development of human, material, and financial resources to the educational enterprise' (p.46). Regrettably, the Australian literature on the economics of education is generally lacking in serious attempts to grapple with these questions.

As reviewers, we find several important questions begged by the Schools Commission's approach. To suggest that a pleasant school life is *sufficient* to justify additional spending eschews all notion of opportunity cost (what if we have to give up kidney dialysis units or better working conditions in factories?). What is efficient and equitable about compensating *schools* which have large concentrations of children with learning difficulties rather than *children* with learning difficulties independently of where they study? How can 'acceptance of the view that the influence of schooling is limited' incline one to accept also the 'practicality' of schools as *the* point of attack on poverty? Why should we expect not to be as disappointed as the British or Americans by the results of compensatory programmes? Even if one accepts parental income as an unsatisfactory constraint on educational choices, the grounds for regarding parental (but not bureaucrats') preferences *en masse* as unacceptable are hard to fathom. The Schools Commission also appears to wish to override the preferences of citizens expressed politically at the State level and to make schools conform to *its* plans rather than the *State* bureaucrats' plans. Equality between the States in schooling inputs is to be promoted although the voters at State level have opted (indirectly) for differences. What is the basis for the fear of 'intolerable diversity' of which private schooling is allegedly redolent?

But perhaps of greatest importance is the lack of clarity surrounding the objective function of the Schools Commission. Without it evaluation of performance becomes almost impossible, in part because the multiple objectives of *Schools in Australia* and McKinnon and Hancock are generally incompatible, and require trading off one against the other. As matters stand, quite different educational policies could be rationalised as being consistent with 'established objectives'.

Section 5 Fees Abolition, Student Loans and Grants, and Vouchers

As noted, the climate over the past decade has been one of increased public outlays and reduced private outlays based essentially on principles of equality. Fees in tertiary institutions were abolished in 1974, no fees have been charged in government primary and secondary schools for many years (apart from limited school appeals amongst parents), financial grants to tertiary students have been increased and shifted from a competitive to a needs basis. Tax deductions for school expenses have been reduced to a fraction of their former real level. Here we present in more detail the Australian discussion surrounding these issues.

5.1 Fees Abolition

Proposals to abolish fees in government tertiary educational institutions are discussed in a comprehensive appraisal by Brennan (1971) and by Mathews (1972, 1973). The actual abolition of tertiary fees in Australia took place in 1974.

Brennan distinguished efficiency and equity aspects of fees abolition. At the time, fees accounted for only 11 per cent of universities' revenue. Although wide differences in marginal costs of education existed in different subjects, Brennan noted a striking uniformity in fees across courses. Unless compensated, the States had most to lose from fee abolition under the then-existing Commonwealth-State tertiary education financial arrangements.

Only students unable to win scholarships or teacher training awards were obliged to pay their own fees. Inclusive of income forgone and living-away-from-home expenses fees were estimated to account for about 22 per cent of students' total educational costs. Since entrance to tertiary institutions was basically meritocratic, fee-paying students were likely to comprise the 40 per cent less able.

Brennan emphasized that fees abolition was part of the more general problem 'of determining the precise nature and extent of the 'appropriate' subsidy to higher education' (p.87). In practice, the question concerns the allocation of places within a given set of institutions and whether willingness to pay or ability should be used in determining places. Brennan suggested that the first criterion is usual in a market economy, while the second is 'rather unfamiliar, and its advantages as a rationing device need to be investigated' (p.97). Brennan distinguished between private and external benefits of education, and argued for subsidisation equal to the value of external benefits created by each individual in conjunction with a set of market-clearing fees. Differential subsidies would be offered to those generating differential external benefits so that the greatest subsidies need not necessarily go to the most able. Practical difficulties of implementation were noted, but not resolved.

Brennan was sceptical about the alleged undervaluation of tertiary education. 'Academics have something of a vested interest in higher education—and it is all too easy to justify subsidies on the basis of authoritarian judgements concerning the inherent value of one's own product' (pp.110–111). The problem of imperfect anticipation of income increases could be solved more cheaply by investment in information dissemination, and although the *ex ante* failure to appreciate the consumption benefits of education is rather intractable, one must note that we have very little *ex post* quantitative information about optimal subsidy levels. Brennan further noted that excessive discounting of future benefits by individuals did not justify subsidising education as opposed to other investments but he did admit a case for some type of interference in the face of capital market imperfections. He concluded, however, that 'the precise magnitude of the market failure associated with these problems is extremely difficult to estimate, and consequently so is the optimum size of the subsidy needed to correct this market failure' (p.113). Moreover, capital market failure that penalises the poor especially may establish a case for a government loan system using competitive interest rates, rather than subsidies.

For economic efficiency, fees are required to be abolished only for those induced to attend by fee abolition. The efficiency argument also has equity implications, since across-the-board abolition subsidises all students and is likely to be regressive. As a method of income redistribution, like most piece-meal approaches, fee abolition appears to be an expensive method. In any case, if ability is used as a rationing device, society is favouring the natural and environmentally determined distribution of intelligence, which some may see as no more desirable than the distribution of income.

Brennan argued that if matriculation results were used to identify ability, we needed to discover the association between matriculation performance and (i) the probability of success in higher education, (ii) the size of private returns to higher education, and (iii) the size of spillover returns thus generated. Although university and matriculation performance are positively correlated, 'matriculation performance is only marginally satisfactory as a predictor of success at university' (p.118), and referred to an ANU study of enrolments which showed that the graduation rate *fell* over the early range of matriculation performance. If student motivation can compensate for poor matriculation performance, the use of a price system may be useful in weeding out students of low motivation.

In sum, these arguments were rather hostile to the concept of higher education as a 'basic right' to be provided at zero price. Ability as a rationing device excludes a very large proportion of the population from the benefits of substantial public expenditures. Moreover, to extend these very costly rights to a large section of the population, independent of ability, must inevitably lead to adjustment of average quality downwards in institutions of higher learning.

5.2 Grants and Loans for Tertiary Education

The use of competitive scholarships to finance fees and living expenses has recently been replaced by a system of tertiary education allowances (TEAS). The permanence of this system is open to doubt; the introduction of student loans either to substitute or supplement TEAS has been mooted, interest culminating at the official level in the Butcher Report (1977).

Mathews (1973) provided a useful taxonomy and analysis of systems of loans and grants at this level, distinguishing seven approaches which could be used separately, or in conjunction.[5] As Mathews noted, various combinations of these schemes have been used historically in Australian education.

We begin our discussion of such schemes by noting an egalitarian dilemma. If students are constrained by their own or their parents' current incomes or wealth, many students will be unable to undertake higher education, which will tend to be reserved for the offspring of the wealthy. This seems unfair. But a system of *grants* from society, even if means tested, is also highly selective in that it picks out an intellectual elite to support. Since most taxpayers will not attend tertiary institutions (or will not graduate from them) a system of pure grants smacks very much of turning Robin Hood on his head. This is true whether the benefits of higher education are those of a capital good or of a consumption good. Nor is future tax liability an adequate justification for grants, since all higher incomes yield higher taxes independently of their source.

Without a means test, the burden of grants on the community is often seen as excessive, and also regressive, since on average, tertiary students come from above median income families. But the application of means tests, according to Mathews, tends to be discriminatory and unenforceable, and presupposes non-existent rights of children to dispose of their parents' income for tertiary education. Many students are presumably willing to pay to obtain some measure of independence in their late teens, and there seems to be no good reason to design a system of financial support that denies this privilege to these children whose *parents* happen to be better off than average.

A system of zero allowances may result in inefficiency in human capital accumulation: part-time studies mean slower progress and fewer years to benefit from higher education. Human capital is probably most efficiently accumulated by specialising in its production: most countries report a higher failure rate among part-time students although the reduction of earnings-loss during training offsets this efficiency loss (Chapman 1977).

Such considerations have led some to consider student loans as a basis for educational finance, or at least supplementary finance. This work includes contributions by Thomson (1974a, 1974b), Thomson and Lindner (1975), Weeden (1970, Blair (1973, 1975) and the Butcher Report (1977).

There are particular characteristics of human capital that sharply distinguish it from physical capital and hence lead to inadequate (or non-existent) markets for the financing of human capital formation. Human capital cannot be offered as collateral to the banking system, since it is, by its nature, embodied in the person producing it. The extremely low liquidity of human capital makes risk-averse banking institutions unwilling to hold claims to it. Further, part of the return is in terms of consumption benefits. Thurow (1970) put the difficulties nicely: 'human capital investments must be made at precisely that age when it is most difficult to borrow for any purpose. Credit ratings and collateral assets are just what young persons do not possess, although they may be possessed by their parents. This is not a perfect substitute, however, since parents and children need not agree on what constitutes a good investment' (p.78).

These arguments appear to give the government an important role in compensating for capital market failure. Nevertheless, as Thomson argued, it may not be sufficient to provide a surrogate for a competitive loans market. The reason is that the demand for education is likely to be positively related to household income, while low-wealth households may be highly risk averse, which led Thomson (1974a) to conclude that 'a decision to compensate for differences in risk aversion or income elasticity of demand effects on, say, grounds of equity, would best be executed via means-tested grants' (p.12).

Turning to the mechanics of a loan programme, the problem of default immediately raises its head. Essentially, what is required is that economically-successful borrowers cover the losses of the unsuccessful—as it may prove impossible to accurately forecast lifetime earnings at the time of borrowing. The real issue is whether income-related schemes are feasible. Nerlove (1975) suspects infeasibility because of adverse selection and moral hazard. The first concerns the *ex ante* acceptability to potential high earners of a scheme that penalises them for their success, and bites more deeply, the more successful they are. Clearly a loan system will not work if the only entrants are those with a high probability of failure. The moral hazard problem concerns the *ex post* choice of market income flow and on-the-job-training investments of loan recipients. Since higher earnings are penalised by higher repayments, loan recipients will be discouraged from choosing such earnings profiles, and will be encouraged to substitute leisure and household work for market work and investment in training. According to Nerlove, 'the income profile for the representative borrower may be greatly affected by the terms of the income-contingent loan repayment plan' (p.165).

Lindner and Thomson attempt to estimate the importance of adverse selection and concluded that the danger in an Australian scheme would be small. They noted, however, that their conclusion was sensitive to some of their assumptions.

Regarding fixed-repayment loans, Thomson distinguished *credit foncier* loans (with fixed repayment schedules) and graduated repayment schedules and made some very detailed calculations of the repayments required in all these schemes.

The Butcher Report recommended two inter-related schemes. The first would provide relatively small loans for unanticipated expenditures, with a 1–2 year repayment period, leaving the administering educational institutions to determine whether or not guarantees and interest payments would be involved. The second scheme would be administered through conventional financial institutions, and permit a total accumulated debt of $8000, the loans to be government-guaranteed and interest rates to be determined by the long run bond rate. It does not appear that repayments are to be generally income-related, and many commentators would be concerned that children from working-class backgrounds would be unwilling to absorb substantial debt unless they could somehow underwrite the risk of failure.

Again, females, on average, spend much less time in the labour force than males, have erratic earnings profiles, and may be discriminated against in labour markets, further reducing their lifetime earnings. They will, therefore, have a lower demand price for education, and perhaps may well merit educational (or, perhaps more general) subsidies for the tricks that nature and men play upon them. On the other hand, some students will have no truck with loans at all. The Butcher Report (Sections 3.14, 3.17) noted that strong opposition to any type of student loan was expressed in a set of 1300 individually signed submissions apparently prepared by student organisations, while the AUS member of the Butcher Committee, Mr M. Gallagher, filed a minority report rejecting the concept in principle and suggested instead a maximum in non-repayable grants equal to at least the minimum wage for every student. One doubts that this suggestion will obtain much public support, unless it is backed by some similar commitment to maintain graduate earnings at something close to the minimum wage for a very long time *after* as well as *during* studies.

Blair (1973, 1975) has provided interesting evidence about incentive effects of some types of educational finance. He compared the performance of 127 part-time students awarded Commonwealth Technical Scholarships at NSW technical colleges with one group receiving no aid, and another aided by employers. Only the *employer*-aided group had significantly better performance than the no-aid group. Indeed, many scholarship recipients reported reducing their educational effort compared to earlier stages. Blair argued that one impact of scholarships may be to give students an inflated evaluation of their abilities. The good performance of the employer-aided group may be due to the personal interest and surveillance of employers, and support being tied to the maintenance of demonstrably adequate standards of achievement.

Another method of financing educational expenditures is the payment of grants or salaries to students during training, and bonding them to the financing institution for subsequent service. For a number of years, the main form of teacher recruitment involved trainees receiving tuition and substantial allowances, while, as a *quid pro quo*, contracting to remain in the State Education Department for several years. The implications of such financing were examined by Burke (1976) and Selby Smith (1973), who found that the terms of the financial provision were substantially in favour of the recipients.

Selby Smith noted that the presence of a fairly flat earnings profile over the teaching life cycle had implications for turnover. Although bonding prevented some immediate resignations, teachers found it profitable to quit early before their human capital became highly specific to the institution employing them. Moreover, the salary structure may have deterred highly motivated and competent potential teachers from entering teaching, and encouraged some to switch to more lucrative administrative duties. The consequence was an expected low average age of teachers, with low retention rates (because of low salary growth rates over the life cycle). The absence of differentials between different schools was seen as leading to lower quality teaching in areas with poorer working conditions, for which random teacher assignment (as in South Australia) can only partly compensate.

Burke examined the Victorian bonding scheme's ability to provide a desired workforce efficiently. Undergraduate education is essentially general, which bonding effectively transforms into *specific* teaching skills for a period of time. The impact of bonding was to reduce resignations temporarily over the first three years of service. Dividing estimated discounted cost per trainee by average length of service gave an estimated cost per year of service equal to about 25 per cent of a beginning teacher's yearly salary, leading Burke to conclude that 'the case against the studentship scheme looks very strong on these calculations' (p.44).

5.3 Vouchers for Education

The concept of educational vouchers, first thoroughly developed by Friedman (1962), has received strong advocacy in Australia from Burke (1970, 1973, 1975). An education voucher is essentially a coupon with a prescribed purchasing power, but assigned to *parents*, who have the freedom to use the voucher to purchase any form of 'approved' education. Certain minimum standards under which schools could offer educational services would be determined, formulated and policed by a central authority, perhaps involving licences of a kind required before professional persons are permitted to enter private practice. The value of the voucher would be financed out of general taxation revenue. State institutions could co-exist with private profit-making firms and could compete on equal terms. Many schemes envisage parents being able to supplement vouchers where extra-curricular activities are desired. Education would presumably still be compulsory until a given age is reached, but education need not be homogeneous across schools.

Burke claimed the following advantages. First, schools would be free to develop to satisfy different parental/student demands. At present, only those parents who can afford to locate themselves suitably, or are willing to meet the very high incremental cost of private education can satisfy demands for a 'different' education, or an education involving 'different' teaching methods, a point emphasized in the position paper prepared by the Curriculum Development Centre (1976). Second, freedom of choice would promote efficiency and an 'appropriate' output composition. Under the present state system there is little pressure to perform well. Cost-minimising techniques would be encouraged, while flexible appointments and promotions would see teaching staff allocated to areas in which the value of their services was highest, aiding both recruitment and retention of competent teachers. With a flexible price structure, the system would be responsive to demand changes and receptive to demonstrated innovations in educational techniques. Thus Burke (1970) concluded that the voucher system 'may lead to a fairly competitive market for educational services, with some consequent stimulus to avoiding waste and to producing the type of schooling desired', while voucher supporters 'forsee not only the growth of choice between existing schools but an increase in the variety of schooling, and hence a greater satisfaction of different (and especially minority) needs' (pp.129–30).

Expansion of choice may also lead to an increase in parental concern and interest in education, to parental encouragement to reinforce a type of schooling that they have chosen with desirable effects on student achievement. At present, there is very little accountability to users of the education industry, and parents may be intimidated in their attempts to have school performance modified to their tastes, because of potential boomerang teacher reaction on their children who are zoned to attend specific schools.

Mathews (1973) argued that vouchers would not avoid the social and distributional disadvantages of a *laissez-faire* system. Even if all students receive the same voucher, richer parents would still be free to supplement educational expenditures from their own resources. Since the equity argument is so vital in the education field, this point of view raises two important issues.

The first is to note that rich people can *always* supplement any 'basic' expenditures on *any* commodity but this has not led to the scrapping of the market system in Australia for most other commodities. As Blaug (1970) points out, some people have a basic objection to the use of purchasing power for distributing educational services. As long as parents are assigned both the duties and the rights to bring up their children as they see fit, it is not altogether clear why this principle is held so firmly.

Reasons which could be advanced include, first, that it may be difficult for many parents to judge the quality of any particular school, especially without first permitting their children to attend for a fairly lengthy period of time. Second, the lack of sensible judgement of other goods and services is often detected and remedied easily because they are consumed by the purchaser; not so for education. Third, in the case of errors of judgement, children rather than purchasers of educational services suffer. Finally, it is arguable that decisions made for the next generation should not automatically build in and reinforce the inequalities prevalent in the current generation.

These arguments are serious, but essentially relate to the *generality of use* of vouchers, rather than disqualifying them entirely. Parents unwilling or unable to evaluate schooling could be permitted to opt out of vouchers and their children assigned state education directly. Schools would have to meet minimal standards and their continuation would depend on their parent/child-assessed quality of output. The second and third objections imply that parents are indifferent or casual or unable to make judgements about their children's schooling. For these parents, vouchers would be cumbersome relative to state education, and presumably would not be chosen. But deeply committed parents capable of detecting school inadequacies and who were prepared to search for high-quality educational services presumably would not be so easily dissuaded from the merits of vouchers.

Mathews (1968) argued that a voucher system would lead to oligopolistic rather than competitive market structures, implying a tendency towards excess capacity and resource waste. Certainly outside large conurbations, this may be a valid point. It is less evident that it would be relevant in Australia's major cities.

The second issue is whether the 'typical' voucher proposal, which might be termed the 'unregulated market model', can be modified to meet the equity arguments since this is where much hostility is evident (Norris 1975). Burke (1975) noted that 'the anticipated result of this proposal would be to increase the advantages of the middle and upper classes in access to school resources and to provide insufficient safeguards to prevent exploitation of disadvantaged children' (p.1). This problem has led to the design of several 'compensatory' voucher schemes.

Burke reported that the implementation of one type of compensatory voucher scheme met with considerable opposition in the U.S., but was introduced in 1972–1973 as a pilot scheme in the eastern suburbs of San Jose, California. Six elementary schools initially participated, followed by another seven. Parental support for the demonstration rose during the year, as did the proportion of parents favouring increased parental influence in school operations. Burke reported the major change to be that to teaching and school administration staff, teachers reporting greater autonomy, teamwork, and ability to innovate, but also reporting additions to workload and some threats to security caused by the mobility of children away from the less well-performed schools.

Could such a demonstration be carried out in Australia? Burke suggested that centralisation of appointments and expenditures makes local demonstration more difficult, but noted that the trend towards decentralisation in recent years makes it easier to think of now.

As matters stand, Australian parents who wish to opt out of government schooling must make substantial sacrifices. An alternative, suggested by Sheehan (1975), would be to make available to *parents* choosing independent schools a basic recurrent grant equal to some proportion of the average recurrent costs of educating a child in a government school. The grant is envisaged as being taxable but would replace state aid to schools and tax concessions to parents. Sheehan argued that poor parents would not be penalised in choosing high quality education, but all parents would pay some price (albeit an income-related price) for the privilege of opting out of the government system. However, Sheehan's scheme requires that schools have access to parents' income-tax data, which surely disqualifies it as a practical proposition.

Another alternative of Mathews (1973) is to provide state aid to private schools which would not be permitted to charge fees. Schools would then be similar to universities, with freedom of curriculum and appointment of staff. It is unclear how excess demand for places in high-standard schools would be removed.

Section 6 Rates of Return to Education

There have been a handful of studies examining the profitability of investments in education in Australia, forming part of the now well-established international literature which has been reviewed recently by Blaug (1976). There is a continuing debate on the meaning of the rates of return to educational investments. 'Human capital' theory argues that the rate of return derives from increases in productive capabilities resulting from skill acquisition during schooling. Other theorists have invoked the so-called 'screening hypothesis' to account for the returns to schooling. This hypothesis asserts that credentials acquired through schooling processes are simply an important sieving device used by employers to sort 'talented' wheat from 'untalented' chaff. Passing the screen yields a *private* return—but no increment of productive capability arises from schooling, so that the *social* returns from schooling are independent of earnings distributions (even if such distributions reflect productive differences among individuals). The meaning of 'social' rates of return to educational investments is problematical; but the meaning of 'private' rates of return (which depend simply on earnings differences, however these arise) is not. Although schooling may serve in part as a screening device, evidence from overseas suggests it is unlikely to be simply or even predominantly a screening device (Layard and Psacharopoulos 1974).

The Australian empirical studies were undertaken by Selby Smith (1975b), Blandy and Goldsworthy (1976), Chapman (1977), O'Byrne (1971) and Davis (forthcoming). In addition, there have been some studies using the human capital model to investigate broad educational policy questions including Parish (1965), Niland (1974), and Maglen (forthcoming). Like all cost-benefit analyses of activities in which perfect markets are not operating (which is generally what inspires such analyses in the first place) these rate of return studies are subject to considerable limitations. They may detect gross misallocations and trends in the economic attractiveness of schooling investments—especially in predicting likely *shortages* in demands for places in educational institutions.

Blandy and Goldsworthy dealt with private rates of return to education in South Australia in 1969. Their cross sectional data on *gross* incomes bias their estimates upwards (especially of private, after tax, rates of return) partly by attributing all of the increment in earnings to the education increment rather than in part to other associated factors (such as family background, native ability, and so on). Also, insofar as the supply and demand balance for different groups of educated workers is changing, the estimates derived from a cross-section may be quite misleading. Last, no account was taken of costs and benefits of a non-monetary kind. These limitations apply to most of the other studies. The rates of return estimated were about 14 per cent to upper secondary schooling and University first degrees (without Commonwealth Scholarship support), which appears to be broadly comparable to other advanced countries' estimates and suggests that in general the incentives to invest in education have been attractive compared with other possibilities for investment. Because of recent occupational downgrading of formal 'credentials' and the recent compression of earnings ratios one suspects that the rates have fallen.

Selby Smith calculated private and social benefit/cost ratios for 1969 for various post-secondary courses in Universities and CAEs, using cross-section data of earnings before tax for the social and after tax for the private estimates. They are subject to the inherent weaknesses of cross-sectional comparisons referred to (although explicit adjustment for long-term change is attempted) and like other studies involve numerous challengeable assumptions.

Selby Smith's results, by and large, show educational investment as less attractive than Blandy and Goldsworthy. Unless students are in receipt of some financial assistance, private benefit/cost ratios were less than unity (the rate of return is less than 8 per cent) for a number of undergraduate degree courses. Social benefit/cost ratios were somewhat greater for these courses but a number were still poor investments, as were most Masters and Ph.D. degrees. Higher degrees were a better investment on a private calculus, however; widespread financial assistance for higher degree students makes these courses appear distinctly attractive. Dentistry, Law, Economics, Medicine and Science emerged as the best investment options both privately and socially.

CAE courses fared somewhat better than University courses—especially the certificate, technician and trade courses, the first appearing to be astoundingly good value for money both as private and social investment.

Chapman examined the private rate of return to holding a degree in the Australian Public Service, using cross-section 1974 earnings data on 77000 full-time officers in the Second and Third Division. After allowing for inflation, he found earnings of graduates close to those found by Blandy and Goldsworthy, though earnings of non-graduates were almost 8 per cent greater. In consequence, the estimated rate of return was less than the earlier South Australian estimate. Chapman confirmed that the estimates were quite sensitive to the earnings or financial support students receive during their studies.

O'Byrne used 1968–69 cross-section data in a linear programming model for educational planning in New South Wales from 1970–1980. He also calculated private rates of return to tertiary education. His estimated rates of return were large—15–16 per cent for CAE and University courses, and 34 per cent for Teachers' Colleges courses! His linear programming model gave the same qualitative results, and led him to conclude that there would be growing excess demand for higher education places throughout the 1970s, a not unpopular conclusion when he came to it, but now rather overtaken by events.

Davis used manpower forecasting techniques to modify cross-section estimates of future earnings, thus estimating the expected future rate of return to medical education in Australian. He critically reviewed the Australian University Commission's Medical Manpower plan for 1971–1991, pointing out that a great 'oversupply' of doctors might well result from that plan. But even if an 'oversupply' of doctors were to materialise, the social rate of return to medical education might still justify the projected rate of output of doctors. The paper highlighted the inadequacies of manpower forecasting for educational planning purposes used independently of techniques which seek to *evaluate* the educational changes involved.

The broad conclusions of these studies for educational policy are that post-secondary education 'pays' both as a private and social investment (or has appeared to do so until recently). Lower-level post-secondary courses are probably a better investment at present than degree or diploma courses. These studies all show (as does Maglen's study), that the level of financial support has very strong effects on the private viability of educational investments. The more recently based Chapman and Davis studies, reveal the possibility that rates of return to tertiary education have fallen or will fall in the future.

The only attempt to consider retraining in Australia from a human capital vantage was made by Niland. No empirical estimates of the viability of manpower retraining are attempted, but Niland proposed a human-capital cost-benefit framework by which such an evaluation could be attempted. He suggested that training and retraining have received insufficient emphasis in Australia because formal education has received the lion's share of government subsidies and because the award wage structure has compressed earnings differences to a degree which has made unsubsidised training unprofitable both for individuals and for employers. He urged a greater use of transfer payments such as negative income taxes and wage subsidies to protect egalitarian income distribution goals, rather than establishing a wage structure which may be associated with strong disemployment effects. He cautioned that without an evaluation system for training and retraining, inefficiency in allocation and inappropriate budget size are likely to be associated with an expanded training effort.

Section 7 Production Functions in Education

In principle, each educational institution can be envisaged as a firm transforming inputs into educational outputs. The 'firm's' decision problem is to maximise an objective function of educational outputs (such as cognitive achievement and affective development of its students) subject to the educational production function, a set of input prices, and, perhaps, a constraint on levels of total expenditures.

Notwithstanding considerable theoretical-estimation problems, a large literature on the effectiveness of educational inputs has emerged overseas. The results of these studies are ably reviewed by Averch *et al.* (1974) and Spady (1973). An appropriate point of departure is the controversial work of Coleman *et al.* (1966), who found systematic influences for peer group and socio-economic status variables in the educational production function, but no such influence for levels of school resource inputs. Averch *et al.* claimed that re-analysis of the Coleman data has failed to establish or disprove the importance of peer group effects found to be of considerable importance in the Coleman study. Secondly, background variables generally emerge as important variables determining achievement, either directly or through influences on students' attitudes and motivation. 'Background' is generally measured by socio-economic status of family and community, and is claimed by Averch *et al.* to account on average for about 15 per cent of variation in educational outcomes. Compensatory education, then, appears to have something to compensate for; the point is, can increases in school resources do the trick?

This is far from clear. Averch *et al.* claimed that school resources are rarely important determinants of outcomes, appearing to add only an additional 1 per cent of explanatory power. They can only explain about 5 per cent of achievement variation in the absence of background factors. Because of the methodological problems involved, however, Averch *et al.* were worried about accepting their own conclusion that 'the resources for which school systems have traditionally been willing to pay a premium—teachers' experience, reduced class size, and teachers' advanced degrees—do not appear to have been of great value' (p.53). Spady, however, claimed that Averch *et al.* reached conclusions that were in places 'too general and somewhat misleading' and believed that his analysis 'supports the principle of concentrating expenditures on personnel rather than on tangible facilities' (Spady, p.201).

It is important to emphasise the tentative nature of these results. The educational production function will differ across pupils, and most studies are highly aggregated, dealing with average school or school district performance rather than individual pupil performance. Summers and Wolfe (1977) argued that the level of aggregation was too high to unscramble the effects of variations in school inputs. In their sample of Philadelphia sixth-grade students certain specific school inputs, particularly teacher quality, school size and peer group effects for low-achievers explained variations in changes in performance on a per-pupil basis. Parents' income had little impact on learning once interactions with school inputs were accounted for, and so did the general physical facilities of schools.

Finally, educational production function studies may omit crucial variables. Positive student orientations towards learning may reflect, according to McDill (1969), the interest that parents (as perceived by teachers) show in the educational policies of the school and the academic progress of their children (p.218). This is of major interest, especially for compensatory education. It may mean that low socio-economic status of parents is not required to be compensated *per se*, but instead parental indifference to their children's achievement, which might be (but surely is not necessarily) correlated with socio-economic status. Moreover, this view may provide some clue to the alleged failure of compensatory education programmes in the US and elsewhere, since an increase in public expenditures on schooling may, as Becker and Tomes (1976) argued, lead some parents to substitute public expenditures for their own outlays of income and time, so that parental reinforcement of schooling may well be lost. These matters have not been explored much, but may well be important in explaining the link between status and achievement, since, at present, it is by no means evident how family income, occupation, and education gets translated into a flow of educational services as opposed to merely being determinants of (or correlated with) aspirations and/or innate ability. The case for a devolution of power over children's schooling from bureaucrats and teachers to parents, by providing parents with the means to make more real choices, garners support from these studies.

Results of Australian studies by Rosier (1973) and Comber and Keeves (1975) have recently been surveyed by Keeves (1975). They refer to disparities in achievement (average performances in word knowledge and science) and attainment (years of schooling) across schools and States in Australia. At the 14 year-old level, no significant differences between States emerged for the word knowledge test, but highly significant differences were observed for achievement in science, the best being Queensland, South Australia, and Western Australia, and the worst being Victoria and Tasmania. At terminal levels, there were significant State differences in achievement with Queensland, South Australia, and Victoria starring in word knowledge, and South Australia particularly meritorious in science achievement.

In general, attainment is higher in independent and metropolitan schools. Independent schools generally outperform the others in word knowledge and science at the 14 year-old level, and in turn, Catholic schools show achievement levels that are generally greater than in government schools. Although it is not clear what the contribution of different resources are to these outcomes, Catholic schools in general are known to 'suffer' from poorer physical school facilities and equipment. In the terminal secondary year there appears little systematic difference between different types of schools, because, it is argued, selection has already taken place.

Data from the International Education Association (IEA) science project have been used to evaluate the effect of socio-economic status and cultural background in explaining achievement. The IEA index is a weighted combination of father's education and occupation, mother's education, use of dictionary, number of books in the household, and family size. Keeves claimed that this measure of the cultural level of households was a better explanatory variable than more conventional indexes of status, explaining 40 per cent of the variation in performance at the 14 year-old level, and 5 per cent at the terminal level.

The IEA science sample has been used to account for low performing schools. Rosier gives some evidence on the reasons for low performance, and finds that only *one* factor associated with resource availability, namely, the quantity of laboratory assistants and ancilliary staff, could account for low (science) performance. Instead, he found that the more time spent by teachers in preparation, the greater their practical experience, the greater the emphasis laid on information content as well as method, and the higher the level of teachers' training in physics, the higher the students' science scores.

Thus, although the Australian evidence is highly fragmentary, many conclusions appear to be in accord with those found in overseas studies. The accumulated evidence suggests that ploughing on with expenditures, especially those which do not induce increases in teacher quality, may be socially wasteful, and would at least seem to require more substantive *a priori* justification.

Section 8 Cost Functions for Australian Education

It is reasonable to expect that teaching costs per student will fall over a sizeable range of output in various educational institutions. But significant diseconomies of large size might also quickly emerge. Stretton (1965) has argued that the idea of efficiency measurement in universities is a useful but hazardous procedure; variations in the quality of graduates, the efficiency of communication within and between departments, staff-student frustrations, and the merit of research are difficult to allow for. Stretton presumes they all worsen as a consequence of larger size. He describes large universities as 'monsters providing the services that only monsters can' (p.89). Hall (1965) also seriously questions the efficiency of large size in universities, believing that unit costs would not fall once 3000–4000 students are reached.

The Australian evidence on this point is provided by Mathews (1968), Williams (1972), Selby Smith (1973b), a substantial recent contribution by Selby Smith (1975d), and Hind (1977). All the work, except Hind's, concerns tertiary education. Mathews 1968 data from the Australian National University suggested a marked difference in marginal costs between science and nonscience faculties, the incremental cost being 3 times as large for an additional science student. Fixed costs are also substantially larger for science enrolments, making average costs highly dependent on departmental size and composition of the student population. The form of the cost function estimated cannot be used to evaluate *optimal* scale at the faculty level, but simply to assert 'the larger the better'.

Selby Smith (1975d), building on his earlier 1973 work on University Faculty costs, demonstrated a very wide disparity in unit costs across CAE's, with the lowest found in the established metropolitan Victorian Colleges. Average costs were also highly variable with engineering, art, and architecture relatively expensive, and part-time certificate and technicians' courses having a unit cost of only about one third of corresponding diploma courses.

Both Williams and Selby Smith estimated average costs per equivalent full-time student in universities. According to Selby Smith, average costs in veterinary science were over 3 times as large as in the least expensive course, economics; over twice as large in agricultural science, medicine, dentistry and engineering; science was some 63 per cent greater, while architecture, arts, education and law courses were slightly higher than for economics. Very similar quantitative results, but using a different data set, are obtained in the Williams study. Comparisons with costs per student in CAE's show much higher average costs in Universities in general, although the cost differences are less dramatic for comparable degree/diploma courses.

There are, however, two major provisos to consider. First, educational output (to which the costs refer) is unlikely to be simply proportional to student numbers. There may be differentials in drop-out, wastage, and repetition rates between CAE's and universities. If these are greater for CAE's, they will appear artificially cheaper vehicles for educational production. The second is that quality may not be homogeneous within and between institutions in a given tertiary sector, and may be quite different between sectors. Unless diplomas and degrees are perfect substitutes, CAE's average cost estimates again may not make useful comparisons with universities. A quick check of income differentials of diploma and degree holders would have provided a rough index of this quality differential, but Selby Smith does not consider this matter.

A major difficulty in interpreting these cost estimates relates to Selby Smith's necessarily partly arbitrary allocation of costs between courses—even where they appear to be truly joint to several courses. The arbitrary procedures seem plausible, but it is well to remember that they remain arbitrary, and to this extent so are Selby Smith's estimates.

Selby Smith also estimated economies of scale in CAE's and Universities, being concerned with the behaviour of average cost as the scale of production rises. Considering the plethora of small, decentralised tertiary institutions developed in Australia in the 1970s, much interest is attached to the scale features of their cost functions.

For purposes of inference, however, certain stringent conditions must be met. What one is ideally looking for is *the minimum cost* of producing a given output level, over the range of feasible output levels. Selby Smith however used the data available to estimate cross-section *average expenditure* relationships with respect to enrolments as of 1969. He noted a considerable number of qualifications to his procedure, finally concluding that 'if analysis reveals that larger scale is associated with lower expenditures per student it is not possible to determine, in the last resort, to what extent this is due to technical economies of scale rather than to administrative decisions which embody rules under which larger scale programmes or institutions tend to be less generously funded per student' (p.37).

Selby Smith first estimated a set of regression equations of expenditures per student in CAE's on varying enrolment levels. A quadratic costs function was used, but he noted that enrolment growth rates were not considered, so that educational institutions were assumed to work at full capacity.

Adjusting for course-mix, but not for differences in educational quality, region, age, or multi-campus institutions, Selby Smith's estimates produced evidence of scale economies in CAE's over a substantial initial range. University cost functions were estimated by faculty and by entire university enrolments, obtaining statistically significant coefficients for all 80-odd faculties. For instance, the implied optimal enrolments of economics students per institution is 1720, and of science students nearly 3000.

We have pointed to the problem of allocation of apparently joint costs, which reduces fixed costs and raises average and marginal costs associated with enrolments. There are also problems associated with the allocation of research costs. But his results of large economies of scale are at least a challenge to those who argue for small-scale institutions, and on a generous interpretation give some idea of the costs associated with not offending the sensibilities of those who believe that small is beautiful.

Hind estimated cost functions for primary schools in rural areas to investigate whether savings could be made from consolidation of rural schools in response to the progressive rural depopulation of New South Wales. Hind, like others, skirted quality problems by choosing an administrator's model of educational *services* (students 'processed'). He found that economies of scale were exhausted when primary schools reach a size of 200 enrolments—both for instruction and for maintenance. In fact, it was only the per pupil costs of really tiny one-teacher schools that were very much above the others. Schools with as few as 70 pupils are hardly more costly (per student) than schools of 200 or more. On the other hand, he found some evidence to show slight *diseconomies* of scale at enrolments of 600 or more. These results confirm U.S. findings.

Hind's paper is particularly interesting for the light it throws on the economics of decentralising the State primary school system into smaller, self-administered units. On Hind's evidence, deschooling characterised, say, by teacher-mothers forming small neighbourhood schools of 50–100 children would not be a very costly option for the education system to pursue. Hind's paper is relevant to the State Aid debate as well, since alleged scale economies have been one of the main arguments advanced by protagonists of centralised State systems against State Aid.

Section 9 *Manpower Planning for Education in Australia*

The observed structure of any education system has been influenced *inter alia*, by educationists and teachers, the demands of individuals seeking education, the 'requirements' of the economy; and, increasingly, by governments involved for reasons of social policy. Governments have tried sometimes to reconcile the different interests. It is not surprising that the reconciliations adopted yield different labour market outcomes for lengthily-schooled people.

Should government attempt to anticipate and take measures against prospective professional labour market imbalances? Here there are broadly three options (Blaug 1970, Chap. 7; Australian Department of Labour 1974a):

(a) leave individuals and institutions or firms to anticipate and adjust to market situations, with little or no government intervention,
(b) plan on the basis of medium to long term forecasts to reduce likely market imbalances,
(c) promote the speedy working of market forces, on the basis of early warning indicators of developing market imbalances, with the aim of lessening the scale and duration of the imbalances.

Most Western countries have tended to move away from (a) both because of the personal hardships involved in incorrect market anticipations, and because of the difficulty of adjusting the public education structure in response to potentially volatile private demands. Also, the countries that have made serious attempts at (b) have sought flexibility in action largely because of the failure of forecasts, particularly long-term forecasts of industrial manpower requirements (Ahamad and Blaug 1973). Thus there has been a widespread and gradual increase of interest in (c) which provides manpower planners with a visible correction of unemployment and shortages of skilled manpower, but which is less obviously effective for educational planners as a means of adjusting educational facilities to the processes of markets.

The problem of imbalance for educational facilities is particularly difficult to solve. The supply of teachers and facilities must be planned on the basis of forecasts of, at the very least, three years ahead; and once the educational institutions are set in their geographical locations it is not easy to dispel excess capacity in response to unforeseen changes in demand (Australian Universities Commission 1976, p.42). Further, the basis of planning is often contentious. Educational systems, from schools through to universities, have been planned so that parts of their activities cover general education and the disciplined development of knowledge for its own sake, independently of the training requirements of industry (whether those requirements have been expressed by employers or students). Thus, education has in this sense a life of its own. But moves in the 1960s and 1970s in most countries towards flexibility of training to lessen the effects of imbalances have begun, slowly, to feed back towards the planning of general education. This process has led to increased liaison between manpower and educational administrators and, through the increasing flow of information into schools about job opportunities, has blurred the distinction between individual choice and industrial needs in education.

Karmel, for example, has been concerned with the impact of rapid tertiary growth on labour market conditions. In fact, in 1975, the annual output of University graduates was double his anticipations thirteen years earlier (1962, p.34). In 1962 he had concluded that 'in the latter part of the 1960's there may well be a relative plenty of graduates' (p.34). By 1977, Karmel claimed that further increases in the graduate output rate 'inevitably means that graduates must accept positions lower in the job hierarchy' (1977a, pp.9–10). Two years earlier he had argued that although increased numbers of graduates may be expected to find jobs (so that structural unemployment among the skilled should not emerge) the jobs might not be those that had been expected, and might be jobs for which degrees were not previously required (1975, p.269). Karmel also invoked the 'screening hypothesis', claiming that 'employers require high qualifications, frequently as a selecting device' (1975, p.208), and that the labour market was becoming 'accustomed' to employing graduates at the expense of young, unskilled persons. A reason for the latter given in 1977 was that unemployment could be expected to be concentrated among the young unskilled workers, since 'an employer will not be prepared to pay a wage to a young person if he believes his contribution to the enterprise is worth less than the wage' (1977a, p.10). Karmel not only rejected the use of manpower forecasting, especially for people with generalised qualifications (because of associated wide forecast errors), but also disagreed with Mathews (1972) who favoured the use of social rates of return to education, or the use of cost/benefit ratios, as guides to optimal levels of educational output (1977a, p.14).

An excess supply of graduates *might* be adjusted by a compression of skilled/unskilled wage differentials, rather than by allocating lengthily—schooled workers to less skilled jobs while the wage structure remains intact. The extent to which relative wages are set independently of supply and demand balances matters greatly. If markets do not adjust by wage flexibility, they will adjust by 'job-flexibility', and those without existing 'property rights' in a job will be severely disadvantaged because all the adjustment will be thrown on such entrants to the labour market, rather than the adjustment being borne over all workers.

Karmel has implicitly taken the view that relative occupational wages are sufficiently 'sticky' in Australia that most adjustment in the graduate labour market will be thrown onto occupational grading patterns of graduates rather than onto relative wage changes. This view receives some Australian support from Freebairn and Withers (1977) who have demonstrated that the coefficient of variation of relative occupational wages is much less than the coefficient of variation of occupational employment, unemployment and vacancies. Similar behaviour in the United States graduate labour market has been observed by Freeman (1976a). As Freeman and Freebairn and Withers have pointed out, this form of market adjustment makes manpower forecasting *more* rather than less viable as a tool for considering the manpower 'requirements' of the economy. Blandy (1978) has recently prepared some manpower forecasts for Australia for the year 2000 based on two scenarios of possible future economic development. Although the scenarios differ greatly, the 'requirements' of lengthily-schooled workers in each (based on 1971 occupational gradings of formal credentials) show much less variation than is observed in current output. Further, in each scenario, dramatically fewer educational resources are required than presently exist.

Hence, Karmel has been quite correct in emphasising the occupational downgrading of graduate credentials likely to ensue from the educational expansion of the 1960s and 1970s. And while we would agree that manpower forecasting (or rate of return analysis, for that matter) is insufficiently accurate to 'fine tune' the capacities of the educational institutions to the economy's 'needs' (even if this were desirable), the gross imbalance which can now be foreseen by manpower forecasting between educational capacity and economic 'needs' suggests that total rejection of manpower forecasting could lead to very costly errors.[6]

Some measure of the potential for occupational downgrading of graduate credentials in Australia (mirroring events in North America and Western Europe) can be gained by observing that in 1957 there were only 3382 new first degree students graduating from Australian Universities; in 1976 there were 23025! This takes no account of growth in the rest of the tertiary education sector. The stock of employed first degree graduates in 1971 in Australia was 128212. This stock is currently being augmented by more than 10 per cent per annum. Since the labour force is growing by much less than 3 per cent per annum, it is clear that the potential exists for a severe downward adjustment in graduates' earnings and job opportunities.

Given such a now-glaring imbalance, it surely cannot be sufficient to reject manpower forecasting or rates of return techniques without specifying some alternatives. Educational expenditure is surely immensely greater at present than would be reflected by purely private demands for education. That there is no objectively optimal level of educational expenditure because decisions on public education are 'political' is not really very helpful, least of all to politicians. Without specific objectives, almost any policy can be rationalised on an *ad hoc* basis. In a world of tightening government budget constraints, demands for social reform cannot simply be translated into licences to spend. We would be dubious both about Karmel's claim that increases in the supply of educated persons has increased the demand for them (and that one cannot separate these effects) (1974, p.267) and his suggestion that society should 're-design those activities in which people spend so much of their lives in order to provide suitable employment for a better educated workforce' (1976, p.15). The latter seems to suggest that society should bear the costs of financing an expanded education system and then bear the further costs of nonoptimal factor proportions and/or output composition so that the excess supply of graduates may be 'suitably' employed. This appears to be the sort of bind that the legitimation of income differences solely through schooling credentials inevitably leads to; (compare 'egalitarian' Communist economies where the oversupply of 'credentialled' workers fit for 'complex' work is of large dimensions contrasting with shortages of supply for simple labour, Szelenyi, 1977).

Forecasts of manpower requirements may be useful—and even vital—for educational planning in detecting potential imbalances of an extreme kind whose consequences would be unacceptable. On the other hand, given the possibility for forecasting errors and flexibilities in markets and institutions, a narrower use of manpower forecasting is likely to be unhelpful.

The best uses for the approach are to provide a reference point for forecasts of specific occupations, and as a means of simulating extreme *possibilities* in occupational and educational requirements as a backdrop to assessing the adequacy of educational plans to meet such a range of contingencies.

Methods are gradually being improved and for this reason their usefulness is increasing (Freeman 1976b).

Only one piece of work on educational planning comparable with overseas techniques has been published in Australia (Blandy 1978). It is likely, however, that more sophisticated simulations of demand for various skill groups will emerge as part of the 'IMPACT Project', a joint research effort of a number of Australian government agencies looking at dynamic models of Australian industry, employment and demographic structure. Australian work in this area has lagged about a decade behind work overseas, possibly because there has been less call to use it in educational planning. The immigration programme has taken some of the pressure off the home education system to provide industrial manpower requirements. The skill-selective aspects of the immigration programme have been based both on Department of Labour assessments of requirements and on employer nominations. This has resulted in educational forecasting attention being focused more on the demand for enrolments.

The Commissions advising the Minister of Education have from time to time reported their views on the manpower implications of specific submissions before them. However, the main responsibility for monitoring supply and demand in each occupational market has lain with the Department of Employment and Industrial Relations (and the Department of Immigration) and their precursors and successors, especially since the post-1960 upsurge of interest in structural unemployment. The Department's published work has focused on both industrial and occupational employment, and has provided a source of data for educational planners.

The early 1960s marked the beginnings of the collection of the detailed data needed. In an address in 1967 on 'Manpower Planning in Australia' (Bury 1967), the Minister for Labour and National Service made clear the government's explicit intention to assist in the workings of markets rather than to plan them on the basis of forecasts. The focus was on the achievement of full employment of people *after* their chosen education was completed and avoiding *comprehensive* planning. *Ad hoc* intervention in matters of manpower usage and in education increased throughout the 1960s and early 1970s.

An overseas mission comprising senior representative of trade unions, employer organisations and the Department of Labour and National Service found that:

> in most countries there is a close link between the general education system and the training of skilled workers and that in many the actual training of skilled workers is regarded as a continuation of the education process and comes within the jurisdiction of the Education Department. In countries where there is an apprenticeship type system of training in the hands of organisations other than the Department of Education, close links are maintained with the education authorities (Australian Department of Labour and National Service 1970, p.13)

This report initiated wide-scale and continuing debate and was the forerunner of a series of six reports (Australian Department of Labour 1974(a); 1974(b); 1974(c); Kangan 1974 and 1975; Cochrane (1975) which provide an inter-related coverage of manpower, training and some educational aspects of labour market analysis. In presenting three of them to the House of Representatives, the Minister responsible, Mr Clyde Cameron, commented:

> Previous governments have sought to tackle the manpower problems arising from change by a series of *ad hoc* methods applied band-aid fashion after the damage has been done. There has been no overall manpower strategy which seeks to integrate the nation's economic requirements with the social needs and aspirations of individual Australians. These 3 reports on Australia's labour market development and policy needs provide the groundwork on which to construct the manpower programmes which will constitute an active manpower policy for Australia. (Cameron 1974, pp.6–7 and 9)

It was seen as necessary to 'head off' situations of labour market imbalance as well as to 'cope' with them (Australian Department of Labour 1974(c), p.124). Forecasts were to be short term: 'periods of three to twelve months ahead and certainly not more' (p.142). In the same context, an 'active manpower policy' was seen to be one of continuing manpower training and re-training (p.129). The basic aim was still the promotion of market flexibility rather than comprehensive planning on the basis of long-term forecasts, although such forecasts were not ruled out as possibly having some value.

There has been a good deal of academic comment on forecasting manpower requirements in Australia (Gates 1972, pp.33–34; Radford 1968, pp.31–37; Molhuysen 1966; Davidson 1970; University of Queensland 1968; Vaizey 1973; Hall 1965; Beaumont 1974; Mortensen 1971). To us, it appears to break little new ground. Niland's reviews of manpower planning (1973, 1974a) made in the wake of six reports, attempted to raise 'fundamental questions' about a possible transition from aiming mainly for flexibility to more positive planning based on projections.

Niland's interest was to have a list of these 'fundamental questions' put before 'unions, employers, government departments and other interested groups' so that they could 'clearly signal their attitude on specific options'. They might indicate general dislike of planning aspects of the options, in which case the present flexible approach based on current data and short-term projections would presumably prevail. Alternatively, some planning options could be taken up. In the latter case educational planners would need to take more account of manpower requirements. The question of how heavily manpower requirements should weigh, or indeed whether there is much conflict between manpower and other purposes, is by no means clear in current debate.

The TAFE Reports 'adopted' the following position:

> There are at least two alternatives to the emphases that can be given to the purpose of technical colleges and like institutions. A manpower orien-

> tation expresses their purpose as being to produce the skilled manpower necessary to the development of the economy. An educational and social emphasis is on their function to enable people to develop their potential as individuals but within the realities of the job opportunities by means of which they are aiming to use their education to earn a livelihood. The Committee has adopted the educational and social purpose of technical and further education as the more appropriate, without overlooking TAFE's vital manpower role. (Kangan 1974, p.xxvii)

The Committee did not attempt to deal with how the *quantitative* manpower needs of industry might be determined.

Another stance taken by the TAFE Committee was to recommend education to promote flexibility of occupational choice. At the same time it placed great emphasis on 'unrestricted access to recurrent education' (1974, p.xxxvi) without ascertaining what benefits the community might reap in return for the costs of training facilities and of lost time by those being retrained.

The last report published, the Cochrane report (1975), led to the establishment of the National Employment and Training Scheme (NEAT). It recommended, *inter alia*, that the Department of Labour collect information on, and monitor, changes occurring in the labour market both in terms of occupations and regions; that an energetic programme of research be directed towards the provision of information regarding Australia's future manpower requirements; and that early action be taken to establish a comprehensive Australian labour market training scheme.

Parelleling the enquiries and missions of the years 1973 and 1974, the Department of Education continued its co-ordinating, liaising and initiating roles in educational matters. But until the IMPACT project was begun at the end of 1974 there was no concrete move towards a full-scale exercise which would permit medium to long-term forecasting of the manpower requirements of the education system. The IMPACT project hopes to analyse the effects of a wide variety of changes on many matters including the scale and structure of industrial output, and the size, age, occupational structure and skill composition of the workforce. The project stretches across many areas of policy and promises to provide us with a good deal of hitherto unavailable disaggregated analysis, for example, on industrial manpower requirements. IMPACT has already made one attempt at estimating the effect of one policy change (tariff protection) on the skill composition of the work force (IMPACT 1977), but it is too early at this stage to assess how useful to educational policy IMPACT will ultimately prove.

Section 10 Postscript

In one sense, our survey of the economics of education in Australia might properly have ended at this point. But, we believe that it may be useful and interesting to readers if we add our own view of the state of the economics of educational *policy* in Australia after having ploughed through a very large body of literature. We should assert at the outset that we began our reading in a dispassionate frame of mind, but what we read left us otherwise.

Our perusal of the literature has suggested the existence of a dominating lobby group effectively determining the course of educational policy in Australia. This lobby group is a loose association involving political, bureaucratic and teacher/student vested interests of a progressive, social reform philosophy. Their distaste for private sector schooling appears to us to be a major stumbling block in the path of an efficient renewal of Australian education. In addition, this 'schools lobby' holds that education is a right, should be child-centred and an end in itself, and that unfavourable evaluation of the capacities of school leavers reflects critically on the nature of society and not on the schools.

The development of powerful interest groups in the service sectors such as education appears to have accelerated in recent times. The distinguishing features of these groups are that they are coalitions of workers and bureaucrats rather than coalitions of capitalists, and that they have a vested interest in the expansion of the public rather than the private sector. But their basic economic function of maintaining demand for their product and restricting competition appears no different from that of the coalitions of capitalists which have been subject to critical scrutiny by economists since Adam Smith.

People complain about the quality of locally-produced cars in Australia, but they should not be surprised when the local oligopoly has been assured of eighty per cent of the market whatever it cares to produce. The state near-monopoly of schooling also holds about eighty per cent of its market, dictates the unfavourable terms on which the private sector competes with it, and has the added advantage that it can require consumption of its product by children below the age of fifteen years. If such an industry were described in the abstract in an economics textbook it would be expected to be X-inefficient, wasteful and arrogant towards the demands of consumers. The elimination of economic 'exit' sanctions on the state monopoly *may* strengthen the prospect of political 'voice' involvement of parents, but at the expense of 'unacceptable' minority groups, and under the inescapable potential threat of 'consequences' for the children of those who rock the boat.

Parents, unless very wealthy or willing to make savage sacrifices are unable at present to escape the sheltered monopoly State system of schools. But a system of competitive schools—many of which might be State operated—would return to the vast majority of parents (at least in urban areas)—a prospect of genuine choice as to the nature and quality of the education their children receive. We do not believe that bureaucrats are more fit to decide the educational fate of children than their parents are—even though the bureaucrats may be better informed at present. If unrestricted, some parents may make unwise schooling decisions on behalf of their offspring. But the state has the *existing* power to put boundaries on the scope for lunatic parental decisions on their children's education. As things stand, there is little incentive for schools to inform parents as fully and accurately as possible on the consequences of choices for these are very restricted. Nor is there incentive for parents to accumulate such irrelevant information. The literature is suggestive, moreover, that parental involvement in their children's schooling is a key element in school success. Yet the present State system provides few incentives for parents to develop their interest. The same State monopoly also deters effective expressions of dissatisfaction —by its power and interest in defending its authority against individual, 'voice' expressions of dissatisfaction. It takes considerable confidence and courage to enter into confrontation with the state machine and its 'experts'. The voucher 'exit' option is less intimidating as a means whereby ordinary people can express dissatisfaction—simply by voting with their feet, and taking their money with them. A devolution of power to parents through a system of voucher-financed, fee-charging schools certainly deserves an experiment, we believe. Such a system is not, of necessity, less egalitarian in resource deployment between socio-economic groups, and we do not see how else a democratic evaluation of schooling processes can be brought to bear.[8] It is a measure of the strength of the 'schools lobby' that no experiments with vouchers have been attempted—even though the Schools Commission has commissioned at least one competent study of voucher systems.

Vouchers have the attraction of placing the schools under pressure to deploy their resources as efficiently and effectively as possible, of enabling salary differentials to be established which have the potential to direct teaching resources more effectively and of promoting diversity in the range of schoolings offered in society. The fear of 'diversity' in schooling (unless controlled by the schools lobby within its own parameters) is one of the most disheartening aspects of the Australian schools lobby literature.

It is a sad commentary on the thirst for homogeneity typifying Australian society that a greater spread of schools *meeting minimum State standards* which happen also to specialise in Marxist propaganda, Buddhist Mantras, rock music, Christian devotionals, or whatever, which parents and their children are free to choose between is seen as a threat by many educators. If there is one feature above all others which makes 'vouchers' appealing in the Australian context it is the prospect of a reduction in the weight of the dead hand of sameness in the schools and eventually in the society.

Similarly, at the tertiary level, there is a case for users of educational services to bear more of the cost of financing those services, through (a) permitting institutions to supplement their resources from fees and (b) replacing or supplementing the present means-tested allowance system by a system of loans to students. These questions have been amongst the more thoroughly explored in the Australian literature. The literature demonstrates that there are ways of reducing the disincentive effects of loan schemes for children from disadvantaged socio-economic backgrounds. The abolition of fees and the (by world standards) lavish allowances paid have benefitted a privileged handful of the community's children behind a smokescreen of egalitarian slogans.

The literature shows that Australian post-secondary education has repaid students (and the society) as an investment at a modest rate of return which seems similar to such estimates in other advanced Western countries. It is a moot point whether developments in the Australian labour market since these calculations were made may not have stripped some of the glitter from educational investments at the post-secondary level. There also seems to be some evidence that the shorter, less prestigious courses are a better return on money invested than the longer, more prestigious courses and that—in Australian as elsewhere—post-graduate education is not a very attractive economic proposition.

The evidence on costs seems to suggest that least-cost operation is achieved at quite small size in primary schools but at larger size than many of our current tertiary institutions. An appealing rationalisation of this pattern is the increasing degree of specialisation of knowledge and spread of programmes as people acquire more years of schooling. The programme at primary school level is relatively uniform, basic and understandable even by parents who are able, often, to reinforce. It is not surprising, therefore, that there is little fixed element in the cost-structure of a properly-functioning primary school. Universities form the other extreme where, because of the overhead costs and specialised resources required, there are very large 'economies of scale'. This suggests that little children can be quite properly cared-for in little schools and offers the prospect of the entry of small 'family-schools' into a voucher network at primary level. In fact, the full benefits of a voucher experiment would require decentralisation of existing school complexes into 'mini' schools. On the other hand, big children and adults can be better cared for in larger units permitting an appropriate range of specialisation at reasonable cost.

While manpower questions have bulked large in many of the reports commissioned in recent years, the capacity of the education system to come to terms with manpower needs remains unresolved. Until recently, the problems of matching demands and supplies were obscured by a happy perpetuation of excess demand for graduates in particular—heavily fuelled by the need to provide extra teachers for the even bigger cohorts of students further back in the education system. With the change in demographic structure, the pressure for more cognizance to be taken of labour market outcomes will intensify. We appear to be ill-placed to accommodate that pressure in a credible way. Some recent econometric research developments provide hope that at least some consistent (although highly speculative) scenarios of future manpower—education imbalances can be explored which will prove instructive for broad policy purposes. But a premium on flexibility and adaptiveness in the skills and attitudes acquired in the schools and post-school institutions is certain to emerge. Some of the adaptation will be taken up by the labour market, but the education system itself will face uncomfortable pressures in a context of probably large excess capacity to become more nippy on its feet than it has been used to. Whether it will be able to respond adequately to the new circumstances is not clear, although one could be forgiven for not being entirely sanguine.

A major source of the present difficulties is the ostensibly 'Progressivist' philosophy which dominates educational policy. This philosophy sees the schools as *the* instrument for social reform. In Australia, the reform hoped-for is egalitarian in a variety of senses. The basic conflict is between elite and mass education. It is observed that—on average—young people who persist furthest up the educational ladder are economically advantaged in their home circumstances and in their later life. Hence, programmes to raise the persistence rates of children from disadvantaged homes provide an avenue for social mobility and possibly also for a more egalitarian distribution of incomes in the society. But it is clear that persistence is also related to intellectual and personality endowments of children which enable them to acquire progressively higher abstract intellectual skills. And the evidence that the *schools* can have a major impact on these endowments is not encouraging.

In these circumstances, we would expect that the 'traditional' curriculum in each grade of schooling would become increasingly inappropriate and unappealing as the proportion of each cohort of children attaining each grade increased. The pressures for a watering down of the curriculum to make it more appealing to the mass rather than an elite, and to encourage persistence, we would expect to become great. The introduction of a less-demanding, 'pupil-centred' curriculum in the post-compulsory reaches of the education system becomes necessary to permit the mass of children to advance to those levels and succeed. This can work as a strictly egalitarian device only if it succeeds in eradicating differences in achievement levels and if employers (including the state) can be tricked into confusing an unchanged credential with a changed level of abstract skill. As Hofstadter has remarked of Progressive-dominated American schooling: '[it is a system which] is more universal, more democratic, more leisurely and less rigorous. It is also more wasteful: class-oriented systems are prodigal of the talents of the under-privileged; American education tends to be prodigal of talent generally' (Hofstadter 1964, p.324). The Progressive philosophy appears to us to be fundamentally anti-intellectual in character.

The Progressive philosophy runs into a self-defeating impasse by its concentration on the schools as *the* lever for egalitarian reform of the society. The Schools Commission, for example, on its own admission is operating its 'resource equalisation' programmes in the *knowledge* that the gains in socio-economic equality are *likely* to be limited, but also in the (unsubstantiated) *hope* that they will not be. This is an important justification for schooling programmes which have raised public expenditure on *schools* by 2 per cent of the Gross Domestic Product in 5 years.

Is this the best hope of committed egalitarians? We scarcely think so. Two per cent of G.D.P. is approximately $1 billion. If, instead of being spent on the schools, it had been spent on children between the ages of 15 and 21 who were not in school, university or college of advanced education it would have amounted to about $1250 per head of the 800,000 young people involved (in 1975). This is not as much as expenditure per head of those staying in the schooling/university/college system. Accumulated over six years at 10 per cent interest the capital sum which could be presented, on his or her 21st birthday, to a person who left school at age 15 would easily exceed $10000, with correspondingly smaller sums for persons who left the system at older ages. We know that early school leaving is associated with socio-economic 'disadvantage', that the children of 'disadvantaged' families on average have less school-relevant abilities, find schooling frustrating, and are under economic pressure to leave school earlier. The schools lobby position is to change the schools so that differential drop-out by socio-economic class will be reduced, particularly in an endeavour to reduce post-schooling earning disparities between children. But what are likely to be the gains in schooling achievement, productivity and earnings of these less willing and less able children encouraged to stay on in the system? Will an increased expenditure on schooling *resources* encourage them to continue? Might not the building-up of their non-human capital have more egalitarian effects than building-up their human capital?

If children have a 'right' to as much human-capital enhancing education as they wish, why do children not wishing to avail themselves of this prospect have no rights to comparable state subsidies to enhance their endowments of physical capital or human capital acquired outside the state-subsidised institutions? Is not the concentration of the society's resources on giving a flying start to some children (who by accidents of birth and upbringing find the abstract pursuits of the mind worthwhile), but not to others, unfair? Why not give all young school-leavers the *right* to an expectation of a physical capital sum as a means for improving their expectations in life (by buying schooling or other life-enhancing investments of their choice) rather than giving a 'right' only to extended subsidised schooling which many appreciate is of little value *to them*? Might not $20000 towards better housing for a young couple who both left school early be a more golden prospect than the slender chance that they can make one of the educational jackpots if they struggle against odds to persist at school?

Such 'life-endowment' vouchers might be restricted in their use—to prevent their being squandered on fly-by-night activities of no lasting value. They might be useable against education expenses later in life, should their recipients decide to return to gain more schooling, or they might be useable for housing, or for financing small business enterprises or simply left invested in approved securities to provide a flow of income over the life of the recipient. The projected fall in education expenditures by one percentage point or more of GDP over the next decade, in fact, yields scope for a beginning on such a 'life-endowment' plan without a concomitant reduction in the current share of other expenditures in GDP. Such a prospect is within our financial capability. We offer it as a serious alternative in egalitarian policy to the present preoccupation with schooling as *the* instrument for egalitarian reform.

Such a plan would enable the schools to concentrate more effectively on their traditional tasks. Ineffective programmes would probably decline as a result of parental influence having greater play. With a recapturing by parents of patronage power based on schooling vouchers—loaded where necessary for parents in identified disadvantaged circumstances, by socio-economic status, by Aboriginality, migrancy, religion or whatever—parents would be able to bring effective pressure on *their* schools where it matters. A parent bearing a withdrawable $1500 ticket, we venture to guess, would receive a somewhat different welcome at her child's school than she receives at present.

A renewal of Australian schools is needed. The parents of Australia's children deserve more direct control over the quality and direction of the schooling their children receive than the current philosophies of the schools lobby allows. We can do no better as a final statement than to quote from Dahrendorf's Reith Lectures:

> ... equality provides the floor of the mansion in which liberty flourishes; it is condition, not purpose; equal opportunities are opportunities for unequal choices ... By starving private schools and mistaking the idea of comprehensive education as aiming at integration rather than differentiation, we sacrifice the reality of liberty for the appearance of equality ... Of course an active policy of full citizenship means that we make every effort to reduce environmental handicaps for people ... But we want to do so in order to offer opportunities; so let us be careful not to destroy them in the process ...
>
> The new liberty is there for people to be different, and not for the differences of people to be levelled and abolished ... (R. Dahrendorf 1975, p.43–44).

Notes

[1] The willingness and capability of parents in transmitting common social values is an empirical matter which appears to be unexplored. Clearly, many supporters of state education are not sanguine regarding either matter.

[2] An ARGC Education Survey of South Australian secondary schools in 1971 revealed that Catholic and other independent schools, compared to government schools, attracted children the incomes of the parents of whom were generally higher in terms of mean and median incomes, but which were also more dispersed.

[3] For an extensive discussion of these themes, see, for instance, Berg (1970) and Bowles and Gintis (1976, Chapters 1–4).

[4] An extensive bibliography may be found in Griliches (1977).

[5] These included—(i) zero living allowances, requiring students without other means of support to study on a part-time basis, (ii) full living allowances subject to a means test, (iii) partial living allowances without a means test, requiring students to supplement resources from parental contributions and/or casual employment, (iv) full living allowances treated as repayable loans, (v) full allowances with bonding, (vi) salaries with bonding, and (vii) full living allowances without bonding, available to all students or to those who perform adequately in pre-entry examinations.

[6] Critics of manpower forecasting frequently allude to large *absolute* forecast errors as indicative of failure, but since *some* view of the future must be taken, it is *relative* forecast error that is important.

[7] This conclusion is also reached by radical economists in the U.S. Thus, 'it is clear to many that the liberal school-reform balloon has burst . . . In less than a decade, liberal preeminence in the field of educational theory and policy has been shattered'. (Bowles and Gintis 1976, pp.5–6).

[8] Radicals, however, would presumably dispute that much good can come from expanded educational choice and a more competitive environment for the production of education. In the view of Bowles and Gintis (1976), the functions of schooling under capitalism are essentially those of 'enhancing workers' productive capacities and perpetuating the social, political, and economic conditions for the transformation of the fruits of labour into capitalist profits' (p.49). Instead, 'An education system can be egalitarian and liberating only when it prepares youth for fully democratic participation in social life and an equal claim to the fruits of economic activity' (p.14). Presumably, only myopic capitalist school-owners would offer courses on 'how to overthrow capitalism' to those demanding them?

Bibliography

Abramovitz, M. (1962), 'Economic Growth in the United States', *American Economic Review*, Vol. 52, No. 4 (September), pp.762–81.

Ahamad, B. and M. Blaug (eds) (1973), *The Practice of Manpower Forecasting* (Amsterdam, North Holland).

Archbold, D.A. (1971), 'Economics and Education' in A.G. Maclaine and C. Selby Smith (eds), *Fundamental Issues in Australian Education* (Sydney, Ian Novak), pp.102–133.

Australian Commission on Advanced Education (1975), *Report for the Triennium 1976–78* (Canberra, Australian Parliamentary Paper No. 244).

Australian Council for Educational Research (1975), *Forty-Fifth Annual Report, 1974–75*, (Melbourne, ACER).

Australian Department of Education (1975), *Report for 1974* (Canberra, Australian Parliamentary Paper No. 166).

—— (1976), *Transition from School to Work or Further Study : A Background Paper for an OECD Review of Australian Education Policy* (Canberra, Department of Education, June).

Australian Department of Employment and Industrial Relations, Economic Studies and Information Branch, (annual), *Employment Prospects by Industry and Occupation, July* (Canberra, Australian Government Publishing Service).

Australian Department of Labor and Immigration (periodical), *Manpower Training Programs* (Canberra, Australian Government Printing Service).

Australian Department of Labour (1974a), *Report of the Australian Interdepartmental Mission to Study Overseas Manpower and Industry Policies and Programmes* (Canberra, Australian Government Publishing Service).

Australian Department of Labour, Hancock, K.J., Isaac, J.E. and D. Ironmonger (1974b), *Report of the Advisory Committee on Commonwealth Employment Service Statistics* (Canberra, Australian Government Publishing Service).

Australian Department of Labour (1974c), *Manpower Policy in Australia : A Report to the OECD* (Canberra, Australian Government Publishing Service).

Australian Department of Labour and National Service (1970), *The Training of Skilled Workers in Europe : Summary Report of the Australian Tripartite Mission 1968–69* (Canberra, Australian Government Publishing Service).

Australian Schools Commission (1975), *Report for the Triennium 1976–78* (Canberra, Australian Parliamentary Paper No. 240).

Australian Universities Commission (1976), *Report for the 1977–79 Triennium* (Canberra, Australian Government Publishing Service).

Averch, H.A., S.J. Carroll, T.S. Donaldson and H.J. Kiesling (1974), *How Effective is Schooling? : A Critical Review of Research* (N.J., The Rand Corporation).

Beaumont, P.B. (1974), 'Some Manpower Implications of Industrial Labour Markets', *Journal of Industrial Relations*, Vol. 16, No. 1 (March), pp.85–87.

Becker, G.S. (1962), 'Investment in Human Capital: A Theoretical Analysis', *Journal of Political Economy*, Vol. 70, No. 5, Part 2, Supplement, (October), pp.9–49.

—— and N. Tomes (1976), 'Child Endowments and the Quantity and Quality of Children', *Journal of Political Economy*, Vol. 84, No. 4, Part 2 (August), pp.143–162.

Berg, I. (1970), *Education and Jobs : The Great Training Robbery* (N.Y., Praeger).

Bieda, K. (1970), 'The Pattern of Education and Economic Growth', *Economic Record*, Vol. 46, No. 115 (September), pp.368–383.

Blair, J.R. (1973), *A Study of the Incentive Values of Financial Aid in Education and the Part-time Student*, B.A.(Hons) Thesis, University of Sydney.

—— (1975), 'Motivation, Money and the Part-time Student', *Australian Journal of Adult Education*, Vol. 15, No. 1 (April), pp.20–26.

Blandy, R.J. and A.J. Goldsworthy (1976), 'Private Returns to Education in South Australia' in G.S. Harman and C. Selby Smith, *Readings in the Economics and Politics of Australian Education* (Sydney, Pergamon Press).

Blandy, R.J. and A.J. Goldsworthy (1977), 'Educational Opportunity in South Australia', Working Paper Series No. 21, Adelaide, Flinders University Institute of Labour Studies, (March 1977).

Blandy, R.J. (1978), 'Effects of Structural Changes on the Australian Labour Market in the Year 2000' in W. Kasper and T. Parry (eds), *Growth, Trade and Structural Change in an Open Australian Economy* (Sydney, University of New South Wales).

Blaug, M. (1967), 'Approaches to Educational Planning', *Economic Journal*, Vol. 77, No. 306 (June), pp.262–87.

—— (1970), *An Introduction to the Economics of Education* (London, The Penguin Press).

—— (1976), 'The Theory of Human Capital: A Slightly Jaundiced Survey', *Journal of Economic Literature*, Vol. 14, No. 4 (September), pp.827–54.

Borrie, W.D. (1968), 'Demographic Trends', National Seminar on Educational Planning, Canberra, Australian National Advisory Committee for UNESCO (September 1968).

—— (1972), 'The Demography of Higher Education', in G.S. Harman and C. Selby Smith (eds), *Australian Higher Education : Problems of a Developing System* (Sydney, Angus and Robertson), pp.55–72.

Bowen, I. (1967), 'The Place of Manpower Planning in Economic Development', paper delivered to the session of ANZAAS, Melbourne, (January 1967).

Bowles, S. and H. Gintis (1976), *Schooling in Capitalist America : Educational Reform and the Contradictions of Economic Life* (N.Y., Basic Books).

Brennan, H.G. (1971), 'Fee Abolition: An Appraisal', *The Australian University*, Vol. 9, No. 2 (July), pp.81–149.

Burke, G. (1970), 'An Economic Approach to Government Aid in Education' in P.J. Fensham (ed.), *Rights and Inequality in Australian Education* (Melbourne, Cheshire).

—— (1972), 'A Study in the Economics of Education with Particular Reference to the Supply of Secondary Teachers for Government Schools in Victoria', (Ph.D. Thesis, Monash University).

—— (1973), 'Financing an Education Authority' in G.S. Harman and C. Selby Smith (eds), *Designing a New Education Authority* Education Research Unit, Research School of Social Sciences, (Canberra, Australian National University Press), pp.233–243.

—— (1975), 'Education Vouchers: Theory and Demonstration', a paper prepared for the Australian Schools Commission (Melbourne, Monash University), pp.1–27.

—— (1976), 'The Economics of Bonded Service: The Case of Graduate Secondary Teachers in Victoria, Australia', *Higher Education*, Vol. 5, No. 1 (February), pp.35–47.

—— (1976), 'Demographic Accounting and Modelling: An Application to Trainee Secondary Teachers in Victoria', *Australian Economic Papers*, Vol. 15, No. 27 (December), pp.240–251.

Bury, L. (1967), 'Manpower Planning in Australia', address delivered to the Sixth Annual Convention of the Australian National Economics and Commerce Students' Association, Hobart, 20–27 May, 1967.

Butcher, M.W.J. (1977), *Student Loans : Report of the Committee appointed to Examine the Desirability and Feasibility of Introducing a System of Loans for Australian Post-Secondary Students* (Canberra, Australian Government Publishing Service).

Cameron, C.R. (1974), 'An Active Manpower Policy for Australia', Ministerial Statement in the House of Representatives, Canberra, (17 July 1974).

Chapman, B. (1977), 'The Rate of Return to University Education for Males in the Australian Public Service', *Journal of Industrial Relations*, Vol. 19, No. 2 (June) pp.146–157.

Cochrane, D. (1968), 'The Cost of University Education', *The Economic Record*, Vol. 44, No. 106 (June), pp.137–153.

—— (1974), *Australian Labour Market Training : Report of the Committee of Inquiry into Labour Market Training* (Canberra, Australian Government Publishing Service).

Cohen, S.W. (1973), *Teacher Education, 1973–5 : Report of the Special Committee on Teacher Education* (Canberra, Australian Government Publishing Service).

Coleman, J.S., E.Q. Campbell, C.J. Hobson, J. McPartland, A.M. Mood, F.D. Weinfeld and R.L. York (1966), *Equality of Educational Opportunity* (Washington, U.S. Government Printing Office).
Comber, L.C. and J.P. Keeves (1973), *Science Education in Nineteen Countries* (Stockholm, Almqvist and Wiksell).
Crittenden, B. (1975), 'Arguments and Assumptions of the Karmel Report: A Critique' in J.C. d'Cruz and P.J. Sheehan (eds), *The Renewal of Australian Schools: Essays on Educational Planning in Australia after the Karmel Report* (Melbourne, Advocate Press), pp.3–20.
Crowther-Hunt, (Lord) (1976), 'Manpower Planning, the U.G.C. and Universities', *Times Higher Education Supplement* (7, 14, 21 May 1976).
Curriculum Development Centre (1976), *Education Vouchers*, (Canberra).
Cutt, J. (1977), 'Resource Allocation for Tertiary Education in Australia', Administration Studies Programme, ANU.
Dahrendorf, R. (1975), *The New Liberty* (London, Routledge and Kegan Paul).
Davidson, F.G. (1970), 'Technical and Manpower Trends' in G.W. Bassett (ed), *Planning in Australian Education* (Melbourne, ACER).
Davis, D.J. (1976), 'Some Effects of Ph.D. Training on the Academic Labour Markets of Australian and British Universities, *Higher Education*, Vol. 5, No. 1 (February), pp.67–68.
—— (forthcoming), 'Manpower Planning, Rate of Return Analysis, and the University Medical Schools', *Higher Education*.
Denison, E.F. (1962), *The Sources of Economic Growth in the United States and the Alternatives Before Us* (New York, Committee for Economic Development).
—— (1967), *Why Growth Rates Differ* (Washington, D.C., The Brookings Institution).
Dufty, N.F. (1969), 'Occupational Choice and the Sub-Markets for Skilled Labour', *Journal of Industrial Relations*, Vol. 11, No. 2 (July), pp.187–193.
—— (1970), 'The Potential for Labour Mobility', *Journal of Industrial Relations*, Vol. 12, No. 2 (July), pp.255–262.
Ellem, G.C. (1970), 'The Relevance of Cost-Benefit Analysis to Private and Public Decision Making in Education', (M.A. Thesis, University of Sydney).
Fitzgerald, R.T. (1970), 'Economic Aspects', in P.J. Fensham, (ed), *Rights and Inequality in Australian Education* (Melbourne, Cheshire), pp.105–126.
—— (1972), 'Emerging Issues in the Seventies', *Quarterly Review of Education*, Vol. 5, No. 3 (September), pp.1–47.
Freebairn, J.W. and G.A. Withers (1976), 'Manpower Cobwebs and Welfare Effects', Economics Working Paper, Canberra, ANU (July 1976).
Freebairn, J. and G. Withers (1977), 'The Performance of Manpower Forecasting Techniques in Australian Labour Markets', *Australian Bulletin of Labour*, Vol. 4, No. 1 (December), pp.13–31.
Freeman, R.B. (1976a), *The Overeducated American* (London Academic Press).
—— (1976b), 'Manpower Requirements and Substitution Analysis of Labour Skills: A Synthesis', Harvard Institute of Economic Research, Discussion Paper No. 152.
Friedman, M. (1962), *Capitalism and Freedom* (Chicago, Chicago University Press).
Gannicott, K. (1972), *Recurrent Education: A Preliminary Cost/Benefit Analysis* (Melbourne, ACER Occasional Paper No. 6).
Gates, R.C. (1972), 'The New Responsibilities of Government: Welfare Versus Growth', *Economic Papers*, No. 39 (January/June), pp.20–40.
Gravell, K. (1973), 'Some Aspects of the Graduate Labour Market', paper delivered to the session of ANZAAS, Perth, (August 1973).
Grewal, B.S. (1976), 'Fiscal Equalization, the Grants Commission and the Schools Commission', Occasional Paper No. 5, Centre for Research on Federal Financial Relations (Canberra, Australian National University Press).
Griliches, Z. (1977), 'Estimating the Returns to Schooling: Some Econometric Problems', *Econometrica*, Vol. 45, No. 1 (January), pp.1–22.
Hall, A.R. (1965), 'Supply and Demand' in E.L. Wheelwright (ed), *Higher Education in Australia* (Melbourne, Cheshire), pp.44–65.

Harbison, F. and C.A. Myers (1964), *Education, Manpower and Economic Growth* (New York, McGraw Hill).

Harman, G.S. (1974), *The Politics of Education* (Brisbane, University of Queensland Press).

Hartman, R.W. (1973), 'The Rationale for Federal Support for Higher Education' in L.S. Solmon and P.J. Taubman (eds), *Does College Matter* (N.Y., Academic Press), pp.271–292.

Hind, I.W. (1977), 'Estimates of Cost Functions for Primary Schools in Rural Areas', *Australian Journal of Agricultural Economics*, Vol. 21, No. 1 (April), pp.13–25.

Hofstadter, R. (1964), *Anti-intellectualism in American Life* (New York, Knopf).

Hollister, D.R. (1966), *A Technical Evaluation of the First Stage of the Mediterranean Regional Project* (Paris, OECD).

IMPACT (1977), P. Dixon, J. Harrower and A. Powell, 'Long Term Structural Pressure on Industries and the Labour Market', *Australian Bulletin of Labour*, Vol. 3, No. 3 (June), pp.5–44.

IMPACT (occasional), Impact of Demographic Change on Industry Structure, *Working Papers* (Melbourne, 608 St. Kilda Road, mimeo).

Jain, S. (1975), *Size Distribution of Income* (Washington, D.C., The World Bank).

Jay, R. (1975), 'The Shift to Specific Purpose Grants: from Revenue Sharing to Cost Sharing' in R.L. Mathews (ed), *Responsibility Sharing in a Federal System* Research Monograph No. 8, Centre for Research on Federal Financial Relations (Canberra, Australian National University Press).

Jencks, C. (1972), *Inequality : A Reassessment of the Effect of Family and Schooling in America* (New York, Basic Books).

Kangan, M. (1974), (Australian Committee on Technical and Further Education), *TAFE in Australia : Report on Needs in Technical and Further Education* (Canberra, Australian Government Publishing Service).

—— (1975), Australian Committee on Technical and Further Education, *Second Report on Needs in Technical and Further Education* (Canberra, Australian Government Publishing Service).

Karmel, P.H. (1962), 'The Pattern of Tertiary Education in the 1960's', *Australian Journal of Higher Education*, Vol. 43, No. 2 (November), pp.31–37.

—— (1964), 'Some Economic Aspects of Education', in R.W.T. Cowan (ed), *Education for Australians* (Melbourne, Cheshire), pp.24–48.

—— (1966), 'Some Arithmetic of Education' in E.L. French (ed), *Melbourne Studies in Education 1966* (Melbourne, Melbourne University Press), pp.3–34.

—— (1971), *Education in South Australia 1969–70 : Report of the Committee of Enquiry into Education in South Australia* (Adelaide, South Australian Government Printing Service).

—— (1972), 'Tensions and Trends in Mass Tertiary Education', Presidential Address, 43rd ANZAAS Conference, University of New South Wales.

—— (1973), *Schools in Australia : Report of the Interim Committee for the Australian Schools Commission* (Canberra, Australian Publishing Service).

—— (1975), 'Some Economic Implications of Educational Policy', *The Giblin Memorial Lecture*, 46th ANZAAS Conference, reprinted in *Search*, Vol. 6, No. 7 (July, 1975), pp.266–272.

—— (1976), 'Roles and Goals of Education', *Sir John Morris Memorial Lecture* (Division of Adult Education, Tasmanian Department of Education).

—— (1977a), 'The Educational System and the Labour Market' in *Australian Economic Policy Essays in Honour of Wilfred Prest* (Melbourne, Melbourne University Press).

—— (1977b), 'Education and the Workforce', *Education News*, Vol. 16, No. 1, pp.12–17.

Keeves, J.P. (1974), *The Effects of the Conditions of Learning in the Schools in Australia* (IEA [Australia] Report 1974, No. 2, Melbourne, ACER).

Keeves, J.P. (1975), 'The Needs of Education in Australian Schools' in J.V. d'Cruz and P.J. Sheehan (eds), *The Renewal of Australian Schools : Essays on Educational Planning in Australia after the Karmel Report* (Melbourne, Advocate Press), pp.38–58.

Kidd, G.A. (1973), 'Professional Manpower in Australia: Prospects, Problems and Policies', paper delivered to the session of ANZAAS, Perth (August).
Kitchenn, R.G. (1976), 'A Case Against State Aid', in G.S. Harman and C. Selby Smith, *Readings in the Economics and Politics of Australian Education* (Sydney, Pergamon Press), pp.85–90.
Layard, P.R.G., J.D. Sargan, M.E. Agar and D.J. Jones (1971), *Qualified Manpower and Economic Performance* (London, Allen Lane).
Layard, R. and G. Psacharopoulos (1974), 'The Screening Hypothesis and the Returns to Education', *Journal of Political Economy*, Vol. 82, No. 5 (September/October), pp.985–998.
Lindner, R.K. and N.J. Thomson (1975), 'Discrimination in Student Loans', *Economic Analysis and Policy*, Vol. 6, No. 1 (March), pp.43–55.
McCloskey, H.J. (1970), 'The Rights of the Parent', in P.J. Fensham (ed), *Rights and Inequality in Australian Education* (Melbourne, Cheshire), pp.3–17.
McDill, E.L., L.C. Rigsby and E. Meyers Jnr. (1969), 'Educational Climates of High Schools: Their Effects and Sources', *American Journal of Sociology*, Vol. 74, No. 6 (May), pp.567–586.
McIntosh, M.K. (1976), 'The Occupational Grouping for IMPACT', *IMPACT Working Papers*, (Melbourne, 608 St. Kilda Road, February, mimeo).
—— (1976), 'Manpower Forecasting for Technical Education in Australia', Paper delivered to Conference of Principals of Victorian Technical Colleges, (31 May 1976).
McKinnon, K. and G. Hancock (1976), *Financing Schools in Australia: A Study of Instruments Used to Finance Primary Education and their Relationship to Educational Policy Issues* (Canberra).
Maglen, L.R. (1973), 'An Evaluation of the Role of Student Assistance Schemes in the Financing of Higher Education: with particular reference to Australia and the Commonwealth Scholarship Scheme 1951–1969', (Ph.D. Thesis, Faculty of Economics and Politics, Monash University).
—— (1976), 'Higher Education: Externalities, The Public Purse and Policy', *Economic Analysis and Policy*, Vol. 6, No. 4 (September), pp.27–43.
—— (forthcoming), 'Student Assistance Schemes and the Supply of Highly Skilled Manpower: The Australian Experience', *Economic Record*.
Martin, L. (1964), *Tertiary Education in Australia: Report of the Committee on the Future of Tertiary Education in Australia to the Australian Universities Commission* (Melbourne, Australian Government Publishing Service).
Mathews, R.L. (1967), *Public Investment in Australia* (Melbourne, Cheshire).
—— (1968), 'Finance for Education', *The Australian University*, Vol. 6, No. 1 (April), pp.59–95.
—— (1969), 'Resource Allocation in Universities', *The Australian University*, Vol. 7, No. 3 (November), pp.171–189.
—— (1972), 'Financing Higher Education' in G.S. Harman and C. Selby Smith (eds), *Australian Higher Education: Problems of a Developing System* (Sydney, Angus and Robertson), pp.73–105.
—— (1973), 'Patterns of Educational Finance', *Australian Economic Papers*, Vol. 12, No. 21 (December), pp.145–161.
Matthews, P.W.D. and G.W. Ford (1966), 'Trade Union Education and Training in Australia', *Journal of Industrial Relations*, Vol. 8, No. 2 (July), pp.158–174.
Molhuysen, P.C. (1966), 'The Australian Universities and Scientific Manpower', *Comparative Education Review*, Vol. 10, No. 1 (February), pp.67–72.
Mortensen, K.G. (1971), *Planning for Technological Change in Australia* (East St. Kilda).
Murray, K. (1957), *Report of the Committee on Australian Universities* (Canberra, Australian Government Publishing Service). Sir Keith Murray, Chairman.
Nerlove, M. (1975), 'Some Problems in the Use of Income-contingent Loans for the Finance of Higher Education', *Journal of Political Economy*, Vol. 83, No. 1 (February), pp.157–184.

Niland, J.R. (1973), 'Manpower Policy for Australia', in G.W. Ford (ed), *Redundancy*, Searchlight Series (Sydney, John Wiley and Sons).
—— (1974a), 'Some Fundamental Questions for Manpower Planning', *Journal of Industrial Relations*, Vol. 16, No. 4 (December), pp.303–313.
—— (1974b), 'Retraining Problems of an Active Manpower Policy', *Australian Economic Papers*, Vol. 13, No. 23 (December), pp.159–170.
—— (1975), 'Issues in Australian Manpower Policy', in J.R. Niland and J.E. Isaac, (eds), *Australian Labour Economics—Readings* (Melbourne, Sun Books).
O'Byrne, G.B. (1971), 'The Application of the Constrained Optimisation Model in Planning Investment in the New South Wales Education System: 1970–1980', (Ph.D. Thesis, Macquarie University).
OECD (1965), *The Mediterreanean Regional Project: An Experiment in Planning by Six Countries—Country Reports* (Paris, OECD).
Parish, R.M. (1963), 'The Economics of State Aid to Education', *Economic Record*, Vol. 39, No. 87 (September), pp.292–304.
—— (1964), 'State Aid to Education', in R.W.T. Cowan (ed), *Education for Australians* (Melbourne, Cheshire), pp.218–238.
—— (1965), 'Education as an Investment', *Current Affairs Bulletin*, Vol. 36, No. 8 (August), pp.115–118.
Parnes, H.S. (1962), *Forecasting Educational Needs for Economic and Social Development* (Paris, OECD).
Paukert, F. (1973), 'Income Distribution at Different Levels of Development: A Survey of Evidence', *International Labour Review*, Vol. 108, Nos. 2–3 (August–September), pp.97–125.
Psacharopoulos, G. and K. Hinchliffe, (1973), *Returns to Education: An International Comparison.* (Amsterdam, North-Holland).
Radford, W.C. (1968), 'Education Needs in Science and Technology', *Economic Papers*, No. 27 (June), pp.31–39.
—— (1969), 'Evaluation of Progress in Education', *Australian Journal of Education*, Vol. 13, No. 2 (June), pp.209–232.
Ritchie, R.G. (1974), 'An Analysis of Costs in Technical Schools in Victoria', (M.A. Thesis, Monash University).
Rosier, M.J. (1973a), *Variation between Australian States in Science Achievement* (IEA [Australia] Report 1973, No. 5, Melbourne, ACER).
—— (1973b), *Science Achievement in Australian Secondary Schools* (Melbourne, ACER).
—— (1974), 'Factors Associated with Learning Science in Australian Secondary Schools', *Comparative Education Review*, Vol. 18, No. 2, pp.180–187.
Segall, P. and R.T. Fitzgerald, (1974), 'Finance for Education in Australia: An Analysis', *Quarterly Review of Australian Education*, Vol. 6, No. 4 (December), pp.1–77.
Selby Smith, C. (1972a), 'Course Costs in Colleges of Advanced Education', *The Australian Journal of Higher Education*, Vol. 4, No. 2 (December), pp.78–92.
—— (1972b), 'Resource Allocation in Higher Education', in *Financing Education in Australia* Conference Proceedings (Burbury, Australian College of Education, Western Chapter, 21–23 April).
—— (1972c), 'The Economics of Education', in R.K. Braine, *Social Science Perspectives on Australian Education* (Sydney, MacMillan), pp.64–120.
—— (1973a), 'An Economic Approach to Teacher Loss and Retention', *Australian Journal of Education*, Vol. 17, No. 2 (June) pp.142–152, reprinted in G.S. Harman and C. Selby Smith (eds), *Readings in the Economics and Politics of Australian Education* (Sydney, Pergamon Press), pp.185–194.
—— (1973b), 'Faculty Costs in Australian Universities', *The Australian University*, Vol. 11, No. 2 (September), pp.87–908.
—— (1975a), 'The Costs of Failure in Australian Universities and CAE's', *The Australian University*, Vol. 13, No. 2 (July), pp.103–129.
—— (1975b), 'Rates of Return to Post-Secondary Education in Australia', *Economic Record*, Vol. 51, No. 136 (December), pp.455–485.

—— (1975c), 'The Macro-economics of Educational Renewal' in J.V. d'Cruz and P.J. Sheehan (eds), *The Renewal of Australian Schools: Essays on Educational Planning in Australia after the Karmel Report* (Melbourne, Advocate Press), pp.117–132.

—— (1975d), *The Costs of Post Secondary Education: An Australian Study* (Melbourne, Macmillan).

Sheehan, B.A. (1972), 'The Organisation and Financing of Education in Australia', *Comparative Education*, Vol. 8, No. 3, (December), pp.133–146.

Sheehan, P.J. (1975), 'The Renewal Programme after the Karmel Report' in J.V. d'Cruz and P.J. Sheehan (eds), *The Renewal of Australian Schools: Essays on Educational Planning in Australia after the Karmel Report* (Melbourne, Advocate Press), pp.163–180.

Snooks, G.D. (1977), 'Personal Income Distribution and its Determinants: The Australian Visual Arts Profession', Working Paper Series No. 22, Institute of Labour Studies, The Flinders University of South Australia, (July 1977).

Spady, W.G. (1973), 'The Impact of School Resources on Students' in F.N. Kerlinger (ed), *Review of Research in Education* (Itasca, Illinois, F.E. Peacock) reprinted in W.H. Sawell, R.M. Hauser and D.L. Featherman (eds), *Schooling and Achievement in American Society* (N.Y., Academic Press, 1976), pp.185–224.

Stretton, H. (1965), 'Problems of University Expansion' in E.L. Wheelwright (ed), *Higher Education in Australia* (Melbourne, Cheshire), pp.75–128.

Svennilson, I., Edding, F. and L. Elvin (1962), 'Targets for Education in Europe in 1970', *Policy Conference on Economic Growth and Investment in Education* Vol. II, Paris, OECD (January).

Sweeney, J. (1969), *Report of the Inquiry into Salaries of Lecturers and in Colleges of Advanced Education* (Canberra, Australian Government Publishing Service).

Szelenyi, I. (1977), 'Social Inequalities in State Socialist Redistributive Economies—Dilemmas for Social Policy in Contemporary Socialist Societies of Eastern Europe', (Sociology Discipline, The Flinders University of South Australia, January 1977).

Thomson, N.J. (1974a), Loans for *Australian Tertiary Students* AACRDE Report No. 2 (Canberra, Australian Government Publishing Service).

—— (1974b), *Economics of Student Loans* AACRDE Report No. 3 (Canberra, Australia Government Publishing Service).

Thurow, L. (1970), *Investment in Human Capital* (Belmont, Wadsworth).

Tinbergen, J. (1975), *Income Distribution* (Amsterdam, North-Holland).

Tomlinson, D. (1976), *Finance for Education in Australia: Developments 1969–75* Australian Education Review No. 5 (Melbourne, Australian Council for Educational Research).

University of Queensland (1968), Conference of Appointments Officers and Student Counsellors of Australian Universities, *Responsibilities of Universities and of Employers for Professional Training* (Brisbane, 16 August 1968).

Vaizey, J.E. (1973), 'The Economics of Education', in R. McCraig, (ed), *Policy and Planning in Higher Education* (Brisbane, University of Queensland Press).

Wade, P.B. (1974), 'Recent Developments in Fiscal Federalism in Australia, with Special Reference to Revenue Sharing and Fiscal Equalization' in R.L. Mathews (ed), *Fiscal Federalism: Retrospect and Prospect* Canberra Research Monograph No. 7, Centre for Research on Federal Financial Relations (Canberra, Australian National University Press).

Webster, A.H. (1969), 'Methods of Financing Australian Education Today', *Australian Journal of Education*, Vol. 13, No. 2 (June), pp.195–208.

Weeden, W.J. (1970), *Report on the Pros and Cons of Student Loans* (Canberra, Department of Education and Science).

West, C.E. (1972), 'Science Ph.D. Graduates: Overproduction or Underutilization', *Search*, Vol. 3, No. 10 (October), pp.357–361.

Wheelwright, E.L. (1963), 'Costs, Returns and Investment in Education', *Australian Journal of Higher Education*, Vol. 1, No. 3 (November), pp.1–12.

Wiley, D.E. (1976), 'Another Hour: Another Day: Quantity of Schooling, a Potent

Path for Policy' in W.H. Sewell, R.M. Hauser and D.L. Featherman (eds), *Schooling and Achievement in American Society* (N.Y., Academic Press, 1976).

Williams, B.R. (1972a), 'University Income and Expenditure', *Australian Quarterly*, No. 2 (June), pp.54–56.

—— (1972b), 'The Escalating Cost of Universities', *The Australian University*, Vol. 10, No. 2 (July), pp.91–113.

—— (1972c), 'The Fifth Report of the Universities Commission', *The Australian University*, Vol. 10, No. 3 (November), pp.214–237.

Williams, H.S. (1961), 'Tertiary Education and Community Needs in the Professions', *Australian Journal of Higher Education*, Vol. 1, No. 1 (November), pp.52–61.

Wiltshire, F.M. (1969), *Report of the Committee of Inquiry into Awards in Colleges of Advanced Education* (Canberra, Australian Government Publishing Service).

Wood, W. (1969), 'Educational Manpower in Australian Schools', *Australian Journal of Education*, Vol. 13, No. 2 (June), pp.167–194.

Chapter 4

Radical Economics in Australia: A Survey of the 1970s

P.D. GROENEWEGEN

University of Sydney

Contents

In the preparation of this survey, I am especially indebted to Bruce McFarlane, Dave Clark and Geoff Harcourt with whom I discussed this project continuously and who gave many suggestions and provided me with much important material which otherwise would have escaped my notice. In revising the survey for publication, I am grateful to three anonymous referees for comments, and to Fred Gruen for his excellent editorial suggestions and comments on the abbreviation of the original draft. Their co-operation and assistance does not absolve me from any of the many errors of omission and interpretation which undoubtedly remain in this survey.

Whenever one uses the term 'political economy' one must be careful to make clear in what sense it is being used. There is no special virtue in the expression itself.
(Chattopadhyay 1975, p.32)

Section 1 Introduction

During the 1970s, Australian economics always just that little bit later than the latest trend in the United States (see Edwards, MacEwan and others 1970; Bronfenbrenner 1970), experienced a re-awakening of radical economics or radical political economy. There is now an Australian Political Economy movement largely consisting of students, workers and some academic staff which has held conferences in Sydney (1976) and Melbourne (1977), which is publishing its own journal, the *Journal of Australian Political Economy*, has conducted first- and second-year courses at Australia's oldest university since 1975 and is now spreading to a variety of other Australian universities, colleges of advanced education and schools. It has produced a number of textbooks and is in the process of producing more.

Viewed in this manner, it seems that Australia, in 1977, has produced a split in the economics profession by the creation of a new and monolithic radical political economy, similar to the creation of the Union of Radical Economists in 1968 in the USA. Such an impression would be wrong. As shown below, the re-awakening of radical economics in Australia in the 1970s is quite different from the picture presented in the editorial of the first issue of the *Australian Journal of Political Economy*, which argued that 'the *national* Political Economy movement really swung into gear with the 1976 Conference . . .'[1] This is highly misleading in some important respects. For example, part of this re-awakening of Australian radical economics has roots in the past which reveal its diverse origins and considerable heterogeneity. Furthermore, the nature of the dissatisfaction with orthodox economics is far from uniform. It has led to a variety of radical critiques of economics rather than to a uniform political economy movement. As the quotation with which this survey starts indicates, we must carefully clarify what is meant by radical economics and political economy because these terms mean different things to different people.

1.1 What is Radical Economics?

Readers of the *Australian Quarterly* in the early 1970s will have gained the impression that radical economics is essentially a critical movement which provides a 'challenge to bourgeois economics'. Gruen (1971, esp. pp.59–60) argued that radical economics charges orthodox economics with being 'unnecessarily theoretical', 'sterile and lacking in relevance' and with pretending 'to be value free whilst in reality it is but an ideology to uphold the existing capitalist system.' Similarly, Wheelwright and Waters (1973, esp. pp.11–12) defined radical economics as a movement critical of conventional economics by confining their discussion (which largely derives from articles published in *URPE*) to the inadequacies of its theories on a series of arguments which they summarise as the 'ideological bias argument', the 'logical invalidity of models argument', the 'practical argument', the 'lack of relevance argument' and the 'constricted methodology argument'. These shortcomings are very similar to those listed by Gruen. They are seen as leading to omissions of topics such as war, imperialism, underdevelopment and the environment from the scope of economics. (Wheelwright and Waters 1973, pp.19–21).

Although these characterisations highlight an important element of radical economics (including Australian radical economics), they are incomplete and insufficient to explain the re-awakening of radical economics in Australia in the 1970s. Criticism of conventional theory has always been a feature of radical economics in the past. It has not always led to a general movement. There are thus other features inherent in the nature of the critiques which must be explored.

1.2 A Working Definition of Radical Economics

Radical economics in this survey is interpreted as the literature of economists who are critical of conventional economists and who, on the basis of that critique, want to construct a new political economy either on classical[2], or on institutionalist or on Marxist, or on Keynes-Kaleckian lines. The critique is basically aimed at the mainstream theory or neo-classical synthesis developed in the post-war period; as characterised at the textbook level by Samuelson's *Economics* (1948) and at the higher theoretical level by his *Foundations of Economic Analysis* (1947). (See, for example, Nell 1972a, 1972b, Hollis and Nell 1975, esp. chapters 1 and 9).

Like Bronfenbrenner (1970), I exclude from this survey those who are essentially liberal reformers, the radical right and those who introduce some economic material in what is essentially non-economic debate (for example, environmentalists and those concerned with questions such as the mining of uranium) and the fringe writers and economic 'cranks' who still contribute to economic discussion on the basis of older, now discredited traditions, such as the present generation of Henry Georgists, still advocating the single tax and the writers associated with the League of Rights, and others, who still publish Douglas Credit material.

A further indication of the scope of this survey can be given by a brief description of the process of selecting the Australian literature included. Three sources of literature were tapped. First, books published in the late

1960s and 1970s which are either written by, or include, contributions of Australians who describe themselves as radical economists. Secondly, there are the political economy articles in the journals—especially the radical Australian journals like *Arena*, *Intervention* and the new *Journal of Australian Political Economy*. Finally, and quantitatively least important, there are some unpublished papers, but there the coverage is obviously not systematic. Broadly speaking, therefore, the survey has been confined to Australian published sources, mainly from the 1970s except for a number of earlier publications required to provide some necessary historical background. Needless to say there are many omissions, partly for the reasons listed by Mayer (1971, pp.65–67) but partly also a matter of deliberate choice.[3] Reasons of space, coupled with the heterogeneity of the material, were also important. Nevertheless, it is felt that this survey presents a basic coverage of the more important Australian radical economics of the 1970s.

Section 2 *Radical Economics: A Grouping of Current Schools of Thought*

Radical economics can be seen to derive from several distinct strands of thought of varying degrees of sophistication. There is first of all, the older, largely populist, highly descriptive and frequently anti-theoretical tradition which lives on in part of the political economy movement. This tradition is partly illustrated in the history of radical economics in Australia. Secondly, there are the Australian institutionalists whose inspiration derives from Veblen and Hobson at the turn of the century (for example, Irvine's work in the early twentieth century) and more recently from Galbraith and Myrdal (for example, much of Wheelwright's work can be described in this way).

In addition, we can discern two further groupings basing themselves on fairly established *theoretical* traditions, that is, the Marxists and the 'post-Keynesians'. These constitute a substantial part of the present writings in radical economics, including some produced by Australians. However, because these groupings overlap to some extent and in order to avoid later confusion, it is important to delineate these groupings further, starting with the post-Keynesians.[4]

2.1 The Post-Keynesians

It is now well known that from the late 1940s onwards there developed a distinct group of economists with international reputations which felt that the Keynesian revolution was being betrayed in the neo-classical synthesis (essentially created by Hicks and Samuelson) which substituted Keynesian economics for the economics of Keynes. (Leijonhufvud 1968 raised this criticism *outside* the post-Keynesian school see also Robinson 1971 and for a survey of post-Keynesian economics, Coddington 1976, esp. pp.1259–1263). Much of this group bases itself on the Marshallian Cambridge tradition, as revitalised by Keynes and Kalecki, and enriched by Sraffa's rehabilitation of classical political economy (that is, from the Physiocrats up to and including Marx).

This group began its task of creating a new political economy by criticising the Keynesian-neo-classical synthesis from fundamental principles: the treatment of equilibrium and historical time; aggregation problems in the development of growth and micro-distribution theory; problems in the theory of the firm, and so on. Much of this criticism culminated initially in the famous Cambridge controversies on capital theory of the 1950s and 1960s (see Harcourt 1969, 1972) which *destroyed*[5] many of the *logical* foundations of neo-classical capital theory and other fundamental principles of neo-classical theory. As a result of these debates, many post-Keynesians regard conventional economics as having retreated into its last bastion, general equilibrium theory, which is reputedly logically sound but irrelevant to practical problems (Kaldor 1972, Hahn 1973). Other post-Keynesians, particularly Garegnani (1960, 1976) have argued that even general equilibrium analysis is not immune from the destructive effects of the capital controversies.

Although many of the criticisms of the post-Keynesians were at first essentially negative (Sraffa 1960; Robinson 1975a)—though Sraffa's positive contributions should not be ignored (see for example, Meek 1967; Roncaglia 1974, 1976, 1977)—attempts are continuing to reconstruct a new political economy along 'Keynesian' lines which are based on Kalecki's 'general theory' rather than that of Keynes (Robinson 1975b). This new political economy has produced several textbooks (Robinson and Eatwell 1973; Kregel 1974) and has been described as a new paradigm to use the currently fashionable Kuhnian parlance (Eichner and Kregel 1975). The relevance of this movement to Australian radical economics is that it has spread to Australain largely through the efforts of G.C. Harcourt, while there are also strong adherents of this school at other Australian universities (for example, Frearson at Monash) including politics departments (for example, McFarlene, one of Australia's most prominent Kaleckians—see McFarlane 1971a, 1977b—is Professor of Politics at Adelaide). Many prominent overseas members of the group as well as the local practitioners have contributed papers on post-Keynesian economics to Australia's economic journals, especially *Australian Economic Papers*[6].

There has been debate in Australian radical economics about the role of this group in the reconstruction of political economy. Many overseas Marxists (for example, de Brunhof 1973; Medio 1972, 1977; Rowthorn 1972, 1974; Roosevelt 1977) have regarded the 'Sraffian Revolution' (Dobb 1973 pp.248–249) with suspicion and these attitudes have rubbed off on local Marxists, an issue explored later. This debate has come to a head with the publication of Steedman's *Marx After Sraffa* which shows that Sraffa's work is not only a powerful instrument to criticise marginalist economic theory but that some of Marx's theorems have been destroyed by it as well. For instance, the transformation problem has been described as a 'chimera', labour values are argued to be irrelevant to the determination of the profit rate and the 'law of the falling rate of profit' has been questioned (Steedman 1977, pp.14–15).

The neo-Marxist versus neo-Ricardian debate highlights the division in the post-Keynesian/Cambridge camp, as Harcourt (1977a, pp.363–367) has shown. There are further differences which relate to the problems being analysed, the scope of the problems being considered and the method of analysis. The neo-Ricardians (see especially Pasinetti 1974) have been largely concerned with abstract problems of pure theory, in particular of long run equilibrium growth but also with the theory of value, production and distribution—that is, with the questions of classical political economy. Others are more particularly interested in developing relevant short run theory to deal with policy issues in the developed capitalist world and in the underdeveloped world as well as the socialist economies (good examples are to be found in the first volume of the *Cambridge Journal of Economics*: for example, Robinson and Wilkinson (1977) Singh (1977), Kaldor (1977) Ellman (1977), Hare (1977), Paine (1977) and Bhaduri (1977)—a recent concise statement of the research programme is Robinson (1977). Furthermore, many post-Keynesians accept Marx's research programme as the one posing relevant problems for economics but at the same time emphasise the need to criticise Marx and Marxists, the necessity to use modern theory and mathematical techniques plus the need for empirical work to analyse the complexities of recent developments in the world economy (a fine example of such critical, empirical work is Smith (1977) on the role of military spending).

2.2 *The Marxist Revival*

During the 1960s there was also a considerable Marxist revival in the western world which spilled over into economics. As Bronfennbrenner has shown (Bronfenbrenner 1970, pp.750–753) much of the American revival of radical economics has been Marxist inspired. Two reasons are advanced for this Marxist revival: first, the publication of important texts in English by Marx himself (Marx 1962, 1961, 1968, 1972 and 1973); second, the publication of translations of works on Marxist political economy (for example, Mandel 1968, 1971, 1975; Emmanuel 1972). Later it is shown that the Marxists have had a particularly strong influence on the development of Australian radical economics in the 1970s, but here again it should be emphasised that the Marxist contribution has been far from homogeneous.

One group (largely associated with Australian journals such as *Intervention*) can be characterised as paying lip service to categories such as the organic composition of capital, rate of exploitation, rate of surplus value but not of integrating these fully into the analysis because of the difficulty of applying these concepts to modern problems in the development of capitalism. Another grouping is largely concerned with conceptualisation of the basic categories of Marx's analysis in *Capital* Volume I; but some of its adherents have also made suggestions for the measurement of these categories as a step in the development of further analysis. In addition, as has already been indicated, many of the post-Keynesians have affiliations with Marx by adopting his research programme and some of his methodology.[7] These distinctions, although difficult to define precisely, are important for the understanding of the heterogeneity of the Australian Marxist radical economics.

2.3 Radical Economics or Political Economy?

So far we have treated radical economics and political economy as synonymous. As the initial quotation indicates, this is not satisfactory because these terms have a variety of shades of meaning reflecting past usage. To a large extent, the definition used here is pragmatic, but some common elements can be stressed. Most important of these is the emphasis in all radical economics (political economy) on the integration of economics, politics and sociology—though the manner in which this is done varies from group to group. This emphasis on the political nature of economic questions leads to a very different view of the scope of economics from that normally posited by positive economics. Political economy extends far beyond economic policy formation with its concomitant value judgements. The meaning to be attributed to these terms is best illustrated by the types of topics selected for discussion in Australian radical economics and the manner in which they are analysed and examined. Some preliminary indications of this have already been given in the introduction and are further pursued in the examination of the historical antecedents of radical economics in Australia.

Section 3 *Historical Antecedents: A Brief Look at the Past*

3.1 The Roots of Australian Radical Economics

Students of early Australian economic thought who turn to Goodwin's massive history (Goodwin 1966) will not find many references to radical economics in Australia in the nineteenth century. This is not because this aspect was ignored by Goodwin but because there was so little radical radical economics in Australia in this period. What there was, however, illustrates great diversity, was highly critical of conventional economics and initially drew its inspiration from anarchists, Owenite socialists, romantic critics of laissez-faire in the Carlyle-Ruskin tradition and above all, a large number of Henry Georgist land reformers. If an Australian radical economics patron saint had been required in this period, it would have been Henry George or Edward Bellamy, *not* Karl Marx. As Goodwin (1966, p.366) put it: 'Deities held sacred by early radicals were Henry George, John Stuart Mill, Herbert Spencer, Thomas Carlyle, and finally, Edward Bellamy . . .' though this list should be expanded to include John Ruskin, Robert Owen and the American populist 'funny money' tradition particularly important in the 1890s (Gollan 1968, chapter 3).

The virtual absence of Marx and Engels should be further commented on, particularly because the Marxist tradition has been so important in the Australian radical economics tradition in the 1970s. Although Mayer (1964, Part I) has shown that some Marxist influence was exerted as early as the 1870s, this influence was ephemeral and overshadowed by such diverse movements as spiritualism and land reform along Georgist lines. For a short period during the depression of the 1890s, Marx and Engels, and lesser lights like Nordau, Bax and Gronlund were influential (Goodwin 1966, p.368) but these flirtations with Marxism were neither profound nor long lasting (McQueen 1970, pp.181–191)[9].

An historical section is required because it sheds light on the present. One example is the criticism of conventional economics but it is also needed to explain the rise of vulgar Marxism in Australia and to stress the reliance on ideas from abroad characteristic of Australian radical (as well as conventional) economics.

One aspect of the criticism of conventional theory derived from what was considered to be the misapplication of British political economy (Adam Smith, John Stuart Mill[10] and Fawcett) to Australian conditions—felt to be different from those prevailing in England. (Examples are the frequent attacks on laissez-faire—e.g. Cinderella (1890a), Goodwin (1870, pp.21, 51) —the debates about free trade and protection, and the tremendous concern with the failure of the land settlement legislation in splitting up large estates.) This led to demands for inheritance taxation and particularly land taxes on Henry Georgist lines (e.g. Hirsch 1901, 1903, 1904; Ogilvy 1898).[11] This type of criticism was not confined to radical critics: it was endemic to much of Australian economic thought at least up to the second world war (as clearly demonstrated by Goodwin 1966, Part I).

This type of criticism also implies a strong association between economics and politics, an association characteristic of much of Australian economics up to the second world war. With the general emphasis on positive economics—American style—in Australian universities after the second world war, the present generation of radical economists has tended to re-assert the earlier interconnection between politics and economics. In some nineteenth century radical economics it was strongly implied that economic problems can only have political solutions (e.g. Goodwin 1878; Andrade n.d., 1888) and by the early twentieth century the need for a unified social science (economics, politics and sociology) was frequently articulated. Francis Anderson, for example, argued that economics 'cannot be taught properly apart from the instruction in the more general social sciences of Sociology and Politics' (Anderson 1912, p.3) and this position was strongly supported by Irvine (1914), Sydney University's first economics professor.[12]

More specific criticism of the conclusions of economic theory focussed on the treatment of factors of production in the theory of distribution (Cinderella 1890 a and b) and the analysis of unemployment and depressions (e.g. Goodwin 1878, Andrade n.d.; Ogilvy 1898, pp.132–139, 208–209) some of which embodied considerable sophistication. Ogilvy, for example, argued that depressions were caused by under-consumption and over-saving. What was therefore required was a more equal distribution of income (to be achieved through land nationalisation, the taxation of interest and inheritance taxation). In addition, as an interim measure during depressions, he advocated the taxation of saving and severely criticised the emphasis on thrift and 'economising'. 'The worst thing a country can do in a financial crisis is to economise by contracting expenditures, stopping public reproductive works and dismissing hands'. In a passage reminiscent of Keynes he argued that it was 'better even to pay men to dig holes and fill them up again than have them idle at the street corner'. (Ogilvy 1898, pp.143–146, 230).

This type of Australian radical economics rose to its greatest heights in the work of R.F. Irvine. Irvine was critical of current developments in economics, emphasised the need for the combination of politics, economics and sociology, had radical monetary views and unconventional remedies for the depression of the 1930s. He was highly suspicious of conventional theory, stressed the need for relevance and for his inspiration on these matters drew heavily on the writings of economic heretics from England and the United States. Irvine's work epitomises much of the current Australian radical economics tradition, as is shown by his criticism of conventional economics presented in 1914:

> 'Political Economy, it may be said, has missed its chance. [This is illustrated] by the almost hopeless confusion in the minds of the older economists between the social and the individual points of view; their tendency to mistake assumptions for facts; their beautifully simple and logical reasoning which, however, is only true of a hypothetical world that never did nor could exist, their numerous false predictions . . . The new school of economics [Jevons and the Austrians] . . . built up another unreal world. The continued neglect of social factors, a new misuse of the dangerous process of abstraction, the adoption of inappropriate methods from Mathematics and Physical Science, which delude by their

very appearance of accuracy, have given economic theory an air of unreality ... which has done much to retard its development ... (Irvine 1914, pp.11–12)[13]

In some of his monetary thinking, Irvine was in advance of contemporary thought and in line with the later thinking of Keynes. In *The Veil of Money* (Irvine 1916) he argued that the burden of the public debt is on the present generation which sacrifices the real resources and not on future generations (Irvine 1916, pp.15–17). The lecture also contains a strong attack on the gold standard and emphasises the need for a more elastic money supply, which gave him the reputation of being an inflationist (Goodwin 1966, p.565). His espousal of unorthodoxy[14] increased his unpopularity and he resigned as Professor of Economics at Sydney, ostensibly for personal reasons.[15] He remained active in his retirement, gave advice to the Labor Party (including E.G. Theodore) during the Depression and advised against wage cuts in 1930–31. His work has been almost completely ignored by the Australian economics profession[16] even though he foreshadowed Keynesian notions of saving, the importance of effective demand and Say's Law (Irvine 1933, pp.14–18, chapter 15). Unfortunately, these ideas were given no lucid theoretical expression and, what probably offended his fellow economists even more, they were combined with lengthy, approving quotations from Keynes' 'economic underworld' (Keynes 1936, pp.353–371)[17].

Generally speaking, this discussion of Irvine's economics shows that much of the present day radical economics has a great deal in common with the older variety. Irvine's 1914 critique of conventional economics is very similar to that of Wheelwright and Waters (1973) a similarity largely explained by the fact that Irvine and Wheelwright were both influenced by Hobson and Veblen and the institutionalists in general. Some present day radical economics also embodies the same lack of theory, populism and the reliance on imported criticism. Another conclusion drawn from this historical digression is that none of the criticism in the past led to a general interest in radical economics; the reasons for the revival of radical economics in the 1970s must be found elsewhere.

3.2 Marxism, the Communist Party and the Development of Radical Economics

The Communist Party's role in the development of radical Marxist thought can best be discerned from the following characterisation: 'The first avowedly Marxist party did not emerge until 1920. Its creators had read little Marx (and no Lenin until 1926!), and their Communism amounted to little more than enthusiasm for the victory of the Bolsheviks. This theoretical immaturity was revealed, and at the same time reinforced, by the subsequent subjugation of the Australian left to Stalinist theory and political practice, [and this] fixed the Communist Party in a barren orthodoxy ....' (*Intervention*,

Editorial, No. 1 April 1972, p.2). The virtual lack of any Marxist influence on nineteenth-century Australian radical economic thought has already been mentioned; the theoretical guidance provided by that 'serious social scientist', J. Stalin[18] perpetuated that lack of influence of Marxism on Australian radical economics for almost half a century.

During the 1940s, the period of maximum influence of the Communist Party in Australia, there was no Australian political economy text for the party faithful. Economic training was provided through A. Leontief's textbook on political economy (Leontief 1935), supplemented by economic pamphlets produced by members of the Australian and British parties, as well as by left-wing members of the Labour Party. In 1954, Campbell's *Political Economy* (Campbell 1954) gave the basis of the Marxist credo, as interpreted by Stalin but with Australian examples. Apart from the crude paraphrasing of Marx's economics, this book contained no theory and was exposed as a piece of plagiarism by McGuinness (1955). In 1958 (second edition, 1964), this text was replaced by the less obviously Stalinist but no less crude *Economics for Workers* (Aarons 1958) which, according to its author, provided an introduction to the more basic of Marx's texts. Again, this pamphlet provided no analysis of Australian capitalism though, like its predecessors, it illustrated the conclusions of *Capital*, Volume I with Australian examples. The vulgarity of these handbooks of fundamentals of Marxian economics has to be seen to be believed, and it undoubtedly accounts for the current lack of sophistication of some of the Community Party cadres in the political economy movement, who still draw partly on these teachers of 'Minto Marxism'.

The more interesting Communist Party material consisted of the pamphlet literature which critically examined the role, functions, importance and inefficiency of private enterprise (see Dobb 1944–the most important of these pamphlets—Wilson 1946, for an Australian version); the efficiency of government enterprise as shown from the historical record and the need for the socialisation of industry (Fitzpatrick 1945; Sharkey and Campbell 1945) and during the bank nationalisation campaign of the late 1940s, analyses of the 'money power' and the case for bank nationalisation (Campbell 1947; Lockwood 1948; and the *Fabian Society* pamphlet, *The Case for Bank Nationalisation* Arndt et al. 1947).

In addition, there was also a large literature on who owns, controls and rules Australia by means of an examination of a number of wealthy families in Australia, their shareholdings, their directorships and their associations with government. (Fox 1940, 1974; Moss 1955; Thomas 1954 but especially, Rawlings 1937 and its final successor, Campbell 1963). This literature can be described as the most important part of the Australian radical economics research programme during the 1940s and to the end of the 1960s. As Encel (1965a, p.4) has argued, the origin of this type of study is probably found in some of the writing of Frank Anstey (e.g. *The Kingdom of Shylock*, 1917 and *Money Power*, 1921).[19]

This literature, although devoid of theoretical content, and particularly Marxist theoretical content, was nevertheless important in the further development of Australian radical economics. It was the product of painstaking research from primary sources in order to discover the 'anatomy of Australian capitalism' in the ownership, control, interlocking directorships and monopoly power of Australia's corporate sector. At a higher level, this type of research was continued by Australian academics during the 1950s and 1960s. Some research focussed mainly on ownership and control of business, including foreign ownership (see especially, Wheelwright 1957; Fitzpatrick and Wheelwright 1965; Sharp 1965; Wheelwright and Miskelly 1967; Rolfe 1967); others focussed more widely on the class and power structure in Australian society (Encel 1960; Davies and Encel 1965; and especially, Playford 1968–69, 1969, 1970, 1972).

This research contributed a great deal of interesting information on Australian business and on the power structure of Australian society but its weaknesses derive from the type of literature from which it developed. It consistently failed to develop a coherent economic theory of modern Australian capitalism and steered most of the research effort of Australian radical economists into a well channelled course by continuing the tradition of descriptive, populist and nationalistic analysis at the expense of advanced theoretical work on the 'laws of motion' of Australian capitalist society.[20]

3.3 The Work of Brian Fitzpatrick

Although Brian Fitzpatrick is mainly known as a radical economic historian, he also published a number of interesting contributions to radical economics. *The Rich get Richer* (Fitzpatrick 1944) provided a detailed examination of industrial concentration in Australia and the decline of competitive industry. The remedy was not nationalisation, the more frequently suggested policy of the Left but the setting up of public enterprises in competition with the largely monopolised sectors of private industry (pp.45, 47, 52). Because public enterprise had then, as it still has, a bad name in Australia, he followed up this argument with an examination of public enterprise in Australia which clearly showed that public enterprise did pay in the past (Fitzpatrick 1945). Fitzpatrick showed the problem was that successful public enterprises were almost invariably sold back to private enterprise by conservative governments: such governments only liked to socialise the losses of essential services: profits should remain with private enterprise. This bolstered up the conventional arguments about public inefficiency and the efficiency of private enterprise. Fitzpatrick's contributions on this subject were influential because his research provided the foundation for further work; his policy of setting up state industry in competition with private industry, thereby avoiding the difficulties associated with nationalisation, was revived in the late 1960s (e.g. McFarlane 1968).

Fitzpatrick's major contribution to radical economic history (Fitzpatrick

1939, 1941) cannot be dealt with here. Although his influence on Australian economic history has now greatly declined, partly as a result of more recent and more widely accepted interpretations by the Butlins and others, his work continues to inspire radical economists in their historical researches. For example, his thesis depicting Australia as the victim of British imperialism has been questioned and has led to new analyses of the historical association between the two countries (Clark 1975, 1978). During the 1970s, Fitzpatrick's economic history contributions have been attacked from the Left as being too populist, nationalistic, insufficiently theoretical and non-Marxist (see e.g. MacIntyre 1972, pp.58–65). They have been subject to a recent methodological debate among economic historians—in which issues were raised which are highly relevant to the methodological disputes among radical economists in the 1970s.

3.4 Radical Economics in the 1960s: some Causes of the 1970s Revival

During much of the 1950s and 1960s, Australian radical economics was in the doldrums. Part of this was due to the then satisfactory nature of Australia's economic performance, its almost complete absence of unemployment (unlike the U.S.A.) and its low and acceptable rate of inflation. The capitalist crises which had inspired radical economics in the past were just not there except for some wishful thinking peddled in some Communist Party literature. Further, the Cold War and the Stalinist hegemony over Marxist thinking prevented the development of independent Marxist analysis; if radical economics was engaged in at all, it kept safely within the confines of the established radical research programme of who owns and controls.[21] These tendencies are illustrated in Playford's analysis of *Neo-Capitalism in Australia* (Playford 1969) and in the contents of the one radical journal, *Arena*, which survived the 1960s and which carefully avoided all questions of political economy.

One important exception to this lack of radical economics, the swallow that heralded the spring as it were, can be noted. This was McFarlane's *Economic Policy in Australia. The Case for Reform* (1968), which attempted to examine a far wider range of economic issues from a radical perspective. The starting point of this book is the criticism of conventional economists who almost invariably advance a 'too rigid separation of politics and economics' and who thereby fail to come to grips with some of the more important problems. McFarlane therefore attempted four interrelated tasks: '(1) the development of themes ignored by economic theoreticians, (2) the tying together of institutional development and the pattern of economic development (3) the presentation of the results of research on economic power and its influence on economic policy .... (4) an evaluation of the advantage of an approach rooted in political economy or 'institutional economics'.' (McFarlane 1968, pp.1–3).

While these themes are largely left implicit, the book broke with established radical left economic traditions by discussing a wide range of practical issues ranging from planning to problems in the Victorian State electricity supply, from health economics to income tax reform, and from the analysis of the institutions and vested interests in policy formation to the problems of economic stabilisation policy. To some, such content provided grounds for criticism in itself; the book was described as just another 'Fabian tract'. But this type of criticism ignores its methodological intent and its theoretical innovations, for example, the use of Kaleckian growth models to explain Australia's economic development.

More important factors, however, brought about the revival of radical political economy in Australia. As Bronfenbrenner (1970) has shown for the United States, a series of events occurred at the end of the 1960s making for an increasing interest in radical economics in the western world. These developments, in so far as they are relevant for Australia, can be quickly summarised:

(1) The radicalisation of the Australian student body, largely associated with the Australian involvement in the Vietnam war and the use of national service conscripts. *In addition*, there was also the demonstration effect of student revolts in many western countries during the 1960s which were not necessarily associated with the Vietnam War, but frequently with the inadequacies of teaching and the organisational framework at the universities and other educational institutions.

(2) Even though Australian performance on the traditional indicators (growth, inflation, employment) was still satisfactory, there was a growing realisation of other unsatisfactory aspects of this economic performance. Attention was increasingly drawn to the existence of a significant amount of poverty in Australia in spite of the affluent society; to the inequities of the tax system; to inequality in income and wealth distribution in Australia; and to problems caused by economic development for the environment through pollution, the destruction of wildlife and national parks, and so on.

(3) Great awareness of, and sympathy with, the Aboriginal problem in Australia, combined with the rise of radical feminism and interest in other 'minorities' in Australia such as migrants.

(4) Starting at the beginning of the 1970s, the change in Australia's economic performance on the established criteria; the rising inflation rate and the re-emergence of unemployment, problems which greatly increased from 1973 onwards.

(5) Dissatisfaction with the safe, conservative governments from the middle of the 1960s onward; the 'time for a change' mentality permeated many facets of life. In addition, from 1974 onwards, though for some much earlier, there was considerable radical dissatisfaction with the performance of the Labor 'alternative' which many argued did not provide a real alternative at all.

Apart from these broad social, economic and political factors, there were also elements at work in the world of ideas. The impact of the Cambridge controversies began to be felt by some economists in Australia's universities, largely as a result of Harcourt's efforts (1969). The revival of interest in Marxism was stimulated by the sudden availability in English of Marxist texts which showed to many that Marxism was not dead and buried under Stalinist dogma but that it had a lively, rich and continuing intellectual tradition particularly in continental Europe (e.g. the works of Lukacs, Gramsci, Korsch, Marcuse, Mandel and Althusser). Finally, there was the well publicised, growing dissatisfaction within the leaders of the international economics profession with the nature of the progress in economic research, and the relevance of that research. Examples of such dissatisfaction are the presidential addresses of such distinguished economists as Kaldor (1972, 1975), Leontief (1971), Gordon (1976), Phelps-Brown (1972), Worswick (1972), Galbraith (1973) and Robinson (1972).

Is it surprising that this conjuncture led to a critical appraisal of conventional economics and a re-awakened interest in radical economics?

Section 4 *A Survey of the Literature of the 1970s*

There are as yet no general Australian texts on radical economics or political economy; the radical economics literature remains highly fragmentary but it differs from the past because there is now a great deal more of it and more topics are now discussed than was previously the case. Furthermore, most of it is written by established or budding academics with a few contributions from students and trade unionist. This means that the general quality of the argument has lifted even though it remains uneven.

The fragmentary nature of the material makes a survey rather difficult, a difficulty enhanced by the lack of coherent theoretical framework of some groups. Neither the Marxists nor the post-Keynesians in their various subgroupings can be said to suffer from this. They have a body of theory—largely imported from abroad—but here there are many examples of poor or inadequate application of theory as well as controversies over both interpretations and local application of that theory.

The best way of handling this heterogeneous material is to group the literature by subject headings. For this purpose, the following headings have been adopted:

(1) Methodology and Criticism (including criticism of conventional economics);
(2) Analysis of Australian capitalism;
(3) The Capitalist Crisis of the 1970s;

(4) The State, Economic Policy and Public Finance;
(5) Technocratic Laborism and the Role of Social Democracy;
(6) Imperialism and Economic Development;
(7) Political Economy and Feminism;
(8) Australian developments in 'post-Keynesian' economics.

4.1 Methodology and Criticisms of Conventional Economics

Issues of methodology have invariably been raised in the context of both the criticism of neo-classical or conventional mainstream economics *and* the reconstruction of the *new* political economy or radical economics. The Wheelwright-Waters (1973) contribution is basically the attack on the abstractions of conventional economics made so frequently in the past by the historical school and the institutionalists because these abstractions lack relevance for what are seen as real world problems. This critique has been enriched by the arguments derived from the Cambridge controversies[22] that many of the abstractions of neo-classical economics do not even have general logical validity.

These aspects have been further developed by members of the Sydney Political Economy Group (Stilwell 1975a, 1975b; Butler and Stilwell 1975; Wheelwright 1971; and especially Jones 1975, 1977). Some of these contributions arose from the methodological debates at Sydney University over the introduction of political economy courses (see Simkin 1975) and involved issues about the nature and scope of economics as well as arguments about rival philosophies and theories of science. The first was largely confined to a discussion of the narrowness of the *scope* of neo-classical economics (Butler and Stilwell 1975; Stilwell 1975b, also Wheelwright 1971) and the lack of realism (that is correspondence with the facts) and/or the logical invalidity of the neo-classical models (Jones 1975, 1977 pp.357–361).[23]

The second, more important argument of the Sydney political economists (see especially Jones 1977; pp.350–356), attacks the Popperian notions of science which had been advanced against them by Simkin (1975). These attacks on Popper's philosophy of science have been largely on Kuhnian lines (Kuhn 1970; Lakatos and Musgrave 1970). It specifically criticises the relevance of positivism and empiricism to the economics as practised in the textbooks especially (scientists do not behave as they *ought* to do) but the canons of positivism and empiricism are largely adhered to (Jones 1975, 1977).

The plea of the Sydney political economy group has therefore been for an intellectual pluralism in economics, embracing all schools of thought, particularly neo-classical, institutionalist and Marxian economics. This pluralist structure is built into the Sydney courses and into the basic text prepared for their students (Wheelwright and Stilwell 1976). The rationale is presumably that we cannot be certain about what is valid or useful; hence the wider the coverage, the more chance we have of being right.

Coupled with this is the anti-theoretical stance of the older members of the group (Wheelwright 1974; Simpson-Lee 1970) which they have described as the 'Sydney tradition'. This is now either a loose form of descriptive writing, with empirical material frequently culled from newspapers and other secondary sources (Wheelwright 1974, Part III provides excellent examples) or, in the case of Simpson-Lee, an appeal to the historical tradition embodied in the work of R.C. Mills and S.J. Butlin who combined painstaking empirical research with practical policy application (Simpson-Lee 1970). This branch of 'current affairs economics' is then presented as the institutionalist approach to economics.[24]

This type of methodological view has been strongly criticised, particularly by Marxists. Goddard makes the pertinent comment on Mermelstein's early American text (Mermelstein 1970) that 'to grab together a host of dispersed and piecemeal 'critiques of economics', with the best intentions and insights, fails to establish the *total* perspective that Marx considered indispensible' (Goddard 1971, p.22). Such concentration on omissions of conventional economics 'emanates from an inadequately established radical framework' (ibid. p.24) and usually leads to the tendency of radical critics 'to play the role of the guilty conscience to the bourgeois economist ...' (Rowley 1971b, p.71). According to Marxists, these critics fail to come to grips with the methodological heart of modern economic analysis (Goddard 1971, p.23).

These criticisms form the basis for White's first two methodological contributions to radical economics (1975, 1976). The first of these is a very critical review of Stilwell (1975a) which particularly complains about his 'failure to confront the positivist canons of science' and 'to acknowledge the centrality of ideology to bourgeois economics [which allows us] to dispense with the positive/normative distinction and its conceptual apparatus' (White 1975, p.91). In his second paper, White argues that the dangers of the rejections of positive science (à la Stilwell 1975a) is that it leads to the 'rejection of the possibility of scientific/objective knowledge' (White 1976, p.1), thereby allowing no possibility for finding criteria of the relative merits of alternative economic systems of thought. This can only develop to a relativist position, one clearly abhorrent to the Marxist who finds his scientific basis in the objective knowledge posited by Marx. On the other hand, White's paper debunks the positive/normative distinction as merely part of the defensive ideology of bourgeois economics and he provides strong sideswipes at empiricism. The problem White does not tackle is how objective knowledge can be established, or, more fundamentally, the presumably Marxist theory of objective knowledge which he espouses. One can guess at the possible contents of this theory, but it would be nice to see it spelled out.

Marxian economists have also attacked the neo-Ricardian (post-Keynesian) attempts at the reconstruction of political economy, as was mentioned earlier in this survey. McFarlane raised this issue in Australia in a paper particularly provocative to fundamental Marxists (1975). Apart from setting out some of the issues raised in this debate, he also provides a useful Who's Who of the leading protagonists (pp.31–32). The main argument is about what the post-Keynesians can and cannot contribute. He points approvingly to their critique of neo-classical economics and to the models developed by Kalecki and his followers because these use the real categories of wages, profit and prices rather than the abstract Marxist categories of value, labour power, surplus value and the rate of exploitation (pp.38–43), a point also made overseas by Steedman (1977, chapters 1–5). McFarlane is also critical of the post-Keynesians. Their failure to destroy the 'phoney fact/value distinction', the limitation of their critique of capitalism to the critique of the rentier (a legacy from Keynes' euthanasia theory adapted by Joan Robinson), and he strongly criticises their flirtations with the technostructure and with the reformist policies for the saving of capitalism by means of income policies and the like (pp.43–46).

Ergas (1975) criticises McFarlane's discussion for its 'lack of theoretical clarity' and for not appreciating the correct role of Marx's theory of value. However, he did not reply to the more basic issues raised in this controversy: the difficulties involved in applying Marxist analysis to the analysis of contemporary capitalism.[25] McFarlane's reply to Ergas (McFarlane 1976b) did not return to this basic issue; instead he concentrated on the defence of the contributions made by the post-Keynesians and the misrepresentations made of this analysis by the 'vulgar' Marxists (pp.90–95).

Similar issues were raised in a debate about radical versus orthodox economic history which was conducted in the pages of *Labour History* (1975, 1976). This controversy started when Snooks (1975) pointed to the difficulties faced by radical historians when, with their rejection of Fitzpatrick, they have increasingly relied in their 'discussion of Australian economic development and cyclical activity upon the *conclusions* of mainstream economists such as Noel and Sydney Butlin' (pp.9–10). Since the work of the Butlins is inspired by 'bourgeois' economic theory such as aggregate production functions and Harrod/Domar models, this is seen as a basic contradiction of radical economic history.

Rowse's contribution to this debate illustrates the Marxist dilemma in radical economics. He gives no real indication what the new radical economic history should consist of, except that it should 'make the concept of the 'mode of production' central to [the] historical narrative', that it should see history as a 'process of class struggle' and that it should use Marxian categories. In such history, 'pure facts' of bourgeois historians like the Butlins can be used, provided that the Marxist historian can see past these 'bland phrases and find the class activity that they tend to mask' (p.16). He also implicitly criticises Australian historians for not estimating 'the rate of exploitation, the organic composition of capital' and so on, though he does not disclose how these categories can be quantified with contemporary, available data.

Clark (1976) and McFarlane (1976a) reply mainly to Snooks by arguing that radical historians must not run away from contemporary economic theory (radical or orthodox), that they have to use critically actual data including national income estimates à la Butlin, but that, at the same time, they must present the radical critique of conventional economic history. Clark (1976, pp.60–61) also replies to the difficulties of Rowse's position, that is, the issue of empirical and historical work within Marxian theoretical constructs. This problem has not been faced up to by a large segment of modern Marxists, while Clark and McFarlane try to remove it by utilising the more basic post-Keynesian theories, especially those by Kalecki.

That such flirtations with 'neo-Ricardianism' are not acceptable to (at least) some groups of Marxists has already been mentioned in the context of the international debate (Schwarz 1977, part V; Rowthorn 1974, Eatwell 1974, 1975; Steedman 1977) and for Australia, in our discussion of the McFarlane/Ergas exchange. Two further Australian Marxist criticisms of the neo-Ricardians (O'Donnell 1977; White 1977) should be mentioned. The first presents a critique of Hollis and Nell (1975) on philosophical and economic grounds: O'Donnell argues convincingly that Hollis and Nell's economic rationalism is antithetical to Marxism and that it suffers from logical difficulties; in the context of the more specific economic part of their argument, he shows that their treatment of production and distribution, and their rejection of a theory of value, is also non-Marxist. His conclusion is that Nell's proposals for the reconstruction of political economy are 'inadequate to the development of [such] a new science'. The major fault of O'Donnell work is some serious misrepresentation of Sraffa's work, ignoring work of other prominent neo-Ricardians (e.g. Pasinetti) and concentrating unduly on Nell's work but generalising the conclusion to all neo-Ricardians.

White's critical discussion of Kalecki's theories of developing countries (1977) is concerned with identifying the precise nature of Kalecki's political economy, its relationship with Marxism and its methodological underpinnings. In particular, White examines the relationship between politics and economics by means of a careful discussion of the complex interrelationships between the 'sectors' into which a 'social formation' can be divided (pp.316–326). The ambiguity in Kalecki's work is then seen as residing in the attempt to produce a class analysis of underdevelopment within a representation of the economic, and this, for White (and like-minded thinkers) raises a major theoretical problem facing political economists: what is political economy and how is it to be conceptually constituted (pp.327–328)?

This long section on methodology has been essential to illustrate some of the fundamental differences of opinion in radical economics in Australia in the 1970s and the dilemmas to be faced by those seeking to develop a coherent, logical and therefore theoretical radical political economy. These controversies reveal that the reconstruction of political economy still has far to go.

4.2 Analysis of Australian Capitalism

There is still little Australian radical economics material on what is considered by many to be its major task: the analysis of Australian capitalism not as a national entity but in its integration with both the imperialist world and the underdeveloped countries. In addition, such analyses should present the effects of economic development on class, on politics and the mutual interactions between politics and economics. In other words, an attempt should be made to understand the workings of Australian capitalism as a totality.

The scarcity of such analysis is testified to by some of its practitioners. Rowley (1972a), for example, laments 'the failure . . . to come to terms with the current realities of Australian capitalism'. The 'voluminous quotations from the classic texts . . . are no substitute for the concrete study of the concrete situation' (p.9). To remedy this, there have been calls for an analysis of the development of Australian capitalism on the lines of Lenin's *Development of Capitalism in Russia* (*Intervention*, No. 1, 1972, editorial, 7; McQueen, 1970, p.16). The need for such a comprehensive analysis it is argued, is heightened by the paradoxical features of Australian capitalism; the high degree of urbanisation, the developed manufacturing sector, the high level of per capita incomes, particularly in the 19th century, the large tertiary sector, the high degree of monopoly in industry, combined with a heavy dependence on foreign capital and an export trade dominated with primary products and especially from the 1960s onwards, minerals. (*Intervention* editorial 1972, p.7: O'Connor 1971; Moore 1972, pp.27–28).

The book of essays, *Australian Capitalism* (Playford and Kirsner 1972) did not remedy this shortcoming, although some of the contributions attempted an analysis of Australian capitalism in its relations with other capitalist countries and the underdeveloped nations of the Pacific area (McFarlane 1972; Rowley 1972b; Evans 1972). Although features of these contributions are examined further, the book as a whole failed to achieve what it set out to do. In the many reviews of it, it was frequently criticised on this ground, though the reasons given in support of this criticism largely reflected the political perspectives of the reviewers (see, for example, Arndt 1972; Colin Clark 1972; Davidson 1972; Osmond 1972).

This intellectual failure of the book is explained by its major fault: short contributions by different authors are no substitute for the unified, exhaustive analysis which the subject requires. Fitzpatrick's economic history is no longer acceptable: partly because it does not cover the post-1945 developments of Australian capitalism, but more importantly, because it is populist and because of its nationalistic view of the relationship between Australian and British imperialism (Rowley 1972a, pp.10–11). However, no radical Australian economist has yet been prepared to undertake this massive task of reinterpretation and after 1972 there have been few broad attempts to investigate the developments of Australian capital even at article length (for exceptions, see Clark 1975, 1978).

It seems desirable to point out some of the basic features distinguishing these essays on Australian capitalism from the more conventional accounts such as, for example, that of the Vernon Committee in the early 1960s. Two differences stand out in particular. First, there is the treatment of Australia as a junior partner in world imperialism—not as a simple victim of the major capitalist economies through foreign investment and multinational control, as presented by older populist and nationalist radical economists such as Wheelwright (1974, pp.55–62). For example, McFarlane's analysis emphasises Australia's dual role in the world capitalist system: as a 'satelite *and* as a metropolis' (McFarlane 1972, pp.50–61). The latter aspect is specifically analysed by Evans (1972, esp. pp.186–197).

The second feature of these analyses is the interrelationship usually drawn between economic development, class structure and politics. The effect of Australia's early high per capita income has been especially examined. McFarlane writes of a labour aristocracy, sharping in the spoils of world imperialism, though he admits that this is too simplistic a picture (McFarlane 1972, pp.48–50). Rowley, on the other hand, argues that these changes have not fundamentally affected the basic features of Australia's working class in the system of capitalist relations. 'More than ever before, the worker today is forced to sell his labour power to the owners of the means of production in order to maintain himself and his dependents' (Rowley 1972b, p.289).

A major shortcoming is the lack of specific analysis of the role of the state in all this. Although McFarlane discussed the role of the state in some detail in 1968 (particularly in chapter 7), the state plays almost no part in his 1972 analysis. Similarly, Rowley's contributions devote little attention to the role of the state, apart from a statement that the State is important, and that the only major change in the role of capitalist governments has been the one of budgetary policy to influence effective demand and so iron out economic fluctuations. (Rowley 1972b, pp.278–281). Moore's (1972) analysis of Australian capitalism completely ignores the state; analysis of this important subject in understanding capitalism is confined to discussions of 'Who Rules Australia?' and neo-capitalism (Playford 1969, 1972) or to the detailed critiques of the Labor government and social democracy presented by the radical economists.

While there are many useful suggestions and fragments for the analysis of Australian capitalism from the radical point of view, what is lacking is their combination into a coherent whole. Part of the reason may be the lack of a theoretical framework for such a project, but the Kaleckian model which has been used by McFarlane (1968, chapter 4) may be of use here. Furthermore, a major fault of the Marxists in this context has been the introduction of theory which has only a very tenuous association with Australian problems.[26] The other reason for this failure is an unwillingness to devote the tremendous amount of intellectual and research effort which has to go into such an analysis. Radical economists have tended to concentrate instead on short 'educational pieces' largely addressed to lay audiences. This type of weakness also underlies the analysis of the capitalist crisis.

4.3 The Capitalist Crisis of the 1970s

Three Australian radical economics analyses of the world capitalist crisis (Hinkson 1974; Rowley 1976a; Wheelwright 1977) have dealt almost exclusively with its international aspects; two (Brezniak and Collins 1977; Silver 1977b) deal with its particular manifestation in Australia. Most of these contributions have an explicit Marxist approach, though with debatable success. All draw heavily on research from conventional economists (especially OECD material) and in their theoretical expositions have obtained inspiration from *Das Kapital*, from the Kondratieff cycle as popularised by Barraclough and from *Late Capitalism* (Mandel 1975).

Hinkson sees the world currency crisis as the major cause of the capitalist world collapse in the 1970s, though he also relies on real factors. 'The general thesis I wish to argue is that the present world economic situation is one of profound *financial* crisis that lies much deeper than the usual Keynesian concerns of production, consumption and investment and threatens economic conditions similar to the 1930s depression. Reinforcing the financial crisis, and in part created by it, is the raw material price boom of 1973–74' (Hinkson 1974, pp.24–25). The long post-war boom of the capitalist world (described as the upswing phase of a Kondratieff cycle—p.25, n.15) suffered from a number of contradictions which in combination created the financial crisis. In this context, he mentions the decline in economic power of the U.S.A. and the mounting economic challenge of Japan and the EEC; the collapse of the world financial system, the 'irrational growth of non-productive producers' in western capitalist economies, the development of multi-national companies, and the growth of a 'synthetic technology' which implies increased reliance on oil and the collapse of markets in raw materials for some underdeveloped countries (pp.21–28). In such a situation, he concludes, the Keynesians' remedies will no longer work; his solution is the construction of new regional economies based on cooperation and relative self sufficiency (including a reorientation of technology away from oil dependence). This paper was written at the height of the first energy crisis; the successful postponement of that crisis has meant that not all his predictions have been fulfilled.

Rowley's analysis (1976a) of the end of the long boom runs along more conventional Marxist lines (it is in fact largely based on Mandel's *Late Capitalism*), though he also argues—again with an appeal to Kondratieff cycles—that this is a special phenomenon and not just an ordinary recession (Rowley 1976a). 'It is essential to realise that the very process of rapid expansion and capital accumulation tends to generate forces which brings it to a halt until such time as the capitalist economy is restructured so that accumulation can proceed on a new basis' (p.54). Classical Marxist contradictions are raised: improvement in the bargaining position of labour with full employment, hence rising wages and falling profits: fluctuations in the 'organic composition of capital' which initially raise profits via technological progress but later lower the rate of profit; while the ultimate lower profitability reduces investment and leads to stagnation.[27] This explanation also provides the preconditions required for sustained world capitalist recovery. These are four: increases in the reserve army of labour to prevent bottlenecks in labour supply from aborting the recovery; modest wage increases; technological development which raises labour productivity without raising the organic compositions of capital, and 'the extension of the basis of capitalist production, either through expansion into new areas of the globe or the development of a new complex of industries with a major impact on output and employment, and which brings about the restructuring of existing sectors of the economy' (p.76). Since all these factors are unlikely to eventuate in the immediate future, Rowley predicts that a 'long wave' of 'secular stagnation and crisis is upon us' (pp.77–8).

Wheelwright's 'The End of Economic Growth' (1977) is essentially a survey article of the growing literature on the end of the post-war boom combined with some speculation on what comes next. The greater part of the article is devoted to the latter, in particular to an examination of the three immediately relevant, future problems: first, 'the retreat from internationalism into trade blocs and protectionism'; second, strongly reduced or negative growth rates leading to the intensification of international struggles over the distribution of world output, particularly resources; third, an increased likelihood of authoritarian regimes, particularly of the right' (p.55). Much space is devoted to the dangers arising from the growth of 'trans-national corporation' for third world countries and for Australia (pp.56–59). He concludes that if his diagnosis of the 'age of uncertainty' is correct, then 'Australian economic policies ought to have more in common with some of the demands of the Third World, than with the 'modified free trade' position of orthodox analysis'. Such policies cannot be achieved unless 'Labor economists' demystify the 'propaganda masquerading as economic science' which emerges from the 'citadels of Western capitalism' (p.60). The major policy recommendation is that Australia should attempt to reduce its integration with world capitalism and become more self sufficient, thereby avoiding the problems experienced by the raw material supplying countries of the Third World in the 1960s. Australia should not become the quarry of international capitalism.

The analysis of the current Australian crisis by Brezniak and Collins (1977) starts off with the premise that 'Australian capitalism is now caught not only in a cyclical but in a profound structural crisis' against which the traditional remedies of Keynesian economics are powerless. A Marxist analysis of the crisis is therefore required, which they aim to provide (pp. 4–5). They briefly summarise what they call the four Marxist theories of crises, that is, the falling rate of profit theory, the under-consumptionist theory, the disproportionality theory and the theory of the profits squeeze (à la Glyn and Sutcliffe 1972). All these are described as inadequate but nevertheless explain 'vital elements', the most important of the four being the falling rate of profit thesis because it provides concepts for 'conducting a concrete historical analysis' (pp.6–7). Unfortunately, this assertion is not justified by the later argument, and in the light of their diagnosis of the crisis as a 'profound stuctural one' it seems strange that the 'disproportionality thesis' is hardly explained by them.

After this 'theoretical' introduction, the readers' expectations of a solid Marxist analysis have largely disappeared. The bulk of the discussion of Australia's post-war economic history rests on a mixture of the 'Gregory thesis' and the Jackson Report analysis (which fits in with their non-Marxist approach to structural problems) combined with analyses of increased imperialist rivalries between Japan and the United States, rising class struggle at the end of the 1960s, and a major transformation of the functions of the state over the same period (esp. pp.16–17). Apart from the required genuflections to Marxist terminology, which leads into some unintended contradictions in the analysis of fluctuations in the organic composition of capital, the account differs little from some of the contemporary journalistic treatments of the current recession. This paper cannot be described as an auspicious start to the *Journal of Australian Political Economy.*

Silver's analysis of the economic cycle in post-war Australia is more successful in presenting an orthodox Marxist analysis (Silver 1977b). He argues that it is 'the inherent contradictions in the capitalist mode of production and accumulation that explain both economic crisis and stagnation' (p.64). After setting out a two-sector model of the Marxist theory of the trade cycle where the level of economic activity is an increasing function of the amount of investment and a decreasing function of the capital stock, he applies this theory to the Australian post-war situation. He identifies six cycles in the period 1959–50 to 1976–77 (Table A) and briefly analyses the long term relationship between productive capacity, GDP, income and consumption. He also comments on the post-war decline in consumption (relative to GDP) experienced by all industrial nations. His solution to the problem of deficient effective demand is to change the motive force for productive activity to the meeting of real human needs 'in areas such as reduced hours of work (more leisure), education, child care, public transport, and quality of life issues . . . .' (p.72).

4.4 *The State, Economic Policy and Public Finance*

Radical economists frequently point to the role of the state, particularly the complex interrelationships between public and private sector in modern capitalist society. Orthodox economic theory presents this largely as a relationship between consumers of public goods and their elected representatives, ignoring thereby the interests and pressures of the producers of these public services which include private corporations as well as bureaucrats.[28] Some of these interrelationships were explored in the analyses of power and control in neo-capitalist society (see, especially Playford 1969; but also Barbalet 1974; Connell 1977). Apart from this, and from some of the material discussed below, little Australian radical political economy analysis has been presented on the role of the state.

McFarlane (1968) for example, was basically concerned with economic policy and developed a variety of models about the role of the state in policy formation which emphasised the interdependence of the state (politicians and bureaucrats) and private enterprise. More recently, Tsokhas (1976) has attempted an analysis of the changes in the role of the state induced by the current Australian recession and by the change in government in 1975. Neither of these present a coherent theoretical presentation of the role of the state but at least they do not ignore it. More importantly, they examine concrete examples of the complex interrelationships involved.

On the other hand, Rowley's long survey of the political economy of Australia since the war (Rowley 1972b) devotes less than a dozen (of nearly 60) pages to the role of the state. The role of protection in Australian capitalism is referred to but his major emphasis is on the use of demand management as the one important change in the nature of government intervention in the post-war period. The section entitled 'The capitalist state' is essentially a study of politicians as the 'personnel of the bourgeois state' (pp.295–296) thus adding little to the power and control research of earlier writers. An analysis of 'Australian Capitalism Today' (Moore 1972) does not even mention the role of the state directly.

However, there have been some discussions of particular aspects of the political economy of the state in Australian capitalism which deal with immigration, pollution control, the welfare state, transport, taxation and federalism. Collins (1974, 1975) for example, has discussed Australia's post-war immigration using Marxist models developed in connection with European guest workers (for example, Gorz 1970). The major role of the immigration programme is described as maintaining the size of the 'reserve army of labour' to slow down the rate of growth of real wage levels, but it has also contributed to increase divisions in the Australian working class (Collins 1977).[29]

This problem is highlighted by Lonie in a review of Wheelwright and Buckley (Lonie 1975). Many contributions to this book e.g. Roe (1975) Sandercock (1975) Lonie notes (pp.94–95) lack 'theory and method' and are little more 'than emotional diatribes about the evils of our economic system'. The same charge can be made against the review of the Henderson Report in *Intervention* (Collins and Boughton 1976), the major thrust of which appears to be that because Henderson is not a Marxist, he cannot really understand poverty. However, there have been better radical discussions of policy issues, the outstanding example being Atkinson's (1976) neat and careful discussion of the 'transport trap' in which he carefully expounds the inherent difficulties in a rational transport policy because of the conflict between private (from labour and capital) interests and the longer term public interest.

Implicitly deploring the lack of economic debate in Australian radical economics, Catley (1975a, 1975b, 1976a) attempts to provide some explanations. He attributes the lack of investigations of Australian economic reality to a confusion between Stalinism (see footnote 18 above) and 'an interest in economic matters' (Catley 1975a, p.17) and partly to an obsession of the Australian left with 'French gurus, American feminists, British welfare freaks or Bolivian bush rangers' (Catley 1976a, pp.117–118).[30] Although his own contributions are not very profound, Catley provides at least a starting point for such discussion.

In 1975 he presented a radical critique of the Hayden budget, which with hindsight can be better applied to its successors, the Lynch budgets of 1976 and 1977 (1975a, pp.3–8), and a diagnosis of vulgar Marxism in which he pointed to the usefulness of Marxian national accounting in the analysis of current Australian trends (1975b, pp.13–17). More importantly, he provides a concise summary of the theories and policy responses to the current recession in Australia (1976a, pp.121–122) and suggests alternative policy objectives: public sector expansion, the need for restructuring of the private sector, in particular manufacturing industry and some suggestions for counter-cyclical policy (ibid. pp.125–129).

A more detailed economic programme, *Australia Uprooted*, published by the AMWSU and written by one of its research officers in collaboration with political economists from Sydney and Adelaide, can also be discussed under this heading. This pamphlet has been highly successful (over 80000 copies sold or ordered) and has been commented on extensively in the radical political economy journals (Wiltshire 1977; Carmichael 1977). It provides a discussion of the problems of inflation and unemployment; the structure, concentration and foreign ownership of Australian industry, particularly manufacturing and the mineral industry; the political manipulation of foreign investment and the government's policies to deal with the crisis. Much of this is similar to the material earlier discussed under this heading and needs therefore no further comment. The one exception to this is the emphasis on foreign influence on the Australian economy: the blame for the Australian crisis is placed on overseas decision makers (p.10).

Attached to this document is a preliminary proposal for a people's economic programme (submitted for consideration to the ALP federal conference and the ACTU Congress). This demands the creation of a Department of Economic Planning, whose workings will be subject to full public scrutiny and which will take over the major policy role of Treasury and some other economic departments. It also advocates nationalisation 'as necessary to control the direction and functioning of the Australian economy' as well as of large sections of the mineral industry, with compensation only when warranted; stricter regulation of trans-national companies, especially in connection with the international movement of funds; changes in the structure of manufacturing industry; a differential interest rate structure particularly geared to favour home buyers; large scale tax reform including the abolition of most indirect taxes; the reduction of monopolistic and restrictive trade practices; aid for small business; and last but not least, that the expanded public sector envisaged in the programme 'will not emulate the authoritarian, hierarchical and undemocratic organisational and decision making practices' of existing public enterprises but 'will move towards the introduction of democratic principles in work relations' (pp.18–19). A great deal is based on the Left's traditional demands. Detailed criticism of the programme is impossible in this survey but part of the analysis contained therein shows a lack of awareness of some of the changes that have taken place in government policy in the 1970s.[31] The document is important because it shows that at least some Australian radical economists attempt to influence the course of economic events in Australia, either through the ALP but preferably to most, through the more militant Trade Unions.

This brief discussion of what little there is in the way of Australian radical economic policy discussion at present further illustrates some of its shortcomings. This is the absence of discussion so far on a firm theoretical footing: why, for example, have there been no attempts to utilise Kaleckian theory (which deals with matters such as the business cycle, stabilisation policy, the role of the state, and the incidence of taxation in a specific capitalist framework; for overseas attempts see Eatwell 1971a and b, 1976; Kregel 1976, Appendix; Asimakopulos and Burbridge 1974) in the exploration of the Australian economy? Furthermore, why is there such general reluctance among Australian radical economists, generally speaking, to come to grips with the basic instruments of the State's interrelationship with capitalism: government expenditure, taxation, the federal system[32], government bureaucracy and decision makers? One explanation lies perhaps in the dilemma faced by many of Australia's radical economists, particularly the Marxists. They appear to believe that to involve themselves in such matters constitutes 'reformism' or 'revisionism' and that therefore such topics should be avoided. This explanation has been provided by Catley (1976, p.129) but Blake has suggested that a reform programme has to be developed by the Australian left, not only to clarify the problems of present day society but also to raise the consciousness of those who seek its implementation (Blake 1975, pp.26–28). A further explanation is the disarray in the current Marxist discussion of the theory of the state (see Gold, Lo and Wright 1975 and for more recent discussion, Holloway and Picciotto 1977; Jessop 1977), though it should also be pointed out that overseas Marxists have begun more serious analysis of the political economy of the state (O'Connor 1973; Gough 1975).

4.5 *Technocratic Laborism and the Role of Social Democracy*

One research programme of Australian political economy which has seen much discussion in the 1970s has been the analysis of social democracy, in particular with reference to the ALP.[33] This research was inspired by the fact that during the 1960s it was recognised that the ALP has undergone a change from emphasis on equality, nationalisation and similar traditional Labor policies to 'technocratic laborism' with an emphasis on efficiency, planning, running the economic system better and a consequent playing down of the earlier, and more radical, policies. The newer laborism is associated with Whitlam, Hayden, Hurford at the federal level and with Dunstan and Wran at the State level, and was considered to be a phenomenon requiring serious analysis from the left. (See McQueen 1971a, 1972).

This discussion is fairly extensive and has already been surveyed elsewhere (Beresford 1975). The explanation usually given is to point to the increased strength of middle class representation in the ALP, not only among the branches and the parliamentary party, but especially among the advisors and aides which the party attracts particularly when it is in office. To attract the middle class votes, regarded as essential to win office, emphasis in ALP policy has shifted away from the older egalitarian welfare and tax measures towards new policies designed to increase equality of opportunity and equality of access to public services. These views were clearly expressed in the manifesto of the new Labor philosophy: the 1972 Policy Speech (see Whitlam 1977, pp.265–307).

As a starting point, a number of case studies was prepared on current Labor leaders to show how unsocialistic Labor policy in action actually was and thereby to crystalise the basic characteristics of technocratic laborism. One of the first of these was the analysis of Hawke (Rowley 1971) which showed that Hawke's initiatives in the ACTU—especially those through business ventures—were essentially designed to streamline and rationalise capitalism and thereby to leave the system 'basically untouched'. Another study presented a detailed analysis of the Dunstan government which drew similar conclusions about South Australia's ALP policy of social reform (Lonie 1971), an examination which was continued by Baguenalt (1973) with special reference to worker's participation as contrasted with workers' control and by Catley (1972) in a review of a book on the 'politics of transition from Playford to Dunstan'. In an article entitled 'Living off Asia', McQueen (1971b) carefully dissected the views, speeches and writings of Dr. Jim Cairns on defence and foreign policy, and on economic issues such as trade, protection and international aid.[34]

The most thorough of these studies were carried out by Catley and McFarlane in connection with the Federal Labor Government of 1972–75. (Catley and McFarlane 1973a, 1973b, 1974a, 1974b, 1975). This attack on federal Labor policies had already started before it was elected. In a review article provocatively entitled, 'The End of Equality' of a book (McLaren 1972) containing the prospective policies of such a government, McQueen (1972) was particularly concerned to attack Whitlam's effective substitution of equality of opportunity for equality of income as well as the welfare and tax policies of Hayden, Hurford and Crean. The later Catley-McFarlane critique of the Labor government was far more wide-ranging. The federal Labor government's strategy was regarded by them as the implementation of long run economic policies devised by the OECD for its member countries. This meant that far from being a 'socialist tiger', the ALP was a party serving the needs of the modern capitalist economy with the techniques of liberal capitalism rather than the blundering heavy-handed interventions associated with the Liberal-Country Party coalition over the twenty years before 1972. (Catley and McFarlane 1974a, p.1). They then discussed the performance of the Labor government in the light of this strategy, concluding that the ALP sees its role as consolidating the structure of the capitalist system over which it imperfectly presides (ibid. p.88). Later contributions on this subject (1974b, 1975) modified this thesis and brought it up to date, as well as replying against criticism (for example, James 1974).[35]

The literature on technocratic laborism has been criticised because of its concentration on the ideas of Labor leaders, for ignoring or inadequately analysing the state relations of capitalist society, and, in the earlier studies (those by Lonie, McQueen and Rowley published in 1971) for neglecting the political economy of the phenomenon. These reviews of ALP reform policies also raise the problem mentioned earlier: the negative attitude of some radical economists to policies of reform because of its association with revisionism and the neglect of current policy discussion to which this attitude leads. Nevertheless, this literature has made some interesting contributions but it must be added that a more general, integrated study of modern Australian social democratic governments is still required.

4.6 Imperialism and Economic Development

Radical economics and political economy examinations of Australia's relations with imperialism have already been commented on; this section contains brief observations on Australian analysis of development and underdevelopment—which, with few exceptions has largely been published in the *Journal of Contemporary Asia.* Prior to the 1970s, there was relatively little of this, apart from work of two authors.[36] The 1970s started with what is undoubtedly one of the most prestigeous contributions of Australian political economy, Wheelwright and McFarlane's *The Chinese Road to Socialism* (1970). This book was translated into more than half a dozen languages and provided an interesting political economy analysis of Chinese economic development in the light of the cultural revolution, which drew on and explained the ideological and political factors lying behind that revolution.

A further analysis of China was presented by McFarlane (1971b) which again emphasised both traditional and modern (Maoist) influences on economic strategy and the need to integrate political, social and ideological factors with the economic in the analysis of economic development. A narrow economic focus cannot provide sufficient understanding of the forces at work. (See also McFarlane 1977a).

Many of the other articles by Australians in the *Journal of Contemporary Asia* are devoted to sharpening the theoretical tools required for Marxian analysis of the problems of the third world. Leaver (1977) in the context of the Frank-Laclau debate suggests that Frank's theories can be seen 'as a reaction to a crucial problem—the problem of correspondence between production relations and modes of production' which Frank solves by scrapping the terminology and thereby evading the problem. (Leaver 1977, p.112). In a similar context, McEachern (1976) discusses the mode of production of Indian agriculture because a proper analysis of this is required not just for theoretical purposes but because such an analysis is significant 'for the assessment of various development programmes and revolutionary strategies' (p.453). For similar purposes, Barbalet (1976a) has attempted to clarify the relationship between underdevelopment and the colonial economy (thereby further clarifying the notion of the colonial mode of production) while Hickson (1975) discusses the relevance of Marxian categories for the understanding of rural development in Java. This material presents the case for a Marxian analysis of third world problems and the need for the sharpening of Marxian tools required. It is a return to critical rather than dogmatic Marxism.

Three further contributions can be mentioned in this category. Following a comparison of the Chinese and Indian economic development models (Bhattacharya 1974); Bhattacharya presented a more detailed discussion of the choice of technology in the determination of development strategies in the third world (Bhattacharya 1976). Finally, Catley (1976b) presents an historical schemata—critical of Marx's concept of the Asiatic mode of production and of the more modern work on 'colonial modes of production' pp.54–55) through which the history of imperialism in South-East Asia can be studied. This last paper is indebted to Dobb's (1937, chapter 7) classification of the stages of imperialism, and even more to the work of Resnick and Hymer (1969/70, 1970).

Some review articles of recent Marxist contributions to the literature on imperialism and economic development can also be included under this heading. One of these is of Emmanuel (1972) which criticises Ricardo's doctrine of comparative advantage. This important book focussed on the deterioration in the terms of trade of many of the underdeveloped countries and in the process of analysing this problem provides a radical critique of both orthodox international trade theory and the Leninist theory of imperialism. An excellent review appeared in *Arena* (Giles Peters 1973), it was also reviewed by Rowley (1973) and has been utilised by Clark (1978) to shed light on some problems of Australian economic history. This book, whose criticism of conventional theory was sufficiently powerful to draw a defence from Samuelson (1973) has been ignored by the economics profession in Australia. A further important review (Leaver 1976) presents a hyper-critical discussion of Samir Amin's *Accumulation on a World Scale* (1974) in which the basic thrust is the weaknesses of Amin's Marxism, in particular Amin's lack of success in reconciling 'his desire to use Althusserian concepts with his empiricist proclivities . . .' (p.115).[37]

This literature on imperialism and economic development published by Australians in the *Journal of Contemporary Asia* is an interesting new development in Australian radical economics. This is partly because this material is addressed to a world audience, but more importantly because this literature shows a growing maturity by revealing a critical attitude of Australian Marxists to both the work of Marx and to the work of some of the international 'gurus'. Unfortunately, this attitude remains confined to a few; far too many radical economists in Australia still faithfully follow the most recent overseas trend in radical criticism.

4.7 Political Economy and Feminism

Radical feminism has had some influence on the resurgence of political economy in Australia. It has formed a not insignificant part of the content of that political economy as conceived by some. For example, at the first Political Economy Conference at Sydney in 1976 half a dozen papers fell into the category—the political economy of women—an indication of the importance which, in Australia and elsewhere is attributed to this topic. Three issues can be identified in this literature.

One concentrates on the more traditional issues of women's participation in the workforce, female/male wage differentials, occupational classification on the basis of sex, sex discrimination in the hiring of labour, etc. (See, e.g. Power 1974, 1975).[38] Some of this material has been integrated into the analysis of class segmentation within the work force which stressed the need to study the working class as something heterogeneous (Collins 1977), and which treats women (like migrants and blacks) as part of the victims of discrimination and exploitation.

A second has focussed on what were considered crucially important Marxist theoretical questions. These involved the specification of the role of domestic labour (housework) in the capitalist economy; the role of the family in the reproduction of labour power; whether there was a specific domestic mode of production separate from the capitalist mode, and more importantly, whether housework created value and surplus value or only use value. This last issue was treated as a preliminary to deciding whether domestic labour was productive or unproductive labour—or neither. This large literature has been well surveyed (the international literature by Himmelweit and Mohun 1977; its Australian counterpart by Brennan 1977, esp. pp.34–40). Much of this argument is now regarded as irrelevant and leading to barren, conceptual debate (e.g. Curthoys and Barbalet 1976).

The final topic could also have been discussed under the heading of technocratic laborism. These are the papers by Game and Pringle (1976,

1977) on the feminist movement, the state, and the Labor Party in which the so-called innovations on women's issues introduced by the federal Labor government are critically examined. Game and Pringle argue that all these reforms were achieved not because they were initiated from within the Labor Party, but that they were pressed onto the government by the feminist movement, particularly by the articulate and highly organised pressure groups such as the Women's Electoral Lobby. They also point out, that when the economy moved into recession, and when expenditure restraints had to be implemented, it was this type of programme that was abandoned or cut back where possible. More importantly, however, the second article (Game and Pringle 1977) poses some interesting and critical questions for the further development of the capitalist state and presents a criticism of the 'economism' (that is, the overemphasis on economic aspects) which they see in Catley and McFarlane's treatment of technocratic laborism (ibid. pp.47–51). The contents of this paper are therefore wider than its title suggests, and further illustrate the totality of a particular situation which political economists seek to analyse.

4.8 Australian Developments in Post-Keynesian Economics

This survey, so far, has not dealt with the Australian post-Keynesian contributions. In the forefront is, of course, Harcourt's work whose efforts in popularising the Cambridge controversies has already been noted. Most Australian contributions by other writers have appeared in *Australian Economic Papers* (a detailed list is given in footnote 6 above) to which must be added Clark's work (1974, 1977c) which places this new economics in some perspective. Three different strands in this Australian literature can be identified: Harcourt's more recent assessment of the significance of the Cambridge controversies; theoretical developments largely starting out from the work of Kalecki and Kaldor; and research into the historical background of neo-Ricardian and post-Keynesian economics.[39]

Harcourt's contribution to the Cambridge controversies fall largely outside the scope of this survey because they belong to international debate, but his more recent papers on the subject (1975b, 1976, 1977a) are included because they shed light on the alternative approaches to the post-Keynesian theory (discussed in Part II). One of these alternatives is to develop the Keynesian/Kaleckian short period analysis—but this approach does not fit well with those concerned with the return to the classical mode of analysis with its emphasis on long period problems. Another alternative is to develop the new theory on Marxian lines, with emphasis on the production process and thereby to provide a more satisfactory theory of the 'laws of motion of capitalist society'. (1975b, p.329; 1976, pp.58–60). Some elaboration of this, including an account of the bitter debates between the neo-Ricardians and the neo-Marxists, is the subject of Harcourt (1977a, pp.363–367). In this, and the other two papers, he reiterates the necessity for an alternative 'vision' which will provide a 'more suitable and richer framework for the analysis of historical developments, past and future' and which does not jettison the 'modern methods of technical analysis'. (1977a, p.369). Basically, Harcourt has therefore concluded his comprehensive series of surveys of the Cambridge controversies by looking at *reconstruction* rather than the *destruction* of *economic theory*.

This positive approach is characteristic of many of the Australian contributions to post-Keynesian theory in the 1970s. These include the theoretical contributions of Riach, a leading Australian post-Keynesian on the micro-foundations of that theory (Riach 1971, 1972). The first of these rehabilitates Kalecki's concept of the degree of monopoly and defends it against some misrepresentations; the second investigates the micro-economic foundations of Kaldor's distribution theory. A further modification of Kalecki's economics—the role of price flexibility/inflexibility in connection with the problem of excess capacity with fluctuating investment rates—is explored by McFarlane (1973). Harcourt and Kenyon (1976), in a highly theoretical investigation of the relationship between pricing policy and investment decisions in the oligopolistic firm, further develops the micro-foundations which are of such interest to the post-Keynesians (see Eichner and Kregel 1975, Part IV).

Two further papers are much broader in content. One (Harcourt 1977b) is essentially an introductory survey of the three major theories and policies on the central economic issue confronting Australia (and the western capitalist world, generally). These are the 'monetarist school', the 'bastard Keynesians' and the post-Keynesians. Such divisions are necessarily rather artificial but Harcourt clearly specifies the major issues which divide these groups: the rule of the market for the 'monetarists' and von Hayek aided by as little government intervention as possible; the intervention in the market for short-run stabilisation purposes (employment and inflation) largely through control of the level of demand, for the 'bastard Keynesians'; while the post-Keynesians point to the difficulties of conventional market analysis in connection with price determination and link the problem of distribution directly with that of the short term level of economic activity. Harcourt, needless to say, prefers the last as providing the only realistic framework for policy analysis in contemporary Australia. In Harcourt and Kerr (1977), the advantages of the post-Keynesian framework for the prescription of short term policy in Australia are further explored. These policies stress the need to 'socialise investment', develop an incomes policy and budgetary policies which allow government to fulfil its 'distributive goals' and provide a 'social wage'. State intervention is therefore seen as something different from 'just organising capitalism more efficiently' and this 'reformist' approach to economic policy is in strong contrast to the literature on technocratic laborism.

Finally, there are four contributions which put post-Keynesian economics in historical perspective. Groenewegan (1972) relates aspects of Ricardo's value and distribution theory to some theorems of Sraffa (1960) and the reswitching debates. In his Smith bi-centenary paper (Groenewegen 1977) he relates Smith's discussion of the division of labour to contemporary debates in economic history and theory. Clark has traced some of the more modern antecedents of post-Keynesian theory: the work of the Kiel school in developing circular production models (1977c) and a careful analysis of the relationship between input-output analysis, Quesnay's *tableau économique* and Marx's reproduction schema (Clark 1974).

In contrast to the relative abundance of Marxian radical economics literature in Australia, post-Keynesian economics is still relatively under-developed. In fact, without Harcourt's contributions, there would have been little to survey. Despite the risks involved in making forecasts about future developments in economics, I would venture to suggest that it is in this area that the most important contributions to Australian radical economics will be made in the next decade, and by an increasing number of scholars. This exciting prospect is liable to eventuate because the best of the young talent in radical economics in Australia is being steered into this area of enquiry.

Section 5 *Some Conclusions*

It is hoped that this survey, despite its shortcomings, will have enlightened my academic colleagues in the social sciences as to the current content of radical economics in Australia and that it will have made them appreciate the fact that radical economics and political economy are not necessarily the hobby of long-haired students to plague their professors but that, to a significant extent, they constitute serious attempts by fellow academics to advance research and instruction in the social sciences by the reconstruction of economics. Although some of the literature of that radical economics is still very scrappy indeed, as has been amply demonstrated above, other parts are of high quality and exhibit standards which cannot be said to disgrace the academy—even though much of it is published in non-academic and non-professional journals designed for lay-readers.

This survey has also shown the varied content of radical economics, largely a result of the different and overlapping groupings which are starting the reconstruction of political economy. Unfortunately, a great deal of this reconstruction remains in the populist tradition and is devoid of serious theoretical content if not consciously anti-theoretical. Furthermore, much of it remains the uncritical adaptation of foreign ideas. Other material, however, particularly that produced by the post-Keynesians and by some of the Marxists is of considerable sophistication, and many of its young authors are well versed in mathematical and statistical techniques. As demonstrated earlier, this has so far not yielded any rigorous analyses of Australian capitalism but to this surveyor of the literature it would not be surprising if a similar survey for the 1980s reached a quite opposite conclusion in this respect.

Radical economics and political economy are now far more strongly based in Australia. Its previous sporadic appearances seem definitely a thing of the past. During the 1950s and 1960s (and of course, earlier), Australian radical economics was the product of less than half a dozen scholars and academics. Although it has not amounted to an avalanche, there are steadily increasing numbers of academics working in the field, while there are also many young and promising undergraduate and post-graduate students who are beginning to contribute to the literature. There is still a formative stage in the development of political economy in Australia but the infant is rapidly growing up.

This means that radical economics will have to be gradually accepted as a legitimate field of study even though some of its conclusions may not be palatable to the more conservative members of the profession. Furthermore, the fact that much of this radical economics is Marxist oriented cannot be used any more for its easy dismissal: gone are the days when Marxism prescribed adherence to the labour theory of value as a theory of relative prices, when Marxists had to believe in a series of prophecies (such as the immiseration thesis) or when Marxism meant aping the latest slogans from Moscow or other Communist capitals. There is, it is true, still a great deal of this vulgar and uncritical Marxism about, but this survey has also shown that it is dangerous to generalise in this regard with respect to the various strands of Marxist radical political economy.

This creates some obligations for radical economists as well. They should not lead a separate existence in a situation of intellectual apartheid (as is the aim of the Sydney University Political Economy group which wants a *separate* department and *separate* courses). Radical economists should interact with their more orthodox colleagues (and vice versa), intellectually confront each other and thereby, it is to be hoped learn from each other. In particular, all radical economists should feel the need for exposure to the dominant (and domineering?) conventional economics, in particular to its mathematical and statistical techniques. This does not mean emphasising the merits of a shallow pluralism which skates over the surface of a variety of schools of thought, but criticism and debate will stimulate both the older conventional economics and the newer radical variety in all their schools of thought.

Notes

[1] Editorial, *Journal of Australian Political Economy*, No. 1, October 1977. This editorial starts with the observation that 'Throughout the seventies there has been a growing rejection of bourgeois economics both inside and outside tertiary institutions. At the same time the capitalist crisis has strengthened the rejection of bourgeois economics and made imperative the necessity for students and workers to critically analyse and challenge the capitalist system . . .'

[2] The reconstruction of political economy on 'classical' lines has a left and right radical development depending on the meaning assigned to 'classical'. On Marx's definition of classical political economy (Marx 1971, p.52) the development has been radical left (for example, the radical Ricardians discussed later); classical economics on Keynes' definition (Keynes 1936, p.3n) has led to a radical right libertarian political economy associated with Chicago (Milton Friedman but going back to Simons and Knight in the 1930s), Virginia (Buchanan and Tulloch) and Austrian (von Mises, von Hayek). Their Australian followers (as pointed out by my referees) include Colin Clark, Heinz Arndt, Ross Parrish, Michael Porter, Peter Swan, John Head, Geoffrey Brennan and Cliff Walsh, and the economists associated with the (Austrian inspired) Institute of Independent Studies such as Colin Simkin, Peter Samuel, Malcolm Fisher and E. Sieper. Reasons of space preclude a critical discussion of the views of these right wing libertarian schools which like the radical left are far from homogeneous.

[3] One such omission is the *Australian Left Review*, the theoretical journal of the Australian Communist Party. This was omitted largely because of its very limited political economy content. Newspaper articles (from *Nation Review*, for example) have also been excluded. Furthermore, collected essays such as Wheelwright (1974) and books of readings largely composed of non-Australian material (Wheelwright and Stilwell 1976) have also been excluded because the material was outside the period or non-Australian respectively. For reviews of these books, see McFarlane (1974) and Schneider (1977).

[4] To clarify this discussion, Fred Gruen suggested the following diagram as being helpful:

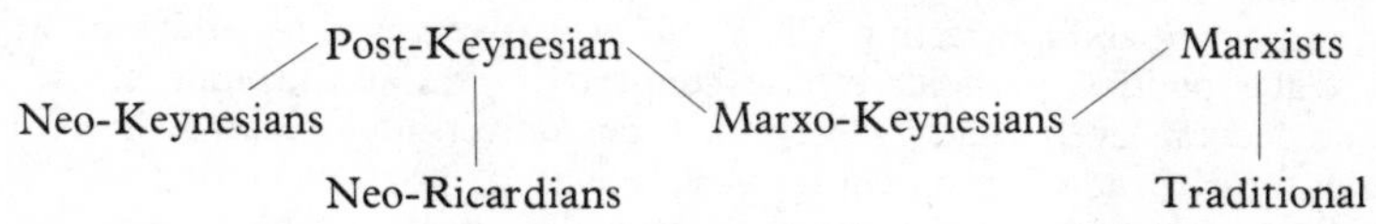

Although there is some merit in this diagram, it blurs the historical parentage of the various schools of thought which is essential to the proper understanding of the divisions. Attempts by myself and others to construct a better diagram to portray these various distinctions *correctly* either became too complicated or missed essential elements. To those unfamiliar with current developments in modern theory in this area the diagram may be useful (qualified by the above mentioned caveat).

[5] Professor Gruen found my use of the word 'destroyed' too strong in this context. Those who think likewise should study Samuelson (1966, 1976) and cannot draw comfort from Blaug (1974) which is filled with factual, methodological and theoretical errors. See esp. pp.39–43. See also Solow (1975), and for the destructive impact of the Cambridge critique, Pasinetti (1969) and Garegnani (1970).

[6] See, for example, Asimakopulos (1969, 1970), Akyuz (1976), Eichner (1977), Harris (1974), Henry (1975), Hodgson and Steedman (1977) Levine (1976) Nell (1968, 1972), Robinson (1969), Roncaglia (1974) and Steedman (1971). Australian contributions include Frearson (1964), Groenewegen (1972, 1977), Harcourt (1963), McFarlane (1973) and Riach (1971, 1972). Reference should also be made to Ng's critical discussion of the Cambridge controversies (Ng 1974 and the subsequent Peacock-Ng exchange 1977).

Australia's other major economic journal, the *Economic Record*, has had relatively fewer contributions on this branch of economics but see Sen (1963), Harcourt (1965), Harcourt and Massaro (1964), Harcourt *et al* (1975), Hieser (1954), Hieser and Soper (1966) and Laing (1969).

[7] Some of these differences are illustrated in the survey of the methodological debates in Australian radical economics in the 1970s: particularly in connection with the Snooks-Rowse-Clark-McFarlane debate in *Labour History* (1975, 1976), the McFarlane-Ergas debate (1975, 1976) and the contributions by White (1975, 1976, 1977) and O'Donnell (1977). The survey of contributions to other topics will further illustrate these substantial differences.

[8] In the original draft of this paper, this section was much longer. Reasons of space have forced its drastic reduction, but the author intends to develop this material elsewhere in a joint project with B.J. McFarlane and D.L. Clark, *Political Economy in Australia.*

[9] The limited Marxist influence and the reasons for this can be illustrated by looking at Holman, the New South Wales Premier. In 1893, Holman delivered a series of lectures on socialism and economics (extracts in Evatt 1945, pp.39–44) in which Marx was singled out for particular praise. In 1905, Holman argued that it was 'a mistake to imagine that English and Australian socialism owed much to Karl Marx . . .' (Holman 1905, pp.328–329).

[10] As the author of the leading text on political economy in the second half of the nineteenth century, J.S. Mill was invariably attacked by these early critics. As the advocate of inheritance taxation, as the land tax reformer, as the qualified freetrader, and as the 'co-operative socialist', Mill was important in stimulating radical critiques in the nineteenth century.

[11] The influence of Henry George on Australian radical economics has been particularly strong, important and longlasting. Clark (1977a) has surveyed his influence on New South Wales politics, particularly that connected with land taxation at the local, state and federal level. Henry George was not universally accepted, however, by Australia's early radical economists; Andrade (n.d. pp.8–9) argued that Henry George cannot provide a real solution to Australia's problems because his land tax would not fall on the landlords; like all taxes, it would be passed to the workers. Cinderella (1890b, p.11) who described him (her) self as a pupil of Henry George, nevertheless criticised him for confining his attacks of landlords and not extending it to the other 'idlers' in society, the owners of capital. Although Georgists are still active on the land question in Australia, they have no influence on the present political economy movement, though one of their number did attend the 1977 Conference.

[12] Anderson (1912, p.9) makes the suggestion: 'I am told that the Chair of Economics at Sydney University was blocked for twenty years because it was thought in certain quarters that the Professor of Economics would think it is duty to preach the doctrine

of free trade.' For a detailed discussion of the painfully slow development of economics as an academic subject at Sydney University, see Goodwin (1966, pp.545–568).

[13] In developing these criticisms of economics, Irvine was undoubtedly indebted to the great 'heretics' of the turn of the century; T.B. Veblen and J.A. Hobson. Some of the critical arguments advanced in 1914 were further developed in Irvine's only book, *The Midas Delusion* (1933, chapters 2–5).

[14] In his years of retirement, Irvine seems to have maintained his strong interest in monetary questions, particularly the work of Keynes, but the main sources of his economics were highly unconventional. His depression economics was especially influenced by Crozier, J.A. Hobson, Veblen, and later, the works by Foster and Catching and Major Douglas. These last undoubtedly aided him in anticipating some of Keynes' later conclusions such as the 'paradox of thrift', though unlike Keynes he failed to build these criticisms into a coherent theory.

[15] In this context, S.J. Butlin (1970, p.9) has written: '. . . apart from suspicion of monetary heresy he antagonised some in his last few years by daring to speak his mind. How far the traditional reason for his enforced resignation was convenient occasion for his opponents I do not know, but when the attack came he was vulnerable and among his enemies were the dominant academics.' (For a more outspoken account, see McFarlane 1966a, pp.12–18).

[16] Goodwin (1966) for example, makes no attempt to analyse his theories of money or business cycles; he only deals with Irvine's activities at Sydney University and his evidence for wage cases. He is not mentioned in the standard economic texts of the time: Mills and Benham 1925; Mills and Walker 1935; and in connection with the depression, by Shann and Copland (1931). In the current standard work on the great depression, (Schedvin 1970) he has also been ignored. For a discussion of his role in this period, see McFarlane 1966a; Clark 1977b, pp.152–157. He has also been ignored by Sydney University's 'radical political economists' (see for example, Simpson-Lee 1970, p.16 who devotes not a single line to Irvine's role in the 'Sydney tradition').

[17] For the use of heretics as texts by Irvine, particularly the work of Major Douglas and the amusement that this caused in more orthodox circles, see Gaitskell (1933, p.348 n.1). Mills and Walker (1935) spend considerable space in criticising Douglas credit, without making reference to the fact that the first holder of the Sydney Chair was influenced by his monetary theory. See also McConnell (1934).

[18] Stalin's influence is particularly noticeable in Campbell 1954, chapter 1. The use of the phrase, 'serious social scientist' in connection with Stalin comes from Meek's *Economic Journal* review of Stalin's *Economic Problems of Socialism in the U.S.S.R.* (Meek 1953). The spectre of Stalin killed serious interest in economic questions among Australian Marxists from the middle of the 1950s to the end of the 1960s because of the identification of economism with Stalinism. Economism refers to overemphasis on the 'economic base' in the analysis of society to the neglect of the 'superstructure'. This overemphasis was a hallmark of Stalin's crude materialism. This meaning of the term should not be confused with Lenin's critique of trade union action and reformism as 'economism'.

[19] For a detailed survey of this type of literature and its American sources of inspiration, see Gollan 1968, chapter 3.

[20] Because much of this academic work has been critically examined recently by Connell (1975, pp.227–235), it is not discussed in detail here. For comments on its atheoretical nature, see Connell 1977 p.36.

[21] Alternatively, the few Australian radical economists of the period provided a commentary on Labor Party policy in the now defunct journals such as *Outlook* and *Dissent*. As stated earlier, the economic content of these journals cannot be surveyed here.

[22] The Cambridge controversies need not be surveyed here, because excellent surveys of their content are available (Harcourt 1969, 1972, and, for a simpler version, 1975). While the inspiration Harcourt provided for the revival of political economy in Australia should not be under-estimated his contributions are given little space in this survey because most of them contributed to the *international* debate in the pages of leading academic journals.

[23] Butler and Stilwell (1975) criticise neo-classical economics for its erroneous treatment of time, but more basically, for its *omission* of power, conflict, the role of the state, property ownership, income and wealth distribution. These omissions are explicitly described as the value judgements of neo-classical theory, so that all neo-classical economics can be described as *Normative Economics*, the title of Stilwell's book (1975a, p.ix). This position is criticised in White's review of the book (1975, esp. pp.90–92).

[24] It has of course little to do with the tradition of American institutionalism in the work of Veblen, Commons and Mitchell, for example, with its thorough empirical research. Wheelwright's earlier work (1957; Wheelwright and Miskelly 1967) is in this institutionalist tradition, his later work is not. Simpson-Lee's papers (1953, 1961) are not really 'institutionalist' in the American sense.

[25] All Ergas had to offer on this issue is the following: 'it is difficult to believe that Marx intended budding academics to go out and measure the rate of surplus value or the organic composition of capital; he wasn't such a crass empiricist' (p.100). This of course completely dodges the issue of Marx's own use of empirical material in the construction of his economic analysis in *Capital*. But cf Rowse (1975).

[26] A good example is the use of Lenin's *Imperialism* (1950) and Hilferding's *Finanzkapital* (1973) in the analysis of Australia's 'finance capital' as in the articles by Rivers and Hyde (1975) and Cochrane (1976).

[27] Some statistical evidence is presented in Table 2 (pp.44–47) in which property income as a percentage of national income and capital consumption as a percentage of GDP are used as proxies for the rate of surplus value and the organic composition of capital respectively. Rowley also discusses other factors such as the rising share of government expenditure (pp.47–48), accelerating inflation in the Western world and its implications (55–58), the collapse of the international financial system (56–62), the energy crisis (62–65) and the decline in world trade (68). Most of the data is from OECD publications. Rowley's paper has been criticised by Silver for failing to use Marx's theoretical framework of *Capital*, Volume III, chapter 13–15 sufficiently (1977a).

[28] The radical rightwing libertarians, especially from the Virginia school, have examined some of these aspects in so far as the interests of the bureaucrats are concerned. For an Australian example, see Sieper (1978). The role of 'citizens' as producers is generally ignored, despite its importance, particularly in the Australian context.

[29] Collins (1977) utilises Braverman's (1974) analysis in this paper, but without going into detail about his analysis of the labour process. My Marxist referee's expressed surprise 'that this book has not been important in Australia' and that 'it has not been a major subject of debate' is worth mentioning. I am not aware of any review of this book in Australia's radical journals, perhaps an indication of their alienation from the problems of the working class.

[30] A prime example of this obsession in Higgins (1975) which presents a working paper on the welfare state which is almost exclusively based on English welfare sources, and which displays no awareness, for example, of the evidence on redistribution resulting from the tax and the welfare system presented in the Asprey report and its commissioned studies. The French Guru refers to Althusser, the spell of American feminists to the long, sterile debate on domestic labour (surveyed later) and Bolivian bushrangers to the 'romantic attractions' of Che Guevara. These detract from the analysis of Australian capitalism.

[31] The following examples suffice. In their tax policy they argue the case for rebates as against concessional deductions (rebates were implemented in the 1975 Budget) and they propose a graduated company income tax, in spite of the cogent reasons advanced against this practice by Crean on its abolition in the 1973 Budget. In connection with foreign investment, they do not point out that both the McMahon and the Whitlam governments actively discouraged certain types of foreign investment in 1972–73, presumably because this would not fit in with their basic thesis of the multi-national conspiracy to destroy the Labor government.

[32] This reviewer has attempted to remedy this situation by providing some discussion of taxation policy and the 'new federalism' as an Australian starting point for the political economy of public finance. (See Groenewegen 1975, 1976).

[33] The British model for such analysis has frequently been Miliband's examination of parliamentary socialism (Miliband 1961); an early Australian analysis is Gordon Childe's book, *How Labour Governs* (Childe 1964, but first published in 1923).

[34] There have been fewer analyses of conservative governments. McEachern and Lonie (1972) presents an analysis of the Playford government in South Australia, and Simms and Tsokhas (1977) analyses the Liberal Party's attitudes and practice towards nationalisation and government enterprise. (I am indebted for these references to Melanie Beresford.)

[35] For critical comments on the Catley-McFarlane thesis by former advisors to Whitlam and Hayden, see McGuinness (1975) and Freudenberg (1977, pp.72–78, esp. pp.74–75).

[36] Wheelwright (1974) contains sections on Latin America and Asia, largely written during the 1960s; McFarlane (1964, 1966b) discusses problems of economic growth, planning and the economics of neo-colonialism.

[37] In the earlier draft of this survey, the material contained in this paragraph appeared in an expanded version in a section completely devoted to a survey of review articles. For reasons of space, this section has been eliminated, despite the fact that it highlighted a feature of Australian radical economics which editors of Australia's academic journals could do well to copy, that is, to allow more space for book reviews and to shorten the gestation period in the publication of book reviews. Many of the radical reviews focus on important problems inherent in modern Marxist thought: for example, the reviews of Bose (1975) by Giles Peters (1976) and Fishburn (1976);

Green's (1975) review of Dobb (1973) and Barbalet's reviews (1975, 1976b) of two re-issued Marxist classics: Riazanov (1973) and Koshimura (1975). Rowley's review of Mandel (1975) is interesting in the light of his later use of Mandel's *Late Capitalism* in his analysis of the end of the long boom (Rowley 1976a and b).

[38] One of my referees has objected to the inclusion of Power's work on the ground that it is hardly radical because it uses neoclassical tools including phase diagrams from T.W. Swan. Power's work has been mentioned because of her association with the Sydney political economy group, which styles itself as radical economists.

[39] Only contributions of the 1970s are discussed: the work of Hieser, Frearson and the early work of Harcourt is therefore excluded.

Bibliography

Aarons, Eric (1958), *Economics for Workers* (Sydney: Current Book Distributors).
Akyüz, Y. (1976), 'A Note on the Marxian Transformation Problem and Income Distribution', *Australian Economic Papers*, 15, June.
Amin, Samir (1974), *Accumulation on a World Scale* (New York, Monthly Review Press).
Anderson, Francis (1907), *Liberalism and Socialism*—Presidential Address, 11th Meeting of Australian Association for the Advancement of Science, held at Adelaide (Sydney: n.p.).
—— (1912), *Sociology in Australia: a Plea for its Teaching* (Sydney, n.p.).
Andrade, David A. (1888), *An Anarchist Plan of Campaign* (Melbourne, n.p.).
—— (n.d.), *Our Social System and How if Affects Those Who Work for Their Living* (Melbourne, n.p.).
Anstey, Frank (1917). *The Kingdom of Shylock* (Melbourne: Labour Call Printery).
—— (1921), *The Money Power* (Melbourne: Fraser and Jenkinson).
[Arndt, H.W., N.G. Butlin, J.R. Wilson and K. Laffer] (1947), *The Case for Bank Nationalisation* (Sydney: New South Wales Fabian Society).
Arndt, H.W. (1972), 'Review of Australian Capitalism', *Australian Quarterly*, 44, June.
Asimakopulos, A. (1969), 'A Robinsonian Growth Model in one Sector Notation', *Australian Economic Papers*, 8, June.
—— (1970), 'A Robinsonian Growth Model in one Sector Notation—An Amendment', *Australian Economic Papers*, 9, December.
—— and J.B. Burbridge (1974), 'The Short Period Incidence of Taxation', *Economic Journal*, 84, June.
Atkinson, Don (1976), 'The Transport Trap, *Arena*, No. 42.
Australian Metalworkers and Shipwrights Union (1977), *Australia Uprooted* (Sydney: AMWSU).
Baguenalt, J. (1973). 'Dunstan's Scheme for Worker Participation', *Arena*, No. 32–33.
Barbalet, J.M. (1974), 'Political Science, the State and Marx', *Politics*, 9, May.
—— (1975), 'Riazanov on Marx and Engels', *Arena*, No. 39.
—— (1976a), 'Underdevelopment and the Colonial Economy', *Journal of Contemporary Asia*. 6, No. 2.
—— (1976b), 'Capital Reproduction and Accumulation: Koshimura's Theory', *Arena* No. 42.
Beresford, Melanie (1975), 'The Technocratic Labor Thesis: A Critique', *Arena* No. 39.
Bhaduri, Amit. (1977), 'On the Formation of Usurious Interest Rates in Backward Agricultural Countries', *Cambridge Journal of Economics*, 1, December.
Bhattacharya, D. (1974), 'India-China: Comparisons and Contrasts 1950–72', *Journal of Contemporary Asia*, 4, December.
—— (1976), 'Development and Technology in the Third World', *Journal of Contemporary Asia*, 6, No. 3.
Blake, Jack (1975), 'Revolutionaries and Reformists'. *Arena* No. 40.
Blaug, M. (1974), *The Cambridge Revolution: Success or Failure?* Hobart Paper No. 6, (London: Institute of Economic Affairs).
Bose, A. (1975), *Marxian and post-Marxian Political Economy*. (Harmondsworth: Penguin Modern Economics Texts).
Braverman, H. (1974), *Labor and Monopoly Capital: The Degradation of Work in the Twentieth Century*, (New York: Monthly Review Press).
Brennan, Teresa (1977), 'Woman and Work', *Journal of Australian Political Economy*, 1, October.
Brezniak, M. and J. Collins (1977), 'The Australian Crisis: from Boom to Bust', *Journal of Australian Political Economy*, 1, October.

Bronfenbrenner, M. (1970), 'Radical Economics in America: 1970', *Journal of Economic Literature*, 8, September.
Butler, G.J. and F.J.B. Stilwell (1975). 'The Teaching of Political Economy', paper presented at Fifth Conference of Economists, Brisbane. (Mimeographed).
Butlin, S.J. (1970), 'The Faculty's Fifty Years'. *Economic Review*.
Cameron, T.J. (1972), 'Understanding the Radical Students' Approach to Economics: A Reply to F.H. Gruen's "The Radical Challenge to Bourgeois Economics"', *Australian Quarterly*, 44, March.
Campbell, E.W. (1947), *People versus the Banks* (Sydney: Current Book Distributors).
—— (1954), *Political Economy. A Simple Outline* (Sydney: Current Book Distributors).
—— (1963), *The 60 Families Who Own Australia*. (Sydney: Current Book Distributors).
Carmichael, L. (1977), 'A People's Programme', *Intervention*, No. 9.
Catley, R. (1972), 'The Politics of Transition', *Arena*, No. 28.
—— (1975a), 'The Budget', *Arena*, No. 40.
—— (1975b), 'Vulgar Marxism', *Arena*, No. 40.
—— (1976a), 'Current Notes on the Economy', *Arena*, No. 42.
—— (1976b), 'The Development of Underdevelopment in Southeast Asia', *Journal of Contemporary Asia*, 6, No. 1.
—— (1977), 'Review of the first issue of Journal of Australian Political Economy', *Bulletin of Marxist Studies*, 3, October.
—— and B.J. McFarlane (1973a), 'An Emerging Man Power Policy', *Arena*, No. 32–33.
—— and B.J. McFarlane (1973b), 'Labor's Plan: Neo-Capitalism Comes to Australia', *Intervention*, No. 3.
—— and B.J. McFarlane (1974a), *From Tweedledum to Tweedledee: The New Labor Government in Australia*. (Sydney: ANZ Book Company).
—— and B.J. McFarlane (1974b), 'The Limits of Technocratic Laborism', *Arena*, No. 36.
—— and B.J. McFarlane (1975), 'Technocratic Laborism—the Whitlam Government', in Wheelwright and Buckley (eds.), *Political Economy of Australian Capitalism* (Sydney: ANZ Book Company), Vol. I.
Chattopadhyay, P. (1974), 'Political Economy: What's in a Name?', *Monthly Review*, 25, April.
Childe, V.G. (1964), *How Labour Governs* (Melbourne: Melbourne University Press). Originally published in 1923.
Cinderella (variously attributed to Hugh Gilmore and Ella McFayden) (1890a), *Money versus Wealth or the Origins of Interest Clearly explained by a Pupil of Henry George and John Ruskin* (Sydney, n.p.).
Cinderella (1890b), *A Manual of Political Economy for Free Men*. (Sydney, n.p.).
Clark, Colin (1972), 'Socialism: The Full Rich Nutty Flavour of Lunacy', *News Weekly*, 11, October.
Clark, D.L. (1974), 'The Origins of Input-Output Analysis: Walras versus Marx', Paper delivered at Fourth Conference of Economists, Canberra. (Mimeographed).
—— (1975). 'Australia: Victim or Partner of British Imperialism', in Wheelwright and Buckley (eds.), *Political Economy of Australian Capitalism* (Sydney: ANZ Book Company), Vol. I.
—— (1976), 'Marx versus Butlin: Some Comments on the Snooks-Rowse Debate', *Labour History*, No. 30.
—— (1977a), 'Single Tax, Free Trade and Land Values Taxation: Henry George and the Sydney Single Tax League' (Kensington: University of New South Wales, Department of Economic History). (Mimeographed).
—— (1977b), 'Was Lang Right?' in H. Radi and P. Spearritt (eds.), *Jack Lang* (Sydney: Hale & Iremonger and *Labour History*).
—— (1977c), 'The Kiel School: Its Contribution to Capital and growth Theory', Paper delivered at the Sixth Conference of Economists, Hobart (mimeographed).
—— (1978), 'Britain and Australia: Unequal Exchange', in Wheelwright and Buckley (eds.), *Political Economy of Australian Capitalism* (Sydney: ANZ Book Company), Vol. III.

Cochrane, Peter (1976), 'Australian Finance Capital', *Intervention*, No. 6.
Coddington, A. (1976), 'Keynesian Economics: The Search for First Principles', *Journal of Economic Literature*, 14, December.
Collins, J. (1974), 'Immigrant Workers in Australia', *Intervention*, No. 4.
—— (1975), 'The Political Economy of Post-War Immigration', in Wheelwright and Buckley (eds.), *Political Economy of Australian Capitalism* (Sydney: ANZ Book Company), Vol. I.
—— (1977), 'A Divided Working Class', *Intervention*, No. 8.
—— and R. Boughton (1976), 'Capitalism and Poverty: A Critique of the Henderson Report', *Intervention*, No. 7.
Connell, R.W. (1975), 'Structure and Structural Change in the Ruling Class', in Wheelwright and Buckley (eds.), *Political Economy of Australian Capitalism* (Sydney: ANZ Book Company), Vol. I.
—— (1977), *Ruling Class. Ruling Culture. Studies of Conflict Power and Hegemony in Australian Life* (Cambridge: Cambridge University Press).
Curthoys, J. and J.M. Barbalet (1976), 'The Domestic Labour Debate', papers presented at the First Political Economy Conference, Sydney. (Mimeographed).
Davidson, A. (1972), 'A Good Book for the Thirties', *Australian Left Review*, No. 37, October.
Davies, A.F. and S. Encel (eds.), (1965), *Australian Society : A Sociological Introduction* (Melbourne: Cheshire).
De Brunhof, S. (1973), 'Marx as an A-Ricardian', *Economy and Society*, 2.
Dobb, M.H. (1937), *Political Economy and Capitalism.* (London: Routledge and Kegan Paul).
——(1944), *The Economics of Private Enterprise.* (Sydney: Current Book Distributors).
—— (1973), *Theories of Value and Distribution Since Adam Smith* (Cambridge: Cambridge University Press).
Eatwell, John (1971a), 'A New Approach to the Problem of Public Goods', Cambridge, Faculty of Economics (mimeographed).
—— (1971b), 'State Intervention and Income Distribution: Some Theoretical Considerations', Cambridge, Faculty of Economics (mimeographed).
—— (1974), 'Controversies in the Theory of Surplus Value: Old and New', *Science and Society*, 38.
——(1975), 'Mr. Sraffa's Standard Commodity and the Rate of Exploitation', *Quarterly Journal of Economics*, 89.
—— (1976), 'A Simple Framework for the Analysis of Taxation, distribution and Effective Demand', Cambridge, Faculty of Economics (mimeographed).
Edwards, R.C., A. McEwan, *et al*, (1970), 'A Radical Approach to Economics: Basis for a new Curriculum', *American Economic Review*, 60, May.
Eichner, A.S. (1977), 'The Geometry of Macrodynamic Balance', *Australian Economic Papers*, 16, June.
—— and J.A. Kregel (1975), 'An Essay on Post-Keynesian Theory', *Journal of Economic Literature*, 13, December.
Ellman, M. (1977), 'Report from Holland: The Economics of North Sea Hydrocarbons', *Cambridge Journal of Economics*, 1, September.
Emmanuel, A. (1972), *Unequal Exchange. A Study of the Imperialism of Trade* (New York: Monthly Review Press).
Encel, S. (1960), 'The Top Men', *Outlook*, 4, December.
—— (1965), 'Power in Australia', *Arena*, No. 6.
—— (1970), *Equality and Authority* (Melbourne: Cheshire).
Ergas, H. (1975), 'Radical Ricardians: Reply to McFarlane', *Arena*, No. 40.
Evans, D. (1972), 'Australia and Developing Countries', in Playford and Kirsner (eds.), *Australian Capitalism* (Ringwood: Penguin Books).
Evatt, H.V. (1945), *Australian Labor Leader* (Sydney: Angus and Robertson).
Fishburn, G. (1976), 'Arun Bose's "Post-Marxian Political Economy": Critique, Clarification and Evaluation', Kensington: University of New South Wales, School of Economics (mimeographed).

Fitzpatrick, Brian (1939), *British Imperialism and Australia 1783–1833* (Sydney: Sydney University Press, 1971), First published, 1939.
—— (1941), *The British Empire in Australia 1934–1939* (Melbourne: Macmillan). First published, 1941.
—— (1944), *The Rich Get Richer* (Melbourne: Rawson's Bookshop).
—— (1945), *Public Enterprise Does Pay* (Melbourne: Rawson's Book Shop).
—— and E.L. Wheelwright (1965), *The Highest Bidder* (Melbourne: Landsdowne Press).
Fox, L.P. (1940), *Monopoly* (Sydney: Research Department, Left Book Club).
—— (1946), *Wealthy Men* (Sydney: Current Book Distributors).
—— (1974), *Australia Taken Over?* (Sydney: for the author).
Frearson, K.S. (1964), 'Recent Developments in the Theory of Economic Growth', *Australian Economic Papers*, 3, June-December.
Freudenberg, Graham (1977), *A Certain Grandeur* (Melbourne: Macmillan Company of Australia).
Gaitskell, H.T.N. (1933), 'Four Monetary Heretics' in G.D.H. Cole (ed.), *What Everybody Wants to Know About Money* (London: Victor Gollancz Ltd.).
Galbraith, J.K. (1973), 'Power and the Useful Economist', *American Economic Review*, 63, March.
Game, A. and R. Pringle (1977), 'The Feminist Movement, the State and the Labor Party'. *Intervention*, No. 8.
Garegnani, P. (1960), *Il Capitale nelle Teorie della Distribuzione* (Milan: Giuffré).
—— (1970), 'Heterogeneous Capital, the Production Function and the Theory of Capital', *Review of Economic Studies*, 37, July.
—— (1976), 'On a Change in the Notion of Equilibrium in recent Work on Value and Distribution', in M. Brown, K. Sato and P. Zarembka (editors), *Essays in Modern Capital Theory* (Amsterdam: North Holland Publishing Company).
Giles Peters, A. (1973), 'Unequal Exchange', *Arena*, No. 32–33.
—— (1976), 'Marxism and Modern Political Economy', *Intervention*, No. 6.
Glyn, A. and R. Sutcliffe (1972), *British Capitalism: Workers and the Profits Squeeze* (Harmondsworth, Penguin Books).
Goddard, M. (1971), 'Critiques of Mainstream Economics', *Arena*, No. 25.
Gold, D.A., C.Y.H. Lo and E.O. Wright (1975), 'Recent Developments in Marxist Theories of the Capitalist State', *Monthly Review*, 27, October.
Gollan, R. (1968), *The Commonwealth Bank of Australia, Origins and Early History* (Canberra: Australian National University Press).
Goodwin, C.D.W. (1966), *Economic Inquiry in Australia* (Durham N.C.: Duke University Press).
Goodwin, J.E. (1878), *Scientific Legislation: or a Theory of Calculated Labour Equivalents* (Melbourne, n.p.).
Gordon, R.A. (1976), 'Rigor and Relevance in a Changing Institutional Setting', *American Economic Review*, 66, March.
Gordon, R. and W. Osmond (eds.), (1970), *The Australian New Left: Critical Essays and Strategy* (Melbourne: Heinneman).
Gorz, A. (1970), 'Immigrant Labour', *New Left Review*, No. 61.
Gough, I. (1975), 'State Expenditure and Capital', *New Left Review*, No. 92.
Green, R. (1975), 'Ricardo or Marx', *Arena*, No. 39.
Groenewegen, P.D. (1972), 'Three Notes on Ricardo', *Australian Economic Papers*, 11, June.
—— (1975), 'Accumulation and Tax Policy', *Arena*, No. 39.
—— (1976), 'Fraser and the New Federalism', *Arena*, No. 42.
—— (1977), 'Adam Smith and the Division of Labour: A Bi-centenary Estimate', *Australian Economic Papers*, 16, 1977.
Gruen, F.H. (1971), 'The Radical Challenge to Bourgeois Economics', *Australian Quarterly*, 43, March.
—— (1972), 'A Rejoinder', *Australian Quarterly*, 44, March.

Harcourt, G.C. (1963), 'A Critique of Mr. Kaldor's Model of Income Distribution and Economic Growth', *Australian Economic Papers*, 2, June.
—— (1965), 'A Two-sector Model of the Distribution of Income and the Level of Employment in the Short Run', *Economic Record*, 41, March.
—— (1969), 'Some Cambridge Controversies in the Theory of Capital', *Journal of Economic Literature*, 9, June.
—— (1972), *Some Cambridge Controversies in the Theory of Capital* (Cambridge, Cambridge University Press).
—— (1975a), 'Much Ado About Something', *Economic Papers*, No. 49, (Sydney: Economic Society of Australia and New Zealand, NSW and Victorian Branches).
—— (1975b), 'The Cambridge Controversies: The Afterglow', in M. Parkin and A.R. Nobay (eds.), *Contemporary Issues in Economics* (Manchester: Manchester University Press).
—— et al., (1975c), 'Decline and Rise: The Revival of (Classical) Political Economy', *Economic Record*, 51, December.
—— (1976), 'The Cambridge Controversies: Old Ways and New Horizons—or dead end?', *Oxford Economic Papers*, 28, No. 1.
—— (1977a), 'The Theoretical and Social Significance of the Cambridge Controversies in the Theory of Capital', *Revue d'économie politique*, March/April.
—— (1977b), 'On Theories and Policies', in J. Nieuwenhuysen and P. Drake (eds.), *Australian Economic Policy* (Melbourne: Melbourne University Press).
—— and P. Kenyon (1976), 'Pricing and the Investment Decision', *Kyklos*, 29, No. 3.
—— and P.M. Kerr (1977), 'The Acceptance of a Mixed Economy', in P. Weller (ed.), *The A.L.P.: Past Trends and Future Prospects*, (forthcoming).
—— and V.G. Massaro (1964), 'Mr. Sraffa's Production of Commodities', *Economic Record*, 40, September.
Hare, P.G. (1977), 'Economic Reform in Hungary: Problems and Prospects', *Cambridge Journal of Economics*, 1, December.
Harris, D.J. (1974), 'The Price Policy of the firm, the Level of Employment and Distribution of Income in the Short Run', *Australian Economic Papers*, 13, June.
Henry, J.F. (1975), 'Productive Labour, Exploitation and Oppression', *Australian Economic Papers*, 14, June.
Hieser, R.O. (1954), 'Review of Steindl, Maturity and Stagnation in American Capitalism', *Economic Record*, 30, May.
—— and C.S. Soper (1966), 'Demand Creation: A Radical Approach to the Theory of Selling Costs', *Economic Record*, 42, September.
Higgins, W. (1975), 'A Working Paper on the Welfare State', *Arena*, No. 40.
Hilferding, R. (1973), *Das Finanzkapital* (Frankfurt A.M.: Europaeische Verlaganstalt). First published, 1910.
Himmelweit, S. and Mohun, S. (1977), 'Domestic Labour and Capital', *Cambridge Journal of Economics*, 1, March.
Hinkson, J. (1974), 'Currency Crisis: Money as a Measure of Capitalist Decline', *Arena*, No. 36.
—— (1975), 'Rural Developments and Class Contradictions in Java', *Journal of Contemporary Asia*, 5, No. 3.
Hirsch, Max (1901), *Democracy versus Socialism* (London: Macmillan).
—— (1903), 'Free Trade and the Empire', in G.H. Reid, *et al. Free Trade and Tariff Reform* (Sydney: Angus and Robertson).
—— (1904), *An Exposure of Socialism* (Melbourne: Renwick Press).
Hodgson, G. and I. Steedman (1977), 'Depreciation of Machines and Changing Efficiency: A Note', *Australian Economic Papers*, 16, June.
Hollis, M. and E. Nell (1975), *Rational Economic Man* (Cambridge: Cambridge University Press).
Holloway, J. and S. Picciotto (1977), 'Capital, Crisis and the State', *Capital and Class*, No. 2, Summer.
Holman, W.A. (1905), 'Is Socialism Possible?' *Journal of the Institute of Bankers of New South Wales*, 15.

Irvine, R.F. (1914), *The Place of the Social Sciences in a Modern University* (Sydney: Angus and Robertson).
—— (1916), *The Veil of Money* (Sydney: 'The Review' Company Limited).
—— (1933), *The Midas Delusion* (Adelaide: The Hassell Press).
James, R. (1974), 'Tweedledee's OECD Plan', *Intervention*, No. 4.
Jessop, Bob (1977), 'Recent Theories of the Capitalist State', *Cambridge Journal of Economics*, 1, December.
Jones, E. (1975), 'The Critique of Positive Economics', *Arena*, No. 38.
—— (1977), 'Positive Economics or What?', *Economic Record*, 53, June/September.
Kalange, O. (1964), 'Academics and Big Business', *Arena*, No. 3.
Kaldor, N. (1972), 'The Irrelevance of Equilibrium Economics', *Economic Journal*, 82, December.
—— (1975), 'What's Wrong with Economic Theory?' *Quarterly Journal of Economics*, 89.
—— (1977), 'Capitalism and Industrial Development: Some Lessons from Britain's Experience', *Cambridge Journal of Economics*, 1, June.
Keynes, J.M. (1936), *The General Theory of Employment, Interest and Money* (London: Macmillan).
Koshimura, S. (1975), *Theory of Capital Reproduction and Accumulation* (North Kitchener, Ontario: Dumont Press).
Kregel, J.A. (1974), *The Reconstruction of Political Economy. An Introduction to Post-Keynesian Economics* (London: Macmillan), first edition.
—— (1976), *The Reconstruction of Political Economy. An Introduction to Post-Keynesian Economics* (London: Macmillan). Second Edition.
Kuhn, T.S. (1970), *The Structure of Scientific Revolution* (Chicago, Chicago University Press, second edition).
Laing, N.F. (1969), 'Two Notes on Pasinetti's Theorem', *Economic Record*, 45, September.
Lakatos, I. and A. Musgrave (editors), (1970), *Criticism and the Growth of Knowledge* (Cambridge: Cambridge University Press).
Leaver, R. (1976), 'Accumulation on a World Scale', *Arena*, No. 42.
—— (1977), 'The Debate on Underdevelopment: On Situating Gunder Frank', *Journal of Contemporary Asia*, 7, No. 1.
Leijonhufvud, A. (1968), *On Keynesian Economics and the Economics of Keynes* (New York: Oxford University Press).
Lenin, V.I. (1956), *The Development of Capitalism in Russia.* (Moscow: Foreign Languages Publishing House). First published, 1899.
—— (1950), *Imperialism. The Highest Stage of Capitalism.* (Moscow: Foreign Languages Publishing House). First written in 1916.
Leontiev, A. (1935), *Political Economy.* (London: Lawrence & Wishart).
Leontief, W. (1971), 'Theoretical Assumption and Non-Observed Facts', *American Economic Review*, 61, March.
Levine, D.P. (1976), 'A Critical Note on the Theory of Production', *Australian Economic Papers*, 15, December.
Lockwood, R. (1948), *Bankers Backed Hitler* (Melbourne, n.p.).
Lonie, J. (1971), 'The Dunstan Government', *Arena*, No. 25.
Lonie, J. (1975), 'Political Economy of Australian Capitalism', *Arena*, No. 39.
Mandel, E. (1968), *Marxist Economic Theory* (London: Merlin Book Club).
—— (1971), *The Formation of the Economic Thought of Karl Marx* (London: New Left Books).
—— (1975), *Late Capitalism* (London: New Left Books).
Marx, K.H. (1962), *Economic and Philosophic Manuscripts* (Moscow: Foreign Languages Publishing House).
—— (1961, 1968, 1972), *Theories of Surplus Value* Parts I–III (Moscow: Foreign Language Publishing House).
—— (1971), *A Contribution to the Critique of Political Economy* (with an introduction by Maurice Dobb), (London: Lawrence & Wishart).

—— (1973), *Grundrisse*, translated with a foreword by Martin Nocolaus (London: Allen Lane).
Mayer, H. (1964), *Marx, Engels and Australia*, Sydney Studies in Politics, No. 5, (Melbourne: Cheshire).
—— (1971), 'Radical Studies: An Australian Project', *Arena*, No. 27.
McConnell, W.K. (1934a), *The Douglas Credit Scheme: A Simple Explanation and Criticism* (Sydney: n.p.).
—— (1934b), *What is Bank Credit?* (Sydney, n.p.).
McEachern, D. (1976), 'The Mode of Production in India', *Journal of Contemporary Asia*, 6, No. 4.
—— and J. Lonie (1972), 'Classless Party for a Classless State', *Arena*, No. 29.
McFarlane, B.J. (1964), 'Maurice Dobb on Economic Growth and Planning in Underdeveloped Countries', *Arena*, No. 4.
—— (1966a), *Professor Irvine's Economics in Australian Labour History* (Canberra: Australian Society for the Study of Labour History).
—— (1968b), 'The Economics of Neo-Colonialism', *Arena*, No. 10.
—— (1968), *Economic Policy in Australia. The Case for Reform* (Melbourne: Cheshire).
—— (1971a), 'Michal Kalecki's Economics: An Appreciation', *Economic Record*, 47, March.
—— (1971b), 'Economic Policy and Economic Growth in China', *Journal of Contemporary Asia*, 1, No. 4.
—— (1972), 'Australia's Role in World Capitalism', in Playford and Kirsner (eds.), *Australian Capitalism* (Ringwood: Penguin Books).
—— (1973), 'Price Rigidity and Excess Capacity', *Australian Economic Papers*, 12, June.
—— (1974), 'Review of E.L. Wheelwright, *Radical Political Economy, Australian Outlook*, 28, August.
—— (1975), 'Radical Ricardians and Their Marxist Critics', *Arena*, No. 39.
—— (1976a), 'The Use of Economic Theory in History: Snooks snookered', *Labour History*, No. 31.
—— (1976b), 'Debate on the Neo-Ricardians: Reply to Ergas', *Arena*, No. 42.
—— (1977a), 'Editorial: Special Issue: Development and Underdevelopment', *Journal of Contemporary Asia*, 7, No. 1.
—— (1977b), 'Review of Feiwell, *The Intellectual Capital of Michal Kalecki*', *Economic Record*, 53, March.
McGuinness, P.P. (1955), 'Capitalism Demolished—A Review of 'Political Economy—A Simple Outline by E.W. Campbell', *Tocsin*.
—— (1975), 'Political Economics: The Art of Deftly Dropping Serious Questions', *National Times*, May 26–31.
McIntyre, S. (1972), 'Radical History and Bourgeois Hegemony', *Intervention*, No. 2.
McLaren, J. (ed.), (1972), *Towards a New Australia Under a Labor Government* (Melbourne: Cheshire, for the Victorian Fabian Society).
McQueen, H. (1970), A New Britannia.
—— (1971a), 'Technocratic Laborism: Introduction', *Arena*, No. 25.
—— (1971b), 'Living Offi Asia', *Arena*, No. 26.
—— (1972), 'The End of Equality', *Arena*, No. 30.
Medio, A. (1972), 'Profits and Surplus Value' in E.K. Hunt and J.G. Schwarz (editors), *A Critique of Economic Theory* (Harmondsworth: Penguin Books).
—— (1977), 'Neo-classicals, Neo-Ricardians and Marx' in J. Schwarz (editors), *The Subtle Anatomy of Capitalism* (Santa Monica: Goodyear Publishing Company).
Meek, R.L. (1953), 'Review of J. Stalin, *Economic Problems of Socialism in the U.S.S.R.*', *Economic Journal*, 63, September.
—— (1967), 'Mr. Sraffa's Rehabilitation of Classical Economics', in R.L. Meek, *Economics and Ideology and Other Essays* (London: Chapman & Hall).
Mermelstein, D. (ed.), (1970), *Economics: Mainstream Readings and Radical Critiques* (New York: Random House).
Miliband, R. (1961), *Parliamentary Socialism. A Study in the Politics of Labour* (London: Allen and Unwin).

Mills, R.C. and F.C. Benham (1925), *The Principles of Money, Banking and Foreign Exchange and Their Application to Australia* (Sydney: Angus and Robertson, second edition).
Mills, R.C. and E.R. Walker (1935), *Money* (Sydney: Angus and Robertson).
Moore, P. (1972), 'Australian Capitalism Today: Structure and Prospects', *Intervention*, No. 1.
Moss, J.L. (1955), Who Owns South Australia? (n.p.).
Ng, Yew Kwang (1974), The Neoclassical and the Neo-Marxist-Keynesian Theories of Income Distribution: A Non-Cambridge Contribution to the Cambridge Controversy in Capital Theory', *Australian Economic Papers*, 13, June.
—— (1977), 'The Cambridge Controversy in Capital Theory—A Reply', *Australian Economic Papers*, 16, June.
Nell, E.J. (1968), 'The Advantages of Money over Barter', *Australian Economic Papers*, 11, December.
—— (1972a), 'Economics: The Revival of Political Economy', in R. Blackburn (ed.). *Ideology in Social Science* (London: Fontana/Collins).
—— (1972b), 'The Revival of Political Economy', *Australian Economic Papers*, 11, June.
O'Connor, J. (1971), 'Australia—An Exception', *Arena*, No. 24.
—— (1973), *The Fiscal Crisis of the State* (New York: St. Martins Press).
O'Donnell, R.M. (1977), 'Rationalist Red Herrings or a New Kettle of Fish for Political Economy. A Philosophical and Economic Critique of Hollis and Nell's *Rational Economic Man*' Sydney: Sydney University, General Philosophy Department.
Ogilivy, A.J. (1892), 'Is Capital the Result of Abstinence?' Report of the Fourth Meeting of the Australasian Association for the Advancement of Science (Hobart: n.p.).
—— (1898), *The Third Factor of Production and Other Essays.* (London: Swan Sonneschein & Co.).
Osmond, W. (1972), 'Australian Capitalism', *Arena*, No. 29.
Paine, Suzanne (1977), 'Agricultural Development in Less Developed Countries', *Cambridge Journal of Economics*, 1, December.
Pasinetti, L.L. (1969), 'Switches of Technique and the Rate of Return in Capital Theory', *Economic Journal*, 79, September.
—— (1974), *Growth and Income Distribution. Essays in Economic Theory* (Cambridge: Cambridge University Press).
Peacock, Frank (1977), 'The Cambridge Controversy in Capital Theory—A Comment', *Australian Economic Papers*, 16, June.
Phelps-Brown, E.J. (1972), 'The Underdevelopment of Economics', *Economic Journal*, 82, March.
Playford, John (1968–69), 'Big Business and the Australian University', *Arena*, No. 17.
—— (1969), *Neo-capitalism in Australia* (Melbourne: Arena Monograph Series No. 1).
—— (1970), 'Myth of the Sixty Families', *Arena*, No. 23.
—— (1972), 'Who Rules Australia?' in Playford and Kirsner (eds.), *Australian Capitalism* (Ringwood, Penguin Books).
—— and D. Kirsner (eds.), (1972), *Australian Capitalism* (Ringwood, Penguin Books).
Power, M. (1974), 'The Wages of Sex', *Australian Quarterly*, 46, March.
—— (1975), 'Women's Work is Never Done—by Men, A Socio-economic Model of Sex-Typing in Occupations', *Journal of Industrial Relations*, 17, September.
Pringle, R. and A. Game (1976), 'Labour in Power: The Feminist Response', *Arena*, No. 41.
Rawlings, J.N. (1939), *Who Owns Australia?* (Sydney: Modern Publishers).
Resnick, S. (1970), 'The Decline of Rural Industry Under Export Expansion', *Journal of Economic History*, 30, March.
—— and Hymer, S. (1969–70), 'The Crisis and Drama of the Global Partnership', *International Journal*, 25, Winter.
Riach, P.A. (1971), 'Kalecki's Degree of Monopoly Reconsidered', *Australian Economic Papers*, 10, June.

—— (1972), 'Microeconomic Motivation in the Kaldorian Distribution Model', *Australian Economic Papers*, 11, December.
Riazanov, D. (1973), *Karl Marx and Friedrich Engels* (New York: Monthly Review Press).
Rivers, L. and J. Hyde (1975), 'The Dominance of Finance Capital', *Arena*, No. 39.
Robinson, J. (1969), 'The Theory of Value Reconsidered', *Australian Economic Papers*, 8, June.
—— (1971), *Economic Heresies* (London: Macmillan).
—— (1972), 'The Second Crisis in Economic Theory', *American Economic Review*, 62, May.
—— (1975a), 'The Unimportance of Reswitching'. *Quarterly Journal of Economics*, 89, February.
—— (1975b), *Collected Economic Papers* (Oxford, Basil Blackwell). Introduction to second edition, Vol. III.
—— (1977), 'What are the Questions?' *Journal of Economic Literature*, 15, December.
Robinson, Joan and John Eatwell (1973), *An Introduction to Modern Economics* (London: McGraw Hill).
Robinson, J. and F. Wilkinson (1977), 'What has become of Employment Policy', *Cambridge Journal of Economics*, 1, March.
Roe, J. (1975), 'Social Policy and the Permanent Poor', in Wheelwright and Buckley (eds.), *Political Economy of Australian Capitalism* (Sydney: ANZ Book Company), Vol. I.
Rolfe, H. (1967), *The Controllers* (Melbourne: Cheshire).
Roncaglia, A. (1974), 'Labour Power, Subsistence Wages and the Rate of Wages', *Australian Economic Papers*, 13, June.
—— (1976), 'The Sraffian Revolution', in S. Weintraub (editor), *Trends in Modern Economics* (Philadelphia: Pensylvania University Press).
—— (1977), 'Sraffa and Price Theory', in J. Schwarz (editor), *The Subtle Anatomy of Capitalism* (Santa Monica: Goodyear Publishing Company).
Roosevelt, F. (1977), 'Cambridge Economics and Commodity Fetishism', in J. Schwarz (editor), *The Subtle Anatomy of Capitalism* (Santa Monica: Goodyear Publishing Company).
Rowley, K. (1971a), 'Bob Hawke: Capital for Labor?' *Arena*, No. 25.
—— (1971b), 'Baran and Sweezy: Marxist Economists?', *Arena*, No. 27.
—— (1972a), 'Pastoral Capitalism', *Intervention*, No. 1.
—— (1972b), 'The Political Economy of Australian Since the War', in Playford and Kirsner (eds.), *Australian Capitalism* (Ringwood: Penguin Books).
—— (1973), 'The Imperialism of Trade', *Intervention*, No. 3.
—— (1976a), 'The End of the Long Boom', *Intervention*, No. 6.
—— (1976b), 'Late Capitalism', *Intervention*, No. 7.
Rowse, T. (1975), 'Facts, Theories and Ideology: A Comment on Graeme Snooks', *Labour History*, No. 28.
Rowthorn, R. (1972), 'Marxism and the Capital Theory Controversy', *Bulletin of the Conference of Socialist Economists*.
—— (1974), 'Neo-classicism, Neo-Ricardianism and Marxism', *New Left Review*, No. 86.
Samuelson, P.A. (1947), *Foundations of Economic Analysis* (Cambridge: Harvard University Press).
—— (1948), *Economics*. (New York: McGraw Hill).
—— (1966), 'A Summing Up', *Quarterly Journal of Economics*, 80, November.
—— (1973), 'Illogic of Neo-Marxism Doctrine of Unequal Exchange' (mimeographed).
—— (1976), 'Interest Rate Determination and Oversimplifying Parables: A Summing Up', in M. Brown, K. Sato and P. Zarembka (editors), *Essays in Modern Capital Theory* (Amsterdam: North Holland Publishing Company).
Sandercock, L. (1975), 'Capitalism and the Environment. The Failure of Success', in Wheelwright and Buckley (eds.), *Political Economy of Australian Capitalism* (Sydney: ANZ Book Company), Vol. I.

Schedvin, C.B. (1970), *Australia and the Great Depression* (Sydney: Sydney University Press).
Schneider, M. (1977), 'Review of Wheelwright and Stilwell (eds.), *Readings in Political Economy*', *Economic Record*, 53, June/September.
Schwarz, J.G. (1977), *The Subtle Anatomy of Capitalism* (Santa Monica: Goodyear Publishing Co. Inc.).
Sen, A.K. (1963), 'Neo-Classical and Neo-Keynesian Theories of Distribution', *Economic Record*, 39, March.
Shann, E.O.G. and D.B. Copland (1931), *The Battle of the Plans* (Sydney: Angus and Robertson).
Sharkey, L. (n.d.). *Nationalisation of Banks* (Sydney: Modern Publishers).
—— and E.W. Campbell (1945), *The Story of Government Enterprise in Australia* (Sydney: Australian Communist Party).
Sharp, N. (1965), 'Who Owns, Who Controls?' *Arena*, No. 8.
Sieper, E. (1978), 'Consumer Protection: Boon or Bane?' Paper presented at Centre for Independent Studies Conference 'What Price Intervention', Macquarie University, April.
Silver, C. (1977a), 'The Long Boom: A Critique', *Intervention*, No. 9.
—— (1977b), 'The Economic Cycle in Post-War Australia', *Arena*, No. 49.
Simkin, C.G.F., (ed.) (1975), *Political Economy versus Economics* (Sydney: University of Sydney). (Mimeographed).
Simms, M. and K. Tsokhas (1977), 'Liberal Party: Ideology and Rhetoric', paper delivered at 1977 APSA Conference, Armidale (mimeographed).
Simpson-Lee, G.A.J. (1953), 'New South Wales Trader's Protection Association 1923–1944', *Economic Record*, 29, November.
—— (1961), 'Dairying in the Next Decade' and 'A Proposed Plan for the Future Organisation of the Dairy Industry', in N.T. Drane and H.R. Edwards (editors), *The Australian Dairy Industry* (Melbourne: F.W. Cheshire).
—— (1970), 'The Sydney Tradition', *Economic Review*.
Singh, Ajit (1977), 'U.K. Industry and the World Economy: A Case of Deindustrialisation?' *Cambridge Journal of Economics*, I, June.
Smith, R.P. (1977), 'Military Expenditure and Capitalism', *Cambridge Journal of Economics*, 1, March.
Snooks, G. (1975a), 'Orthodox and Radical Interpretations of the Development of Australian Capitalism', *Labour History*, No. 28.
—— (1975b), 'The Radical View of Australian Capitalism: A Reply', *Labour History*, No. 28.
Solow, R. (1975), 'The Unimportance of Reswitching—A Comment', *Quarterly Journal of Economics*, 89, February.
Sraffa, P. (1960), *Production of Commodities by Means of Commodities* (Cambridge: Cambridge University Press).
Steedman, I. (1971), 'Marx on the Falling Rate of Profit', *Australian Economic Papers*, 10, June.
—— (1977), *Marx After Sraffa* (London: New Left Books).
Stilwell, F.J.B. (1975a), *Normative Economics: An Introduction to Micro Economic Theory and Radical Critiques* (Sydney: Pergamon Press).
—— (1975b), 'Alternative Courses in Economics', *Arena*, No. 38.
Thomas, P.H. (1955), *Who Owns Queensland?* (Brisbane, n.p.).
Tsokhas, K. (1976), 'On the Constitutional Crisis', *Arena*, No. 44–45.
Wheelwright, E.L. (1957), *Ownership and Control of Australian Companies* (Sydney: Law Book Company).
—— (1971), 'Radical or Bourgeois Economics?', *Journal of Contemporary Asia*, 1, No. 4.
—— (1972), 'Concentration of Private Economic Power', in Playford and Kirsner (eds.), *Australian Capitalism* (Ringwood, Penguin Books).
—— (1974), *Radical Political Economy. Collected Essays* (Sydney: ANZ Book Company).

—— (1977), 'The End of the Age of Growth', *Journal of Australian Political Economy*, 1, October.
—— and K.D. Buckley (eds.), (1975), *Political Economy of Australian Capitalism* (Sydney: ANZ Book Company).
—— and B.J. McFarlane (1970), *The Chinese Road to Socialism* (New York: Monthly Review Press).
—— and J. Miskelly (1967), *Anatomy of Australian Manufacturing Industry* (Sydney: Law Book Company).
—— and F.J.B. Stilwell (eds.), (1976), *Readings in Political Economy* (Sydney: ANZ Book Company).
—— and W.J. Waters (1973), 'University Economics: A Radical Critique', *Australian Quarterly*, 45, September.
White, M. (1975), 'An Australian Political Economy?' *Arena*, No. 39.
—— (1976), 'Ideological and Scientific, Positive and Normative: Issues and Non-Issues in Political Economy', Paper given at First Australian Political Economy Conference, Sydney. (mimeographed).
White, Michael (1977), 'Kalecki's Theories of Economic Growth and Development', *Journal of Contemporary Asia*, 7, No. 3.
Whitlam, E.G. (1977), *On Australia's Constitution* (Camberwell: Widescope International Publishers).
Wilson, J. (1946), *The Inefficiency of Private Enterprise* (Sydney: Current Book Distributors).
Wiltshire, Ted (1977), 'Australia Uprooted: A Discussion', *Journal of Australian Political Economy*, 1, October.
Worswick, G.D.N. (1972), 'Is Progress in Economic Science Possible?' *Economic Journal*, 82, March.

Chapter 5

Australian Economics 1968–78: A Survey of the Surveys

F.H. GRUEN

Australian National University

Contents

I am indebted to W.M. Corden, R.G. Gregory, T.W. Swan, P.A. Volker for helpful overall suggestions and to R. Beale, S. Richardson and T. Valentine for useful comments on individual sections.

Section 1 Introduction

An attempt will be made here to summarise those major economic debates of the last decade covered in the surveys and, in particular, to highlight the interaction between changing events and the economic literature. Reference will also be made to the growth of econometric modelling of the Australian economy—an important activity of Australian economists not much explored in the surveys.

The chapter begins with some more general reflections about Australian economics during the last decade. Judging from statistics available from two major employers of economists (the Federal Government and universities), Australian economics has been one of the 'growth industries' over the last seven to ten years—with annual rates of growth of nine to twelve per cent in numbers of academic staff in 'economics, commerce and government' and in numbers of Federal public servants with professional training in economics. However both universities and the Federal public service face a period of distinctly slower future rates of growth—if not actually declining numbers in some cases.

A further impression one gets is that a greal deal of extra writing and research work is being done; for instance the number of professional papers given at Conferences has increased rapidly. There has also been a substantial upgrading both of university staff and of economists in the Federal Public Service in terms of professional qualifications. Again, an increasing number of Australian academic economists now frequently contribute to the international literature—with Corden, Harcourt, Kemp, Ng and Turnovsky being perhaps the best known but by no means the only examples.

Section 2 The Changing Climate of Australian Economic Opinion 1968–78

The Radical Critique

In spite of this impressive development of the profession (at least within universities and the Federal Public Service) there has been a growing disenchantment both with the discipline itself and with such traditional indicators of economic success as economic growth, price stability and full employment. This disenchantment was evident both from outside and from within the profession and has occurred both in Australia and overseas. In this respect—as in others which we will be recording here—Australian views have been largely derived from overseas intellectual trends. Since this disenchantment pre-dates the traumatic economic events of 1974/75 and of later years, it was largely rising expectations rather than falling standards of performance which were responsible. Groenewegen (1979, p.185) has summarised the series of events and the intellectual trends in the late sixties and early seventies which led to this increasing disenchantment. The critics raised a long list of issues ranging from degradation of the environment and of the quality of life generally, to Vietnam and growing awareness of poverty and of discrimination against such groups as Aborigines, migrants and women. They regarded these as resulting inherently from the prevalent economic organisation of society. Further study of existing modes of economic organisation (without encompassing major institutional changes of such economies) was unlikely to be rewarding.

The ensuing radical critique has been equally wide ranging. Although, as Groenewegen points out, Australian radical left economists are a diverse group and often hostile to one another, there is agreement on one underlying, if sometimes only implicit, proposition: whatever the issue under consideration, existing defects/problems could be alleviated if not cured by the abolition of the private ownership of the means of production—or at least by the substantial subordination of private interests to public guidance, regulation or dictation. This is at least a necessary, if not a sufficient, condition for the solution of our problems. Or, as some of the radicals would put it, inequality, alienation, discrimination and imperialism are inherent in the nature of capitalism. This view is, of course, the result of the Marxist intellectual heritage of the radical revival. But the attempted demonstration of the causal connection between capitalism and these evils is not very rigorous. Inequality, alienation and discrimination are probably inherent in the minute division of labour which is common in all wealthy societies (whether capitalist, socialist or different degrees of 'mixed'). Again these evils may be inevitable—though it is hoped that they can be mitigated—when an economy is characterised by decentralised decision making and a reliance on economic incentives. Finally, they may be inevitable to some degree in any economy because of the limited changeability of human nature. 'Maoist man' appears as much a myth as was 'Soviet man' in the 1920s.

The radical emphasis is largely on critiques.[1] The inherent difficulties of their implicit or explicit solutions tend to be skated over—though this is a trait common to many critiques, not only to radical ones. Thus at least the newer radical groups—both in Australia and elsewhere—have been critical of both markets and of co-ordination of economies through bureaucratic planning techniques—without suggesting any known viable alternative co-ordinating mechanism. Further, one major suggested solution—namely citizen participation—is beginning to the queried (Sandercock 1978). The impact of radical critiques was probably at its greatest during the late sixties and early seventies—that is during the closing years of the Vietnam War, and before the election of the Labor government in December 1972.[2]

The Labor Government

A good deal has been written about the Labor government's style and about its economic performance; here the focus is on the climate of economic attitudes in the country. In this connection, two aspects require reference here.

First there was the liberating influence of the Labor government. This was especially felt by artists and writer—but also by many social scientists. A large number of academic and other 'outside' economists were commissioned by the Labor government to re-examine the various economic and social issues confronting the country. The contrast was particularly great with the prevalent pre-Labor (and post Labor?) practice of avoiding open (i.e. non-public service) investigations of such problems whenever possible, or alternatively setting up 'semi-amateur' committees of inquiry with no professional membership—or strictly minority representation of professional economists. Corden (1968, pp.49, 59) referred to this anti-intellectual tendency in his earlier survey. Whether this plethora of Labor-sponsored inquiries, task forces and commissions contributed to better decision-making by government is another question; some political scientists and students of public administration have misgivings on this point (Hawker 1977). Only a small minority of the economists thus involved were committed ALP supporters—of some two dozen names of economists which readily come to mind only about half a dozen stand out as committed ALP supporters.[3] The much beloved jobs-for-the-boys criticism applied to two or three prominent appointments which were probably unrepresentative of the whole.

Scondly, there was the basic orientation of Labor's programme towards equality of opportunity. To quote a recent summary of it by Ralph Willis, MP, the present Labor shadow Treasurer:

> we argued that people of all income levels should have the right to decent education, proper health care, efficient trasport, adequate recreation facilities, and a non-polluted environment, and that the only way that such rights could be guaranteed was for the State to play a much greater role in their provision than hitherto. (Willis 1978).

But, as Edwards (1976) has pointed out:

> Labor also arrived in office with an unresolved, almost unrecognised, conflict over the means by which it would promote equality.

On the one hand there was the increasing role for the State in the provision of services; on the other hand there was need for extra public revenue to finance transfer payments for more adequate social services; yet again, the trade union members of the government expected greatly to improve their members' real living standards and the share of GNP going to wage earners. Squaring this very round circle was an impossible task for any government. Critics—and perhaps even the electorate as a whole—may indulge in the luxury of espousing mutually inconsistent policies, but a government's inconsistencies are inevitably exposed publicly. After two and a half years in office, Prime Minister Whitlam recognised some of these problems in his 1975 Chifley Memorial Lecture:

> .... In a sense the Party of reform in a democratic system carries a self-created handicap as a reforming Government. In Opposition, its essential task is to raise the public perception of the need for change, the need for reform. That is, its task is to raise expectations. The nature of politics, founded as it is on human nature itself, is that there will always tend to be a gap, a shortfall, between expectations aroused and expectations met.
>
> A conservative Government survives essentially by dampening expectations and subduing hopes. Conservatism is basically pessimistic; reforming is basically optimistic. The great tradition which links the American and French revolutionaries of the Age of Reason with the modern Parties of social reform is the tradition of optimism about the possibility of human improvement and human progress through the means of human reason. Yet inevitably there will be failures, and the higher expectations rise, the greater the likelihood of at least temporary failure to meet them.

In the event, even if there had been no world recession, these unavoidable conflicts would have needed to be faced—and would inevitably have led to some disillusionment among Labor supporters. As it turned out, the impossible task Labor set itself considerably aggravated subsequent levels of inflation and unemployment. While high rates of inflation and unemployment were shared in part (though not to the same extent) by all other OECD countries, they were to provide a very potent impetus for the ensuing widespread disillusionment with Labor. This is not the place for a detailed discussion of the Labor government's economic policies—or of what we can learn from this particular episode.[4] The emphasis here is restricted to the effect of this period on the climate of economic opinion.

The Libertarian Responses

Paralleling the earlier history of American disillusionment with President Johnson's 'Great Society', there has been a similar disillusionment with government here. This has been coupled with a growth in Libertarian economics—or what one might term, alternatively, the economic philosophies of Milton Friedman, George Stigler or Friedrich Hayek (if we can, for the purpose of broadbrush characterisation, ignore the differences between their philosophies).

Both at ANU and at Monash (and perhaps at other univerisities) the Libertarian stance has become—if not the new orthodoxy—at least the predominant intellectual movement among the younger members of the discipline. In addition a new libertarian organisation—the Centre for Independent Studies—sponsored an impressive professional conference on 'What Price Intervention' at Macquarie University in April 1978. (The papers by McGregor, Parish, Porter and Sieper are listed in the bibliography).

The libertarians regard their basic positive stance as protective to the maximum extent possible of the liberty of the person. (In addition, there is a basic negative stance—i.e. against government—of which more below). Power over a person should be exercised only to protect others, not to protect man from himself or to achieve any other social goal. If freedom and the satisfaction of consumer wants are regarded as THE most important ends which public policy should serve, the predominant prescription of the Libertarians—rely on the market in practically every situation—follows logically. Those who believe that the world is more complicated, that government needs to bear in mind other considerations as well, cannot endorse such universal remedies. To take one example, the health of groups in the community is often regarded as a legitimate concern for governments which might, for instance, justify publicly financed anti-smoking campaigns, or discriminatory taxes on such products, or even the prohibition of tobacco advertising.[5] However, to the true Libertarian this type of do-good public meddling is deeply suspect and, at least one prominent Libertarian—Milton Friedman (in his *Newsweek* column)—has attacked both governmental anti-smoking campaigns ('Government has no business using the taxpayer's money to propagandize') and prohibition of tobacco advertising as 'hostile to the maintenance of a free society.' (Cited by Mishan 1976, pp.160–161).

Again, there is the awkward question: at what age does the individual become a sufficiently good judge of his welfare to make his freedom such a paramount goal? Perhaps of greater basic importance is Rawls' question—whether society (and by implication policy) can be adequately judged in terms of the fulfilmant of *given* wants since society (the interaction of groups and individuals) has an important role in influencing and shaping these wants.

> Everyone recognizes that the form of society affects its members and determines in large part the kind of persons they want to be as well as the kind of persons they are. It also limits people's ambitions and hopes in different ways, for they will with reason view themselves in part according to their place in it and take account of the means and opportunities they can realistically expect. Thus an economic regime is not only an institutional scheme for satisfying existing desires and aspirations but a way of fashioning desires and aspirations in the future. (Rawls 1977, pp.159–165)

The Libertarians' deep suspicion of government is probably a useful antidote to the previous implicit view of many economists that governments can be relied upon to perform the role of Platonic guardians who, in a disinterested fashion, determine the best course amongst alternative possible outcomes for a particular economy. Whatever one may think of the Libertarians' suspicious (value) judgements about government, valuable work on both the theory and the empirical consequences of governmental regulation of private economic affairs has resulted from this general orientation—though even here non-Libertarian economists will not follow them all the way.

Thus there is now a general consensus among (non-Marxist) economists that little good can come of governmental attempts to regulate those competitive industries giving rise to neither externalities or informational deficiencies; but when confronted with such situations or with natural monopolies we are in the realm of the second best. Here general principles remain elusive and case-by-case examination and (uncertain) judgements about policies are still required.

As Joskow and Noll point out in their excellent and comprehensive overview of the US literature on regulation in theory and practice:

> ... the inherent inefficiencies of regulation that flow from these theories have no natural normative consequence, although one would not deduce that from the tone of the literature. That regulation fails to reach a Pareto optimum is fairly uninteresting if no institutions exist which can reach a point that Pareto dominates regulation. For regulatory interventions that deal with empirically important market imperfections, the departure of regulatory equilibrium from perfect competition is not normatively compelling. (Joskow & Noll 1978, p.61).

Section 3 *Macro-economic Policy*

3.1 Econometric Modelling of the Australian Economy

The operation and continuing refinement of sizeable econometric models of the Australian economy provides one important difference between Australian economic policy discussion when Max Corden wrote ten years ago and the current position. Such modelling began with a series of individual academic efforts by Nevile (1962), Kmenta (1966), Zerby (1969) and Evans (1972). While academic modelling of the present Australian economy and of such relevant past periods as the 1930s depression (Valentine, 1978) is continuing, attention is focussed here on the considerably larger and more elaborate models constructed by econometricians working either directly for government or for such statutory organisations as the Reserve Bank and the Industries Assistance Commission.

Of the four existing official models three are concerned with the type of short to medium run macro-economic policy problems which are under consideration here. The first is the National Income Forecasting (NIF) model originally designed by Chris Higgins and Vince FitzGerald and now operated by a team from Treasury and the Australian Bureau of Statistics led by Neil Johnston. Then there are the Reserve Bank models—in particular RBA 1 originally designed by a team led by Bill Norton—and RBA 76 designed by Peter Jonson and his co-workers.[6]

Developing and maintaining the larger models requires sustained team work as well as gifted individual research efforts. This type of work is done more easily within governmental organisations than in universities—at least as presently structured. It is unfortunate that all regularly used and publicly documented models are operated by government and/or statutory organisations.[7]

Broadly speaking there are three major purposes of models—to increase understanding of the structure of the economy, to provide conditional forecasts and to evaluate the effects of past and of proposed policy changes. These aims may be conflicting; a model designed primarily for forecasting may have unsatisfactory features from the point of view of consistency or of economic theory; whilst a model for policy simulations may give relatively worse predictions. Like policy makers, model builders often have to choose between alternative ends and settle for trade-offs which can then be attacked by those with different aims and priorities. For reasons of space only sketchy characterisation of the models is possible here.[8]

The Treasury (NIF) and Reserve Bank (RBA 1) models naturally concern themselves particularly with short-run macro-economic questions. They are quarterly models used both for forecasting and for policy analysis. New forecasts are produced every quarter as new sets of quarterly national accounts statistics become available. They have strong Keynesian features; gross national product is mainly determined by effective demand; but there is considerable treatment of inventories in a buffering role and also of capacity constraints—especially in the longer run. RBA 1 has a more detailed modelling of the monetary sector than the NIF model (at least so far, but see below). RBA 1 is also more 'monetarist' in the sense that real wealth and price expectations tend to have more influence on expenditure than in the NIF model.

Comparison of the predictive errors of the two models suggest that the predicitive performance of the NIF model is generally superior.[9] There have been seven annual re-estimations (and partial re-specifications) of the NIF model so far which have no doubt added considerably to the realism and sophistication of the model. The model as it stands now is a good deal more elaborate than the original Higgins-FitzGerald model.

Some of the major changes made to the NIF model over the years include:

1. A more fully elaborated model of public-private sector interactions enabling fiscal policy changes to be analysed more adequately.
2. Investment relationships have been studied intensively and probably modelled more satisfactorily.
3. The influence of real wage changes on unemployment has been included in the model in various forms since 1975.
4. Expression of relevant flows at constant prices with the provision of the appropriate national accounts data.
5. The elaboration of a more fully developed incomes sector.

Work on a fully fledged model of the financial sector was reported at recent professional conferences and will be incorporated in the next (1978) re-specification of the model. Inadequate monetary-real sector interactions have been a subject of some past criticism.[10]

RBA 76 is very different from the successive NIF versions and RBA 1. It pays more attention to long-run consistency and is primarily designed for medium and longer run analysis than for short-term (conditional) forecasting. It is more 'neo-classical' and monetarist. Demand for commodities and assets are modelled in two steps: long run equilibrium levels depend on relative prices and the relevant constraints, whilst actual demands and supplies gradually adjust to these (changing) long run equilibrium levels. Buffer stocks, consisting of money in the case of households and of goods inventories in the case of firms, play an important role smoothing the adjustment paths in the face of unforeseen disturbances. RBA 76 is estimated using more sophisticated full information maximum likelihood techniques than the models discussed earlier. It has been the subject of very open discussion; for this discussion selected ousiders' experimentation with the model has been encouraged.[11]

It is probably too early to assess the full impact of official and semi-official econometric modelling of the economy—either on government or on policy, or on the economy itself. However, since I am one of the few academic economists who has had the regular opportunity over a period of 2½ years or so to read the quarterly NIF model-based forecasts, some personal speculations on this topic may not be inappropriate. My impression is that the development and continuing operation of these models has considerably advanced understanding of the economy—in particular the understanding of those who operate the models and those who see the conditional forecasts and the policy simulations. This is basically because the models attempt in a systematic and precise way to trace through the relevant interactions and interdependencies within the economy. Regular quarterly operation continually throws up questions as to why certain unexpected events occur. This presents challenges and gradually improves understanding. The formal nature of the models means that this understanding can then be passed on to others, while the informal and intuitive knowledge of other 'economy watchers' is less readily transmittable.

One should not overstate the advances in understanding which are possible as a result of the development and operation of these models. The available data often will not allow us to choose conclusively between rival models and their policy implications. Model building will always contain a skill which is not wholly subject to scientific rules. In the words of the builders of the NIF model:

> The nature of the data with which our profession must work requires the imposition of a high degree of prior specification if the facts are to be discovered. On the other hand, if the imposition of specification is taken too far the modeller is in danger of 'discovering' only what he hid. (FitzGerald and Higgins 1977, p.177).

Again official forecasting with models can never be self-contained: the models can only predict how the economy is likely to behave once a large number of exogenous variables (variables not determined within the model) are specified and fed in to produce forecasts—forecasts which are then conditional on the values of the exogenous variables having been correctly specified. National econometric model forecasts are based on some international trade and external price assumptions; the National Wage decision of the Arbitration Commission and farm output are also exogenous.

In practice the number of variables to be thus specified is large—in the case of the NIF model there are over 100 exogenous variables. However, many of them are policy variables—for example the company tax rate. Hence forecasting with econometric models is always conditional. Cynics might argue that since one can never get the future paths of so many variables right, one is never really likely to get the forecast right. While it is true that the future is really unknowable, governments and other economic agents act (either explicitly or implicitly) on the basis of a likely future. Models then provide them with an explicit efficient information tool, a systematic storage and processing framework for the large quantities of information used by forecasters, whatever method they might wish to use.

The economic structure the model builders are trying to capture is a changing one, so that understanding can never be complete. There is evidence that the Australian economic structure changed rapidly during the seventies, probably in response to the much higher rates of inflation and the lower levels of economic activity. To give just one example: Davis and Lewis (1978) cite evidence suggesting that the demand for money functions estimated with data of the 1950s and 1960s exhibited considerable instability during the 1970s. A change or evolution in the parameters creates considerable problems for statistical estimation. Also, the structure could change just because different policies are followed.[12]

In spite of these drawbacks, econometric models have firmly established their role both in forecasting and in policy simulation, both in Australia and elsewhere, notably the United States, the United Kingdom, the Netherlands and Norway. According to Eckstein (1976), a leading US model builder, virtually all serious national economic forecasting in the US is now done with the aid of large-scale econometric models. Just as politicians rightly consult fallible public opinion polls as giving them the best available information, so economic policy advisers consult fallible econometric models before either making their own forecasts or recommending appropriate policy stances.

Partly as a result of the development and operation of these large—scale models, there appears to be a substantial gap in understanding and expertise on the Australian economy between the economists in the central policy-making departments (the members of the 'official family' as they sometimes call themselves) and those outside who do not have regular access to these and other internal applied economic research and policy memoranda. A good deal of this gap would seem to be unnecessary for protecting the formulation and the giving of confidential advice from senior public servants to Ministers.[13]

3.2 Some Basic Issues—Keynesians versus Monetarists and/or Neo-classical Economists[14]

> . . . The 'monetarist counter-revolution' has attracted remarkably little attention by Australian economists, who are mostly confirmed Keynesians, and steadfast in their belief in the necessity for an active fiscal policy (Nevile and Stammer 1972 p.9).

Since these judgements were made, monetarists have become much more prominent and belief in the necessity for an active fiscal policy—in the 1972 sense of demand management—is less steadfast. Belief in the efficacy or otherwise of fiscal policy is in fact one of the basic differences between Keynesians and monetarists. Some prominent Australian economists would now deny the need for—or the desirability of—an active anti-cyclical fiscal stabilisation policy (Porter 1978, McGregor 1978). They follow the view of monetarists in other countries that:

> There is no serious need to stabilise the economy; that even if there were a need, it could not be done, for stabilisation policies would be more likely to increase than to decrease instability; and . . . even in the unlikely event that stabilisation policies could on balance prove beneficial, the government should not be trusted with the necessary powers. (Modigliani 1977 p.1).

While such views would represent a minority opinion—at least as of 1978—there has been a definite move away from a belief in the efficacy of 'fine tuning'—that is of a very active stabilisation policy. Again official government statements in 1977 and 1978 from time to time denied the possibility of the government's being able to stimulate directly the level of output and employment. While such statements may be made partly for political purposes (to escape the odium of responsibility of presiding over an economy with a high and rising level of unemployment) some of the government's economic advisers do appear to believe that various leakages would eliminate positive aggregate real demand and employment effects from any fiscal stimulus. They point to the dramatic increase in unemployment during 1974–75 in spite of a very expansionary fiscal policy stance. While there was at first some direct expenditure and product increase (though little employment response) to fiscal stimulus, this was much less than might have been expected on the basis of previous experience—that is adverse private sector reactions (through consumption, investment as well as external responses) neutralised a good deal of the stimulus within the year. On the other hand, given the long lags shown by the econometric models it is perhaps not very surprising that the stimulatory action of 1974–75 had so little real effect within the year.

Another difference is that monetarists interpret the unsatisfactory economic developments of the seventies in terms of key monetary developments—the balance of payments disequilibrium of 1970–72, the monetary explosion of 1972–73, the credit squeeze of 1974 and the exchange rate instability from 1974 onwards. Keynesians, on the other hand, place more emphasis on flows of income and expenditure than on changes in stocks of money and other assets; on demand influences, and on inflationary transmissions from other countries through commodity prices, increased export incomes etc. They place more emphasis on real, and less on purely monetary, phenomena.

Neo-classical economists identify relative price imbalances—in particular the overall level of real wages and the relative wages for some workers (e.g. juveniles and the unskilled) as crucial influences on the level of unemployment. Neo-classical economists such as Corden (1978), Snape (1977) and the authors of the *Australian Bulletin of Labour* (e.g. issue 3, 1977) believe that a reduction in real wages (relative to productivity) is a necessary condition for a reduction in unemployment. It is not, however, a sufficient conditions and needs to be accompanied by an increase in real demand. Whether an increase in *nominal* demand is also required is one of the points at issue in the debate between Keynesians and neo-classical economists.

(a) Tax Cuts and Wage-Tax Trade-Offs as Anti-stagflationary Weapons

> Between then [1973] and the end of 1974 Australian economists appear to have reached an impressive consensus on prices and incomes policy. Practically all economists who discussed inflation in this period went on record as favouring the immediate introduction of a prices and incomes policy. . . . Typically the suggested policy took the form of a 'package' consisting of proposals for wage and price restraint accompanied by a variety of suggested 'carrots' and 'sticks'. The carrots proposed usually included a guarantee that wage restraint of the required degree would be rewarded by substantial tax concessions, varying from a reduction in

> excise charges and sales taxes on essential items to personal tax indexation. (Hagger 1978, p.175).

More recently the Melbourne Institute of Applied Economic and Social Research has, on a variety of occasions, called for cuts in indirect taxes and government charges and cuts in income taxes in return for reductions in the rate of money wage increases. Such measures, it is argued, would simultaneously reduce inflation and provide a real stimulus to economic activity.[15] Similar suggestions for 'innovative policies to slow inflation' have been made recently in the United States at the twenty-fifth Brookings Conference on Economic Activity (April 1978), with suggestions for a substitution of direct for indirect taxes and proposals for a tax-based incomes policy. (*Brookings Papers on Economic Activity*, No.2, 1978).

Using the model of the Australian economy in his Fiscal Policy text, Nevile (1977) has examined tax cuts as an anti-inflationary weapon. His simulations suggest that indirect tax cuts reduce the rate of inflation mainly in the year in which they are made and taper off in the following two years. After that the increases in demand resulting from the tax cuts will tend to worsen inflation. Coghlan's 1978 simulations with the NIF model also suggest that the anti-inflationary effects of indirect tax cuts decline substantially after the first year (Coghlan 1978).

The proponents of an exchange or so-called 'package' argue that such simulations do not allow for the 'deal' under which either money wage growth and/or the growth in unit labor costs will be slowed down. This depends of course on how far the growth in money wages *can* be centrally controlled if and when unions' bargaining power increases.

A further argument against such proposals is that they tend to be one-off operations which need to be renegotiated every year or so—with government likely to run out of bargaining counters.

Expansion of real economic activity can also run into other constraints. If indirect taxes are reduced and real output and expenditure increased as a result, some spill-over into extra imports is likely.[16] Again part of the increased budgetary deficit is likely to be financed eventually by an increased external current account deficit. Corden has pointed out some of the possible problems with such a solution:

> . . . from a national point of view foreign borrowing . . . or a running down of reserves makes possible the restoration of full employment at a constant post-tax real wage. Australia would be temporarily living above its means until its means catch up with its somewhat high living. In assessing this proposal one has to decide how much can be borrowed without generating speculative capital outflow and to what extent it pays Australia to mortgage the future so as to subsidise wages. A mitigating factor is that a good part of the gains from pre-tax wage reduction would go to profits which would, to a considerable extent, be invested in Australia.
>
> The overwhelming difficulty is probably to strike the bargain in the

> first place and to hold real post-tax wages for a sufficient time. Even if a bargain could be struck one year, would it not be harder the next time round? For how long is the Treasury to be prevented from increasing taxes? Should the government ever make so inhibiting a commitment, bearing in mind that it has enough trouble keeping the deficit within limits. Of course, if the bargain *could* be struck *and* were adhered to, *and* then led to a significant increase in employment, the extra deficit might, after a time, turn out to be quite small or even non-existent. (Corden 1978).

A similar proposal envisaged the introduction of a tax-based incomes policy—a policy of taxing excessive wage increases—either by taxing companies granting such excessive wage increases or by taxing individuals receiving them. This was popular in Australia during the period of the Labor government and was the subject of an official inquiry which pointed to a variety of possible administrative problems and injustices as between firms placed in different circumstances, (though it concluded it was possible to introduce such a scheme).[17] A more recent, public, assessment of similar US proposals by two US Treasury officials concurred in this overall evaluation. They were perhaps somewhat more positive:

> TIP [a tax based incomes policy] would entail significant administrative problems for the Internal Revenue Service and compliance problems for businesses. These problems could be reduced to a manageable size if TIP were applied only to business taxpayers, if it were limited to wages, if the hurdle approach were adopted, and if it did not apply to small companies. The administrative compliance problems, however, still would be significant. (Dildine & Sunley 1978, p.389).

These administrative and compliance problems must of course be weighed against the expected gains from a tax based incomes policy in moderating wage and price increases and—Keynesians would add—the costs of alternative methods of making progress against inflation. It is widely conceded—even among those who favour the use of restrictive policies to cure inflation—that the gains are disappointingly slow and the costs in a purely economic sense (let alone in social terms) very great. Those who still favour such restrictive policies maintain that the alternative would either not work or would work only for a very limited period. Apart from any balance of payments and/or inflationary problems a fundamental obstacle to getting back to full employment, as many of the 'restrictionists' see it, is the tendency of wages to rise faster than productivity (and at an accelerating pace) when unemployment is low and relative union bargaining strength high.

(b) Wages and Unemployment

The Australian economic debate about the connection of wages and unemployment has many varied and inter-twining facets. One aspect has been historical—how important was the 1974 wage explosion in the subsequent dramatic rise in unemployment rates from around 1½% to 2% of the labour force to 1978 levels of 6% or so? The official position argues that it was very important. This view was presented in many submissions to the Arbitration Commission in national wage cases[18] and in several Budget statements. This position received support from the 1978 OECD survey of Australia. It pointed out that, whereas the fall in output in the most recent recession was not as severe as in the 1951/52 and 1960/61 recessions, the growth of unemployment was much greater. An examination of the relevant equation in the NIF forecasting model suggests that 2 to 2.8% of the 4 to 4½% increase in unemployment between 1974 and 1978 is attributed by the equation to wage costs in excess of gains in labour productivity (Gruen 1978). While the Melbourne Institute has criticised such estimates, according to the most recent issue of the *Australian Economic Review* (No.2, 1978, p.10) there is now agreement that

> the real wage rise and profit squeeze were important factors in the rise in unemployment during 1974–75. The current issue, on which we would differ from many economists and from the recent OECD report on Australia, is whether the levels of real wages and profits obtaining in 1977 and 1978 are significant influences on the present level of unemployment in Australia.

Differences also arise when attempts are made to identify and quantify the relevant gap between movements in real wage costs and in labour productivity—the so-called 'real wage overhang'. The empirical issues separating the various proponents revolve around the best base period for such comparisons, the appropriate sector of the economy for productivity estimates (i.e. whether it should be the non-farm *market* sector or the non-farm sector of the economy), whether actual or trend productivity should be used and, if the latter, whether trend productivity has changed significantly in recent years. The various empirical issues are canvassed in Treasury (1978, pp.15–25): Stammer (1978) and *Australian Economic Review* (No.2, 1978, pp.8–10). However, such a debate is necessarily inconclusive; even if there is no real wage overhang, the level of real wages may be too high to re-establish full employment. Risk premiums may have increased since the base period and both investment and economic activity generated might not return to previous full employment levels—unless either profitability exceeds previous trend levels, or some alternative methods of stimulating labour-using investment is devised. Again external factors (such as a reduction in the long run level of capital inflow) could make the real wage too high to re-establish full employment.

The third and possibly most important issue is whether a reduction in real wages (relative to productivity) is a necessary and/or sufficient condition for a reduction in unemployment. Here there are wide and apparently unbridgeable disagreements between the various groups. The issues are canvassed in detail in the March 1978 CAER paper *Real Wages and Unemployment* and in Corden's Presidential address (Corden 1978). The arguments for the importance of real wages rely on the cost-minimising behaviour of economic agents and the evidence that the demand for labour is negatively related to the wage rate (Freebairn and Withers 1977). Those arguing against cite the male-female employment puzzle—female wages have risen much faster than those of males, yet this does not appear to be reflected in relative employment levels (Gregory and Duncan 1978)—and the fact that the reduction in demand has been responsible for a large part of the rise in unemployment. The last is countered by the earlier group's contention that any government-induced increase in nominal demand is likely to lead to balance of payments problems and/or price rises rather than to output and employment increases—unless real wages fall (at least relative to productivity.)

Finally, there is the question how far changes in the rate of growth of money wages really affect changes in real wages. As Riach and Richards (1978) have pointed out, it is in fact very rare to find periods when large increases in money wages have squeezed profits and led to large real wage gains. From the opposite side of the political fence there is the suggestion in the 1978/79 *Budget Papers* (Statement No.2, pp.40–41) that a deceleration in the rate of growth of money wages might, on balance, affect the real wage level very little.

3.3 Monetary Policy

As is shown by Davis and Lewis (1978) the quantity and quality of research in the field of monetary economics has grown remarkably during the last decade. In spite of this, the issues involved in some of the major areas of work by Australian monetary economists are, according to Davis and Lewis 'far from resolved'. This may be too harsh a judgement in some respects. There is a good deal of agreement that 'money matters' more—both for the determination of levels of economic activity and rates of change of prices[19]—than was generally accepted say a decade ago, though there is ongoing policy debate on the financial constraints upon fiscal policy.

Also, there is debate about the transmission mechanism through which monetary policy becomes effective. The older view—embodied for instance in the pre-1976 structural models—emphasises the effects of monetary policy on a narrow well defined range of assets and expenditure categories (consumer durable, private dwelling and fixed investment expenditure). More recent work emphasises that portfolio choices of firms and households can affect a larger range of assets, each with different yields and other characteristics. This suggests that monetary policy may, in due course, impinge on a very wide spectrum of asset prices and yields. The length of the adjustment lags and their variability is an issue which has not been resolved. This has an important bearing on the wisdom of and scope for discretionary monetary policy; the longer and the more variable the lags in the transmission of monetary influences, the less likely it is that discretionary monetary policy can be pursued in a stabilising direction.

Another aspect of the monetary policy debate concerns the practicality and the advisability of controlling the rate of growth of the money supply. Davis and Lewis regard the analysis of the determination of the Australian money supply as 'in general' in an unsatisfactory state. This is because unique institutional features affecting the money supply have not been adequately modelled. Neither the assumption of perfect substitutability between banks' cash and government securities, nor the assumption of no substitutability is satisfactory. The real world requires some more complicated relationship of which these are two polar cases. Whether it is practical to control the money supply depends partly on the issue of modelling this relationship adequately. It is also a question of the flexibility with which other instruments of policy are operated (taxes, expenditures and interest rates), or as other economists would put it, whether other policy instruments are subordinated to a money supply target. How far it is sensible to give priority to a money supply target in the presence of a wide variety of possible disturbances has not, as yet, been discussed adequately in the Australian literature.

The recent move towards more flexible exchange rates should make it possible for governments to pursue a more independent monetary policy —though even with fixed exchange rates, exchange controls, restrictions on borrowing and sterilisation policies provided some room for independence.

> Whether this independence is a matter of weeks, months or years lies at the basis of the conflicting interpretation of past monetary policies, as surveyed here. (Davis & Lewis, 1978, p.78).

Again, the openness of the economy, the integration of world capital markets and the growth of offshore financial markets affect the possibility of pursuing independent monetary policies.

3.4 A Taxonomy of Failures of Stabilisation Policies in the Seventies

Why has Australian stabilisation policy failed in response to international disturbances? Garnaut (1978) distinguishes three sources of failure; first the failure to identify optimal policies—the identification problem; second political difficulties in implementing optimal policies and third institutional barries to the implementation of the right policies.

Garnaut lists three identification problems. (1) Unemployment levels in 1972–74 were an inadequate indicator of the level of slack in the economy. This led to inappropriate expansionary responses, while unemployment (at that time) was largely the result of such other factors as increased mismatching (possibly due to reduced immigration), higher real wages and/or higher unemployment benefits. (2) Failure to identify correctly the cyclical and temporary nature of the improvement in Australia's terms of trade in 1972 and 1973 made it more difficult to institute restraint in expenditure during the boom period and to accumulate large foreign reserves for a later time (and sterilise some part of them). (3) Identification problems were also important after 1975 when low levels of export growth and foreign capital inflow were regarded as temporary phenomena likely to disappear with the world recession. (These factors are of course, much more easily discernible with the benefit of hindsight!)

The political problems Garnaut isolates are also three. (1) The McMahon non-Labor government's failure to appreciate in late 1971 laid the groundwork for the massive subsequent destabilising capital inflow. (2) The intense electoral competition during the whole of the calendar years 1972, 1974 and 1975 was not conductive to firm policies designed to insulate Australia from world-wide inflation and recession. (3) The new Labor government's political commitment to expand public expenditures on education, health and welfare payments without increasing tax *rates*—contributed to the subsequent difficulties.

Finally the principal institutional constraint Garnaut cites is the complex system through which wages were fixed in Australia, which prevents governments having complete constitutional authority over wage policy.

Some may quarrel with this particular interpretation of the events of 1970–75; but the distinctions between problems of identification, political problems and institutional ones seems useful. It reminds us that solutions to economic problems involve not only correct analysis and identification, but also have to be institutionally and administratively feasible and remain within the political constraints under which different governments operate.

Section 4 The State and Economic Activity—Microeconomic Policy

4.1 Protection

There is a long tradition of government protection of selected economic activities in Australia. During the last 10–12 years this policy of protection has come under increasing attack—from academics, individual politicians, government appointed commissions of inquiry and from the Tariff Board and its successor, the Industries Assistance Commission. Perhaps one could single out three individuals as playing key roles in this gradual change of opinion—Corden at the academic level; Kelly in the Federal Parliament and the Rattigan in the bureaucracy.[20]

As Lloyd (1978) has pointed out, in recent years there has been less stress on the major traditional arguments for high individual or high average levels of protection (such as fostering diversification, improving Australia's terms of trade, or increasing real wages and immigration). Instead the focus of the debate has shifted to alternative methods of bringing greater uniformity into the structure of protective rates and to the most desirable pace of reform towards a much lower level of protection—if not towards completely free trade.

The first tentative steps towards both lower and more uniform tariffs were taken on the initiative of the Tariff Board under Mr. Rattigan's leadership in the so-called Tariff Review (suggested in the 1967/68 Tariff Board Annual Report and accepted by the government in May 1971). In a variety of ways, this represented a clear break with earlier principles. Tariffs were to be reviewed if they were unusually high or had not been examined for some time. Tariff inquiries were previously normally held on the initiative of those manufacturers who had convinced the relevant government department that they were unduly hurt by import competition. Since review of protection was mainly at the request of the injured party, this naturally led to a gradual upward trend in levels of protection.

The Tariff Review represented an attempt to reverse this process. It was, therefore, not surprisingly, hotly contested by those manufacturing groups who had been beneficiaries of the earlier approach. The concept of 'effective protection'—which was to be used for the purpose of the Tariff Review—became the subject of detailed Australian criticism by Gunnerson (1970), Evans (1972) and Norman (1975). While the formal validity of some of these criticisms is now generally granted, there is, as Lloyd pointed out

> still a presumption that an industry with a relatively high effective rate of protection has attracted resources away from industries with lower effective rates. This is the essential idea of effective protection theory (Lloyd 1978, p.250).

In addition, the international and the Australian debate has resulted in the accumulation of a sizeable stock of knowledge—both in terms of making theory more applicable to the complexities of the practical world and in terms of generating knowledge about levels of protection actually prevailing.

The most dramatic act in the field of protection policy was the Labor Government's 25 per cent across-the-board tariff cut in July 1973. This decision was taken partly for the purpose of improving the allocation of resources within the Australian economy, but more importantly as an instrument for reducing the level of excess demand operating in the economy at that time—in order to enable the Labor government to achieve more of its ambitious social and economic programme (e.g. to channel more resources towards education, health, urban development etc). Partly because of its dramatic nature and partly because it provided a convenient scapegoat, the quantitative economic importance of the tariff cut in reducing employment in Australian manufacturing industry has been greatly exaggerated. There is a consensus among those who have seriously attempted to quantify its importance, that the 25% tariff cut was much less important as a cause of increased import competition than the combined effect of exchange rate changes and the very large wage increase taking place during 1973–75 (Gruen 1975, Gregory & Martin 1976, IAC 1977a, p.83).

According to Gregory and Martin the tariff cut had its major effect on the volume of imports in the third, fourth and fifth quarter after the event—providing evidence of the difficulty of correctly timing tariff cuts with the business cycle. Since an across-the-board tariff cut is normally more 'digestible' in periods of buoyant economic activity, the long lags of 1973/74 illustrate the difficulties of achieving proper timing (though supply shortages overseas at that time may have made the lags longer than normal).

The dramatic and sustained growth in the level of unemployment beginning in 1974, has led to a sizeable reversal of policy. Average rates of effective protection for manufacturing industry appear to have remained relatively constant, rising in some years and falling in others. But average effective rates remain substantially below 1968/69 levels (IAC 1978, p.130). On the other hand, the variability of effective rates between different sectors of manufacturing industry has widened—with especially high levels of protection given in the form of quantitative import restrictions to a small group of industries already highly protected—in particular clothing and footwear, textiles and motor vehicles.[21]

Lloyd deplores the slow pace of reform (and dismantling) of the Australian system of protection:

> the very high differentiation of the structure of assistance in Australia relative to other developed countries has continued along with these sophisticated debates, debates which have had only a slow influence in reforming the structure. Clever analysis is not sufficient for sound policies. (Is it even a necessary condition?)
>
> Why has the structure of assistance changed so slowly? (Lloyd 1978, p.288).

While Lloyd's pessimism about the slow pace of reform is understandable, it is not surprising that the most serious and deep-seated recession for some four decades should have given rise to increased protectionist sentiment and policies—as it has in other countries. Nevertheless the weight of uncommitted opinion seems to be gradually moving in favour of both lower all round levels of protection, and less inter-industry variability. The basic problem consists in translating these general policy attitudes—enunciated in the annual reports of the Industries Assistance Commission and fairly widely endorsed—into the difficult individual assistance decisions affecting particular firms and their employees. However, with the notable and important exceptions of clothing and footwear, textiles and transport equipment (which between them account for only about 12½% of the value added of all manufacturing industries), the trend in levels of average effective protection has been downward—even since the 1973 tariff cut (IAC

1978, p.33). As shown in the accompanying table there has been a sizeable shift towards lower rates of effective assistance between 1968/69 and 1976/77 (though the proportion of industry receiving extremely high effective protection has increased).

TABLE 1
Estimated Percentage of Manufacturing Industry (in terms of value added) with Different Effective Rates of Assistance 1969 and 1977

Average effective rates of assistance# (per capita)	Percentage of value added*	
	1968/69	1976/77
Negative	10.4	10.6
0–10%	9.9	12.9
10.1–20%	7.5	25.5
20.1–30%	11.7	20.4
30.1–40%	18.3	14.5
40.1–50%	11.9	7.4
50.1–100%	25.6	3.2
Above 100%	5.0	6.0

Source: IAC 1978, Figure 2.2, p.132.
*Totals do not sum to 100.0 due to rounding
#An attempt has been made to allow for the protective effects of quantitative restrictions.

4.2 The Gregory Thesis—Interrelations between Mining and Other Industries

The rapid growth of the mining sector in the last decade or so has had important consequences for the rest of the economy. While these had been realised by economists for some time, the issues were highlighted by a simple model and some rough, but spectacular 'order of magnitude' estimates by Gregory (1976).

The growth of a new major export industry such as the Australian mining industry provides the economy with an alternative (substitute?) source of export income. It can also be viewed as enabling the economy to increase its spending on overseas goods and services. In this case, the growth of mining exports might be regarded as providing additional 'competition' for the import competing sector of the economy. The mechanisms through which the mineral export growth harms the traditional export sector or the import competing sectors can be either by an appreciation of the Australian currency or by a faster internal inflation than in those countries which are Australia's trading partners. Either of these mechanisms will have adverse financial effects on both traditional exporters and import competing industries.[22] Lindner (1978, p.43) suggested that 'the eventual effect of the mineral boom is likely to be an increase in the level of domestic prices by about 12 per cent.'

Gregory suggested that, from the point of view of traditional rural exporters the rise of mineral exports had been about as harmful financially as a doubling of all tariffs; whilst from the point of view of import competing industry it was more harmful than the total abolition of all tariffs—let alone the 25% general reduction of tariffs which industry was both complaining about, and suffering from, at that particular time. While these were very rough orders of magnitude which are sensitive to Gregory's assumptions about supply and demand responses, the actual numbers (or orders of magnitude) do not appear to have been challenged subsequently. What has been challenged are, first, the policy implications which some have drawn from the model and from the estimates and second some theoretical simplifications in the Gregory model.[23]

The damage to traditional export industries and to import competing industry by the growth of mineral exports has been cited as an important argument for a slower future rate of development of Australia's mineral deposits[24]; but mainly by those opposed to mineral developments for other reasons—such as the resultant damage to the environment or to aboriginal ways of life in their remaining tribal areas. These are, of course, quite distinct arguments which have no necessary connection with each other. Thus one may oppose mining in aboriginal reserves and yet believe that the damage to other industries is not an adequate reason to defer mineral development—and vice versa. But mixing up the issues often makes it politically easier to take one side—because of the cumulative reinforcement provided by the separate arguments.

4.3 Agriculture

> During the past decade the rural sector has experienced extremely volatile prices and incomes. Underlying these forces however has been a steady erosion of the competitive position of agriculture in the Australian economy (Miller 1976, p.29).

Miller's quotation focuses on two of the major agricultural problem areas—instability and declining trends in farm incomes (relative to non-farm incomes) and in the competitive position of agriculture. The instability of farm incomes has been well documented (Working Group on Rural Policy 1974; Table 4.1). What is less certain is whether government action is desirable and if so what form it should take. Reduction of (producer) price instability and of uncertainty through the use of more stable (and normally higher) home prices—often administered by governmentally enforced monopolistic marketing boards—has been a major Australian response to such instability. In this form, reduction in price instability usually involves some form of financial assistance—either from local consumers or taxpayers. Whether—and under what conditions—such assistance is justifiable on efficiency grounds has been one area of economic debate. A good deal of this debate has taken place under the heading of whether agriculture is entitled to 'tariff compensation'. The argument is well summarised by Lloyd (1978, pp.265–8) and requires no elaboration here. There is now a greater wariness among professional economists in condemning low levels of protection in rural industries whilst not accepting the very sweeping claims for financial assistance sometimes made by rural spokesmen in the name of 'tariff compensation'.

Another strand of the debate concerns the connection between price and income instability. The contribution of price variability to gross income variability varies from close on 100% for wool to relatively minor figures for the main cereal crops. In the latter case increased price stability can make little contribution to the stability of producers' incomes. In addition, reduction of price instability may lead to losses as producers' rational responses to changing market opportunities are inhibited or delayed. For this reason, agricultural economists have generally favoured income—over price-support schemes. Even the former may not be easily justifiable on efficiency grounds and raise possible 'moral hazard' problems—that is they reduce the incentive to guard against the uncertainties and instabilities of nature. (Even if not justifiable on efficiency grounds, many may favour cushioning farmers against very severe income falls on equity or distributional grounds.)

The reasons for the declining relative income position of farmers are very deep seated and unlikely to be fully reversible by government actions. One thinks not only of the growth of the mineral industry already mentioned, but also of the low-income elasticities of demand for farm products, of the high and apparently irreversible levels of agricultural protection in many of Australia's trading partners—including the growing use of export subsidies to unload embarrassing domestic surpluses. This declining (relative) income position of farmers has given rise to demands for action on a variety of fronts. The demands for 'tariff compensation' have been mentioned. Policies of fostering 'development' (land-clearing and preparation for farming purposes) and of 'closer settlement' (compulsory subdivision of larger farms) have given way to 'reconstruction' policies. These are designed to help farmers cope better with adverse economic conditions. Such reconstruction programmes have led to the provision of concessional credit and of financial assistance for farm amalgamation. The economic (efficiency) case for either provision does not appear particularly compelling; however, one can certainly regard them as lesser evils than the policies they replaced. The former tended to reduce the real incomes not only of the community at large but also of agricultural producers as a whole.

Edwards and Watson's (1978) survey of agricultural policy covers these and other major policy issues in Australian agriculture. Another important change in agricultural policy in the last decade to which they draw attention has been the establishment of the IAC with its brief to recommend also on assistance to agriculture. One effect has been a greater public scrutiny both of claims for assistance and of the public institutions servicing the farm sector. This is particularly welcome where a good deal of marketing is undertaken by secretive governmental agencies which have often successfully prevented an adequate arms-length examination of their performance —both of their overall pricing policies and of their technical marketing functions (in how far their grading, storage, financing and transport operations are carried out efficiently).

4.4 Urban Economics

Nowhere has the role of government in Australian economic life been more controversial than in the urban field. Federal Labor believed in large—scale federal funding of urban infra-structure and of new growth centres. It also favoured stricter governmental regulation of land use, betterment taxes on increases in land values resulting from growth and/or re-zoning of land. The ALP also believes in more public transport and in using governmental land and urban policies to improve the distribution of incomes and/or locational access for lower income groups. In the name of freedom and of less central government interference in essentially local issues, non-Labor believes in none of these things—or at least downgrades them markedly. The effect is that a period of federal Labor rule leads to a good deal of federal urban activity generally and in particular increased expenditure on perceived urban problem areas, while urban and regional development becomes one of the major avenues for economies by succeeding non-Labor governments (Lloyd and Troy 1978).[25]

This synoptic sketch of federal Australian urban policies over the six-six-year period 1972–1978 provides the background against which to examine Australian urban economics during the last decade. As pointed out by Neutze and Bethune (1979), urban economics is a late-comer to the scene of Australian urban studies which have tended to be largely interdisciplinary in nature To an economist not schooled in the particular subdivision of the discipline, a good deal of Australian urban economics appears to lack rigour and the types of definitive studies which elsewhere provide the basic building blocks for further research. Thus, urban economics is one area where, as a result of proximity and interdependence of the various economic agents, one would expect externalities and market failure to be important facts of life. Unfortunately it is not easy to find clear statements of the principal areas of externalities and market failure in the Australian context (although Beale's (1978) brief discussion and Paterson's (1975) illuminating survey of historical developments of housing and planning standards provide important clues).

While market failure and externalities provide an *a priori* case for *examining* government involvement, the latter appears to have produced its own inefficiencies (Neutze and Bethune 1979; Harrison 1978). A promising avenue for research may be to examine how government involvement can be made to perform a variety of tasks better than at present. Neutze (1977, p.190) points out that while statutory urban landuse planning has not been a very effective means of achieving urban policy goals it has succeeded in some things—for example protecting the environment in sensitive areas and in reducing the extent of scattered development at the fringe of urban areas. Many economists would want to ask whether marginal cost pricing by the providers of urban services could not have done this as well or better, though more adequate pricing policies could not cope with some urban problems; inconsistent urban uses in close proximity such as tanneries in residential areas is an example that comes to mind. Growth of developers' contributions to infra-structure costs is a move in the direction of using prices to affect allocative decisions.

As in most other western economics, the three post-war decades have seen major improvements in the quantity and quality of the housing stock (*Social Indicators* Nos. 1 and 2; Section 7 Housing). By world standards Australian *average* housing standards are good. Home ownership has been fostered by large-scale government assistance through tax concessions and concessional interest rates. The benefits of these policies have probably been regressive. On the other hand, a private rental market has been preserved by the absence of rent controls and perhaps of capital gains taxes. Public housing programmes have catered less adequately for the poor or the aged and least adequately for Aborigines.

An important area of work in Australian urban studies has been 'whether a policy of diverting some growth from the largest cities to smaller centres should be undertaken' (Neutze and Bethune 1979 p.66). While there has been a considerable groundswell of opinion in earlier years in favour of siphoning off some of the growth—especially from Sydney and Melbourne—there is little definitive evidence of either the costs or benefits associated with such policies. With the decline in birth rates and in levels of migration since 1970 the issue has become a less pressing one. Other similar issues which have become less pressing as a result of changed economic conditions include urban land policy—for example whether to have betterment taxes; whether to use government land commissions to develop land in competition with private developers.

Finally there is some interesting modelling of city interdependencies being undertaken currently—into the relationships between housing, transport and employment (e.g. Alexander 1978).

4.5 Economics of Education

The most difficult issues of political economy are those where goals of efficiency, freedom of choice, and equality conflict. It is hard enough to propose an intellectually defensible compromise among them, even harder to find a politically viable compromise (Tobin 1970).

In their review of the economics of education, Blandy, Hayles and Woodfield (BHW) raise a large number of important issues—even though many (non-economist?) social scientists will disagree with their strong commitment to choice and efficiency (at the expense of equality?). They document the large increase in relative expenditure in education (as a proportion of gross domestic product); much of this increase (since the mid-sixties) being accounted for by improvements in teacher/student ratios and in other quality indices, with practically no increases required for demographic reasons. They then ask some awkward questions about the basic justification for such substantial increases in the proportion of GDP spent on education.

> The accumulated evidence suggests that ploughing on with expenditures, especially those which do not induce increases in teacher quality, may be socially wasteful, and would at least seem to require more substantive *a priori* justification (BHW, p.145).

In addition to a very large increase in total educational expenditures, there has been a dramatic increase in the share of central government financing of education over this period. Some part of this has been at the expense of private expenditure. Is this basically desirable and why? Most of the government's increased spending at tertiary level has almost certainly been regressive (including the abolition of fees). As BHW put it

> . . . at the tertiary level, there is a case for users of educational services to bear more of the cost of financing those services, through (a) permitting institutions to supplement their resources from fees and (b) replacing or supplementing the present means-tested allowance system by a system of loans to students. . . . The abolition of fees . . . have benefitted a privileged handful of the community's children behind a smokescreen of egalitarian slogans (BHW, p.156–7).

Many will part company with BHW in their wholehearted endorsement of the market as obviously the most desirable mechanism for allocating educational services.

> In what sense is education a very special commodity? . . . why cannot most households afford modest educational expenses? Most households agree that they cannot afford a Mercedes Benz, but governments do not seem obliged to fill the breach in cases like this (BHW, p.122).

As Blaug (1970) has pointed out, the degree of government intervention in education *generally* observed in market economies cannot be justified in terms of the normal economic arguments embraced under the general heading of market failure. Tobin's notion of limiting the domain of inequality to luxuries and the less essential amenities—*or in this particular case to those commodities affecting the present generation*—may provide a clue for the predominant behaviour patterns in most market economies with respect to education. As Tobin puts it:

> The social conscience is more offended by severe inequality in nutrition and basic shelter, or in access to medical care or to legal assistance, than by inequality in automobiles, books, clothes, furniture, boats. Can we somehow remove the necessities of life and health from the prizes that serve as incentives for economic activity, and instead let people strive and compete for non-essential luxuries and amenities? (Tobin 1970, p.450).

Specific egalitarianism of this kind can take a number of forms more fully spelt out by Tobin (who also discusses education in this context).

BHW recommend experiments with the use of government-issued vouchers for use in payment (or part-payment) for education. This is a move away from Tobin's specific egalitarianism towards allowing market forces greater influence. With vouchers a great many different variations are conceivable; a recent Schools Commission (1978) discussion paper lists six basic options. The Schools Commission appears to agree with BHW's assessment of vouchers as a likely means for revolutionising the structure of Australian education and for transferring power from professionals to parents.

> Payments to individuals, if introduced, as a new approach to financing school-level education, may well revolutionise the structure of Australian education systems, between users and schools, at least from that which currently exists in government systems. Such a voucher-type scheme, if 'full cost' in nature and applied to all children, would depend for its success on a number of factors. Parent awareness of what different schools have to offer, and their capacity to make an informed choice would be important. So would the ability of schools to adapt their curriculum, teaching-learning styles, and administrative procedures. The availability of physical space to accommodate fluctuating demands would help to determine success. So too would the nature of conditions laid down regarding enrolment policies and preferences, and levels of compulsory fees which could be charged. *However, perhaps the most important factor of all would be the degree to which those who exercise the most immediate control over schools at present—the professionals (teachers and officials)—were prepared to countenance a shift in the locus of power* (Schools Commission 1978, p.61—my italics).

On the other hand, the one American experiment with vouchers at Alum Rock—a school district in San Jose, California—does not appear to have led to such far-reaching changes. According to Hind (1978) parental involvement in advising and decision-making *diminished* as the Alum Rock demonstration progressed; by the third year only half the parent advisory committees established in the beginning were still functioning. However there may be special factors behind the failure of the Alum Rock experiment and it cannot be regarded as conclusive evidence of the effects of the voucher method of financing (or partially financing) education. This is not necessarily an argument against attempting such an experiment.

One possibly valid counter-argument is that it may increase the inequality of access to educational resources. Reducing the cost of non-government education by the provision of vouchers to parents would increase the demand for such education, drawing teachers and other resources into this area—partly (especially in the short run) from government schools. Whatever its merits in encouraging parent involvement, greater competition and innovation, such a voucher proposal would seem likely to increase inequality in the consumption of educational services. In the short run, a substantial proportion of the better teachers (employed in response to greater competition for the parents' vouchers) would come from the predominant government system. In the long run these teachers would be replaced, but there would probably remain a greater variability in per pupil expenditure on education—a variability related not only to parents' tastes but also to their incomes. On the other hand BHW argue that special compensatory voucher schemes might be designed to counteract such tendencies.

Section 5 Inequality—Some Economic Issues

As pointed out in Richardson's survey (1979), a great deal of extra information has become available on inequalities of income and expenditure in Australia in the last ten years. This has led to much extra research of an empirical nature. While a good deal of this research is using increasingly sophisticated statistical tools, in Australia it is unfortunately too often conducted in the absence of any relevant theoretical framework—for example of a theory of how incomes are determined. In other branches of economics measurement without theory seems to have been increasingly displaced by the quantitative testing of theories; it would be surprising if the economic issues of inequality require such different treatment. Academic economists overseas have found it useful to examine distributional questions within the normal neo-classical economic framework (e.g. Tinbergen 1975), though this is not to deny that another theoretical scaffolding could also be fruitful.

5.1 The Extent of Inequality

Income appears to be much more unequally distributed—both in Australia and in countries with comparable living standards—than such other human characteristics as height, IQ etc. Wealth is even more unequally distributed. We do not yet know enough about the reasons for existing inequalities; how far are they the result of injustices and/or discrimination and how far do they correspond to differences in age and/or work intensity, to longer periods of training or just to good or bad fortune. As Richardson (1979) makes clear there are a good many hazards in drawing conclusions from the raw statistics—or even from historical or international comparisons of inequalities. Some may feel despite this that her approach has been too negative; others adopt the approach of examining 'the extent to which the figures are deficient and to try and assess how far this affects the conclusions drawn' (Atkinson 1975, p.257).

What are some of the hazards concerning inequality statistics? There is, first, the need to compare like with like. Generally income inequality indices for individuals exceed those for families; income inequalities exceed expenditure inequalities; again incomes for a year appear to be more unequal than lifetime incomes. Hence comparisons should refer to the same categories—or alternatively an attempt should be made to make the necessary adjustments. Second, changes in inequality indices may arise from very many causes; for example from such social trends as the growth of two-income families as an increasing proportion of married women enter the paid work force. In other words it is desirable to go behind the reasons for changes in inequality indices. Third, an inequality index attempts to summarise the magnitude of the dipersion and skewness of a frequency distribution by the use of a single number. It is easy to show that this can produce paradoxical results.[26]

Richardson refers to the fact that the income distribution literature concentrates mostly on the examination and explanation of trends in earnings of full-time adult males. This concentration is partly the result of data limitations; until 1966 there were no available statistics on household incomes or expenditure. But it is also the result of the existence of a fairly centralised arbitration system—which has encouraged an academic and perhaps litiginous interest in the structure of earnings and of pay. As Richardson shows, while there have been alternative periods of compression and widening of male pay rates and earnings over the last 60 years, there is no evidence of any long-term trend—either towards compression or diperson.

The absence of such a long-term trend does not necessarily imply stability in differentials between different occupations. But Freebairn and Withers suggest that there is little evidence that changes in relative award rates respond to relative market pressures—either on an industry or occupation basis (Freebairn and Withers 1977, pp.22–23)—casting doubt on the efficacy of markets in this area. On the other hand, Phelps Brown (1977) attributes the almost universal unequal structure of pay largely to economic or, more narrowly to market, forces—though he does not deny that social and cultural factors may modify (by how much?) the extent of differentials and some of the rankings. The ranked pay structure—so that work requiring more education, skill and experience and carrying more responsibility is more highly paid—embraces not only Western but also Soviet-type economies, not to mention China and Cuba.

A good deal of attention has been devoted to estimating trends in the functional distribution of income—in particular the labour/non-labour share. Again the interest appears to be related to proceedings and argument in front of the Arbitration Commission. Little work has been done on integrating—or even relating—the functional income distribution with either the personal or the household distribution of income. Probably because of inheritance, wealth is more unequally distributed than total income. Income from property is therefore also likely to be more unequally distributed than income from wages and salaries. Yet it cannot be taken for granted that an increase in labour's share in national income will necessarily reduce the inequality of the total income distribution—since a disproportionate share of property income may go to some of the poorer groups (e.g. the aged). Complete answers to these questions would probably require a large scale model allowing for all the different inter-relationships.[27]

According to Murray (1978) differences in income by sex, age and education 'accounted' for some 65% of all income inequality in 1968/69. (This appears to be a larger proportion than in the USA.) While this decomposition helps in a statistical sense to account for income differences, it may not help us greatly in explaining the phenomenon of income inequality. For instance, the evidence from Britain, USA and Australia suggests that income inequalities tend to be smaller within younger than older age groups—that is the within-age Gini-coefficient tends to rise as age increases.[28] This is compatible for instance with human capital theory—that some income earners acquire increasing skills as they get older and thus obtain higher earnings. But it is also compatible with segmented labour market theories—that there exists a 'career' labour market and a secondary market where there is little or no 'learning by doing'. Again it may be compatible with hierarchical, sociological theories of inequality.

While Richardson accepts the historical comparison suggesting a decline in income inequality since the 1914/15 war census, she is cautious of international comparisons suggesting that Australia was a country with a relatively more equal income distribution than most. Perhaps a good example of the need for caution is provided by examining two international comparisons —Roberti's (1978) examination of income inequality in 18 western countries and the OECD's (1976) comparison of poverty in eight of these countries. Roberti finds Australia's 'dwarf' incomes (and those of Germany and the UK) 'exceptionally high'. 'Dwarf' here refers to the share of income received by the lowest 10% of income earners (using mainly family and household data). On this basis one would except that Australia would register relatively less poverty on a standardised definition of relative poverty than at least five of the eight countries in the OECD study. Yet the OECD study finds 8% of the Australian population in poverty (using standardised definitions) compared with 3% in Germany, 3½% in Sweden, 5% in Norway and 7 % in the U.K.

5.2 Poverty and Redistributive Policies

Ronald Henderson of the Melbourne Institute stands out for his work on poverty in Australia. Not only was he responsible for organising and conducting the original 1966 survey of living conditions in Melbourne from which economists' interest in postwar Australian poverty can be said to date; as Chairman of the Australian Government Commission into Poverty he commissioned a good many studies which have added to our knowledge and influenced a variety of policy initiatives to reduce poverty. Thus the Henderson Report proposed a greatly increased level of endowment payment as a replacement for tax deductions for children—a proposal implemented since then. The strong rise in the real value of social benefits set in train by the Labor government and more or less maintained since, probably owes a good deal to Henderson's support and advocacy. All this is not to deny some of the intellectual criticisms of the Henderson surveys regarding both the original discussion of the poverty line chosen and particularly its subsequent updating.[29]

As pointed out earlier, an international study (OECD 1976) based on 1973 statistics suggests that Australia had a good deal more poverty—using standardised definitions—than a number of Scandinavian and European countries with whom Australia is sometimes compared. Since 1973 the improvements in both the relative value of social service benefits and of child rebates would have reduced the incidence or the severity of poverty, while the increase in unemployment would probably have increased it. Further detailed fact-finding studies are needed to ascertain the net effect of these recent economic and policy changes.

Poverty obviously needs to be used as a relative concept. It needs to be defined in relation to some average of consumption prevalent in the community at a given time. It is a measure of inequality at the lower income end. This does *not* imply that poverty (as defined say by Henderson) need always be with us because the real income poverty line is always shifting upwards; its abolition requires an increase in the proportion of the community's total income going to the lowest 5 or 10 or 15 per cent of families ranked in terms of income (or some more complete measure of need).

This is likely to require an increase in governmental income—maintenance expenditure—on pensions etc.—though over the long haul improvements in other social programmes designed to reduce for instance, educational, health and legal disadvantages of the lowest income groups could have longer run beneficial effects. A familiar argument against more generous governmental income maintenance expenditure is its possible effect on incentives to work and save. Little empirical work has been done on these issues in Australia.

As Richardson points out, there has been a major debate among those concerned with inequality and equity in various guises whether some social welfare benefits should or should not be earnings-related—whether the alleviation of poverty should have absolute priority over such other social goals as alleviating hardship resulting from large *declines* in income. Most western countries have earnings-related public pension schemes, with Australia, New Zealand and the Netherlands appearing to be the exceptions (OECD, 1976, p.75). One advantage of non-earnings related schemes is that 100% of the public funds voted for pensions goes for the relief of poverty. The issues are adequately canvassed by Richardson (1979, p.69–73).

In Australia as elsewhere income guarantee schemes have been proposed as the neatest and most direct method of ensuring adequate resources for the bottom 10–20% of the population. It is doubtful whether sufficient public support can be generated to take this proposal beyond the realm of academic theorising and debate. As Richardson puts it:

> welfare policies appear to face political constraints which are not fully recognised by economists . . . to concentrate redistributive benefits solely on the poor . . . has limited political appeal (p.80)[30]

Another reason for doubting the practicality of such a simple and direct approach is provided by the manysided nature of social and equity issues. As Downs put it in relation to housing policy:

> A . . . myth that prevails concerning American social policy in general is that it could be vastly improved if only we would develop a single comprehensive and cohesive 'national strategy' for closely coordinating the actions of all relevant public and private agencies. . . . But experience with the relationship between housing policies and families proves the futility of this demand. America's decision-making and action machinery—in both the public and private sector—is far too decentralised and fragmented to make the implementation of a single plan possible—especially where such fundamental items as housing or family life are concerned. Every fundamental social reality is influenced by dozens, or hundreds, of policies and actions carried out by various specialized agents, each focused upon some narrowly defined subject (Downs 1977, p.164).

Instead 'disjointed incrementalism' is the order of the day and, barring major crises, seems far more likely to determine the shape of future policy—both in the tax and welfare fields.

Section 6 Conclusion

This account has been mainly confined to those areas covered in the commissioned surveys. For instance, there has been no attempt to survey the literature on Federal-State financial relations. Our attempt to commission a survey of the voluminous official reports made during the decade on the Australian tax system was, unfortunately, unsuccessful. Again there has been a good deal of discussion of the economic implications of alternative methods of financing health care which could with profit have been discussed and the changes in trade-practices law, and the debates they have given rise to among economists and lawyers have been another area of neglect.

Finally, it may be appropriate to revert briefly to the previously mentioned disenchantment with economics. Originally this disenchantment was partly the result of rising expectations; growth of living standards, full employment and price stability became taken for granted; while lifting our horizons we managed to forget that these achievements could be lost if we did not go on working at them.

Our recent unsatisfactory economic performance—and the spectre of economists disagreeing about the solutions—have no doubt accelerated this disenchantment. I believe some of the disenchantment is unjustified. Whatever may have been the mistakes of economists and of economic policy advisers, political and institutional failures have loomed large in recent, inadequate, economic performances. This inadequate performance started with the failure to appreciate in 1971 (against the predominant professional advice at the time)—the unduly expansionary fiscal policy stance in 1972/73 (essentially to avoid losing an election) and in 1973/74 (to keep election promises) set the stage for many of the subsequent difficulties.

On the other hand, inadequate economic growth rates, high levels of inflation and unemployment have been shared in greater or lesser degree by most if not all other OECD economies. Economic problems have become more threatening and are therefore more challenging than in the sixties. Can economic analysis come up with worthwhile solutions or are the political constraints too restricting? The dissatisfaction with the development of the discipline felt by many leaders of the profession internationally, is referred to above (Groenewegen 1979, p.186). In a recent survey of the current state of economics, Thurow is agnostic about the future intellectual progress of economics. He believes that the development of the profession proceeds

> in a manner similar to gold mining. Some great, or lucky, prospector strikes a vein of high-grade ore in the form of a new paradigm, technique or vision . . . ordinary miners go to work to mine much of the actual gold. Eventually . . . the miners must work harder and harder. . . . The intellectual rewards of further research along that line get smaller and smaller.
>
> In the last half century the great intellectual gold strikes have been the national income accounts, Keynesian economics (a development that also allowed monetary economics to be rebuilt or rediscovered), mathematical economics, and econometrics. Lesser gold strikes include the analysis of

oligopoly, growth, human capital, and the random walk. Some of these strikes are still being worked in the last half of the 1970s, but most of them seem to have reached relatively low-grade ore. The last decade has not witnessed a major or even a lesser gold strike. To rejuvenate its internal intellectual growth the profession needs a gold strike, but as with all actual gold strikes, no one knows where, or if, it will occur. (Thurow 1977, pp.33–34).

Of course economists themselves could contribute to their professional standing by not being quite so opinionated and appearing certain on the basis of scanty and often inscrutable evidence. Let me close with Robert Solow's recipe for public statements by economists:

> Can anything be done? Your guess is as good as mine. I would like to see us stick to fundamentals in public, and to robust, well-established empirical relationships. Understanding about supply and demand, and marginal cost, and discounting, and the national income identity, and stocks and flows, and substitution, and the simpler macroeconomic models, and the limitations of those models—all that already gives us a comparative advantage over others. Why not stick to it? *Tomorrow* the world. (Solow 1978, p.40).

Notes

[1] In terms of their wider impact, perhaps the two most important critiques of the economy emanating from Australian radical economists concern the piecemeal nature of planning by McFarlane (1968) and the growing importance (dominance?) of foreign ownership by Wheelwright (Wheelwright & Miskelly 1967; Wheelwright 1974).

[2] On the other hand, in terms of conferences and radical magazines there is a good deal of continuing activity. Three Australian Political Economy Conferences have been held, each attracting large numbers. Sizeable and active conferences have also been held of Labor Economists. Again there are a number of active journals such as the *Journal of Australian Political Economy, Arena, Intervention*, apart from papers by radical economists appearing in the non-radical literature.

[3] The names of those who were involved in government during this period include: Brennan, Brogan, Cochrane, Deeble, Gates, Gregory, Gruen, Hancock, Holmes, Ironmonger, Isaac, Karmel, Keating, A.G. Lloyd, Mathews, Mauldon, Parish, Pincus, Porter, Scotton, Selby-Smith, Snape, T.W. Swan and Wheelwright.

[4] I have contributed elsewhere to this type of exercise (Gruen 1976).

[5] For the economist who wants to maintain the supremacy of freedom and of consumer choice as goals, the externalities of smoking can be used as valid gounds for interfering with consumers' choice. (i.e. the nuisance to others and the additional public health costs.) But this does not meet the (paternalistic) argument that there is a case for discouraging patently impulsive and unwise choices which will often be regretted in the future when the consequences of the, often irreversible, choices become apparent (e.g. smoking, the non-wearing of seat belts or safety helmets on motor bikes).

[6] Lastly there is the Impact project, headed by Alan Powell and Peter Dixon and a group assembled under IAC auspices. This work has been described in the first progress report of the Impact project (Powell 1977; Dixon, Ryland, Parmenter and Sutton 1977). Since it is basically designed for medium term (5–7 years) and longer term (over 10 years) policy analysis, whilst the emphasis here is on shorter-run macro-economic questions, the discussion here deals with the other three models.

[7] One should mention the Melbourne Institute's annual model—not as yet publicly fully documented but operated for some of its clients.

[8] For a detailed discussion see Challen and Hagger 1979. I am indebted to the authors for an early copy of their book in manuscript form.

[9] Jüttner 1978. However, as Jüttner points out, his comparisons are not conclusive, partly because the NIF forecasts are wholly within the sample period whilst about 10% of the RBA 1 forecasts are for an out-of-sample or post-sample period.

[10] See Jüttner 1977 and 1978.

[11] Peter Jonson and the Bank should be commended for these endeavours. The papers and proceedings of a two-day conference on RBA 76 in December 1977 are published as *Conference in Applied Economic Research*, Reserve Bank of Australia, December 1977.

[12] Lucas (1976) has argued that these changing structures cannot, in principle, be estimated sufficiently accurately to enable us to provide policy makers with useful information as to the actual consequences of alternative economic policies. For one possible reply, see Gordon 1976.

[13] In Britain and many other European countries (e.g. West Germany, Sweden, Norway, Netherlands and Ireland) economic policy analysis by official and statutory institutions such as central banks is a good deal more open and more informative than in Australia.

[14] In Australia monetarists tend also to be neo-classical economists; but the converse is less often true.

[15] Examples of such proposals are to be found in the Institute's House Journal—the *Australian Economic Review* No. 3, 1974, pp.48–51; No. 3, 1976, pp.12–13; No. 1, pp.9–15. See also Whitehead 1977, pp.31–34, though Whitehead prefers a cut in direct to a cut in indirect taxes.

[16] This is also shown in the Coghlan simulations as one of the effects of an indirect tax cut.

[17] Some of the points made by the committee conducting the official inquiry were: It would of course be necessary for the government to lay down a norm for permissible wage increases. The Australian Bureau of Statistics estimates each month Average Weekly Earnings using payroll tax statistics and a similar method is used in the formula for Reimbursement Grants to the States.

But greater difficulties arise in an attempt to produce a corresponding figure for individual firms which might be used to determine what are 'excessive' wage and salary payments. While such a figure could be produced for each firm there would be many anomalies and the Government would be enforcing penalities which in many instances would clearly be unjust. This is because it would be impossible from award determination, or from other sources, to determine how changes in *pay rates*, occupation by occupation, will affect *payrolls*, firm by firm and quarter by quarter. Even if no wage rates increase, the average payroll might rise because of a different mix of skills and because of variations in overtime, holiday pay, etc. A firm could be penalised for a pay increase which did not arise from any excessive change in rates because of accidental factors such as weather, strikes, shortages of material or power etc . . .

No doubt some of these defects could be set right in the course of administration but it would be impossible to hope for more than the roughest of justice. It may be that rough and ready justice can be tolerated if it is the price of coping with the inflationary situation. But if the injustices were sufficiently common and glaring there would be widespread resentment against the scheme even if it would help keep price down. There might also be industrial unrest and unexpected failures of businesses . . .

But it would be possible to give effect to such a measure, and if applied as part of a total program it could help contain cost inflation. It would, however, be impossible to sustain such a plan for any considerable period of time. If employed it should be seen essentially as a short term measure.

Source: the report of the committee was released to the Press on 21 October 1974 but it was never officially printed.

[18] See, for instance, Hagger 1978, pp.170–2.

[19] Davis & Lewis believe the relation between monetary policy and price inflation is in some doubt. For the most recent study of the relationship see Volker 1978.

[20] Of Corden's writings on Australian protection, perhaps two articles were particularly influential; his uniform tariff article (1958) and the 1967 Joseph Fisher Lecture. C.R. Kelly's many speeches on individual tariff proposals in the House of Representatives and his very readable column in the Financial Review and in a number of rural papers hammered the theme of private gain at the public's expense with a good deal of effect. Kelly's reminiscences have been published recently (1978). Rattigan's very effective espousal of reducing protection—as Chairman of the Tariff Board and the IAC has not yet been adequately documented. Four of his major speeches are listed in the bibliography.

[21] In June 1977 10% of manufacturing output was protected from import competition by quantitative restrictions (IAC 1977b, p.92).

[22] There are of course other avenues of spending extra foreign exchange—e.g. increased overseas investment by Australian individuals and corporations. These would not then have the adverse consequences for the other two sectors referred to above. Cf. Lloyd (1978, pp.269–271).

[23] Snape (1977) has pointed out some of the theoretical simplifications in the Gregory model. These relate to the partial equilibrium type of analysis which necessarily abstracts from important interrelations—including the differential rate of growth in real income resulting from the mineral discoveries and tariff reductions and the income and substitution effects on industries which are neither import competing nor export industries—so-called non-tradeables.

[24] This parallels similar debates in Norway, Holland, the United Kingdom and in some of the petroleum exporting countries.

[25] Some of these programmes would probably not now be embraced by a Federal Labor government; the Wran government in NSW has not initiated any new growth centres and the South Australian Dunstan government has suspended the Monarto programme.

[26] For instance, between 1968–69 and 1973–74, the family income Gini index fell from 0.33 to 0.31—i.e. in the latter year family incomes were more equally distributed. Yet the bottom 30% of families received a slightly lower percentage of aggregate family income in the latter year (21.6% cf. to 21.8%).

[27] In addition there is of course the issue discussed earlier of the relationship of increases in labour's share and the level of employment—or unemployment.

[28] Atkinson (1975, p.68) for British and US data. Similar estimates can be prepared for Australia from official statistics for the 1973–74 income distribution.

[29] Richardson (1979, pp.30–31), references given there and in Pritchard and Saunders (1978, p.18). A good summary and evaluation of the Henderson Report and the associated literature can be found in Pritchard and Saunders (1978).

[30] Instead the progressive state and federal relaxation and removal of gift and estate duties and land taxes which has taken place in recent years has predominantly benefited those at the other end of the income/wealth spectrum (Raskall 1978).

Bibliography

Alexander, I. (1978), 'The Impact of Office Dispersal on Work Journeys and Metropolitan Travel Patterns', Paper presented to 3rd Annual Meeting of the Regional Science Association, Monash University, December 1978.

Atkinson, A.B. (1975), *The Economics of Inequality* (Oxford, Clarendon Press, 1975).

Australian Bureau of Statistics (1976), *Social Indicators*, No. 1 (Canberra, AGPS, 1976).

—— (1978), *Social Indicators*, No. 2 (Canberra, AGPS, 1978).

Beale, R. (1978), 'Joint Ventures' in Troy, P.N. (ed). *Federal power in Australia's cities* (Sydney, Hale & Ironmonger, 1978), pp.71–92.

Blaug, M. (1970), *An Introduction to the Economics of Education* (London, Penguin Press).

Budget Papers (1978/79) Statement No. 2 (Budget Speech 1978–79, Canberra, AGPS, 1978).

Challen, D.W. & A.J. Hagger (1979), *Modelling the Australian Economy* (Melbourne, Longman—Cheshire, 1979).

Coghlan, P.L. (1978), 'Simulation with the NIF Model of the Australian Economy', Paper presented to the Simulation Special Interest Group Conference, Canberra, September, 1978, mimeo.

Corden, W.M. (1958), 'Import Restrictions and Tariffs: A New Look at Australian Policy', *The Economic Record*, December 1958, pp.331–346.

—— (1967), 'Australian Tariff Policy' *Australian Economic Papers*, December 1967, pp.131–154.

—— (1968), *Australian Economic Policy Discussion: A Survey* (Melbourne University Press, 1968).

—— (1978), 'Wages and Unemployment in Australia', Paper presented to Seventh Conference of Economists, Macquarie University, Sydney, 1978 (mimeo).

Davis, K. & M. Lewis (1978), 'Monetary Policy' in Gruen, F.H. (ed.) *Surveys of Australian Economics* (Sydney, George Allen & Urwin, 1978).

Dildine, L. & M. Sunley (1978), 'Administrative Problems of Tax-Based Incomes Policies', in Okun, A.M. & G.L. Perry (eds.), *Brookings Papers on Economic Activity 2* (Washington, The Brookings Institution, 1978).

Dixon, P.B. (et.al. 1977), *Orani, A General Equilibrium Model of the Australian Economy* (Canberra, A.G.P.S., 1977).

Downs, A. (1977), 'The Impact of Housing Policies on Family Life in the United States since World War II', *Daedalus*, Spring 1977.

Eckstein, O. (1976), 'Econometric Models and the Formation of Business Expectations', *Challenge*, March/April, 1976, pp.12–19.

Edwards, G.W. and A. Watson (1978), 'Agricultural Policy' in Gruen, F.H. (ed). *Surveys of Australian Economics* (Sydney, Allen & Unwin, 1978), pp.189–239.

Edwards, J. (1976), 'Labor's Record' in Mayer H. & H. Nelson (eds.) *Australian Politics, A Fourth Reader* (Melbourne, Cheshire, 1976).

Evans, H. (1972), *A General Equilibrium Analysis of Protection* (Amsterdam, North-Holland, 1972).

Fitzgerald, V.W. & C.I. Higgins (1977), 'Inside RBA 76', *Conference in Applied Economic Research*, Reserve Bank of Australia, December 1977.

Freebairn, J. & G. Withers (1977), 'The Performance of Manpower Forecasting Techniques in Australian Labour Markets', *Australian Bulletin of Labour*, December 1977, pp.13–31.

Garnaut, R. (1978), 'The International Transmission of Instability: Recent Australian Experience', Paper prepared for the Brookings/Japan Economic Research Centre project on the international transmission of instability 1978 (mimeo).

Gregory, R.G. (1976), 'Some Implications of the Growth of the Mineral Sector', *Australian Journal of Agricultural Economics*, vol 20, No. 2, August, pp.71–91.

Gregory, R.G. & R.C. Duncan (1978), 'The Relevance of Segmented Labour Market Theories: The Australian Experience of the Achievement of Equal Pay for Women', Paper presented to Seventh Conference of Economists, Macquarie University, Sydney, 1978 (mimeo).

Gregory R.G. and L.D. Martin (1976), 'An Analysis of Relationships between Import Flows to Australia and Recent Exchange Rate and Tariff Changes', *Economic Record*, March 1976 (vol 52, No. 137) pp.1–25.

Groenewegen, P.D. (1979), 'Radical Economics in Australia: A Survey of the 1970s' in Gruen, F.H. (ed.) *Surveys of Australian Economics, Volume II* (Sydney, George Allen & Unwin, 1979).

Gruen, F.H. (1975), 'The 25% Tariff Cut; was it a Mistake?', *Australian Quarterly*, June 1975, pp.7–20.

—— (1976), 'What Went Wrong? Some Personal Reflections on Economic Policies under Labor', *Australian Quarterly*, December 1976, pp.15–32.

—— (1978), 'Some Thoughts on Real Wages and Unemployment' CAER Paper No. 4, March 1978, p.65–80.

Gunnerson, T.H. (1970), 'The Effective Rate of Protection and the Tariff Board', *AIDA Special Bulletin* (1970), pp.1–7.

Hagger, A.J. (1978), 'Inflation', in Gruen, F.H. (ed.) *Surveys of Australian Economics* (Sydney, George Allen & Unwin, 1978).

Haig, B. & M.P. Wood (1977), 'Trading Price Changes Through Stages of Production: Australia, 1968–1977', Paper presented at the 15th General Conference of the International Association for Research in Income and Wealth, York, England, August 1977, *Review of Income and Wealth*, Yale.

—— (1978), 'The Relationship Between Costs, Intermediate and Final Prices: Australia, 1968–1977', Paper presented at Seventh Conference of Economists, Macquarie University, Sydney, August 1978, (mimeo).

Harrison, P. (1978), 'City Planning' in Scott, P. (ed.) *Australian Cities and Public Policy* (Melbourne, Georgian House, 1978).

Hawker, G. (1977), 'The Use of Social Scientists & Social Science in the Inquiries of the Labor Government', Paper presented to the Sociology Section of ANZAAS 1977, (mimeo).

Henderson Report (1975), *Poverty in Australia* (Canberra, Australian Govt. Commission of Inquiry into Poverty, 1975).

Hind, I. (1978), 'An Analysis of the Ideas Behind the Evidence on Education Vouchers', Paper presented at the Annual Conference of the, Australian Comparative and International Education Society, Macquarie University, Sydney, November 1978, (mimeo).

Industries Assistance Commission (1977a), *Structural Change in Australia* (Canberra, AGPS, 1977).

—— (1977b), *Annual Report 1976–77* (Canberra, AGPS, 1977).

—— (1978), *Annual Report 1977–78* (Canberra, AGPS, 1978).

Joskow, P.L. & R.G. Noll (1978), 'Regulation in Theory and Practice: An Overview', *MIT Economics Working Paper* No. 218, 1978.

Jüttner, D.J.P. (1977), 'Economic Policy, Inflation and Unemployment', *Economic Papers* (Economic Society of Australia & New Zealand; NSW & Vic Brauclies), January 1977.

—— (1978), 'An Evaluation of the Performance and a Critique of Econometric Models of the Australian Economy', mimeo., 1978.

Kelly, C.R. (1978), *One more nail* (Adelaide, Brolga Books, 1978).

Kmenta, J. (1966), 'An Econometric Model of Australia, 1948–1961', *Australian Economic Papers*, vol 5, No. 2, December 1966, pp.131–64.

Lindner, R.K. (1978), 'Inflationary Implications of the Growth of the Mining Sector', *Australian Economic Papers*, June 1978, pp.37–50.

Lloyd, P.J. (1978), 'Protection Policy' in Gruen, F.H. (ed.) *Surveys of Australian Economics* (Sydney, George Allen & Unwin, 1978).
Lloyd, C.J. & P.N. Troy (1978), 'A History of Federal Intervention' in Troy, N. *Federal power in Australia's cities* (Sydney, Hale & Iremonger, 1978).
Lucas, R.E. (1976), 'Econometric Policy Evaluation: A Critique', *Carnegie-Rochester Conference on Public Policy Vol. 1* (Amsterdam, North Holland, 1976).
McFarlane, B.J. (1968), *Economy Policy in Australia. The Case for Reform.* (Melbourne, Cheshire, 1968).
McGregor, L. (1978), 'On the Rationale of Stabilisation Policy', Paper for Centre of Independent Studies Conference, 'What Price Intervention', Macquarie University, 1978, mimeo.
Miller, G. (1976), 'Intersectoral Competition and Rural Prosperity: Some Policy Issues', *The Australian Economic Review*, 4th Quarter 1976, pp.29–38.
Mishan, E.J. (1976), 'The Folklore of the Market: An Inquiry into the Economic Doctrines of the Chicago School', Samuels, J. (ed.), *The Chicago School of Political Economy*, Michigan State University.
Modigliani, F. (1977), 'The Monetarist Controversy, or should we foresake Stabilisation Policies?', *American Economic Review*, March 1977, pp.1–19.
Murray, D. (1978), 'Sources of Income Inequality in Australia 1968–69', *Economic Record*, August 1978, pp.159–169.
Neutze, M. (1978), *Australian Urban Policy* (Sydney, George Allen & Unwin, 1978).
Neutze, M. & G. Bethune (1979), 'Urban Economics', in Gruen, F.H. (ed.) *Surveys of Australian Economics Volume II* (Sydney, George Allen & Unwin, 1979).
Nevile, J.W. (1962), 'A Simple Econometric Model of the Australian Economy', *Australian Economic Papers*, vol 1, June 1962, pp.79–94.
—— (1974), 'Inflation in Australia: Causes and Cures', *Economic Papers* (Economic Society of Australia & New Zealand, NSW & Vic Braudies), March 1974, pp.6–16.
—— (1975), *Fiscal Policy in Australia, Theory and Practice*, Second edition (Melbourne, Cheshire, 1975).
—— (1977), *Tax Cuts as an Anti-Inflationary Weapon* (Sydney, Centre for Applied Economic Research, 1977), Paper No. 3.
Nevile, J.W. & D.W. Stammer (eds.) (1972), *Inflation and Unemployment—Selected Readings* (Ringwood, Victoria, Australia, Penguin, 1972).
Norman, N.R. (1975), 'The Effective Rate of Protection' (Canberra, AIDA, 1975).
OECD (1976), *Public Expenditure on Income Maintenance Programmes*, Studies in Resource Allocation No. 3, July 1976.
Parish, R. (1978), 'Industrial Censorship'. Paper presented at Macquarie University Centre for Independent Studies Conference, 1978, (mimeo).
Paterson, J. (1975), 'Social and Economic Implications of Housing and Planning Standards', in Priorities Review Staff *Report on Housing*, (Canberra, AGPS, 1975).
Phelps Brown, H. (1977), *The Inequality of Pay* (London, Oxford University Press, 1977).
Porter, M.G. (1978), 'Stabilisation Policy and Misplaced Entrepreneurship', Paper for Centre of Independent Studies Conference, 'What Price Intervention', 1978, mineo.
Powell, A.A. (1977), *The IMPACT Project: An Overview* (Canberra, AGPS, 1977), First Progress Report of the IMPACT Project.
Pritchard, H. & P. Saunders (1978), 'Poverty and Income Maintenance Policy in Australia—A Review Article', *Economic Record*, April 1978, pp.17–31.
Rawls, J. (1977), 'The Basic Structure as Subject', *American Philosophical Quarterly*, April 1977, pp.159–65.
Raskall, P. (1978), 'Who's Got What in Australia: The Distribution of Wealth', *Journal of Australian Political Economy*, June 1978, pp.3–16.
Rattigan, G.A. (1967), 'The Tariff Board and today' Address given to Associated Chambers of Commerce, Perth, May 1967, (roneoed).
—— (1968), 'The Tariff Board: Some Reflections', *Economic Record*, March 1969, pp.17–26.

—— (1971), 'Protection and the Principle of Public Scrutiny' Giblin Memorial Lecture given on 27 May 1971, (roneoed).
—— (1976), 'Comparison of IAC and Jackson Committee approaches to industrial development', G.L. Wood Memorial Lecture given on 19 October 1976, (roneoed).
Reserve Bank of Australia (1977), *Conference in Applied Economic Research*, December 1977.
Riach, P.A. & G.M. Richards (1978), 'The Lesson of the Cameron Experiment', 1978, mimeo.
Richardson, S. (1979), 'Income Distribution, Poverty and Redistributive Policies', in Gruen, F.H. (ed). *Surveys of Australian Economics Vol. II* (Sydney, Allen & Unwin, 1979).
Roberti, P. (1978), 'Income Inequality in Some Western Countries: Patterns and Trends', *International Journal of Social Economics*, 5, 1978, pp.22–41.
Sandercock, L. (1978), 'Citizen Participation: The New Conservatism' in Troy, P.N. (ed). *Federal power in Australia's cities* (Sydney, Hale & Iremonger, 1978).
Schools Commission (1978), *Some Aspects of School Finance in Australia* (Canberra, AGPS, 1978).
Sieper, E. (1978), 'Consumer Protection—Boon or Bane?'. Paper presented at Macquarie University Centre for Independent Studies Conference 1978, (mimeo).
Snape, R.H. (1977), 'Effects of Mineral Development on the Economy', *Australian Journal of Agricultural Economics*, vol 21, No. 3, December 1977, pp.147–156.
Stammer, D.W. (1978), 'Real Wages and Unemployment' in CAER Paper No. 4, *Real Wages and Unemployment*, March 1978.
Thurow, L.C. (1977), 'Economics 1977', *Daedalus*, Fall 1977, pp.79–94.
Tinbergen, J. (1975), *Income Distribution—Analysis and Policies* (Amsterdam, North-Holland, 1975).
Tobin, J. (1970), 'On Limiting the Domain of Inequality', *Journal of Law and Economics*, 13, October 1970, pp.263–277.
Treasury (1978), 'The Measurement of Real Unit Labour Costs', *Round-up of Economic Statistics: Special Supplement*, 68, September 1978, pp.15–26.
Valentine, T. (1978), 'The Battle of the Plans: An Econometric Analysis', Paper presented at the Seventh Conference of Economists, Macquarie University, August 1978, (mimeo).
Volker, P.A. (1978), 'Influences on Australia Inflation: A Causality Analysis', 1978 (roneoed).
Wheelwright, E.L. (1974), *Radical Political Economy. Collected Essays* (Sydney, ANZ Book Company, 1974).
Wheelwright, E.L. and J. Miskelly (1967), *Anatomy of Australian Manufacturing Industry* (Sydney, Law Book Company, 1967).
Whitehead, D. (1977), 'Inflation versus Unemployment: A Non-Monetarist View', Paper presented to the 48th ANZAAS Congress, Melbourne, 1977, (mimeo).
Willis, R. (1978), 'Sound Economic Managers or Agents of Social Change?' Keynote address to the Second National Conference of Labor Economists, University of Queensland, June 1978, (mimeo).
Working Group on Rural Policy (1974), *Rural Policy in Australia* (Canberaa, AGPS, 1974).
Zerby, J.A. (1969), 'An Econometric Model of Monetary Interaction in Australia', *Australian Economic Papers*, December 1969, pp.154–177.